REVIEW 12

REVIEW

Volume 12   1990

Edited by

James O. Hoge
*Virginia Polytechnic Institute
and State University*

James L. W. West III
The Pennsylvania State University

University Press of Virginia

Charlottesville

THE UNIVERSITY PRESS OF VIRGINIA
Copyright © 1990 by the Rector and Visitors
of the University of Virginia

First published 1990

ISSN 1090-3233
ISBN 0-8139-1310-1

Printed in the United States of America

The editorial assistants for volume 12 of REVIEW are LaVerne
Kennevan Maginnis and Robert M. Myers, both of The Pennsylvania
State University.

PENNSTATE

Funding for *Review* is provided by the generous gifts of Mr. and Mrs. Charles O. Gordon, Jr., and Mr. and Mrs. Adger S. Johnson to the Virginia Tech Foundation, and by a grant from the College of the Liberal Arts, The Pennsylvania State University.

Contents

Tennyson and His Bibliographers   1
   by William E. Fredeman
      Review of Christopher Ricks, ed., *The Poems of Tennyson;*
      Cecil Y. Lang and Edgar F. Shannon, eds., *The Letters of*
      Alfred, Lord Tennyson

Farquhar Complete and Sheridan Under Construction   37
   by Judith Milhous
      Review of George Farquhar, *The Works of George Far-*
      quhar, ed. Shirley Strum Kenny; Bruce Redford, ed.,
      The Origins of The School for Scandal: *"The Slanderers"*
      [and] "Sir Peter Teazle"

No Common Parlance: Recent Linguistic Approaches
to Nineteenth-Century American Authors   53
   by Michael West
      Review of Joan Burbick, *Thoreau's Alternative History:*
      Changing Perspectives on Nature, Culture, and Language;
      Christanne Miller, *Emily Dickinson: A Poet's Grammar;*
      David R. Sewell, *Mark Twain's Languages: Discourse, Dia-*
      logue, and Linguistic Variety

Stepping Outside Ourselves: Tanselle's Universal Text   69
   by D. C. Greetham
      Review of G. Thomas Tanselle, *A Rationale of Textual*
      Criticism

Chaucer and the Stars   81
   by Derek Brewer
      Review of J. D. North, *Chaucer's Universe*

What's in a Text? 89
  by Marshall Brown
    Review of Jerome J. McGann, *The Beauty of Inflections: Literary Investigations in Historical Method and Theory;* Jerome J. McGann, *Social Values and Poetic Acts: The Historical Judgment of Literary Work;* Jerome J. McGann, ed., *Textual Criticism and Literary Interpretation*

Art, Elitism, and Gender: The Last of the Aesthetes 107
  by Regenia Gagnier
    Review of Karl Beckson, *Arthur Symons: A Life*

Reading Mary Shelley, Well— 119
  by L. J. Swingle
    Review of Paula R. Feldman and Diana Scott-Kilvert, eds., *The Journals of Mary Shelley: 1814–1844;* Anne K. Mellor, *Mary Shelley: Her Life, Her Fiction, Her Monsters;* Emily W. Sunstein, *Mary Shelley: Romance and Reality;* Karl Kroeber, *Romantic Fantasy and Science Fiction*

Pound Among the Women 135
  by James Longenbach
    Review of Omar Pound and Robert Spoo, eds., *Ezra Pound and Margaret Cravens: A Tragic Friendship;* Thomas L. Scott and Melvin J. Friedman, eds., with the assistance of Jackson R. Bryer, *Pound/The Little Review: The Letters of Ezra Pound to Margaret Anderson*

Pentimenti: The Georgia Edition of Smollett 159
  by Hugh Amory
    Review of Tobias Smollett, *The Adventures of Ferdinand Count Fathom*

Dreiser's Long Foreground 179
  by Robert H. Elias
    Review of T. D. Nostwich, ed., *Theodore Dreiser's "Heard in the Corridors": Articles and Related Writings;* T. D. Nostwich, ed., *Theodore Dreiser Journalism, Volume One: Newspaper Writings, 1892–1895;* Yoshinobu Hakutani, ed.,

Contents ix

Selected Magazine Articles of Theodore Dreiser: Life and Art in the American 1890s

Dictating Taste in the Eighteenth Century: New Lights on the Careers of Robert Dodsley and John Almon   187
   by Beverly Schneller
      Review of James E. Tierney, ed., *The Correspondence of Robert Dodsley, 1733–1764;* Deborah D. Rogers, *Bookseller as Rogue: John Almon and the Politics of Eighteenth-Century Publishing*

Through Forthrights and Meanders: Notes on Notes on Walking   197
   by Elizabeth Sewell
      Review of Jeffrey C. Robinson, *The Walk: Notes on a Romantic Image*

Mr. Badman, Presented   205
   by Jim Springer Borck
      Review of John Bunyan, *The Life and Death of Mr. Badman: Presented to the World in a Familiar Dialogue Between Mr. Wiseman, and Mr. Attentive*

Confronting Nightmares: The Dalhousie Manuscripts   213
   by Arthur F. Kinney
      Review of Ernest W. Sullivan II, ed., *The First and Second Dalhousie Manuscripts: Poems and Prose by John Donne and Others: A Facsimile Edition*

The Not-So-Little Lower Layer   229
   by Michael Anesko
      Review of David S. Reynolds, *Beneath the American Renaissance: The Subversive Imagination in the Age of Emerson and Melville*

Reading Wharton's Letters   235
   by Katherine Joslin
      Review of R. W. B. Lewis and Nancy Lewis, eds., *The Letters of Edith Wharton*

Bernard Shaw on Progress 249
   by Henry J. Donaghy
      Review of J. L. Wisenthal, *Shaw's Sense of History*

Exploring the Dialogue 255
   by Peter J. Manning
      Review of Theresa M. Kelley, *Wordsworth's Revisionary Aesthetics;* Paul Magnuson, *Coleridge and Wordsworth: A Lyrical Dialogue;* Nicholas Roe, *Wordsworth and Coleridge: The Radical Years*

Market Studies and Book History in American Literature 273
   by C. Deirdre Phelps
      Review of Michael Anesko, *"Friction with the Market": Henry James and the Profession of Authorship;* Cathy N. Davidson, *Revolution and the Word: The Rise of the Novel in America;* Michael T. Gilmore, *American Romanticism and the Marketplace;* Christopher P. Wilson, *The Labor of Words: Literary Professionalism in the Progressive Era;* R. Jackson Wilson, *Figures of Speech: American Writers and the Literary Marketplace from Benjamin Franklin to Emily Dickinson*

Realism Revisited: Darwin and Foucault Among the Victorians 303
   by Peter Allan Dale
      Review of George Levine, *Darwin and the Novelists: Patterns of Science in Victorian Fiction*

The British Stage Corrected, 1660–1737 323
   by Robert Adams Day
      Review of Peter Lewis, *Burlesque Drama: Its Place in the Tradition*

Contributors 327

Editorial Board

Felicia Bonaparte
City College, CUNY

Anthony J. Colaianne
Virginia Polytechnic Institute and State University

Paul Connolly
Yeshiva University

A. S. G. Edwards
University of Victoria

Ian Jack
Cambridge University

James R. Kincaid
University of Southern California

Cecil Y. Lang
University of Virginia

James B. Meriwether
University of South Carolina

Hershel Parker
University of Delaware

George Stade
Columbia University

Peter L. Shillingsburg
Mississippi State University

G. Thomas Tanselle
John Simon Guggenheim Memorial Foundation

Stanley Weintraub
The Pennsylvania State University

Tennyson and His Bibliographers

William E. Fredeman

Christopher Ricks, ed. *The Poems of Tennyson.* Second Edition Incorporating the Trinity College Manuscripts. Longman's Annotated English Poets. 2nd ed., 3 vols. London: Longman, 1987; Berkeley: University of California Press, 1987. Vol. 1: xxxi, 662 pp.; Vol. 2: ix, 746 pp.; Vol. 3: xi, 674 pp.

Cecil Y. Lang and Edgar F. Shannon, Jr., eds. *The Letters of Alfred Lord Tennyson,* I, 1821–1850; II, 1851–1870. Oxford: Clarendon, 1982, 1987; Cambridge: Belnap Press of Harvard University Press, 1982, 1987. Vol. 1: xxxviii, 366 pp.; Vol. 2: xii, 584 pp.

In what may well be the sole recorded instance of Hallam Tennyson's levity, the Laureate's son acknowledged receipt of Thomas J. Wise's bibliography of his father: "Thanks for the Bibliography: it is just the book my father would have HATED."[1] Throughout his life, Tennyson had an aversion to both critics and biographers. Disregarding Arthur Henry Hallam's advice, he fulminated, to his later regret, against John Wilson's *Blackwood's* review in February 1832, ransacking Walker for "usty" rhymes to lambaste "Tipsy Kit" (Christopher North), and later widened his sights to include the whole race of scribblers in "Poets and Critics." As hostile as Browning in "House" to exposing his personal life to public scrutiny, Tennyson invoked Shakespeare's curse on biographical quidnuncs, whom he castigated as clowns and knaves in "To—After Reading a Life and Letters"; and he took Froude to task in "The Dead Prophet" for his too frank treatment of Carlyle's private life. In "Poets and Their Bibliographies"—variously titled in the notebooks "Old Poets," "Book-making," "Poets and Bibliophils," and "On publishing every discarded scrap of a Poet"—he inveighed "against raking together and publishing the fragments of a deceased poet," envying the Ancients—especially Virgil, Horace, and Catullus—that they flourished "Before the Love of Letters, overdone, / Had swamped the sacred poets with themselves." "Poets and Their Bibliographies" appeared untitled just over a hundred years ago in *Tiresias and Other Poems* (1885), when only 1144 of the 5147 items listed in Kirk H. Beetz's *Tennyson: A Bibliography* (1984) had appeared. During the intervening century, that number has swelled exponentially, and includes, among other important studies and editions besides Beetz, Robert Martin's 1980 biography, *Tennyson: the Unquiet Heart,* Christopher Ricks's parthenogenic "three-tomed prodigy"—his second edition of the *Poems,* originally published in 1969—and Cecil Lang and Edgar Shannon's two (of a projected three) volumes of Tennyson's letters, plus critical editions of three of the major works: John Pfordresher's variorum edition of the *Idylls* (1973), Susan Shatto and Marion Shaw's *In Memoriam* (1982), and Susan Shatto's *Maud* (1986). Were the Laureate alive, the two monumental works reviewed here, leaving aside the other five and the nearly 4,000 other items published since his death in 1892, treating his biography and literary output, would likely inspire in him a fatal attack of apoplexy!

Ricks's own subtitle to this second edition, "Incorporating the Trinity College Manuscripts," invites close comparisons with the 1969 version. Because the achievement of that edition, universally acclaimed at the time of publication, a view subsequently corroborated in classrooms around the world, has proved over two decades indisputable, there is no necessity in this review to challenge Ricks's editorial principles by subjecting the basic methodology, retained in the second edition, to microscopic scrutiny. Professor Ricks, in the new edition, has addressed "Hoti's business," dotting and crossing a number of "i's" and "t's" inevitably overlooked in so prodigious an undertaking;[2] supplied many of the lacunae of the first edition; added new factual biographical and publication information, much of it drawn from the still in progress Lang-Shannon edition of the letters; rearranged some sections; and updated the scholarly reference with which the head and textual notes abound. But the main feature of the second edition—and, indeed, its principal justification—pertains to the textual intercalations in the notes and appendices of unpublished drafts, rejected readings, fragments, and new poems—made possible by the availability of the manuscript notebooks at Trinity College, Cambridge, and a few other manuscripts in the Cambridge University Library, the "in perpetuity" interdiction of which was lifted, largely owing to the efforts of Sir Charles Tennyson and Lord Tennyson, within months of the publication of the first edition of the *Poems*.

In a front article entitled "The Tennyson Manuscripts" in the *TLS* for 21 August 1969, Ricks first reported on some of the more important textual revelations in the Trinity notebooks, printing for the first time variant readings, corrections of Hallam Tennyson's mistranscriptions, and new poems that in his edition he could allude to only by the frustrating and oft-recurring siglum "Trinity MS. which may not be quoted." The three-volume format required to accommodate more than 250 pages of new and revised material in the second edition is only the most obvious of the external differences between the two works. Unlike its predecessor—an extraordinary bargain at four guineas in 1969—the new edition, owing to its price ($225 in the U.S.; £120 in the U.K.), is almost certainly destined to be relegated to library reference shelves, a drawback that, unfortunately, is not altogether remedied by the recently published abridged edition.[3]

Most readers will not concur in the *Daily Telegraph* reviewer's assessment of Professor Ricks's 1969 edition of Tennyson, that "his notes are almost as great a pleasure to read as the poems." But as a broad indication of the solid research that buttresses both editions, the hyperbole is not wholly undeserved: few modern editors can match the hard-core scholarship and unpretentious erudition evident in every aspect of this impressive recreation of the Laureate's canon. If the first edition was, as another reviewer called it, "indispensable for future Tennyson scholars and critics," the second, freed from the textual constraints imposed by Hallam Tennyson's deposit embargo on the Tennyson manuscripts at Cambridge, approaches definitiveness, although Professor Ricks is too keenly aware of the hubristic consequences of that term to emulate the recent editor of *Maud,* who substitutes on the title-page for Tennyson's own subtitle to the poem, "A Monodrama," one less accurately descriptive of the work in question: "A Definitive Edition."

While there is no cumulative list of contents for the entire set—each of the separately paginated volumes contains its own listing of the poems included—this disadvantage has been partially offset by printing the complete Index (and the list of abbreviations) in each volume; and the inclusion of page numbers opposite the titles in the Contents removes one of the major inconveniences of the first edition. Among several innovations in the second edition are the contents-breakdowns provided for the two longer appendices (A and B) and the introduction of a new Appendix D, which identifies the poems (by Ricks number) in the ten volumes of collected poems from 1842 to the posthumous *The Death of Oenone* (1892), in which the sequence of the poems is not necessarily chronological. Poems in the first three volumes are printed in sequence and the volumes indicated in the Contents. The basic text of the first edition, including the numbering of the poems, has been retained, with newly identified poems inserted into the running sequence. The introduction of literally hundreds of additions, interspersions, revisions, corrections, and deletions has necessitated a major restructuring of the 1969 text, but while the second edition is in no way a scissors-and-paste reprint, it does not, in an absolute sense, constitute a complete resetting.[4]

The subtitle of the new edition notwithstanding, the editor says in his Preface that he "has tried to resist the temptation to find the Trinity MSS more interesting (than, say, the good old Harvard ones) simply because they used to be under interdiction" (I xiv). Clearly, however, the Trinity variants constitute the major textual interest in the new edition, both for editor and reader, especially since the poetic texts are virtually unaltered. The single textual error in the 1969 edition—the misplacement of line 66 in "The Grandmother," which is now restored to its rightful position in stanza 17—has been rectified, as have one or two collational slips, such as the ambiguous conflation of two variants from *Maud* (from H.Nbks 30–31) assigned to Part I, xix in 1969 (1071), which in the new edition are distinguished and separated, the longer of the two relocated to Part I, v (see II 533–34, 558).[5] Other changes affecting the text involve the addition of new poems (designated by "A" numbers), alternative drafts, fragments and trivia, and the relocation of three poems (No. 285A/B formerly 287/288 in Vol. II; No. 365A formerly 408 in Vol. III) within the chronological composition sequence, which are also assigned "A" numbers.

A textual comparison of the two editions is revealing. The first edition contained 17 unpublished poems, plus a number of drafts and fragments; restored 180 poems to the canon from various primary and fugitive sources: *Materials, Memoir,* and Tennyson's own volumes; periodicals, gift books, annuals, and other published sources; and posthumously published volumes, such as Sir Charles Tennyson's *Unpublished Early Poems* (1931). In his Preface to the second edition, Professor Ricks notes that "new to this edition are about a dozen poems, about a thousand lines of verse, and countless variants" (I xii). The "abouts" in this statement are significant since the reservation obviously hinges on definition. In fact, only seven new poems are introduced into the body of the text—three from the Trinity MSS (all printed by Ricks in *TLS* 1969), four from other published sources—none of them major:

1) 1A "Three Translations from Horace" (A. Pollard, *TRB* 1982, 140 lines)
2) 54A "The musky air was mute" (T Nbk 19, 16 lines)
3) 58A "The Invasion of Russia by Napoleon Buonaparte" (T Nbk 19, 96 lines)
4) 152A "Madonna, wise and mild and rare" (A. Vail Motter, *TLS* 1970, 15 lines)
5) 245A "To Georgina 1834" (Robert Martin *TRB* 1980, 6 lines)
6) 276A "Wherefore, in these dark ages of the press" (T Nbk 26, 34 lines)
7) 297A "'Yours & caetera' O how cold" (A. Day *TLS* 1981, 10 lines)

Besides these seven new titles, "Semele" (No. 220) in the new edition is printed in a fuller and revised text (from T.MS B), replacing Hallam Tennyson's conflated text in the one-volume *Works* (1913) used in the first edition.[6] Similarly, stanza three of No. 137, "To-[Thou mayst remember what I said]," deleted by Hallam, is restored from T. Nbk. 23. One poem remains anomalous, "Sonnet: Salve Lux Renata!" (No. 134, I 304), the canonicity of which has been challenged by Aidan Day, who suggests that it may be by Arthur Henry Hallam. This is the single poem in the edition that is printed in the body of the text and also listed among the "Doubtful Poems" in Appendix C (No. vii).[7] The remainder of the new titles and verses appear in the first three appendices—five, twenty-two, and two in A, B, and C, respectively.

Appendix A contains alternative drafts of fifteen poems printed in the edition, including the nine sections and two fragments of *In Memoriam* which Tennyson did not publish, here collected "since they might detract from the final sequence of the poem" (III 592).[8] Of these, one (section iiiA—presumably the eighth of the "about a dozen" new poems) was first printed by Ricks in *TLS* and subsequently reprinted by Shatto and Shaw; two (ii and iii) and the fragments were unpublished until the first edition; one was printed in Valerie Pitt's *Tennyson Laureate* (1962); the remainder were printed by Hallam Tennyson in the *Memoir* (iv, first in *Materials*). The tenuousness of the evidence for dating individual sections of *In Memoriam,* to which Ricks alludes in his headnote to the poem (II 310), is confirmed by the disparity between his ordering of these additional poems and that adopted by Shatto and Shaw, who claim to follow the "assumed chronology of the manuscripts in which they appear," and who also regard the final poems in their series (Ricks's iv and i) as independent poems on Hallam, "[not] known to have been intended for inclusion in *In Memoriam*" (148).

Among the new drafts in Appendix A, nine of which are new, one is of particular interest: that for "To the Queen"—a draft of the dedication in the seventh (1851 "Laureate") edition of *Poems* (1842) employing the *In Memoriam* stanza—is printed from a MS version of No. 299, formerly in the Drexel Institute, Philadelphia

Tennyson and His Bibliographers 7

(later sold at auction and now unlocated), which was published in Richard Jones's *The Growth of the Idylls of the King* (1895). Hallam Tennyson, as Ricks notes (III 600), printed a three-stanza "unpublished version" as the dedication to the *Memoir*, conflating the first two stanzas of the Jones text with a variant of stanza five in the 1851 text. Presumably, because there is no manuscript authority for the *Memoir* version, or because it represents an arbitrary conflation, Ricks does not record either the three substantive variants in stanza one between the *Memoir* and the Jones text or the major variants between stanza three in the *Memoir* and stanza five in the 1851 version. He does, however, print both a different version of stanza two from *Materials* (III 600) and a variant of stanza three from a proof quoted in Eversley (II 463), the last line of which—"Your nature true as you are great"—closely echoes the wording in the final line in stanza three of Hallam Tennyson's dedication:

> I give this faulty book to you,
>   For tho' the faults be thick as dust
>   In vacant chambers, I can trust
> Your woman's nature kind and true.

While the compositional sequence is uncertain—Tennyson probably abandoned the reading owing to the repetition in the first two lines—the stanza deserves to be preserved as another example of the difficulties, evidenced by the many extant revisions and drafts, that the poem caused the Laureate (Ricks II 463).

Of the thirteen "Poems and fragments still unpublished" and "Fragments previously printed but not included here" listed at the end of Appendix B of the first edition (1804), only one—a reworking of some lines by Patmore—remains unpublished in the second edition (III 640):[9] three are incorporated into the text as new poems (1A, 58A, 276A); the remainder, except for the comic quatrain relegated to "Doubtful Poems" (Appendix C), all appear in Appendix B, which contains twenty-two new uncollected fragments and trivia, thirteen of which are not mentioned in the first edition. Of the twenty-two, five from the Trinity MSS were printed by Ricks in *TLS;* another eight are from various manuscript sources, including the letters; three are from recently published sources, including the epitaph to John Brown printed by Elizabeth Longford in *Victoria R.I.;* another four are from published sources missed by Ricks in the first edition; and two, described in 1969 as "illegible," are now printed from transcriptions by J. Rutter. While Ricks does not give these fragments and trivia full canonical status, a few (e.g., xxiC/D, xxvB) are self-contained poems that vie with some of the slighter works like "Epigram on a Musician, whose Harp-strings were Cracked from Want of Using" (No. 32, from *Poems by Two Brothers*) that are canonical. Others are clearly false-starts for unfinished works or unadopted passages; still others belong to that category described by Hallam Tennyson as having been omitted from the canon "for some forgotten reason" (III 609). Even in a collected edition which makes no pretense at being definitive, these trifles had to be included for the sake of completeness; but for aficionados, they are all of interest, providing further evidence about the workings of Tennyson's creative imagination and reinforcing the hundreds of textual variants, which compromise the major contribution of the new edition.

The revisions to this second edition are so extensive that it is not possible to provide more than a general summary of their nature and scope, the range and complexity of which are inadequately indicated by the simple comparison made by a number of reviewers of the pagination in the two editions—discounting preliminary matter, 2082 in the second versus 1835 in the first. In fact, every section of the edition, from the prelims to the Index, has been totally revised. Changes in the Contents have already been noted. The Preface adds an initial subsection on the second edition, revises the account of the Trinity manuscripts, updates the references to scholarly publications, and introduces some new material, as in the subsection on *Poems by Two Brothers*. Even the minor sections have been heavily revised: new debts are paid in the Acknowledgements; a few significant readjustments are made in the Chronological Table, including the relocation (from 1833 and 1838) in the previous year of Hallam's and Tennyson's respective engagements to the two Emilys in 1832 and 1837. Twenty-five new entries have been added to the Abbreviations.

Each poem in the edition represents a tripartite entity, consisting of headnote, text, and annotations. Headnotes vary from single-line entries providing the merest publication details, as for the "Sonnet [Shall the hag Evil die with child of Good]" (No. 109)—"Published *1830,* not reprinted"—to the extended essays introducing each of the major works—the longest of which, for *In Memoriam,* occupies eleven pages—which provide fully documented discussions of the background of the poems, the history of their composition and publication, their biographical significance, and information on sources, dating, prosody, or other concerns relevant to the poems. New material is introduced in at least half the headnotes to the poems, and literally hundreds of new annotations have been added. As in the previous edition, the annotations are of several kinds: manuscript source descriptions; variant readings in manuscript and printed texts, from single words to verse paragraphs; parallel passages in other literary works; verbal echoes, borrowings, and adaptations from Tennyson's own works; literary allusions, including Biblical and Classical references, and narrative summaries; explanatory notes on Tennyson's literary, historical, and biographical sources, his diction, and his reading; Tennyson's own notes on his poems and commentary by other critics; and documentary references to secondary sources, including the forthcoming third volume of the Lang-Shannon letters. While not all poems are annotated, the vast majority are.

Assessing the new material in the headnotes and annotations in so massive an edition is no small task. However, because Ricks appears to have total recall of Tennyson's entire canon (not to mention his life and the whole corpus of English literature!) and to have engaged virtually the whole of post-1969 scholarship on the poet, collation is likely to prove for most readers more educative than numbing—invaluable preparation for that next graduate seminar on the Laureate. Considering the extent of the variants supplied for the major long poems and for the other poems ("Ulysses," etc.) that Ricks regards as "important" (see the criteria delineated in the Preface [xiv]), it is difficult to credit that the listing of variants is in fact "selective," though a cursory examination of the published volumes of the Tennyson Archive (Garland Publishing, edited by Ricks and Aidan Day) will confirm the accuracy of his contention. A close examination of the critical apparatus in any of the post–1969 scholarly editions of the *Idylls, In Memoriam,* and *Maud* will further confirm the instinctive correctness of Ricks's decision to forgo the kind of vacuum-cleaner comprehensiveness attempted in those editions, none of which approaches the level of critical editing evident in, say, Jerome McGann's *Byron*. What Ricks achieves is a reliable and readable text that reproduces in an admirably economical format almost all the substantive and significant variants, without imposing on the reader the clutter of minutiae that too easily obscures rather than illuminates the text.

Major revisions in the headnotes and annotations exist for so many of the poems that no partial listing would be fairly representative; however, some sense of the general nature of the revisions can be gleaned by comparing Ricks's treatment of "The Epic" and "Morte d'Arthur" (Nos. 225/226) in the two editions. The two poems occupy pages 582–98 in the first edition, 1–19 of Volume II in the second. The headnote to "The Epic" is unchanged. To the "Morte" Ricks has added quotations from correspondence from R. J. Tennant to Tennyson and from Tennyson to Spedding from the *Letters* together with a note from Ellen Hallam and a comment from Martin's biography; replaced the "may not be quoted" rubric with manuscript details in the note on the text; and inserted four citations to recent scholarship. In the annotations to both poems, there are seventy textual variants (nine of them inserted into or appended to existing notes) cited from Trinity MSS, including one passage of three and another of seven lines, plus two more from the Heath MS.; three references to literary sources in Tennyson, Pope, and Horace; nine notices of literary sources suggested by other scholars (Mason, Turner, Gray, and Kolb); one extended quotation from a letter from Hallam to Gladstone from Kolb's edition (line 238); and two deletions—one correcting an error in the annotation to line 223, the other excising a generalization glossing line 255: "Bound by gold chains about the feet of God."[10]

Tennyson and His Bibliographers 11

While there are fewer revisions in "The Epic" and "Morte d'Arthur" than in some other of the shorter works, these poems are adequate to convey Ricks's general editorial practice, though in some instances the notes are all essentially new, as for "Doubt and Prayer" (No. 457), in which Ricks substitutes for collations with "The Christian Penitent" (No. 186)—the early version of the poem (1832, first published in 1969)—new readings from three early manuscript texts. For a number of poems, such as "Audley Court" (No. 136) and "Edwin Morris" (No. 275), some manuscript variants occupy nearly a page of reduced text (see II 136 and 143); for others, additions, such as the lengthy note by Boucher-James on the quasi-burial of lepers in the Middle Ages (III 193–94) printed by Tennyson at the end of "Happy: The Leper's Bride" (No. 424) in *Demeter and Other Poems* (1889) and inadvertently omitted in 1969, swell the entries.

Revisions to headnotes and annotations in the long poems bulk fairly large in the new edition, amounting in all to over seventy pages. The textual notes to the *Idylls* generally are comparatively slight, and only twenty-eight new ones have been added, but the documentary annotations, especially citations from Malory, are extensive. Ricks draws heavily on the post–1969 research of J. M. Gray, John D. Rosenberg, David Staines, and Cecil Y. Lang, as well as on the letters, incorporating references to these works in eighty new notes; but he makes no attempt to key his textual notes to Pfordresher's "variorum edition" (something of a misnomer in view of the paucity of critical commentary), perhaps because he had already established his text, which in any event poses fewer problems, several years before the publication of Pfordresher's edition. In contrast, *The Princess*, the only long work that has not since Ricks's first edition been separately edited, contains in toto only seventy-six new notes, but of these over fifty are textual readings from manuscripts in the University Library, Cambridge (ULC) and a few other sources. Predictably, owing to the overwhelming importance of the released Trinity manuscripts, the significance of the works, and the scholarly attention devoted to them in recent years, the new textual readings are most prominent in *Maud* and *In Memoriam*. Because Susan Shatto's *Maud* appeared in 1987, after Ricks had corrected the third proofs of his second edition and a year before publication, in re-editing the poem, though he introduces some 350 textual variants and another twenty-five explanatory and documentary notes, he was unable to incorporate more than a handful of references to her edition; but he did, as already mentioned, correct one of the more serious blunders in his earlier work. His indebtedness to Shatto and Shaw's edition of *In Memoriam,* however, is generously acknowledged (as theirs to his earlier edition was not) in more than sixty new and revised notes. As arguably the greatest poem in the Tennyson canon, *In Memoriam* rightly receives a lion's share of Ricks's critical attention, and it is one of the few poems for which all textual variants are recorded. Of the roughly 1050 notes to the poem, about 200 of them, both textual and documentary, are new to this edition. Another 120 have been substantially revised, the additions ranging from brief notations of Trinity readings to the long excerpts from three of Hallam's letters to Emily Tennyson written in 1831 and 1832 with which Ricks glosses sections c–ciii, dealing with the move from Somersby in 1837.

Only the minutest comparison of the two editions of *The Poems of Tennyson* will reveal the magnitude of Ricks's revisions, which are only partially (and inadequately) conveyed in this abbreviated survey. Beyond the textual variants, which number in the thousands, and the hundreds of documentary and explicatory annotations, myriads of minor revisions that fall under the general heading of "editorial housekeeping" also required attention: every page cross-reference to the edition itself had to be altered and the appropriate volume added; letter and manuscript sources required updating; British Museum citations changed to British Library; lead-in phraseology to new material rewritten; typos and factual errors corrected; necrology accounted for; and the Index totally reworked. In all, the new edition is a staggering undertaking, made even more difficult by the complications involved in balancing the placement of these extensive revisions within an existing format designed initially to insure the integrity of the poetic texts, to which the apparatus is intentionally, and properly, subordinated. The revisions to the second edition are truly impressive, but in the final analysis they merely complement, without in any sense overshadowing, the splendid editorial achievement of the first.

That said, there are, inevitably, caveats, for Ricks, no less than Homer (or even Milton, whom he knows almost as well as Tennyson and whom he cites often in the notes), occasionally—but only occasionally—nods: the few editorial peccadilloes spotted in fine-combing the edition are herein relegated to footnotes.[11] Every reader will have his own wish-list of apparatus that the editor might have included: an index to the wealth of documentary material cited in head and footnotes would be invaluable, if unconventional and perhaps impractical; but it would be useful to have a checklist of the fugitive sources—periodicals, annuals, gift books, and anthologies—in which the poems first appeared, if only to further our understanding of the Laureate's complicated bibliography.

The three-volume format of the new edition does have some drawbacks (other than cost), but in general it serves both the aesthetic and chronological presentation of the text far better than the original, rather dumpy, single-volume format, enabling the reader to encounter, with the single exception of the *Idylls*, the early, middle, and late poems in self-contained volumes, and providing a convenient overview of the major stages of Tennyson's poetic development. Some problems are posed by paired and pendant poems, especially when their composition and publication dates are separated by several years, sometimes decades, but Ricks provides adequate editorial guidance to clarify most of these anomalies.[12]

While the breaks between volumes may have been arbitrary, determined in part by publication exigencies, one suspects they were deliberate. Volume I includes the poems composed to the mid-1830s, most of which were published in the poet's first three volumes, and ends with No. 224, "Love's latest hour is this" (1834), distinctly a young man's poem about the frustrations of romantic love. Volume II begins with "The Epic" and "Morte d'Arthur," the framed poems that introduced the second volume of new works in *Poems* (1842), includes three of Tennyson's major works—*The Princess, In Memoriam,* and *Maud*—plus "Locksley Hall," "Tithonus," "Enoch Arden," and most of the domestic idyls, and concludes with No. 356, "The Spiteful Letter" (1868), on the unenviable lot of the public poet. Volume III opens with "In the Garden at Swainston," Tennyson's mini-elegy on the third intimate friend he had lost to death, Sir John Simeon (1874), includes most of the poems from his last seven published books, and concludes (leaving aside the *Idylls*), as Tennyson wished all editions of his works after 1889 to end, with "Crossing the Bar" (No. 462).

With this choice there can, of course, be no quibble. Concerning the penultimate poem, however, the last composed work by the aged Laureate, there are grounds for debate. Ricks, following Hallam Tennyson's note in the *Memoir* that it was "the last poem he finished," places "The Dreamer" immediately before "Crossing the Bar." While Hallam's authority is normally unimpeachable, "The Silent Voices," which occupies the antepenultimate position in Ricks, may, in fact, have a greater claim for this distinction. The poem was first printed in the Order of Service in the program for Tennyson's funeral at Westminster Abbey on 12 October 1892.[13] Following the Lesson, two anthems were sung: "Crossing the Bar" (also printed in the program), "Composed (at the request of the Family) for this Service by Professor Bridge, Mus.Doc."; and "The Silent Voices." Against the latter poem appears the following rubric: "The latest poem by Lord Tennyson. Music by Lady Tennyson. Arranged for four voices by Dr. Bridge. (Both are copyright, and printed by special permission)." The point is trivial, perhaps, but closures being what they are today—consider *In Memoriam*'s "One God, one law, one element,/And one far-off divine event,/To which the whole creation moves," with its emphasis on unity; or "Mourn in Hope!," the last three words of the last poem in Tennyson's last volume—"On, and always on!" (the final line in "The Silent Voices") may be a more fitting capstone to Tennyson's poetic career than the cliché that ends "The Dreamer": "And all's well that ends well,/Whirl, and follow the Sun."[14]

The ghost of two Hallams hovers no less over Lang and Shannon's edition of the *Letters of Alfred Lord Tennyson* than it does over

Ricks's edition of the poems. The dearest friend and closest companion of Tennyson's youth, whose untimely death fired the poet's imagination, the first Hallam, Arthur Henry, occupies a recurring symbolic position in the poetry. The emotional epicenter of *In Memoriam*, Hallam also figures, at least tangentially, in a succession of lesser elegies and threnodic verses, including Tennyson's mortuary tributes to the Duke of Wellington and Prince Albert; more prominently in a number of the major lyrics, especially "Ulysses," and in the series of "one-1" English Idyls. And he assumes heroic stature in Tennyson's quasi-epical portrayal of the Great Arthur of the *Idylls,* whose passing in the "Morte," composed in 1833–34, under the press of his immediate grief over the death of Hallam, presaged the poet's lifelong obsession and thematic love affair with loss and death.[15]

The second Hallam, namesake of the first, his father's amanuensis and intermediary after Emily Tennyson's breakdown in 1874, the Laureate's "Sole Literary Executor," and compiler and censor of the *Materials* and the "official" *Memoir,* played an equally focal role in Tennyson's life. But whereas the first Hallam, alive, fostered and, dead, perhaps even fulfilled Tennyson's poetic destiny, the second, determined to protect his father's posthumous public image, in essence rewrote Tennyson's life to conform to the family's vision of the man and poet. Paradoxically, Hallam's carefully constructed and sanitized account of his father almost certainly backfired and was at least partially responsible for the extended "reaction" against the poet that dominated Tennyson criticism during the first four decades of this century.

The adverse effects that Hallam Tennyson's deposit interdiction on the Cambridge manuscripts had on Ricks's first edition have already been discussed. Though frustrating in the extreme in 1969, Hallam's embargo, parodoxically, paved the way for the production of Ricks's greatly elaborated and much improved second edition. No such ameliorative construction, alas, can be put on his deliberate and irrevocable acts of omission and commission affecting the Tennyson life documents entrusted to him. "With a few exceptions," Cecil Lang writes in the Introduction to the letters, "everything we know about Tennyson's life we know by his son's leave" (I x).[16]

Assisted by his mother, his wife Audrey, Henry Sidgwick, Francis Turner Palgrave, and others, Hallam systematically destroyed thousands of incoming letters and outgoing family correspondence, preserving, for example, only snippets of Tennyson's early letters to Emily Sellwood.[17] Other materials he either destroyed, truncated, or severely bowdlerized. Tennyson's innate shyness (I 331) and his avowed aversion both to letter writing and to the "publication of letters not intended to be published" (I 341) doubtless influenced to some degree Hallam's editorial practices. Although masterfully ironic in their treatment of Hallam's role, Lang and Shannon tend to be overly generous in assessing his shortcomings; for, whatever credit may be owed him for his textual work—on the Eversley Edition, for example, Ricks's copy text—and for salvaging vast quantities of his father's papers, Hallam still remains the nemesis of Tennyson scholarship, equally as responsible for most of the lacunae as for what survives. Indeed, in the Lang/Shannon edition of the letters, Hallam functions, as he no longer does in Ricks's revised edition of the poems, as a silent and unwelcome third collaborator, though the editors are at pains to minimize this fact: "The well-loved blameless son, by slow prudence, made mild this rugged matter and subdued it to the useful and good" (xviii).[18]

While final assessment of any edition of letters would normally await the publication of the last volume, these two volumes, containing just over half of Tennyson's extant letters,[19] offer ample evidence, which the third volume is certain to confirm, that the completed edition will occupy a place of prominence in Tennyson scholarship, alongside Hallam's publications—the *Materials,* the *Memoir,* and *Tennyson and His Friends*—Sir Charles Tennyson's biography, and Ricks's edition of the poems as one of a handful of absolutely indispensable research tools. But the LS *Tennyson* differs radically from the growing series of major editions of correspondence of the great Victorians, whose letter-corpus, not surprisingly since most of them flourished before the invention of the telephone, is extensive. Four of the earliest modern scholarly editions, for example—Gordon Ray's *Thackeray* (4 vols., 1945–46), Gordon Haight's *George Eliot* (7 vols., 1954–56), Cecil Lang's *Swinburne* (6 vols., 1959–62), and Clarence Cline's

Meredith (3 vols., 1968)—each contain roughly 2000 letters, though, except for the last, many letters surfaced too late for inclusion in the editions and supplementary volumes either have already been published or will be in the near future. The letter-corpus of other leading Victorian writers for whom ongoing editions are in progress—Browning, Carlyle, and Dickens—is even more enormous, running into the tens of thousands and necessitating what might be labelled epistolary encyclopedias to contain them. Even Dante Gabriel Rossetti's letters will occupy an estimated nine volumes.

By contrast, the number of surviving letters of *the* major Victorian poet is embarrassingly small, and the editors, faced with a paucity, rather than a wealth, of riches were forced to include other documents to flesh out the running life-narrative that constitutes the principal virtue of collected editions of letters.[20] Paradoxically, their decision adds a special interest to the edition, for whereas most editions of letters are largely restricted to the single perspective contained in the writer's outgoing correspondence, the LS edition, drawing on incoming letters to Tennyson, on extensive family correspondence, on letters by others about the poet, on Tennyson's own journals and Emily Tennyson's *Journal* and letters, on published and manuscript recollections and the diaries of associates and friends, and on the *Materials* and *Memoir* and other printed accounts, provides multiple perspectives that, in effect, constitute a new scholarly genre, somewhere between biography and an edition of letters. No small part of LS's achievement lies in the selection of documents which complement the surviving correspondence. What in essence they have produced is a set of materials for a new life of Tennyson, fashioned along lines resembling the *Materials* that Hallam gathered in preparation for the *Memoir,* but much more selective and discriminating.

While the two volumes of LS published to date have a common format, there are important differences between them beyond obvious changes in the apparatus.[21] Running heads in both volumes refer to the earliest date on the page, but in vol. II annotations are letter rather than page oriented, as they are in the first volume. Since letter notes are separated by horizontal bars, there is no possible confusion, even when three brief letters with one note each appear on a single page or when a letter with multiple notes extends into successive pages.[22] The shift clearly underscores the editors' later concern to emphasize the discreteness of individual letters, but it also raises questions about their decision not to number the letters, as is done in most editions, including Professor Lang's *Swinburne Letters*. The obvious advantage to numbering letters is ease of cross-reference; the disadvantage of not numbering them is the need for extended citations in referring to a particular letter. At the very least, cross-references to LS will require citing volume and page, and when more than one letter appears on a page (there are five to Emily Tennyson, for example, on II 263) the date will also need to be given.

The letter-texts are drawn from a variety of printed and manuscript sources, duly described in the Introduction. Printed texts, mainly from the *Materials* and *Memoir*, are more common for the early than for later letters, and the editors have been assiduous in scouting libraries, private collections, and printed resources in order to make the collection as complete as possible. Certainly the edition is comprehensive. The editors have partially restored several mutilated manuscripts (for one, see II 155); another is conflated from three separate sources (II 169); one is a major editorial recovery of a partially published letter from Edward FitzGerald to Tennyson (I 133 and n2), a task which involved, according to the note, "enlarged photographs, infra-red photography, prolonged, intense scrutiny with fluorescent and ultra-violet lamps of several frequencies, plundering of other FitzGerald letters, intuition, outside help, and occasionally pure guess work (indicated by question marks)."

No known letters appear to have been missed out. Tennyson's letter accepting the Laureateship (see I 342n2), however, must have been sent and might be recoverable.[23] The justification for printing both the unsent draft and the formal letter to Princess Alice on the occasion of the death of Prince Albert as separate entries is not immediately clear, but his comparison of her loss of her father to his own grief for Hallam in the draft clearly argues for its preservation in the text. By contrast, Tennyson's autograph draft note to the heroes of Balaclava, a revised version of which was published with the "soldier's version" of "The Charge of the Light Brigade" (II 117), is relegated to a footnote but it surely deserves separate letter status, Emily Tennyson's reservations notwithstanding.[24] The only other omission of any substance is the exclusion of the drawing accompanying the letter to William Cox Bennett (II 381). The visual effect is clear enough from the long discursive description given in the note, and it has been published (though in a not so recent or readily available source), but the drawing is more interesting than the three sketches that are reproduced in the text (I 205, 215, 335).

Not unsurprisingly, there are a few typos and an occasional inconsistency in the two volumes, but these are more than offset by the scrupulousness of the transcriptions, the clarity of presentation of the letters and notes, and the quality of the annotations.[25] The letter-texts are by and large clean and uncluttered: variant readings, indicated in angled brackets, "sics," and square-bracketed insertions are kept to a minimum. Sensibly, there has been no attempt to produce diplomatic texts of the letters.[26]

One editorial decision is more controversial, however, and some users may, even at the risk of being branded "otiose" by the editors, take exception to the exclusion of details relating to the publication history of the letters. It is easy to agree with the editors' reasoning for omitting this information, but, lacking it, most readers have no way of determining either the number of new letters in the edition or the extent of the editors' contribution in restoring the full texts of letters hitherto only partially printed; in correcting corrupt texts; and in accurately dating letters which have been misdated elsewhere. Even more important to the biographer and critic, the publishing history makes it possible to determine with precision the date at which the contents of a given letter entered the public consciousness and became part of the poet's life record.

Most of the notes discussing editorial questions relate to problems of dating, but anyone at all familiar with the letters will appreciate the complexities the editors faced in editing them. A quick flip through the volumes reveals the high proportion of undated letters, and considerable attention has been given to this aspect of the editing, which is candidly reported, often amusingly, in the annotations, which are the most distinctive feature of the edition.[27]

The annotations in LS, unlike the letters they gloss, are never dull or perfunctory; ranging from simple, single-line cross-references to long, detailed bio-genealogical surveys, they are always informative and entertaining. Even an unidentified recipient can inspire an interesting speculation, such as the note on Sir John Richardson, the Arctic explorer (II 251); and the briefest of letters, such as that to Novella of 30 April 1860 (II 256) can spark an extended 350-word identification. The volumes contain such a wealth of fascinating annotations that it is difficult to discriminate among them, but those treating the villains in Tennyson's life are of special interest: Matthew Allen, whose *Pyroglyph* venture nearly sent the entire Tennyson family into bankruptcy in the early 1840s (I 183); Richard Herne Shepherd, whose "cool impudence" over his 1869 piracy of Tennyson's *Window* taxes credulity (II 535); and Thomas Jackson, the publisher of *Poems by Two Brothers* who blackmailed Tennyson by threatening in 1865 to capitalize on the Laureate's popularity by reissuing the volume, of which he envisioned selling "*at least 10,000* copies" (II 391).

Beyond the patent erudition of the annotations, the most singular quality evident is their humor, a feature too seldom associated with scholarly editing. These personal assessments from Vol. II are not uncharacteristic: Sir Francis Palgrave, father of the Golden Treasurer: "The reason of his superiority lay in his name, which was Cohen, and his mind which was Cohen also, or at least not English" (27, quoted from *The Education of Henry Adams*); Frederick William Farrar, Dean of Canterbury: "He was also a novelist of no distinction, a philologist of some . . . , and, as a theologian, variously of none, some and much" (35); James Furnivall: "enthusiastic and intemperate scholar, sculler, editor, antiquary, teacher (Working Men's College), Christian Socialist (for a while), and polemicist (all his life). . . . His virtues, though numerous and conspicuous, did not include moderation or modesty, self-restraint or self-doubt" (79); William Kirby, Canadian novelist, who after defecting to the United States, eventually

Tennyson and His Bibliographers

returned to Canada, where: "He remained more royalist than the Queen, more loyalist than her first minister, more Tory than Walter Scott (his great original), more Anglican than Fielding's Parson Thwackum" (486); Daniel Barron Brightwell, unauthorized compiler of the first concordance of Tennyson (1869): "[He] remains as obscure as even Tennyson could have wished him" (534).

But editorial levity is not restricted to descriptions of individuals. Of the Moxon *Tennyson*, the editors note, "Financially, the edition was a failure, historically a triumph, artistically a toss-up" (89). Risibility is sometimes subdued, seemingly accidental, as it is in the twin alternative identifications of "F" in Allingham's *Diary* (447) or in the attribution acknowledgement to Priscilla Metcalf (349). More often, however, it is calculated: glossing Tennyson's remark to Dr. Mann that "it is a loan I shall accept with fear and trembling," the editors write, "Probably not *Much Ado about Nothing*, II, iii, 203, or 2 *Henry IV*, IV, iii, 15–16, or even Psalm 55:5" (132). Annotating a line in a Tennyson scrap to Emily, written from Lyndhurst on 4 June 1861 reading, "The postmistress here has written wanting to take my portrait," they quote (from a 1912 Maggs catalogue) an untraced letter fragment to the photographer Herbert Watkins dated the previous day declining a similar request, but endorsed, "He did it later on." This is followed by a thoroughly documented discussion of the "problematical photograph" in Wheatcroft's *The Tennyson Album*, concluding, "Herbert Watkins, the well-known photographer of the period ... was probably not the postmistress at Lyndhurst" (276). The most amusing note in the entire edition, however, is the gloss to Tennyson's use of the word "Geschwister" in a letter to Edmund Lushington: "Sister or brother, or brother and sister, or brothers and sisters. Lushington having eight sisters and three brothers, the total number of identifications possible could be 68,588,312," a figure subject to alteration by subsequent information given in the same note (I 200n2). The catalogue could be greatly extended, but the examples cited are sufficient to convey the flavor of the annotations.[28]

There are occasional lapses in the editing, but these are mainly in cross-references, as in the failure to cite their own printing rather than the *Memoir*'s of the famous "Yours with aversion" letter on *Maud* (119n2) in the annotation to Tennyson's letter to A. T. Gurney (137n4); or to signal the reader that the "poetic wine-dealer" mentioned in Bayard Taylor's letter to E. C. Stedman in 1867 (453) is almost certainly the Charles Ellis, Manager of The Star and Garter Hotel in Richmond, to whom Tennyson wrote in October 1853 (73n1); or to cite (along with two other cross-references in 452n1) Tennyson's actual letter to *The Times* about printing errors in the "Exhibition Ode" (305). A different sort of lapse is the repetition of the information on Frederick Tennyson's son, Julius, who "was reputed the strongest man in the British army" (54n5 and 364n1). Such slips are of little consequence given the general level and accuracy of the annotations. Indeed, the only factual error spotted in the entire edition is the publication date of Rossetti's "My Sister's Sleep," which first appeared not in 1850, as the editors state (554n1), but in *La Belle Assemblée* in 1848.

Of course, the justification of the edition, however carefully and skillfully edited, rests finally on the value of the letters themselves. Readers of the *Tennyson Letters*, as opposed to those who merely turn to the volumes for reference purposes, will encounter a far less intimate Tennyson than that conveyed in his poetry, a fact Mary Howitt astutely recognized after only a brief acquaintance with the poet nearly a hundred and fifty years ago: "We seemed to have known him for years. So, in fact, we had, for his poetry is himself" (I 269n3).[29] His letters—unless these that survived the posthumous conflagration are completely untypical, and there is no reason to think that they are—contain precious few revelations about either the poet or the poet's mind, but they do provide a realistic portrait of the man to balance against the official stereotypes of Laureate, Sage, *Sacer Vates*. "In these letters," the editors write, by way of summary, in the Introduction,

we see not the type of the *Memoir*, not the Poet-Laureate, not the Voice of the Age, not the Pre-eminent Victorian, but the living, pulsing, breathing, *man*, husband, father, homeowner, householder, income-earner, worrier, patient, invalid; selfish, self-indulgent, self-pitying yet generous, egotistical and altruistic, introverted and extroverted, gruffly sentimental, vulnerable and studiously self-protective, anti-social recluse and social lion (and, in the old sense, lionizer). We see a man with a capacity for enduring friendships, loyal to his friends. (Indeed, the "old boy network," of which so much is seen in the first volume, gives the letters some value in social as well as literary history.) And, finally, we see a thoroughly professional poet. [I xxviii–xxix]

Prose was not Tennyson's natural mode, and by no stretch of the epistolary imagination could he be ranked with the great literary letter writers, such as Keats, Swinburne, or Virginia Woolf. But it would be gross misrepresentation to say that his letters are devoid of interest, color, humor, or emotion.[30] The fact is he detested letter writing too intensely to regard it as more than a perfunctory exercise. But he did his duty when occasion called, writing sixty letters (five of which are printed in LS) on the occasion of the still birth of his first son in April 1851: "as grand looking [a] little fellow as ever I saw"; "Dead as he was I felt proud of him" (II 13; 14). Two years later, he composed another sixty announcing the birth of "the little brick-faced monkey," Hallam, "who does anything but what Hamlet says Osric did in his nursery days" (II 41). An "enemy of polyonomy" (II 40), he capitulated to Emily's desire to name the baby Alfred, but he informed Henry Hallam, "we intend his second name to be, with your permission, Hallam"; and, inviting his friend's father to stand as godfather to his son's namesake, assured him the request was no "mere compliment or piece of civility nor without reference to times now remote but never to be by me forgotten" (II 39).

Both sides of the correspondence between Tennyson and Hallam were destroyed, and there are extant only contemporary related letters to suggest the intensity of Tennyson's response to Hallam's death, which, as the Reverend John Rashdall confided in his diary, anticipating *In Memoriam*, "seems to have left his heart a widowed one" (I 106). Still, Hallam's memory lingers subtextually in Tennyson's consciousness till the end, and it surfaces often in the letters in passing glances and casual asides, as in the parallel he draws to his own loss in the draft letter of condolence to Princess Alice on the death of Prince Albert, already mentioned.

The portion of Tennyson's life spanned in these two volumes (1821–1870) is too great to survey through extensive quotation. Most of the major events of his personal, publishing, and professional life are recorded in the letters, but as the editors candidly observe,

> Individually or collectively, they are in no way literary—they do not characteristically discuss his reading, they are not carefully constructed compositions, they do not often deal with poetry. They reveal no aesthetic creed, no theory of poetry, they conduct no inquiry into the sources of inspiration, they offer no observations or insights that we recognize, gratefully, as the germ of a poem, no speculative delving into the mystery of the creative process, and no hieratic claims for the role of the poet, or of poetry, in society. Nor are his letters egotistical, or even personal, in the sense of expressing emotional overflowings. Nor do they gossip. [xxviii]

Gossip may have been his "total abhorrence," as the editors conclude the above paragraph, quoting from his letter to Sophia Rawnsley Elmhirst (II 9), but the letters in Volume II abound with other, equally strong, prejudices, the most frequently mentioned of which is letter writing.[31] He also hates illustrations 456); "writing out my own poems after they have been printed"—this "usque and nauseam" (17); claret, perhaps because of his susceptibility to gout (339); contributing to annuals and magazines (346); publishing (474); writing about his own compositions (485); "this horrible age of blab" (23); polyonomy, mentioned above (40), and, most of all, poetasters (*passim*). With good reason, going back to "School Miss Alfred" days in 1846, when Bulwer in a "barefaced lie" (I 253n1) denied his authorship of *The New Timon*, Tennyson swore never again to read his novels, but he broke his vow in 1855 on the recommendation of Sir John Herschel (II 125).[32]

Tennyson's resentment of the laureateship—he writes in 1858 that he is "in the eighth year of my persecution" (II 193)—probably derived less from the onerousness of his official duties—"You may tell [the Rector of Trevena]," Tennyson wrote to Palgrave in 1866, "that I never laureatize except for the Queen and at her express desire, and then not willingly" (II 441)—than from the

Tennyson and His Bibliographers

claims made on him by poetasters who persisted in sending him complimentary copies of their slim or thick volumes, with the expectation of receiving for their generosity a reply if not an assessment: "200,000,000 poets of Great Britain deluge me daily with volumes of poems—truly the Laureateship is no sinecure. If any good soul would just by way of a diversion send me a tome of prose. O the shoals of trash!" (II 45). When he wrote those words, Tennyson was only two years into his post and Emily was fielding most of his official correspondence. As his laureateship wore on, he would have mounting evidence to confirm his early view that "of all books the most insipid reading is secondrate verse" (I 249).[33]

However interesting individual letters—and the barest sampling has been given here—it is the bringing together of Tennyson's letter-corpus under a single roof, buttressed with those related documents that provide the tuck pointing for the interstices left by the missing letters, that gives authority to the LS edition. From dozens of manuscript and printed sources, the editors have gathered Tennyson's letters and relevant related documents to present the Laureate in a completely new perspective. Given the number of single recipient letters in the collection, and the fact that Hallam and his helpers had no means of extending their scorched hearth policy to the bulk of Tennyson's outgoing letters, it is not unreasonable to assume that the publication of the edition will in time cause additional letters to surface, both singles and caches which were not unearthed despite the evidence that Lang and Shannon appear to have left few stones unturned. The editors are probably correct in their assertion that, with the two notable exceptions of his letters to Hallam and Emily Tennyson, "If we had all the letters Tennyson ever wrote, instead of merely the remnants that survive and have been traced, there is no reason . . . to suppose that our view of him as a letter-writer or a poet or a man would differ in any significant way from what it is now" (I xxvi). But the "now" in that assertion is critical syntactically, for it is only subsequent to Lang and Shannon's admirable edition of the letters, which complements so fittingly Ricks's edition of the poetry, that Tennyson scholars and enthusiasts have at last an opportunity to see Tennyson whole.

Notes

1. Quoted in a letter, dated 11 April 1908, from T. J. Wise to H. B. Forman in the Pforzheimer Collection (presumably now in the HRC at Texas), printed in *A Sequel to* An Enquiry, ed. Nicolas Barker and John Collins (London: Scolar, 1983) p. 196.

2. As an indication that no error is too minuscule to evade detection and correction, see the inserted caret in the notes to *The Princess* (between ii and iii, last line II 219), inadvertently omitted in 1969.

3. *Tennyson: A Selected Edition* (London: Longman; Berkeley: Univ. of California Press, 1989) arrived too late to be worked into the body of the review. As a recension of the three-volume edition, however, whose $48.50 price in hardback will make it more attractive to individual student and faculty purchasers, it deserves to be discussed in tandem with the longer work, to which, save for those poems actually included, it is intentionally keyed: in the numbering of the poems and in the notes; in Appendix II (the Contents pages of the complete edition, which does not appear in the original); and in the Index.

Like its parent, this selected edition, which is approximately half the length, is subtitled "Incorporating the Trinity College Manuscripts." In the Preface (x–xii; the thirteen-page Preface to the complete edition is also printed [xii–xxii]), Ricks outlines the major strength of the edition: that it includes the complete texts of the four major poems, *The Princess, Maud, In Memoriam*, and the *Idylls*, as well as "all the masterpieces: onwards from *Mariana, The Lady of Shalott, St. Simeon Stylites, Ulysses, Tithonus*" together with "the entire annotation (headnotes, footnotes, and alternative drafts) of the complete edition." Spatial restrictions necessitated a single guiding principle: the exclusion of any title which Tennyson did not incorporate into his collected edition, "whether left unpublished or published by him and later rescinded." When even this retrenchment proved insufficient, the editor had to make further cuts.

How drastic these cuts were, and their effect on his design to present in the selections the wide scope of Tennyson's poetry composed over sixty years, is revealed by a survey of the Contents. The three-volume edition prints 477 numbered poems. Besides the three major works in Vol. II, each of which is assigned a single number (286, 296, 316), the *Idylls*, which occupy Nos. 463–476, and the "Songs from the Plays" (477), there are 460 titled poems in the complete edition, only 66 of which are printed in *Selected Poems*—23 of 224 in Vol. I, to 1834; 26 of 129 in Vol. II, covering the years 1834–68; and 17 of 107 in Vol. III, 1870–92.

One suspects that the constraints imposed on the editor were governed more by economic than by critical considerations, but it is by no means clear precisely what audience the publishers have in mind in issuing the volume. The claim on the dust jacket that "this is the only fully annotated and comprehensive selection of Tennyson's poetry, and for the first time it provides teachers, students,

Tennyson and His Bibliographers

and the general reader with an affordable edition of the central body of the work which the *Sunday Telegraph* described as the best edition of this century of the best poet of the last century" certainly does not misrepresent the quality of Ricks's editing or, in a sense, the value of the selected edition. But, if textbook adoptions are foreseen, it must be said that *Selected Poems* has distinct pedagogical disadvantages.

The scholarly apparatus, especially the profusion of manuscript variants, will appeal more to graduate than undergraduate students, but the exclusions are likely to prove unduly limiting for use in either undergraduate surveys or graduate seminars. Too many poems which, if not debatable "masterpieces"—"The Poet," "The Poet's Mind," "The Hesperides," "The Voyage," "Tiresias," "The Ancient Sage"—are at least invaluable teaching texts, are not included. But the more serious omissions are broadly taxonomical: most of the juvenilia, including the whole of *Poems by Two Brothers* and *The Devil and The Lady* (the first poem printed is "Mariana," no. 73); many of the dramatic monologues, particularly the later ones; dozens of lyrical, occasional, and Laureate compositions; all of the sonnets; a high proportion of the English Idyls; a number of the paired poems; and virtually all of those poetic tirades and effusions treating literary squabbles cited in the opening section of this paper. None of the new poems in the three-volume edition is printed in the selected edition.

Though it may be cynical to say so, the *Selected Poems* gives every indication of being the publisher's solution to having priced the revised Longman's Annotated Tennyson beyond the reach of the individual purchaser, in particular the student and classroom market. While this assessment in no way affects the scholarly worth of the selected edition, which retains Ricks's invaluable annotations for all the poems included, it is clear that the editor was faced with an unresolvable dilemma in making his selection within the allowed space limits. It is also clear that the students of an earlier generation who had access to Ricks's original 1969 edition of the *Complete Poems*, with his extensive annotations and at a price that was genuinely "affordable," were better served than their counterparts today, who cannot consult in toto both Tennyson and Ricks between the covers of a single volume.

4. Revisions, even on such a grand scale, would be relatively simple were no more required than updating computerized headnotes, text, and notes. Given the early date of the first edition, however, it seems unlikely (though I am prepared to stand corrected) either that Ricks's original text was machine-readable or that the first edition was computer set. Variations in ink density in the second edition give some clue as to new material, but the disparity is not uniform through the three volumes. The restructuring of the text is so skillfully done that much survives page-for-page, often even following major revisions. Only occasionally, as in No. 206 "Life of the life within my blood" (I 548), does the restructuring produce any awkwardness.

5. Though many errors in 1969 are silently corrected when no specific source is involved, Ricks is as scrupulous in acknowledging his sources as he is honest

in calling attention to previous slips. In this instance, he notes that "this edition (1969) erred badly in its placing of the lines (now corrected thanks to S. Shatto), but the attribution—which Shatto does not accept—of the lines to *Maud* (because of movement, plot, and tone) still holds" (II 533). For other examples in all three volumes, see the note to "The Gardener's Daughter" (I 563 11 185–208) that "the sequence of lines was misdescribed in 1969" (I 563); the long addition to the headnote of No. 350 on Charlotte Yonge's *Book of Golden Deeds* (1864) as a source for "The Victim" (II 694); and the rectification of the "wrongly hazarded" date for Epigrams XXI and XXII, transposed in the new edition (III 13–14).

6. In two instances in the notes (II 257 [v 241] and 282 [vii 89]), Ricks keys line cross-references to "Semele" to the old rather than the new text. Similarly, he also retains in the index the exclamation mark following the first line of "The Baby Boy," one of the unadopted songs in *The Princess*. In the text, however, following the ULC MS, he drops the exclamation marks added by Hallam to lines 1, 3, 10, and 14 in *Materials* (see headnote II 302), from which his 1969 text was printed.

7. No. 65 "To Poesy" ["Religion be thy sword"] (I 186) has long been known to be a joint poem by Tennyson and Hallam.

8. In both the headnote to *In Memoriam* (II 311) and in Appendix A (III 592), Ricks retains the 1969 reference to eight unpublished sections, overlooking (iiiA) "'The Light that shone when hope was born,'" first printed by him in *TLS*.

9. The second edition adds, however, two further fragments: an adaptation of "Sir Patrick Spens" in H. Nbk 48 entitled "The King of Scotland," and an "eight-line impromptu on Edgar of 'The Promise of May'" (III 640).

10. While the thrust of the revised edition is to add new material, a number of notes have, in fact, been deleted, presumably (but not certainly) intentionally. The examples cited below (keyed to pagination in the 1969 edition) are intended to suggest the range of the deletions:

760 (*The Princess*): ii 46 Ourself] 1862; ourselves 1847–61.

829 (*The Princess*): vi–vii 13 take] bear HnMS (the new edition substitutes ULC reading).

889 (*In Memoriam*): xxix 3 chains regret] fetters thought Eversley.

909 (*In Memoriam*): liv 12–13 notes presence in T.MS of four lines "saying there has not been such a revelation of after-life to man; deleted presumably for religious reasons." The stanza is quoted in the second edition without comment (II 370).

916 (*In Memoriam*): lxii 5–7 long note on parallels between "Locksley Hall," based on passage in *Hamlet*.

973 (*In Memoriam*): cxxiii 8–9 two lines describing four lines quoted from a proof of HT's edition, deleted in T.MS; a fact not noted in the new edition (II 443).

982 (*In Memoriam*): E 31–2 reference to Catullus.

1525 (*Idylls of the King*): "The Marriage of Geraint" headnote reference to the Canford Manor printing.
1632 (*Idylls of the King*): "Launcelot and Elaine" 422 identification of Uther, Arthur's father.
1775 (Appendix A, headnote to [vi] "Let death and memory keep the face"): details of transcriptional and placement errors in Valerie Pitt's *Tennyson Laureate*.

11. In a work of this length and complexity, some errors and inconsistencies are inescapable, but careful and close editorial control has reduced these to an acceptable minimum. Only a single typo has been discovered in the text itself, and that in Appendix A, where the first line of "The Ring" (III 577) reads "Litte" for "Little." Of the few other typos and inconsistencies that survive, most are trivial: in the headnote to "Song [Who can say]" (I 493), III 618 should read III 619; *Maud* i 76 (II 526) should read 75, and the note for i 715–16 (II 558) II 517 should read II 516; the quotation marks in the headnote to "Ode: O Bosky Brook" (I 289) have not been corrected from 1969. Potentially more serious are transcriptional discrepancies in Tennyson's letter to Sophy (Rawnsley) Elmhirst, printed in the headnote to the new poem 297A " 'Yours & Caetera' O how cold" (II 461), first identified by Aidan Day in *TLS* (11 Dec. 1981; not checked). Ricks quotes the letter from Day rather than the new edition of the letters; collation with the Lang/Shannon text (II 4) reveals four substantive and five accidental variants from their text.

Owing to the publisher's refusal to make final proof of the Index available to the editor, that section of the new edition contains over seventy errors. Professor Ricks kindly made available to me photocopies of his corrected Index and generously sanctioned my using them in this review. Many are insignificant slips in spacing, capitalization, or punctuation; but a few are substantive, sometimes amusing, typos affecting the reading of titles and lines: *Death of Oenonel* for "Oenone"; "Gee *opp* whoa!" for "oop"; "The *must* in the rain" for "mist"; "They found her buried in the *moon*" for "moor"; *To Princess Frederic on Her Marriage* for Frederica; *Wage* for *Wages*; "We know him, *our* of Shakespeare's art" for "out"; "With blackest moss the flower-lots" for "flower-plots"; and "You ask me, why, though *ill a tease*" for "ill at ease." One first line has been omitted—"O Sun, that wakenest all to bliss and pain" (III 313); one—"Prophecy whose mighty grasp"—is redundant." Over sixty are errors in volume and page citations, all but thirteen of which have been corrected in the abridged edition (see note 3 above), which prints the full index to the three-volume work. The citation errors are too numerous to be listed in this note. Interested users can make their own collation of the two indices; however, the following first lines and titles of poems included in the abridged edition have not been corrected, as citations are to the one-volume rather than the three-volume edition:

At Frances Allen's on the Christmas Eve: for II 3, read II 1.
Baby Boy, The: add III 592.

Below the thunders of the upper deep: for II 269, read I 269.
Come in, the ford is roaring on the plain: for III 335, read III 334.
Idylls of the King: add 602.
Lancelot and Elaine: add 602.
Midnight—in no midsummer tune: for III 145, read III 45.
Morte d'Arthur: for II 18, read II 3.
Not to Silence would I build: for III 628, read III 629.
The constant spirit of the world exults: add III 574.
To Alfred Tennyson My Grandson: for III 384, read III 70.
To the Queen: for II 299, read II 462; add III 599.
Turn, Fortune, Turn thy wheel and lower the proud: for III 335, read III 334.

One general stricture can be made about the Index. The sixty first-line titles in the text are placed within quotation marks in the text; in the Index, however, there is no way to distinguish these titles from ordinary first lines, a problem compounded by the inclusion of the first lines of Tennyson's nineteen untitled Sonnets and nine untitled Songs (which are all double indexed, once italicized in square brackets, then separately with neither quotation marks nor italics), the fragments in Appendix B, and the Doubtful Poems of Appendix C.

A few cross-references to poems in the edition or appendices have been omitted, such as to "The Ruined Kiln" (I 663) and "The Invasion of Russia" (II 288). Some others have simply not been updated: in the Preface, for example (I xviii), in noting that the edition begins with "four" poems antedating 1827, the new translations from Horace (1A) are not accounted for; and in an error repeated from 1969 (in the same paragraph) "No. 123" (which should read 183) is retained as the demarcation point between the undatable (to 1832 *Poems*) and datable poems. Similarly, the gloss to section lxxxv of *In Memoriam* (II 397) places the engagement of Tennyson and Emily Sellwood in 1838, overlooking the shift in that date to 1837 in the Chronology (I xxvi). There are occasional inconsistencies in abbreviations: *SP (Studies in Philology),* for example, is unaccountably dropped from the Abbreviations but later used in the headnote to "Merlin and the Gleam" (III 205); and in a note to *The Princess* (II 291), *Paradise Regained* is abbreviated PR, whereas the titles of Milton's long works are normally expanded. Dates of publication given in the headnotes are sometimes too elliptical. The newly added Appendix D provides a ready reference for poems appearing in the major volumes Tennyson published from 1842 onwards. However, shorthand dates such as 1851 for No. 199 "The Eagle" or 1865 for No. 266 "On a Mourner" will be recognized only by readers who already know that the seventh edition of *Poems* (1842), the so-called Laureate edition, appeared in 1851, or that 1865 is the date of the Tennyson selection in the Moxon Miniature Poets series.

While Ricks's notes are unusually generous, there are lacunae. The hostile reception of his "Jubilee Ode" (No. 418) is part of the publication history of that poem, and some mention might have been made of the spate of parodies by

Swinburne and others that the poem engendered. In another area, the headnote to "Hail Briton!" (No. 194) should include a reference by title to the selection from the poem printed in the *Memoir*. Ricks notes that "H.T. printed stanzas of the poem, *Mat.* i 128–30, *Mem.* i 110–11." In fact, Hallam selected twelve stanzas from the manuscript of "Hail Briton!"—one of which, not finally included in the poem, Ricks prints in the notes (I 524)—which he published under the title "The Statesman" in a general section labelled "Unpublished Poems of the Period" (1831–33) that also included "Youth," dated 1833 (No. 223). Although, as printed by Hallam, "The Statesman" is a non-poem, both it and "Youth" have footnotes indicating that they were "Copyright, 1897, by The Macmillan Company." In a parallel case, "This Earth is wondrous, change on change" (No. 201), Ricks records in the headnote the fragmentary printing of lines 21–28 in the *Memoir* as "The Moon" (I 540).

12. Ricks argues convincingly in the Preface (I xviii), using the examples of "The Epic" and "Morte d'Arthur," the case for making individual decisions about the placement of related poems, invoking Hallam Tennyson's precedent for those he elects to separate on grounds of chronological priority. In most instances Ricks's rationale is clear, unobjectionable, and, because he usually cross-refers displaced titles at the point in the chronological sequence where they would normally occur (see, for example, No. 419 "To Professor Jebb, with the Following Poem," which is cross-referred in III 216), unambiguous. There is sometimes a case to be made, however, for overriding the chronological sequence in the interest of preserving Tennyson's intent, as in No. 425 "To Mary Boyle With the Following Poem" (III 194) and No. 193 "The Progress of Spring" (I 516). Admittedly the poems were written fifty-five years apart, but the 1833 poem was not published until *Demeter and Other Poems* (1889), and then in heavily revised form. Printing the poems together, in either volume, would be misleading in terms of their compositional chronology, but, given the intimate nature of the introductory poem, a more prominent signal of their relationship than a cross-reference in the headnote to "The Progress of Spring" would seem to be required.

13. Ricks makes no reference either to the program text or to the separate pamphlet—privately printed for copyright according to T. J. Wise (*Ashley Catalogue* VII 157), with a facing facsimile of the title page—issued by Macmillan in 1892.

14. The importance of this closure was first pointed out by T. Herbert Warren in *Essays on Poets and Poetry Ancient and Modern* (London: John Murray, 1909), p. 325.

15. For recent accounts of Hallam's presence in the *Idylls*, see Cecil Lang's *Tennyson's Arthurian Psycho-drama* (Lincoln TRC, 1983); also John D. Rosenberg's "Tennyson and the Passing of Arthur" and William E. Fredeman's "The Last Idyll: Dozing in Avalon," in *The Passing of Arthur: New Essays in Arthurian Tradition*, ed. Christopher Baswell and William Sharp (New York: Garland, 1988).

16. The Introduction, signed by both editors, is written in the inimitable style of the editor of *The Swinburne Letters*, as are many of the notes in these first two volumes. "A wit as well as a connoisseur of wit" (a phrase used to gloss Goldwin Smith in the note to Tennyson's letter to Emily Tennyson on New Year's Day 1856 [II 140]) applies equally to Cecil Lang and doubtless accounts for the trenchancy and humor of many of the notes. Without in any sense presuming to assess the degree of editorial collaboration in these volumes, I have ventured in this instance to cite Lang singly; most subsequent references to the editors, in both the text and notes, are designated LS.

17. The extent of the materials available to Hallam was enormous— "upwards of 40,000" is the figure he gives in the *Memoir*. Emily reports in a letter of 18 November 1893 that Palgrave had "looked over about twenty three thousand letters for us and Hallam about as many more" (*Letters of Emily Tennyson* 365); and Palgrave noted in a letter of 14 October 1893 (in the TRC) that "the 10,000 & odd letters which you entrusted to me are now completely dealt with. About 1500, I reckon, have been preserved." Assuming Hallam's and Palgrave's figures to be accurate—and, incidentally, there is no evidence that Palgrave's decisions were subject to family veto—and that his ratio roughly matched Hallam's own, only about 6,000 letters would have escaped destruction. While most of these would have been incoming correspondence, which so "penny-post maddened" the Laureate—(for Tennyson's amusing drawing of the deluge of letters to which he was subjected, see his drawing [verbally described, not reproduced in LS] II 381n1; see p. 19 of this review)—much family correspondence must also have been destroyed. For the best account of the building of the *Memoir* and of Hallam's editorial practices, see Philip L. Elliott, *The Making of the Memoir* (Furman University, 1968).

18. In part two of the Introduction, the editors carefully weigh the influence of Hallam, who is portrayed as a kind of Telemachus to Ulysses-Tennyson (I xxii), and the importance of the *Memoir* in sculpting the portrait of the Laureate transmitted to posterity. They defend both Hallam's motives and the book against the charge of hagiography, arguing that the genre of the *Memoir* more nearly approximates fable or typology (I xviii), but Max Beerbohm's caricature of *Woolner at Farringford, 1857,* particularly its caption, may more accurately, if retrospectively, foreshadow the motives behind the shaping of the *Memoir:* "Mrs. Tennyson: 'You know, Mr. Woolner, I'm one of the most un-meddlesome of women; but—when (I'm only asking), *when* do you begin modelling his halo?'"

19. The *actual* number of letters by Tennyson in the two volumes is difficult to ascertain with precision since no letter numbers are employed; the Index of Correspondents (which in both volumes excludes Tennyson) cites correspondents and recipients indiscriminately, and the general index includes only descriptions of the poet. Complicating the letter-count further, many single entries contain more than one letter, especially in the second volume, in which most of the surviving notelets to Emily appear. In a page-by-page survey, I

Tennyson and His Bibliographers 33

recorded a total for the two volumes of 1019 full or fragmentary letters by Tennyson (259 in Vol. I; 760 in Vol. II) plus another 32 written jointly, mainly with Emily (7 in Vol. I; 25 in Vol. II) for a grand, albeit uncertain, total of 1051. Based on the editors' own estimate that "the whole collection from 1821 to his death numbers less than 2,000" (I xxv), approximately another 900 letters will be printed in the final volume when it appears, sometime in 1990.

20. With a few notable exceptions—journals kept by Tennyson on trips to Cornwall and the Continent, Emerson's journals, Sir Francis Hill's "Craycroft Diary," and some recollections under the general head "Tennyson Observed"—the supplementary documentation in the first volume draws most heavily on family correspondence, especially for the early years for which the number of extant letters is extremely sparse. Prior to Hallam's death, for instance, only twenty-five letters survive, just over twice as many as the editors print by Hallam to correspondents other than Tennyson from Kolb's edition; between 1833 and the publication of *Poems* (1842) only eighty-nine, hardly sufficient to give a sustained account of the poet through three decades. Volume II, covering the years 1851–70, with far more letters by Tennyson, relies on some supplementary correspondence, such as Bayard Taylor's letter to E. C. Stedman recounting his visit to Farringford in 1867, headed by LS "Sartar Resartus," which had for him unfortunate ramifications (453–54) and the two accounts of a similar visit by Longfellow in the following year (II 495–98); but most of the documentation consists of extracts from the journals and diaries of William Allingham, Marian Bradley, Moncure Conway, Carolyn Fox (see "Chauntecleer and the Colfox" [II 266]), Anne Gilchrist, Nathaniel Hawthorne, Francis Turner Palgrave, John Addington Symonds, Hallam and Emily Tennyson, J. R. Thompson, and others.

21. Vol. I contains a twenty-four-page Introduction and two appendices, the first providing extended biographical information on five Apostles mentioned in an 1832 letter from Arthur Henry Hallam to William Henry Brookfield (I 70): William Hepworth Thompson, Robert Montieth, Francis Garden, John Moore Heath, and Richard Chenevix Trench; the second an 1831 letter by Hallam to Edward Moxon discovered too late for inclusion in Jack Kolb's edition of Hallam's letters (1981). Vol. II has six appendices containing supplementary documentation to letters in the text, but whereas bidirectional cross-references are provided in Vol. I, in Vol. II cross-references appear only with the letters. Both volumes print the Editorial Principles and the list of Abbreviations, to which five new entries have been added in Vol. II. Each volume contains an Index of Correspondents and a general index of names of people and places associated with the Tennyson circle and of Tennyson's works mentioned in the text. Annotations will be picked up in the comprehensive index to the set in Vol. III.

22. Referring to these multiple notes can, however, be ambiguous; see the end of note 27 below.

23. Tennyson drafted two letters—one accepting, one rejecting, the invita-

tion from the Queen conveyed in the letter of 5 November 1850 (received on the 9th?) from Charles Beaumont Phipps, Keeper of Her Majesty's Privy Purse, following the famous dream recorded in Emily's Tennyson's *Journal*.

24. Emily wrote across the top of the manuscript, "It would be pleasant to write to the soldiers only one is afraid it looks too regal to do so" (II 118n1); John Foster redrafted Tennyson's note to make it more formal. To Foster, Tennyson wrote indicating his preference that his letter be sent separately, adding that "in case the letter be already printed on the same slip as the Poem then of course it had better go . . . as my desire is that the soldiers should have it as soon as possible." The editorial gloss, "It was, and thus it went" (II 119n1), underscores the point that Tennyson clearly construed his prefatory note as a letter.

25. In general, the first volume appears to have been more carefully proofread than the second. Only two minor typos were spotted in Vol. I (147, 191); Vol. II contains at least seven (26, 57, 390, 356, 506, 515, 524), in the main trivial—transposed, omitted, or doubled letters; an omitted word, or the substitution of an "!" for a "£" sign—but, in addition, nine "000s" have not been altered in the footnotes (19, 68, 140, 145, 335, 344, 392, 346, 436). A number of queries are also raised by discrepancies between the names of correspondents as given in the text and in the Index: Charles Edward Cockbin (511 and n1) is Cockin in the Index; Olding, Osborne and Co. (403) is Odling; and Lady Franklin is Lady Jane Franklin. While only the two letters from and to Emily Tennyson on page 5 appear to have been left out of the Index of Correspondents, Tennyson's letter to Sir Francis Palgrave (212), who is not listed, is attributed to his son, Francis Turner. And the page reference in the Index to Tennyson's letter to Charles Kegan Paul should be 386 rather than 286.

26. The handful of pedantries that have been allowed to stand are not numerous; but "I have been and am very fat [sic] from well" (I 27) would have been better silently corrected, as would the [)] in the letter to Frederick Locker (II 517). Puzzlingly, Rossetti's name is allowed to stand with one "s" in the joint letter of Tennyson and Hallam in Vol. I (77) but added in square brackets in the note on Thomas Moore's "The kiss" (II 348).

27. The Cecilisms explaining the reasoning behind assigned dates are one of the delights of the edition. Dates are variously described as "conjectural" (I 105n2) or even "conjectured without confidence for the evidence is tenuous" (I 165n1); "a guess" (I 157n1), one a "mere guess" ("though the handwriting seems to belong to the period" [I 202n2]); another "audacious and possibly foolhardy" (I 189n3), one even "desperate" (II 187n7); arrived at "by circular reasoning and a leap of faith" (I 202n1); negative ("The evidence for the date is persuasive primarily because there is none against it" [I 221n2]); an "editorial convenience" (I 168 n2); and "a *pis aller*" (I 314n1). Although the editors seldom rely on the dates of others, they provide the counter-evidence for alternative dating where relevant. The letter to Matthew Allen, for example, they date [12 May 1841] "solely on the basis of the handwriting," but they acknowledge that

"Schooling dated this note '(about 1843)', and he may well be right; for the same reason (and with little confidence) we prefer 1841, and we may well be wrong" (I 191n2). The most ingenious and ingenuous note on dating occurs in reference to Tennyson and Emily's letter to American poet F. G. Tuckerman, dated 17 October 1855, relating to his review of *Maud* in *Putnam's Monthly Magazine,* which appears to be a reply to his letter printed in *Materials,* where it is dated 22 October: "It seems to us (since only editors can fully appreciate and enjoy the impossibility of this date) that it was mistranscribed from 2 October. In Eidson, *Tennyson in America,* p. 246, the original, still untraced, is incorrectly said to be at Harvard" (II 132 [the second] n1).

28. The humorous footnotes are more common in the second than in the first volume, but they are found there also, as in the description of John Tomlin, the postmaster of Jackson, Tennessee, who is perpetuated as a "minor (if not minimal) poet" (203); and of Matthew Allen's "awesome" handwriting, owing to which "the text of this letter may be to some extent made, not begotten" (197). More nostalgic (or romantic) than humorous is the note on a reference to "Rosa" in an 1854 letter to Sophia Rawnsley Elmhirst: "Conceivably Rosa Chawner ... but more probably, as one hopes, Rosa (Baring) Shafto, with whom Tennyson was in love in the thirties" (II 92). If so, it is the sole remnant of this old romance in the letters. Whether Tennyson and Rosa Baring actually exchanged billets-doux is not recorded.

29. Quoted by LS from her *Autobiography* (I 269n3).

30. Stylistic peculiarities are of special interest in Tennyson's letters, such as his exclusive use of "thee" and "thou" in communications with his wife. His coinages and fondness for esoteric diction should also be noted; among many examples: "paidagogue" (I 86), "flagitiously" (I 246), "monticule" (II 299), "vendibility" (II 391), and "niaiseries" (II 448).

31. Tennyson's comments on letter writing are so numerous as to become a persistent apologetic leitmotif in the correspondence: "I am no letter-writer, as all my friends either know or should know," he informs Mrs. Hogson in 1858 (II 208). As early as 1845, he writes to his Aunt Elizabeth Russell, "I should think I write fewer letters than any man of my standing in Great Britain" (I 245). Realizing that he often seems to be slighting his friends, he informs Rawnsley in the same month, "Truly my love for my friends must not be measured in the quantity of black and white into which I put it" (I 246). His refusal to write long letters (II 364) probably accounts for the shortest letter in the collection, to Coventry Patmore: "My Dear Patmore/Say Friday/Ever Yours/A. Tennyson" (I 284). Though he sometimes couches his dislike in humorous terms—closing a note to Jowett, "Loving you and hating letter-writing" (II 198); or commencing one to Dr. and Mrs. Mann, "You know that any day I would as soon kill a pig as write a letter" (II 211)—the sentiment is always serious. That Tennyson would probably have been comfortable in today's computer environment is suggested by his most extended diatribe against the intrusion of letter writing on his time and energies, sent to Rawnsley on the eve of his receiving the Laureateship in

November 1850: "I have dozens of letters to write this afternoon and I cannot help wishing that I could hire the Electric Telegraph once a month and so work off my scores with the wires at whatever expense. This oldworld pen-and-ink operation is behind the age" (I 343).

32. In the nearest Tennyson ever comes to bawdiness in his letters, he wrote of Bulwer to Richard Monckton Milnes in 1837, "big as he is, [Bulwer] sits to all posterity astride upon the nipple of Literary Dandyism and 'takes the milk for gall'" (I 147–48).

33. Tennyson's disposition towards valetudinarianism—"this really great man thinks more about his bowels and nerves than about the Laureate wreath he was born to inhabit," Old Fitz wrote to E. B. Cowell in 1848 (I 296)—was almost certainly exacerbated by the plague of petty poets who persistently pestered him, including, as Hallam reports, one anonymous abusive correspondent who wrote him on the appearance of each volume. In what amounts to virtually a prose paraphrase of "The Spiteful Letter" (Ricks No. 256), he complained to Rawnsley in 1845, "I doubt not that I shall meet with all manner of livor, scandal, and heartburning, small literary men whose letters perhaps I have never answered, bustling up and indignant that they are past by" (I 248).

Farquhar Complete and Sheridan Under Construction

Judith Milhous

George Farquhar, *The Works of George Farquhar,* ed. Shirley Strum Kenny. Oxford: Clarendon Press, 1988. Two volumes. xxv, 664 pp.; xvii, 636 pp.

Bruce Redford, ed. *The Origins of* The School for Scandal: *"The Slanderers" [and] "Sir Peter Teazle."* Princeton: Princeton University Library, 1986. 165 pp.

The two editions under consideration here both concern what is traditionally thought of as "eighteenth-century laughing comedy," but they represent radically different sorts of writers and utterly different varieties of modern scholarly editions. Both are fine pieces of work and can be given an enthusiastic welcome. Fortuitously, they provide an occasion to look at two familiar writers we are perhaps unduly ready to categorize and forget. Farquhar and Sheridan have enjoyed the blessings and suffered the results of writing two or three enormously popular plays. Critical perception of the rest of their canons remains skewed by the prominence of those plays, leaving both writers, for better or worse, prisoners of their own success.

George Farquhar (1677?–1707) is now remembered primarily for his last play, *The Beaux Stratagem* (1707), though he wrote seven others. *The Constant Couple* (1699) had more performances its first season than any play in theatrical memory. It was thus the greatest success of his short lifetime. The "fifty Audiences in five months" that Farquhar bragged about were not bettered until the phenomenal run of *The Beggar's Opera* in 1728 (I, 142, n. 24; 405). Yet only *The Recruiting Officer* (1706) and *The Beaux Strat-*

agem have been regularly reprinted, studied, and even revived in the twentieth century—and the former is often cited as much because Brecht used it as the basis of his *Trumpets and Drums* (1955) as for its own merits. *NCBEL* treats Farquhar as one of the nine "major" dramatists of the Restoration—heir to Etherege, Wycherley, and Congreve, and fellow of Vanbrugh. The critical cliché about Farquhar is that he represents the last gasp of the satiric tradition of "Restoration comedy," with the corollary that his early death robbed the "anti-sentimental" school of its great white hope. Critics have generally enjoyed the "country" air of the last two plays (set, respectively, in Shrewsbury and Litchfield), while tending to deprecate their cheerful tone and lightweight satire as evidence that Farquhar was making concessions to an increasingly sentimentalized popular taste.

Farquhar received a competent *Complete Works* from Charles Stonehill (2 vols., 1930) and enjoys praise in virtually all critical surveys of eighteenth-century drama, yet he has been the subject of remarkably little criticism. There have been a handful of articles about the last two comedies, but only two critical books have been devoted to Farquhar—Eric Rothstein's competent but very literary Twayne volume (1967) and an uninspired monograph by Eugene Nelson James (Mouton, 1972). In part, this neglect is attributable to the simplicity of the plays: they were effectively contrived stage vehicles, but they pose few difficulties for the reader. They are not in need of explication. Farquhar's claim to a full-dress Oxford *Works* at $230 may not be obvious. If such texts are for critics, and there is little critical attention, do we need the text? One answer is that the text should help generate more accurate assessment of Farquhar's achievements—and, I hope, academic productions of some of the less familiar plays.

Ironically, Farquhar's high reputation in the twentieth century was thrust upon him for almost entirely the wrong reasons. His familiar comedies of manners are close enough to "wit comedy" to pass in some anthologies for "Restoration," yet in others they supposedly mark a shift toward sentimentalism. These are strange distortions. Farquhar is more boisterous than witty, and he writes nothing remotely like the polished drawing-room comedy of his supposed predecessors, Etherege and Congreve. His

Farquhar and Sheridan

view of the comic forms he inherited is decidedly sardonic. E. N. James has pointed out that Farquhar's very first ramshackle effort, *Love and a Bottle* (1698), burlesques those forms (*SEL*, 1965). Jackson I. Cope considers *The Constant Couple* "a comedy of wit; a burlesque; a scandalous *roman-à-clef;* and a problem play focused upon the ethical paradoxes shared by the role-playing societies on both sides of the proscenium" (*ELH*, 1974). The bitterly satiric *Twin Rivals* (1702) comes close to tragicomedy and is like nothing else in the period. Farquhar never settled down comfortably in the standard comic patterns of his time, and this is one of the reasons interpretive analysis is overdue.

A reader approaching Farquhar with a mind disencumbered of inherited truisms ought to be able to gauge the degree to which he was hostile to the critical strictures of his time. He even stated his feelings explicitly. Euphoric over the success of *The Constant Couple,* Farquhar published a marvellously biting "Discourse upon Comedy in Reference to the English Stage" (1702). One of the odder conspiracies of silence—or ignorance—in the history of modern criticism of "Restoration comedy" is the one that has bundled this essay out of sight and ensconced Farquhar as an establishment figure. But then the playwright who gleefully ridicules Aristotle is probably lucky not to find his entire *oeuvre* ignored.

Unless one is a member of the Heil Aristotle club, the enthusiasm Farquhar shows for debunking Established Neoclassical Criticism is extremely entertaining. As a practical man of the theatre, Farquhar has nothing but contempt for rules, models, and theory. With Johnsonian commonsense he hoots at "Aristotelian" decorum and the rules of time and place. He finds realism and probability as propounded by critics simply irrelevant to English theatrical practice. For the likes of Rymer, Gildon, and Dennis—or even Dryden the theorist—Farquhar exhibits a cocky disrespect that sets him apart from the playwrights of his time.

Lookee, Sir, don't be in a Passion, the Poet does not impose Contradictions upon you, because he has told you no Lie; for that only is a Lie which is related with some fallacious Intention that you should believe it for a Truth; now the Poet expects no more that you should believe the Plot of his Play, than old *Æsop* design'd the World shou'd think his *Eagle* and *Lyon* talk'd like you and I; which I think was every Jot as improbable.... If you are so inveterate against improbabilities, you must never come near the Play-House at all; for there are several Improbabilities, nay Impossibilities, that all the Criticisms in Nature cannot correct; as for instance; In the part of *Alexander* the Great, to be affected with the Transactions of the Play, we must suppose that we see that great Conquerour ... at last miserably ending his Life in a raging Madness; we must suppose that we see the very *Alexander*, the Son of *Philip*, in all these unhappy Circumstances, else we are not touch'd by the Moral, which represents to us the uneasiness of Humane Life in the greatest State, and the Instability of Fortune in respect of worldly Pomp. Yet the whole Audience at the same time knows that this is Mr. *Betterton*, who is strutting upon the Stage, and tearing his Lungs for a Livelihood. And that the same Person shou'd be Mr. *Betterton,* and *Alexander* the Great, at the same time, is somewhat like an Impossibility, in my Mind. [II, 383–84]

Much more important, in his view, is providing for the demands of various parts of an English audience. "The Scholar calls upon us for *Decorums* and *Oeconnomy;* the Courtier crys out for *Wit* and *Purity of Stile;* the Citizen for *Humour* and *Ridicule;* the Divines threaten us for Immodesty; and the Ladies will have an Intreague" (II, 366). Comedy, as far as he is concerned, is "no more ... than a *well-fram'd Tale handsomly told, as an agreeable Vehicle for Counsel or Reproof"* (II, 377). This definition emphasizes the didactic function more than Farquhar normally does in his plays. He makes no exaggerated claims for the utility of theatre except as entertainment. As a playwright he is far more concerned with actors, audience, and theatrical impact than with literary genre and critical precepts.

Farquhar's special gifts were recognized by his less hide-bound contemporaries to be energy, impudence, and "air." These qualities are most apparent in his first two plays, after which he suffered a crisis of confidence not altogether repaired until his last two. A judicious assessment of him was voiced in the anonymous obituary that appeared in *The Muses Mercury* (probably by Peter Motteux):

Mr. *Farquhar* had a Genius for Comedy . . . rather above the Rules than below them. His *Conduct,* tho not *Artful,* was *surprizing:* His *Characters,* tho not Great, were Just: His Humour, tho *low, diverting:* His *Dialogue,* tho *loose* and *incorrect, gay* and *agreeable;* and his *Wit* tho not *superabundant,* pleasant. . . . His Plays have . . . a certain Air of *Novelty* and *Mirth,* which pleas'd the Audience every time they were represented: And such as love to laugh at the *Theater,* will probably miss him more than they now imagine. [II, 14]

Very true: though he works with standard materials, Farquhar does not conform to standard patterns. Critics can easily amass lists of antecedents to his character types and plot devices while missing his charm altogether. Just what is meant by "Novelty" in this context? Let me point to some very specific examples.

Farquhar loved to tease his audience, and his attitude toward critical abstractions is nowhere more apparent than when he subverts conventions. He ends his first and last plays with scenes that poke fun at the last-minute revelations of comedy. The conventions governing portrayal of sexual relations were another favorite target. Thus the last scene of *Love and a Bottle* begins with the spectacle of Roebuck, "unbutton'd," on his way from his rooms to those of his wealthy new wife to consummate their marriage, when the revelations of the plot forcibly detain him (V.iii).

Farquhar was partial to the tease of calling to mind scenes from other plays, and the theatrical privilege of crossdressing also tickled his imagination. Earlier in *Love and a Bottle* he enlivens a formulaic older woman-young man courtship by inverting a crucial exit borrowed from Vanbrugh's popular comedy, *The Relapse.* In Farquhar's rendition, the sex-starved maid, Pindress, carries a pageboy off to bed on the pretext of searching him for her lost smelling salts bottle. The overpowered page protests, both against the woman's aggressiveness and because "he" is in fact a heroine in breeches who does not wish to be discovered. The page summons aid and prevents discovery with the line, "Help! help! I shall be ravish'd!" The original audience, given this set-up, would inevitably have recalled Vanbrugh's scene, which ends with Berinthia "very softly" protesting as Loveless carries her off, "Help! help! I'm ravished! ruined! undone! Oh

Lord, I shall never be able to bear it!" (*Relapse*, IV.iii—an allusion Kenny could usefully have pointed out in her notes). Farquhar thus got the additional joke of recalling a successful seduction, even as he averted this attempt at rape. The echo is now lost to all but specialists; nevertheless, the effect was beautifully calculated.

Likewise, at the end of the play when the fake clergyman is revealed to be a woman, part of the joke is that she is the most improbable character Farquhar could have chosen for that impersonation (V.iii). He had found a way to send up the gimmick of the friend disguised as priest, familiar from *The Country-Wife* and many other plays. The followers of Jeremy Collier who were then attacking theatre as an institution were not amused. (Farquhar relented so far as not to ordain any more women, but he did bring back the false priest in Irish guise in *The Stratagem*.)

Farquhar quickly learned to use ambiguous situations as a more subtle tease. Lady Lurewell, the female half of the title pair in *The Constant Couple*, is being courted by at least three men, not one of whom has honorable intentions toward her. The solution to her part of the plot depends on their not being sure to whom she dispenses sexual favors. The [male] audience should also be well-lured but unsure, until she proves chaste and can be rewarded (!) with marriage to the man who originally seduced her. In the sequel, *Sir Harry Wildair* (1701), Farquhar lazily retains Lurewell's reputation and does not even bother to give her a married name. But sexual teasing turns out to be harder to defuse with a joke after marriage than it was before. When Lurewell's husband discovers circumstantial evidence of a liaison between her and Sir Harry, Farquhar plays up the embarrassment Sir Harry feels at trying to make alibis to a friend. This farcical situation is presumably amusing because the audience knows that his attempt on the lady was interrupted. But the comedy does not quite cover up the ugliness of facts which do no credit to either side. Sir Harry's pursuit of his friend's wife resulted from her efforts to blacken the memory of his late wife.

The cheerful afterpiece, *The Stage-Coach* (winter 1701–February 1702), however durable, shows little improvement in Farquhar's skills. Both his Fletcher adaptation, *The Inconstant* (1702), and the uniquely serious *Twin Rivals* represent new departures, but neither proved fruitful. *The Inconstant* diverges radically from *The Wild Goose Chase*, yet is not wholly original, and it is far from "Artful" in its balance. Farquhar's Preface is defensive about his borrowing, to which he did not stoop again. *The Twin Rivals* explores the peculiar case of a younger twin's usurping the family estate while his elder brother is away on his Grand Tour. Primogeniture triumphs, but the attempt towards the end to shift blame from the younger twin to his wicked advisers is unconvincing. The plot is original, but not really plausible, even within the realm of tragi-comedy.

A man in skirts in *The Twin Rivals* was apparently so controversial that Farquhar felt obliged to include an apology for the character in his Preface. Mother Midnight is a composite of all the Nurses we have ever heard reminisce over the infants once in their charge. She appears to have officiated at the births of most of the dramatis personae, a joke that runs through the play. By the developmental logic of comedy, she now earns much of her living as a bawd, since her "children" have grown up. The rotund William Bullock in skirts should have suggested no connection to reality, cooing over memories of one character after another, yet willing to swear to a reverse birth order for the titular twins, if sufficiently rewarded. Still, to portray a midwife was daring, and Farquhar reports that "The Ladies . . . were told no doubt, that they must expect no less than a *Labour* upon the Stage" (I, 499–500).

When he returned to the theatre after a four-year silence, Farquhar had regained his own voice, and with it better control of situations. He encourages the audience to jump to conclusions about the country girl, Rose, in *The Recruiting Officer,* gleefully planting signs that Plume has seduced her in one scene, denying them in the next. The ambiguity is not finally resolved until Plume swears to a Justice of the Peace—to whom a gentleman would not lie—that Rose "had no harm" from him (V.vii). *The Beaux Stratagem* offers Farquhar's most attentive exploration by far of the woman's side of an unsatisfactory marriage. Mrs. Sullen means to keep her vows, however tempting she finds the "footman," Archer. She is innocent of his entrée into her bedroom, so the audience can enjoy their talking at cross purposes until Archer resorts to the use of superior physical force against her. Farquhar deflects this rape attempt with the comic intrusion of Scrub, crying "Thieves, murder, popery!"—whereupon Archer is transformed from ravisher into rescuer. Titillation and threat are more skillfully balanced than ever before.

The problems Farquhar poses to an editor are many and difficult. The texts are surprisingly problematical, and contextual allusion to both contemporary life and literature demands a lot of explication. The edition Dr. Kenny and Oxford University Press have given us offers a well-annotated old-spelling text, liberally embellished with pictures and music where available. The provision of printed and manuscript music (as well as lyrics) is especially welcome and ought henceforth to be considered de rigueur in standard editions of classic plays.

The most important contribution made by this edition is unquestionably the study of printing history on which Kenny has drawn in constructing the texts. Farquhar was quick to sell his plays to printers but also perfectly willing to emend them in rehearsal or during the first run. The initial printing does not always reflect such late changes. The case of *The Stage-Coach* is so confusing that scholars had long despaired of making any sense of its date or its textual history—until Kenny published her dazzling solutions in *Studies in Bibliography* in 1979. The multiple—albeit lost—manuscripts she deduces behind various printed versions do, finally, make sense of printed texts whose discrepancies once seemed inexplicable. Kenny would hardly claim that her hypotheses are unquestionably "true," but they certainly account for the data we possess. Again, in the case of *The Recruiting Officer,* cuts and substitutions in the second edition reflect the play audiences actually saw for most of the century. Kenny prints the new Q2 material, but gives the Q1 original at the foot of the page, so that either text is easily recovered.

I would argue that on the logic of the previous case, Kenny might have done something even more radical and adopted the revised *Beaux Stratagem* as copy-text. To what degree the dying Farquhar approved the changes reportedly made in the first production we have no way of knowing, but we do know that the entire Count Bellair subplot was cut almost immediately—tradition claims as early as the second night. During the eighteenth century the shortened version held the stage undisputed. It considerably reduces the seriousness of the marital discord plot and eliminates Mrs. Sullen's flirtation with adultery. In one sense, we falsify history when we read a text quite different from the one that established the play and won it many decades of popularity. I cannot really quarrel with Kenny's decision to stay with the first quarto: it is a very familiar text; it is the more interpretively serious text; and we cannot be sure Farquhar even knew about changes in it. Thanks to Kenny, however, the would-be critic can make an informed choice here.

Each text seems to me well-constructed, and textual policies are sensible and unobtrusive. I call the attention of all future editors of plays to the decision to expand speech tags, which enormously improves readability. There are, unfortunately, more literals and minor errors than there should be. A few examples: "Queen's College" for "Queens" (I, x); "I fancy, Sit" for "I fancy, Sir" (I, 74); "John" for William Archer (I, 651); a speech misassigned to Foigard (II, 191, *l.* 167); "a notably playwright" (II, 568); and *Love à la Mode* for *Marriage A-la-Mode* (II, 579). Most of these are easy to recognize and of no great importance. But the publisher should be chided for unevenness of photo-reproduction which sometimes makes whole pages difficult to read. Diacritical marks become virtually invisible. The letters O and Q are prone to separate into parentheses that enclose nothing, a particularly annoying defect for anyone trying to pursue textual variants. Notes fade into illegibility, especially the italicized words: I hope page 472 of volume II in my set is atypical. All in all, however, we may fairly conclude that these texts will be standard for our time, and we can use them with confidence.

Kenny provides only a brief general introduction—a thoroughly defensible decision, in my opinion. Not a great deal is known about Farquhar's life, and critical arguments are best left for other venues. Any such overview tends to solidify the flux of critical opinion, but then becomes dated (often painfully so) when critical opinion shifts. Both volumes contain a detailed chronology, which serves many of the functions that would be accomplished by an overview of the life and career.

The lack of materials for a serious "life" has led too many

commentators to extract a life from the works. Farquhar makes a good case on which to test the relevance of biography in the interpretation of works. Because a maid in his third play refers slightingly to Jews, are we to declare Farquhar anti-Semitic (I, 261)? Compare his plea for religious toleration in one of the letters from Amsterdam (II, 321). He published a few love letters, and others attributed to him appeared in various collections. Whether these are "real" or strictly literary exercises will probably remain undeterminable. Kenny doubts but does not refute traditional suppositions. Farquhar's name has long been linked with those of Susanna Carroll (later Centlivre) and Anne Oldfield, but the evidence of such affairs is extremely thin, and, more important, I know of no convincing arguments that either woman had significant influence on Farquhar's work.

Perhaps sexist bias explains this silence; but if we are willing to contemplate the possibility that a woman playwright influenced Farquhar, we must then ask what evidence would make such a claim worth taking seriously. He might have learned all kinds of things, from critical terminology to practical conventions, from Centlivre; the difficulty is proof. What the alleged connection does tell us is something about how Farquhar chose to pursue his career.

Compare Congreve and Southerne, each of whom was willing to serve a long apprenticeship under the critical eye of Dryden. Farquhar arrived in London too late to gain much benefit from the grand old man, even had their interests overlapped more, and no single figure replaced Dryden as arbiter of taste after 1700. Even so, had Farquhar been more willing to be taught, he could have put in the time with Congreve and Southerne. Colley Cibber might have provided practical advice couched in less theoretical terms. But Farquhar chose to write as he pleased and did not acknowledge debts to predecessors. Our heritage is the spontaneity that wafts through his first two plays. Had they been worked over, they might have been improved technically, but they would almost certainly have lost in "Spirits." Assuming that Farquhar did not ask for advice on his first two plays, or refused it, he was then naive in expecting to be praised for flouting decorum. The fabulous success of *The Constant Couple* made him deaf to constructive criticism, but he was hurt by the carping of the envious, as his preliminaries to that play and some other prologues and epilogues show. His next two plays were already both more self-conscious and less spontaneous. The only names we can associate with this point in his career are Carroll/Centlivre and Motteux, who, although they had their virtues, were probably not ideal advisers for him. But all this speculation gets us no further with the plays: it concerns only the milieu that produced them.

Likewise, Farquhar's so-called discovery of Anne Oldfield, reading plays to enliven her lot as a barmaid, was quickly turned into a love affair between them by the expansive power of anecdote. Identification of Farquhar and Oldfield in published love letters has proceeded enthusiastically, "proving" the story. Kenny reports the rumor, dubiously, because it bears on attributions. But even if we grant Farquhar an affair with Oldfield, what visible effect did it have on his writing? Significantly, there is no contemporary tradition that Farquhar wrote "for" Oldfield, despite the precedents of Otway's writing for Elizabeth Barry and Congreve's for Anne Bracegirdle. We should note that all but two of Farquhar's plays were completed before Oldfield found her bearings as an actress; and the truth is that playwrights cannot always recognize the swan potential of fledgling performers. Oldfield's influence on Farquhar was, then, peripheral and undocumented. It is a red herring that should not figure in future critical assessments of his work.

The bulk of the annotation in Kenny's edition is highly satisfactory—erudite and helpful. In a large proportion of cases, the reader who goes to the endnotes in search of illumination will find it. Farquhar's many topical allusions are faithfully run down and explained, and this is a great assistance to the reader. The one realm in which I sometimes found myself frustrated or dissatisfied is staging and stagecraft. Kenny is certainly a great deal more conscious of matters pertaining to actors than she was in 1971 when she published *The Plays of Richard Steele,* but the technicalities of a changeable-scenery theatre do not, apparently, interest her. Nor does she seem sensitive to the intensely theatrical texture of the plays.

Farquhar's anti-theoretical bent and his performing experience in Dublin (albeit limited) usually led him to give reliable stage directions. Only occasionally does he fluff an exit or scene change (II, 73, *l.* 302). Because his directions are comparatively detailed, they also demonstrate the continuing life of a number of the conventions pointed out by Alan C. Dessen in *Elizabethan Stage Conventions and Modern Interpreters* (1984). Travelers appear in riding habits in all the plays except *The Constant Couple*. Justice Ballance marks the passage of time in *The Recruiting Officer* when he makes an entrance "with a Napkin in his Hand as risen from Dinner" (II, 117). "Dark lanthorns" and night caps establish the darkness that facilitates the resolutions of *The Stage-Coach* and *The Beaux Stratagem*.

But in *The Constant Couple* Farquhar neglected two stage directions that have a controlling influence on plot, and unfortunately Kenny overlooks them also. In IV.i, Wildair and Standard begin a conversation, are interrupted by a mob, and later return to the stage. While they are offstage they arrange a test of Lady Lurewell, whom both are pursuing. Standard dares Wildair to give him ocular "Demonstration" which of them she prefers: her acceptance of a ring Standard provides will prove her favor. The ring turns out to be a token Lurewell gave Standard twelve years before, when he seduced and unwillingly abandoned her, and it in fact serves to reconcile them and identify the "constant couple" of the title.

However, the ring may be only half of the men's pact. In a farcical early scene in the play Wildair cudgels the merchant Smuggler, trustee of Lurewell's estate. Smuggler "tumbles over and over, and shakes out his Pocket-book on the Floor; *Lurewell* enters, takes it up" (II.v; italics reversed). At the very end of the play Standard uses evidence of illegal wine imports recorded in the pocket-book to force Smuggler to return Lurewell's papers and property to her (a solution much like the blackmail at the end of *The Beaux Stratagem*). But Lurewell is the last person *stated* to have the pocket-book: how does Standard get it? This is the sort of thing editors tend not to "see" and directors must agonize over. Taking the theatrical point of view, I would argue that editors of plays should concern themselves with staging implications as much as with topical allusions and printing history.

I can see two solutions to the problem I have just pointed out, neither of which is covered by the stage directions. The simpler, and probably the better, is to have Lurewell give the pocket-book to Standard on the spot, since by then the lovers have been reconciled. The other is to have her give it to Wildair at the end of II.v and to have him offer it to Standard as an ocular "Demonstration" of her preference, which Standard keeps as security for the ring. In the theatre both props would be visible when the men return from making their offstage agreement in IV.i, and Wildair's lines would connect their upcoming competition for Lurewell to Wildair's with Smuggler over her. Wildair defeated the merchant in the earlier scene by throwing snuff in his eyes, as he reminds the audience when he says to Standard, "we'll wait on her together: You shall draw your Sword, I'll draw my Snush-Box . . ." (IV.i). Because the "business" was clear in the theatre—probably explained by Farquhar during rehearsals—he did not bother to put it in the written text. The prompter might have noted "ring and pocket-book," but not the details. However the pocket-book was managed, Farquhar was sloppier than usual in his directions about it.

The "literary" reader will not, of course, be disturbed by "performance" complexities. But if Farquhar deserves an Oxford standard edition (and I believe he does), then his deserts rest more on his long popularity in the theatre than on his literary profundity. Seven of his plays were successes, and six of them became eighteenth-century repertory staples. I suspect, however, that most of the plays will strike nonspecialists as thin and contrived. To re-animate them requires a large investment of imaginative effort. To do them full justice will also require comparison with the comedies they played against. Kenny's fine edition will make this project easier.

Lacking first-hand evidence, we can only speculate as to how Farquhar went about writing his plays. Thanks to Bruce Redford and the Friends of the Princeton University Library, however, we can now look over the shoulder of Richard Brinsley Sheridan as he composes. In *The Origins of* The School for Scandal, two batches of drafts and notes from the Robert H. Taylor Collection are reproduced in sharp, full-sized photofacsimile with transcription on facing pages. Although Cecil Price studied these manuscripts, they are only discussed, not transcribed, in his 1973 Oxford Sheridan; hence Redford's edition of these fragments greatly enlarges public access to the texts. While certain kinds of scholarship will always require consultation of the original, this facsimile will be more than adequate for most purposes. It also has the virtue of permitting coherent citation of the manuscripts, one of which was long ago bound out of order in a grangerized volume of the Moore biography.

As a glance will show, Sheridan's writing is a paleographer's nightmare. It varies so much that it can seem like several different hands. Professor Redford has coped manfully with most of the difficulties, but in a few instances a reading might have benefited from consultation. Here are three examples of places where I read passages rather differently than Redford does. On page 69 the manuscript appears to me to say, "But if she drinks acid, & *hauls* her fat sides every morning / behind a coach Horse to be sure she is to be pitied"; Redford prints "*hurts[?]*, her fat sides." "Hauls" makes better sense than "hurts," and the mark Redford reads as a comma looks to me like a false start on another word, not punctuation. On page 133 "and Isaac will fill" makes more sense than "and Lease[?] with fifty." And at the top of page 135 there are simply not enough strokes in the first word to produce "Roundhead[?] in Barber[?] Lesson," but "Round *em*" conjures up a stage picture. Sheridan's hand is difficult enough that reproducing these manuscripts in full is not merely a luxury: no transcription, however careful, can take us entirely out of the realm of doubt.

In the absence of comparable drafts of earlier playwrights' work, I cannot agree with Professor Redford that "Never did such humble beginnings . . . lead to such a brilliant outcome" (p. 11). I see no reason to think that the wit of earlier playwrights came more easily to them than Sheridan's came to him. Farquhar never bothered to polish as much as Sheridan, but he might well have worked just as chaotically. Sheridan's notebooks contain every stage of creation from random jottings to fairly advanced scene drafts. Where the hand is most regular and the corrections fewest, we are (I suspect) seeing Sheridan make fair copy from drafts no longer extant. If inspiration struck as he was copying, he might turn several pages and jot down a single phrase or idea. Many of these random thoughts were not developed, at least not in these manuscripts. Thus on pages 99–131 we have the famous screen scene (IV.iii) in what, for Sheridan, is flowing script, virtually unrevised. Halfway down page 131 we leap into the midst of the Backbite-Crabtree competition in rumors about the duel (V.ii). Page 137 is devoted to the memorandum, "Crabtree to wear a Muff," and page 139 begins a fair copy of IV.i. In view of this muddle, I cannot believe that the passage from the screen scene is the product of a single inspiration.

Professor Redford notes that "Sheridan excelled at the subtle adjustment of witticism: the core of a particular *mot* will often be preserved intact, but its setting rearranged for greater cumulative impact. . . . [Thus] an exchange in 'The Slanderers' between Mrs. Sneerwell and Sir Christopher Crab . . . is reassigned without qualm to Mrs. Candour and Lady Teazle" (pp. 10–11). What this tells us is that to a large extent the exchange of scandal makes members of the college interchangeable. It does not demonstrate that "plot exists for the sake of aphorism" (p. 11). Few lines from the screen scene could be redistributed without affecting the plot.

Despite my quibbles, this handsome volume makes available an important source, and one that is by no means overstudied. We can be grateful that fate preserved these foul papers rather than, say, those for Farquhar's *Sir Harry Wildair* or Sheridan's own *St. Patrick's Day*. Redford has given us ready access to a primary source decidedly difficult to read and assimilate, and he has made the process of comprehension mercifully easy. He has provided only a minimal introduction, one that does not pretend to discuss the full implications of these fragments in relation to the completed play with which we are so familiar. This will be a subject for future critics, and a good one. The best of recent Sheridan criticism, particularly Mark S. Auburn's *Sheridan's Comedies* (1977), has moved toward analysis of theatrical impact. Having these early versions readily available will be a decided advantage to critics inclined to pursue this subject.

Different as they are, both of these editions offer us something of real value. Legible reproduction of significant literary manuscripts is a genuine service, and especially so when the handwriting is nasty and full transcription is provided. The utility of a standard edition hardly needs to be defended, even at current prices. The Kenny *Farquhar,* like most other recent Oxford editions, gives critics the kind of base on which to build that should facilitate informed and sophisticated analysis of the material it makes available. Farquhar's textual puzzles and many contemporary allusions fairly cry out for this sort of treatment—and what critic is going to stop in mid-analysis to check printing history or run down answers to oddities in the text? Personally, I would welcome a more theatrical perspective in editions of plays, but both critics and theatre historians need to acknowledge the value of full-dress editions. Anyone inclined to be dismissive about such work should try doing a bit of it. To work from Readex microcards or Garland facsimiles puts us in an altogether different position, and not a happy one. A major reassessment of turn-of-the-century drama is an urgent desideratum, and Kenny's edition will unquestionably be a cornerstone for this rethinking.

No Common Parlance: Recent Linguistic Approaches to Nineteenth-Century American Authors

Michael West

    Joan Burbick. *Thoreau's Alternative History: Changing Perspectives on Nature, Culture, and Language.* Philadelphia: University of Pennsylvania Press, 1987. xii, 174 pp.

    Christanne Miller. *Emily Dickinson: A Poet's Grammar.* Cambridge: Harvard University Press, 1987. 212 pp.

    David R. Sewell. *Mark Twain's Languages: Discourse, Dialogue, and Linguistic Variety.* Berkeley: University of California Press, 1987. xvii, 188 pp.

Three recent studies examine the attitudes toward language held by Thoreau, Dickinson, and Twain. Alas, one finds oneself wishing that two of the academic authors had scrutinized their own attitudes toward language with similar intensity. Jargonized or poorly organized, their books are not always very readable. Indeed, literary scholarship seems increasingly to view clarity as a sign of intellectual weakness. Rather than seduce a lay reader or two (heaven forbid!) into ambling down the garden path of criticism, too many humanists now write as if their aim were to cow a tenure committee with lingo as impenetrable as any scientist's. What passes for philosophical rigor in literary academia is in too many cases, I fear, *rigor mortis*. Although none of the books under review sounds the knell of humanistic learning, it's regrettable that all three studies treat their authors in substantial isolation from other literary figures. For example, none shows any awareness of C. Carroll Hollis's *Language and Style in Leaves of*

Grass (1983), as though the findings of a Whitmaniac could have no relevance to work on Thoreau, Dickinson, or Twain. To isolate American linguistic theories from their matrix in European culture is questionable enough; it's even riskier when individual authors are analyzed in hermetically sealed studies and shelved separately for coteries of specialists. The idiolects of these three authors were grounded in a common language, but too often their exegetes write as if disdaining common understanding. The awkwardness of much academic prose nowadays is not a necessary condition for sophisticated literary scholarship. Instead it suggests that the books flooding from university presses are not written to be read but to be counted. Do they crave any real audience save a handful of specialists, whose needs for technical information some computer data bank could supply much more cheaply?

In her study of Thoreau, Joan Burbick deploys an amorphous concept of "language." When this is blended with notions like "nature," "culture," and "history," and these big abstractions are allowed to change throughout Thoreau's life, her prose thickens like multigrade motor oil in December. Ideas, however, remain slippery enough: "At Walden, Thoreau establishes a culture that both critiques civilization and validates the redemptive history of Walden Pond. In this culture, nature is not severely harnessed or pushed to the boundaries of the uncivil, but is the essential foundation of the cultural. Accordingly, this history moves beyond the individual observation of nature to the description of a cultural plan, enhancing the observation of redeemed time.... Walden, a spot on a map and a cultural entity, becomes the 'sedes,' or seat, from which the uncivil history of the natural world can be fully known" (pp. 59–60).

"My method is often rhetorical," Burbick explains, "lingering on the finely tuned moments of crafting language, following the figure of speech to its completion or demise, or it is cultural, contrasting Thoreau's literary strategies with those of poets, historians, and naturalists, and linking these differences to the ideological battles of nineteenth-century America" (p. 12). But if we linger on "the finely tuned moments of crafting language," we may come to feel that this cloudy phrase is itself not very well crafted, nor is the whole sprawling sentence, with its squinting impersonal pronoun, finely tuned. This book's graceless style persistently undercuts its claim to rhetorical expertise.

It is instructive to compare Thoreau's own prose with Burbick's analysis of it. "The tortoises rapidly dropped into the water, as our boat ruffled the surface amid the willows," Thoreau wrote in 1845. "We glided along through the transparent water, breaking the reflections of the trees." Burbick's reaction to what she terms "this strikingly beautiful passage" is to explain that it "describes the activity of a natural phenomenon as observed by a moving perceiver, located in space at particular moment in time" (p. 39). The central critical act here seems neither explanation nor evaluation (we might not choose this passage for an anthology of great moments from Thoreau) but obfuscation. Redundant philosophical diction strives to raise portentous restatement of the obvious to the level of novel insight.

Apropos of the walk described in another journal entry, Burbick observes, "The movement through the topography of Concord imparts what Barthes and other structuralists call the 'reality' effect. Enough details of time and place accumulate to create the illusion of the 'here and now'" (p. 42). Only a singularly obtuse audience would need structuralist sanction to agree that, by haphazardly amassing concrete images of time and space, descriptive writers can give a good impression of physical reality. There is no reason why this stupendous bromide must be credited to Barthes rather than to Aristotle, Dreiser, or any rhetorical handbook of the past century—no reason save the academic author's desire to seem *à la mode*. Toward that end quotation marks help greatly to establish the proper philosophical tone. Simply enclose a humdrum term like "reality" with them, and presto! deep thinking is obviously taking place. Perhaps such cerebration even attains the dignity of the "rethinking" so much in vogue.

Italics also serve the aspiring oracle well in lieu of argument. "Thoreau's hut is like Martin Heidigger's concept of a dwelling, in which 'to dwell, to be set at peace, means to remain at peace within the free, the preserve, the free sphere that safeguards each thing in its nature. *The fundamental character of dwelling is this sparing and preserving.*' " Does this solemn pronunciamento really clarify *Walden*'s wonderfully zany analysis of shelter? Be that as it may, Burbick does not dwell on Heidigger's concept of dwelling, summoning another philosopher instead to eke out our understanding of Thoreau's cabin: "Even though the house becomes what Gaston Bachelard calls a 'center of concentrated solitude' from which true culture, in the sense of the awakening of the soul, is made possible, it reinforces a split between matter and spirit" (p. 64). One can only say that in the absence of homeowner's insurance for such perils, Thoreau tolerated this hazard surprisingly well.

Burbick admits that Thoreau has been judged "a contradictory, ambivalent, and even deeply ironic figure" (p. 10), but that is not a view with which she seems deeply familiar or sympathetic. Like the playfulness of his prose, his humor largely eludes her. From "a series of urgent directives for writing" in the *Journal*, she quotes this one: "It is a rare qualification to be able to state a fact simply and adequately, to digest some experience cleanly, to say 'yes' and 'no' with authority . . . to conceive and suffer the truth to pass through us living and intact, even as a waterfowl an eel, as it flies over the meadows, thus stocking new waters. First of all a man must see, before he can say." This prompts a ponderous psychological interpretation. "The digestive analogy, operating as a prerequisite for 'true' writing on the level of declaration, becomes anything but that on the level of description. . . . The metaphor . . . suggests both the violence of consumption and the inevitability of death as necessary stages in the digestive process, while at the same time it suppresses them by the image of the eel 'living and intact.' However much an eel may look like feces, Thoreau cannot allow the possibility of excrement upon the scene of writing" (pp. 55–56). If that were so, it's odd that elsewhere in the *Journal* during that same period he cheerfully described himself returning from a day afield like a "farmer driving into his barn-yard with a load of muck" for fertilizer, except that "my barn-yard is my journal" (19 January 1852). *Walden*'s vision of fecal creativity in the railroad cut suggests that this author did not need to "repress death and decay as necessary stages of being in history" quite so much as Burbick proposes;

indeed, he soliloquizes tediously about his poor health. What she reads as an "urgent directive" is in fact a cheerful hyperbole. Far from stating "a fact simply," Thoreau gaily multiplies metaphors that almost cancel each other out. Like the snappy "see-say" epigram that follows, the eel metaphor is not an oracular summation but only one more exuberantly provisional exploration of truths about writing. These truths are not so much described as wittily enacted, deliberately but not evasively distorted.

Burbick presents Thoreau as a man obsessed by history but at odds with the providential progressivism of nineteenth-century historians. From natural history he derived a less anthropocentric yet potentially redemptive sense of time; to expound it he created for himself the role of an "uncivil" historian. Though "the implications of his counter-history . . . are not systematically apprehended within the text . . . read from a cultural perspective *A Week* becomes a knot of accusations against historians and an attempt to seize their power to tell the story of America" (p. 17). Their notion of history as a theatre for heroic events yields to Thoreau's imaginative cartography, his preoccupation with mapping events precisely in time and space. But he rejects the false objectivity of scientism and insists on first-person observation. Therefore "what begins to confront Thoreau during the 1850s is not only the complexity of perception but also the status of language in natural description" (p. 51). Scanting *Walden*, Burbick is chiefly concerned to trace these preoccupations throughout the journals. "The journal entry in its ideal form reflects the dialectic between time and timelessness," she argues; therefore it "required a 'natural' or 'transparent' language, that is, one shaped not by history and culture, but by the force of universal consciousness" (p. 54). But she largely ignores the relevance of Thoreau's philological studies to that aim as sketched by Philip Gura, myself, and others, just as she ignores Lawrence Willson's careful studies of Thoreau's historicism. Her claim that the journal format "continually strained his understanding of language" dwindles into an unedifying demonstration that as a writer Thoreau always struggled for *le mot juste*.

Tracing Thoreau's perspectivism yields better results. Whether or not "vision itself becomes an open-ended phenomenon, capable of endless analysis" (p. 114), the chapter devoted to that topic forcefully rebuts the received opinion that "the late Journal is largely a compendium of scientific facts" since "in reality it argues against any strictly 'scientific' description of natural phenomena which does not permit delight" (p. 120). But one lays the book down with the feeling that only that chapter really needed to be in print. "The importance of history to American thought from its colonial beginnings cannot be overstated," is the guiding assumption (p. 2). With some justice Burbick suggests that Thoreau did not inhabit the new world of R. W. B. Lewis's American Adam but rather a fallen world abounding in the vestiges of a more remote past than we normally imagine. But exaggeration, vagueness, special pleading, a lack of balance, bogus obiter dicta, and just plain bad writing all mar an argument that depends too heavily on its own stipulative abstractions.

Christanne Miller also succumbs to exaggeration at times— e.g., by blandly asserting that "Dickinson has created a language as meaningful and as free of determined meaning as any English can be" (p. 19). But her study of the poet's idiolect is more often sober and enlightening. She focuses upon the distinctive grammatical features of Dickinson's language, often at odds with standard English usage, that contribute to the basic traits of her poetry: "multiplicity of meaning, indeterminacy of reference and degree of personal involvement in the poem, and the establishment of a diction that swings between stylized aphorism and the informality of speech" (p. 18). Compression of various kinds "allows for protective ambiguity, conveys a sense of the speaker's withheld power and implies a profundity beyond the obvious import of its message" (p. 27). The poet's characteristic grammatical deletions of implied pronouns, auxiliary verbs, and repeated subjects or verbs are sometimes easily recoverable, sometimes not. Like Lawrence's prose, Dickinson's highly paratactic verse uses deletion as a stylistic alternative to conjunction, with effects that range from childlike artlessness to Biblical profundity. Syntactic doubling, where one word or phrase functions in two nonparallel syntactic contexts, "frequently occurs . . . where the speaker of the poem becomes indistinguishable from her subject as the agent of some action" (p. 38). The compressed, monosyllabic quality of Dickinson's largely Anglo-Saxon vocabulary permits extraordinary effects with contrasting Latinate polysyllables, which she often reserves for the endings of poems. Since few Latinate polysyllables have a final stress, "her poems end on a mediate, holding note, with a chord quietly or only partially resolved rather than with the clean 'masculine' rhyme of most nineteenth-century poetry" (p. 44).

Under the sprawling category of "disjunction" Miller groups a great variety of devices, not always illuminatingly. Treating manuscript variants as stylistic devices in their own right seems needlessly deferential to the author. More persuasive is the exegesis of Dickinson's idiosyncratic punctuation as generally designed to violate rather than to reinforce syntactic order. Miller does not make it clear why Dickinson's form-class experimentation is better regarded as an example of disjunction than simply as another form of compression, but she describes one result perceptively: "When mass or plural nouns are made singular and when adjectives and nouns are transposed, they lose as much specificity from the impossibility of literal reference as they gain from the suggestion that some distinction of singularity or reference is possible. Nouns create the illusion of thingness in Dickinson's poems, but they do not direct us to particular events or things." Often capitalized into virtual abstractions, "they give instead the sense that the world is as mobile and flexible as her perception of it. The events of her brain are as concretely and substantially present as the events in her garden" (p. 63). The predilection for uninflected verbs that critics have either decried as ungrammatical or construed as subjunctive forms suggesting doubt, Miller defends as a deliberate and legitimate stylistic device for fusing the particular and the absolute. While Sharon Cameron sees in these uninflected verbs Dickinson's "overriding concern to escape the historicity of time, to make herself in some way timeless and thus safe from the forces of death and loss," Miller argues that they "point more toward a concern with ongoing process, revelation, continuous perception and change than toward the lyric suspension . . . on Keats's Grecian urn" (p. 75).

Miller writes well of Dickinson's fondness for nonspecific pronouns and for definite pronouns sans antecedents, which "stand for the kind of hole in knowledge that Dickinson tells us 'a certain Slant of light' . . . may create" (p. 76). In the poem "It was not Death, for I stood up," the use of repetition certainly endows the impersonal pronoun with peculiar suggestiveness. Whether foregrounding words of relation while omitting transitional phrases between sentences constitutes "one of the most curious and distinctive elements of her poetry" is less clear. "This is not egocentrism . . . but a recognition of how foreign everything beyond the self must be," Miller argues; "for this poet, things (and people) gain significance as they affect oneself" (p. 83). Perhaps, but in the absence of comparative evidence one suspects that most poets invest the world with significance on the same basis.

" 'No' is the wildest word we consign to Language," Dickinson wrote to her suitor Otis Lord, and Miller combs the concordance to support her contention that the poet "uses the word *not* more often than any words but articles, a few prepositions, and *and, it, is,* and *that*" (pp. 99–101). Agreeing with prior critics that Dickinson's is a *poesis negativa,* Miller speculates about the roots of this condition in Dickinson's situation as a woman. The poet's reliance on adversitives suggests "Derrida's ideal of *différence* and of negative or deconstructive interpretation. Using Derrida's language, one might say of Dickinson's poems generally . . . that they do not acknowledge a center of meaning. Because there is no semantic or linguistic center, no focal word of origin or meaning (and in particular no Christian word that explains all), there is expansive play of language and of analogy, which is to say of the mind" (p. 102).

But in his chapter on negation in Whitman, Hollis presented statistical tables of the frequency of negation in eleven nineteenth-century American poets. According to his figures, a much higher percentage of Whitman's lines contain negatives than is true for any other nineteenth-century American (or British) poet, while only Whittier, Holmes, and Lowell rank below Dickinson in the percentage of lines involving negatives. A skewed sampling technique helps account for the surprisingly low incidence of negation that Hollis found in Dickinson's verse: calculating the percentage of lines involving negatives rather than the frequency of negative words in a poet's vocabulary makes negation loom largest in a poet who favors long lines like Whitman's while minimizing the importance of negation for a poet who prefers short lines like Dickinson's. But blithely ignoring Hollis's contradictory statistics on this point makes Miller seem guilty of impressionism and cavalier disregard of comparative evidence. Does Dickinson's negation require a feminist explanation when, like Whitman, Bartleby was male, Thoreau's was also a rhetoric of contradiction, and Hawthorne's "No! in Thunder" reverberates in the dialectic of Transcendentalism? Similar unawareness of Hollis's work on Whitman's metonymy flaws Miller's contention that "Dickinson's predominantly metonymic figurative structures . . . may link her with a history of women's use of language" (p. 111).

Miller's general observations on Dickinson's style are the best part of this book. Less successful is her attempt to illustrate them by recurring throughout to five poems. It makes for too much repetition and incoherence. In "Essential Oils—are wrung," we may grant a powerful pun on *expressed* but feel that finding sexual wordplay in *Screws* and *Lady's Drawer* expresses more literary oil than we need: "As manipulator of 'Screws,' as object crushed by the process of expression, and as wearer of drawers, the Lady creates her Attar as well as using it" (p. 4). Likewise, about "To pile like Thunder" we are told that "the sexual connotation of 'coming'—with its literary resonance of both divinity and death—strengthens the identity of poetry, love, and religious epiphany in ecstatic consummation" (p. 128). But *come* was not common erotic parlance even for improper Victorians like Whitman (as Stephen Marcus observes, they normally *spent* rather than *came*), so one wonders whose imagination is at play in this passage. Miller's ironic interpretation of "This was a Poet" also seems strained. Her reading of "My Life had stood—a Loaded Gun" as "an adolescent fantasy about coming of age that breaks down before what should be its happy conclusion—powerful adulthood" is more plausible, but not in its conviction that the speaker "*chooses* to guard her Master rather than share his bed" (italics mine). Arguing that "with a kind of hysteria, the speaker adopts his perspective on allies and enemies; where he hates, she kills," Miller ignores the fact that both gun and master seem stoic killers as passionless as Natty Bumppo (pp. 123–24). Alas, linguistic criticism has done little to end the controversy over this poem.

One chapter surveys sources that may have influenced Dickinson's distinctive attitudes toward language: the Bible, seventeenth-century stylists, Watts's hymns, the American plain style, Noah Webster's lexicography, Emerson's theories of language, and nineteenth-century women writers. "Dickinson has greater affinity with the lexicographer, the scientist of language seeking to clarify each word's various meanings," Miller concludes, "than she does with the Romantic *Ur*-poet Adam" (pp. 147–48). Dickinson's many definition-poems surely reflect the influence of her dictionary, but Miller might have pushed this insight further by linking other stylistic traits with contemporary textbooks. "Despite the enormous compression of her poetry generally, there is little elision in Dickinson's polysyllables," Miller notes. "The clarity of each syllable, with its individual stress level and sound, gives a weight and delicate edge of wonder to these words that is unlike any other poetic effect I can think of" (p. 43). Of course, nineteenth-century students were drilled in "orthoepy" as part of the pedagogical mania that made Webster's speller the nation's best-seller. Likewise, the poet's peculiarly malleable verbs may reflect the yeasty speculation that led some schoolroom grammars to proclaim invalid distinctions like that between transitive and intransitive verbs. Miller should have consulted works on nineteenth-century grammatical theory. Dennis Baron's *Grammar and Good Taste: Reforming the American Language* (1982) is uncited, for example, to say nothing of Rollo Laverne Lyman's still-standard study. These might have proved as rewarding as the feminist theory surveyed in a final chapter consecrated to "The Consent of Language and the Woman Poet."

In his study of Twain's attitudes toward language, David Sewell levies aid from various sources. Genuflecting deeply to Bakhtin, his book draws eclectically upon semiotics and sociolinguistics. But Sewell does more than the other scholars under review to deploy his extra-literary terminology gracefully. Like mid-nineteenth-century philology, Twain lacked a vocabulary to articulate his intuitions about linguistic pluralism. But as Sewell says, Twain knew that "since we each bear ultimate responsibility for our language, we should not hide ourselves behind borrowed discourse in the hope that like some Wizard of Oz's screen, it will make us appear greater and more terrible than we are" (p. xii). Sewell's awareness that "my own critical vocabulary confronts Mark Twain's language in a manner embarrassingly reminiscent of the parson's talk with Scotty Briggs" marks him as an unusual academic indeed. (If only Burbick had shared this awareness!) Written not only with insight but with clarity, tact, and humor, his is a surprisingly readable book.

The Transcendentalists articulated a philosophy of language stressing semantic unity. As "Adam's Diary" suggests, Twain was seldom comfortable with it. Emphatically no philosopher, through his experiences in different social strata he nonetheless intuited the truth that Wilhelm von Humboldt insisted upon as the basis for his dialogic conception of language: "No one when he uses a word has in mind exactly the same thing that another has.... All understanding, therefore, is always at the same time a misunderstanding" (p. 5). Babel and Pentecost were the era's dominant myths about linguistic variety, both positing an unhappily lost divine speech. For Twain, however, the essence of language was like Bakhtin's *heteroglossia,* where a healthy conflict of voices fosters change and forestalls tyranny. But viewed from another angle heteroglossia seems cacophony, the babble of reciprocally incomprehensible voices in an absurd universe. In Twain's later years speech became increasingly cacophonous.

A fascinating chapter traces Twain's ambivalence toward "grammar." Despite his cheerful burlesques of schoolroom parsing, "Twain never faulted the rules of grammar themselves, only the instruction that made them impenetrable" (p. 20). He carped constantly about the poor speech habits of Americans; indeed, Whitman came closer to championing a genuinely demotic standard. "Raised on Kirkham's *Grammar* and the Presbyterian Bible, Twain retains to the end a Protestant conviction that the authority of the Book is to be taken on faith. The ghost of Kirkham's grammar walking always beside him prevented him from celebrating without reservation an ungoverned heteroglossia" (p.

35). He prided himself upon the purity and correctness of his own English as if that made him one of the elect, yet was haunted by a frequently expressed conviction of linguistic original sin—that it was impossible for him or anyone else to obey all the rules prescribed by the textbooks. "'Natural grammar,' according to Kirkham, was as insufficient to linguistic salvation as natural religion to Christian redemption" (p. 21). Twain's dialect humor was a scarecrow that flapped merrily in the breezes; but a rigid faith in the possibility of "perfect grammar" supported it, and it guarded the pumpkin patch of propriety.

During the year that he worked with Warner on *The Gilded Age* (1874), Twain bought a copy of Richard Grant White's *Words and Their Uses* (1870). The linguistic prescriptions of that influential and essentially conservative authority undergird the novel's satire of genteel pretentiousness. In an acquisitive democracy swayed by mass media, White argued, corrupt language and social corruption go hand in hand. Like paper money, words are inflated until the currency of opinion is debased. The only safeguard against this tendency is the vigilance of a linguistic elite. "Language and economics meet in the word *speculation* . . . baseless ideation and worthless investment," White implies, and Sewell deftly demonstrates that "to the social climbers who populate the novel, money and language are interchangeable means of speculation, of promising, of bribing. Both an issue of worthless stock and an hypocritical Sunday-school speech are symptoms of a society whose favorite activity is to get something for nothing" (p. 44).

"On perhaps no American author has the impact of foreign languages been so great as on Mark Twain," Sewell proposes (p. 51). This insouciant thesis is sustained by a chapter examining Twain's mediocre abilities in German, French, and Italian and his consequent preoccupation with the comedy of incomprehension. Reducing adults to second childhood, foreign tongues made discourse seem comic by emphasizing its mechanical element. Twain was fascinated by the social cachet and the expanded mental horizon that they promised, but repelled by the awkwardness, isolation, and abusive power to which they lent themselves. If Twain's treatment of linguistic incompetence in

The Innocents Abroad aligns him at times with philistinism and cultural imperialism, a far more sophisticated sense of linguistic relativism imbues his too-often-neglected revision of "The Jumping Frog." ("In English. Then in French. Then clawed back into a civilized language once more by patient unremunerated toil.") "Twain's burlesque of the German language . . . is a temporary victory of the pleasure principle over the reality that language is always an imposition" insofar as we are denied telepathy and forced to segment our inner thought into units of semiotic discourse governed by rules (p. 75). By the time he wrote *Meisterschaft: In Three Acts,* where four young American lovers must court exclusively in phrases culled from German phrasebooks, his macaronic humor had led him to wonder how profound "love" could be if generated by superficial conventions, linguistic and social, "that do not necessarily correspond to any inward reality? Substitute *Herz*—or even the English word *heart*—for *Hund* in the . . . dialogue, and would the lovers really understand one another better?" (p. 84).

Challenging the conventional notion that *Huck Finn* celebrates the vernacular at the expense of genteel speech, Sewell argues that "there are, in fact, . . . different vernaculars and . . . standard languages in the novel" (pp. 86–87). In figures like Judge Thatcher and Dr. Robinson, correct English with a genteel tinge is linked to natural goodness and moral authority. So powerful is this convention equating grammar with virtue that to obey it Twain alters his initial characterization of Mary Jane Wilke's dialect. But a professional con man like the Duke appropriates standard English as a tool of the trade, so that it seems less a token of moral authority than a pose. Colonel Sherburn's address to the mob "is the supreme example of the misappropriated standard," Sewell believes. "The heroic ethos he means to project is in truth a persona, a mask, a role. The veneer of *Murray's Grammar* that covers his Southern village speech is the verbal equivalent of whitewash on a sepulcher" (p. 93).

More persuasive, perhaps, is Sewell's trichotomy of the vernacular into an idealized *folk speech* linked to innocence and creativity in figures like Huck, Jim, Judith Loftus, Aunt Sally, and the raftsmen; the *ornery speech* of characters like Pap Finn and the

Bricksville loafers, who deliberately choose vicious language to express their hostility to the upper classes and whose phatic repetition of formulaic phrases suggests the ghastly monotony of cramped imaginations; and the *speech of pretentious ignorance* (the term is Richard Grant White's) exemplified by Tom, the King, and the Grangerfords, where an essentially colloquial dialect is unsuccessfully disguised with fragments of genteel rhetoric. "Speakers of the misappropriated standard are too dangerous to be funny, but the vernacular of pretentious ignorance continuously deflates itself with needles borrowed from Mrs. Malaprop" (p. 96).

In creating this "literary simulacrum of linguistic diversity" Twain comically exaggerated several types of speech. "Huck Finn, in particular, is a linguistic impossibility. He speaks an unfallen Adamic dialect that names objects as if they had never been named before. His language is logically impossible, for it is a plenum, a fully functioning system, that is nevertheless innocent of the social conventions imposed by the social roles that language must play" (p. 109). Though "Huck and Jim are the only characters in the novel who freely and joyously embody all six of Jakobson's functions" in language, "neither Twain nor Huck is mounting a demotic attack on genuine high culture. Instead the major conflict is between an idealized folk better than its real prototype and a debased pseudo-gentility parasitic on its prototype" (pp. 108, 100). Huck admires Emmeline Grangerford's poetry. Ultimate moral authority is reserved to the sophisticated adult reader, whose knowledge of high culture permits him to appreciate properly all the languages that compose the novel.

In *Pudd'nhead Wilson*, free interplay between many alternative languages vanishes. Instead there is a Manichean struggle for power between only two languages, black and white. Characters no longer strive to improve their own speech but to impose it on others. The key issue is not propriety but power, and the central speech-acts involve commands or judgmental naming. With Wilson's assimilation into the culture there remains no morally authoritative variety of standard English. "*Tom Sawyer Abroad*, published in 1894, marks Twain's entry into the linguistic absurdity of the final phase, in which the basic mechanisms of all semiosis, rather than the particularities of individual dialects, create barriers to understanding, and interpretation becomes a guessing game. Inquiries into the connection between thought and language become more and more insistent" (pp. 127–28). Around 1905 Twain wrote several pieces that explore the theme of interpretation; in them "typically Twain mulls over a text whose meaning is finally undecidable" (p. 143). In writing *Christian Science* (1907), his attack on Mary Baker Eddy, Twain came "close to stating a general theory of incomprehensibility" (p. 142). His sketch "That Day in Eden" suggests that, "to paraphrase Wittgenstein, if God could talk, we could not understand him" (p. 147). Yet longing for unimpeded communion between souls led him into parapsychological speculation about "mental telegraphy." During his last years he wrote sentimental sketches like "My Platonic Sweetheart" about "the perfect communication that can be recaptured only in dreams and visions" (p. 153). If such mute communication haunted him, it also terrified him, for he associated it with "absolute stasis . . . speechlessness, the absence of dialogue" (p. 154). Thus an unfinished tale, "The Enchanted Sea-Wilderness," envisions a sinister Sargasso called the Everlasting Sunday where sailors becalmed in eternal peace lose the habit of language. Twain remained ambivalent to the end, but his deeper allegiance was to the heteroglossic paradise that he imagined in *Captain Stormfield's Visit to Heaven,* where voices from all nations, races, and faiths joyfully mingle.

Sewell's illuminating study of Twain reflects praiseworthy curiosity about linguistic currents elsewhere in the American Renaissance. Thus he is the only scholar under review to cite David Simpson's *The Politics of American English, 1776–1850* (1986). Doctoral candidates understandably eager for limited bibliographies guarantee that many of the manuscripts submitted to university presses will take the form of single-author studies. For that reason it behooves editors and reviewers to insist that such limited projects be decently informed about parallel developments in the field. Heteroglossia is a comforting notion insofar as it sanctions critical disagreement and promises full employment for members of the guild. It's less appealing, however, as a rationale for scholarly laziness and parochialism.

Stepping Outside Ourselves: Tanselle's Universal Text

D. C. Greetham

G. Thomas Tanselle. *A Rationale of Textual Criticism.* Philadelphia: University of Pennsylvania Press, 1989. 104 pp.

A Tanselle book without footnotes or internal documentation, virtually without citations or the naming of names? Clearly, *A Rationale of Textual Criticism* is something different in kind from the exhaustive and encyclopaedic articles published in *Studies in Bibliography* and elsewhere, articles which, in their very scope and depth, can cumulatively be read as a history of textual criticism and bibliography in the last twenty or thirty years. This new book is also a history (or rather a book *about* history as an enabling device), but it is a history dependent upon the force of a highly abstract argument, a history which relies not upon the careful exposition of empirical evidence but upon a discursive, occasionally polemical, and always clearly articulated engagement with the basic issues of text, textuality, and textual criticism. Tanselle's *Rationale* is thus a book of *theory* rather than practice, but it is, of course, a theory which has emerged out of a lifetime of practice—his own and others', for the role of scholiast to the discipline which Tanselle has assumed has given him a unique authority in drawing together the activities of the various wings of what he calls "the great enterprise" of textual criticism, in all the fields where it may be practised.

Much of the *difference* in the *Rationale* could be explained by its occasion, as a record of the Rosenbach Lectures given at the University of Pennsylvania on 21, 23, and 28 April 1987. As lectures, the three sections of the book are inevitably tighter, less expansive, and less dependent on documentation than would be a typical Tanselle article on final intention, or the editing of historical documents, or descriptive bibliographies, or any of the other specific areas Tanselle has covered in the last few years. But that is only part of the story, for intention and historical documents and the rest are all inferentially or substantively present in the new work, but all subsumed under a more general, more "philosophical" confrontation of the questions that are "of fundamental importance to all who read books, or attend lectures and plays, or listen to music and folk tales, or watch dances and films, or use printed and written matter in their daily lives" (p. 9).

These are large claims, but they have always been a *donnée* of Tanselle's interdisciplinary and political agenda. Like Fredson Bowers before him (and like his frequent intellectual antagonist, Jerome J. McGann), he has always maintained that literary and textual criticism are inevitably linked, if not identical, activities, and that it is an intellectual as well as a professional mistake for textuists in apparently "different" disciplines (history, literature, and so on) to behave as if the issues they confront are unique to their disciplines. In the *Rationale*, these claims inevitably recur (e.g., "any text that a textual critic produces is itself the product of literary criticism," [p. 35]), but now their articulation and implementation permeate the very method of the argument itself. Partly this is a matter of the theoretical level employed, where a general dictum (e.g., that "the instructions for a work are not the same thing as the work itself," [p. 22]) can be seen to apply negatively or positively to all forms of communication, but partly it is a result of Tanselle's determination not to accord literature a privilege over other media as the *primary* or most sophisticated or most problematical or most rewarding of transmissions. Thus, while he will occasionally invoke literary works as the *locus* for speculation (e.g., Keats on the Grecian Urn, [pp. 11–13], or Wallace Stevens's woman on the Key West strand, [pp. 67–68]), these citations are not used for their specific "literary" value or for their significance to literary criticism or to a theory of literary editing, but are employed as provocation for an interrogation of ontological or epistemological questions relevant to *all* media. In the case of Keats, the problem resides in the "ineluctable entity" of the work, as opposed to its "reproduction" (p. 14), and for

Stevens, in the difficulty of separating the "evidence" of a work (usually a "document," visual or aural) from the work itself (pp. 68–69).

Once these general positions have been staked out, by concrete illustration or otherwise, the highly discursive argument of the *Rationale* may turn almost anywhere, and to any medium, for development. As the preface promised, they are all here: literature, film, history, dance, painting, sculpture, oratory, and music—even book collecting and librarianship.

The organization of the book is, however, narrative or procedural rather than generic or taxonomic, beginning with a chapter on the "nature" of texts, then moving to a consideration of the "reproduction" of texts of documents, and concluding with the problems of the "reconstruction" of texts of works. The first section is thus primarily involved with ontology, and attempts to draw distinctions based on Keats's address to the corporeal and immutable reality of the Grecian Urn, as opposed to the "abstraction" of the verbal constructs of non-concrete work. This distinction, a familiar one, will lead Tanselle to a related distinction between the previously mentioned "ineluctable entity" of the work and its "reproduction" and between the "instructions" for a work and that entity. The divisions set out in this opening chapter will thus motivate the further division of the rest of the book, for Tanselle is continually at pains to demonstrate that "text" and "work" are *not* identical (a perhaps expected persuasion for an author known for his long and articulate defense of Greg-Bowers eclecticism and thus of the "text that never was"). His definition of textual criticism is therefore similar to Eugene Vinaver's, who insisted that the very phrase implied a "distrust of texts," and Tanselle dutifully chastises the "naive faith" (p. 16) of most readers in their acceptance of text as if it were work. Again like Vinaver, he sees that the concept of "error" implies that verbal statements are not "coequal with oral or written presentation" (p. 15), and that it is the responsibility of textual criticism to adjudicate between the accidents of physical artifacts and "meaning." This is not an easy task, for Tanselle recognizes that the very survival of artifacts is a form of meaning, and that we may have a "social obligation to pass along intact what we have received," an obligation mitigated by the different responsibility to correct or "repair" what may be "misleading guides" to the past (p. 21). This dilemma can be seen partly as a mediation between "best text" and "eclectic" editing, but in its foregrounding of the social dynamic of texts, it is also a recognition that there might be a place for the historically derived "bibliographical codes" of McGann's social textual criticism, a question taken up at more length in the final chapter.

The speculations on text and work lead Tanselle to some astute comments on media other than literature, noting, for example, that in painting we cannot have both the work and the historical evidence for it, since "the work and the artifact are in battle for the same physical space" (p. 29). This means that there can be more textual *certainty* in the non-sequential media (like painting or sculpture), for we may *know* what a painting consists of, in a way that we can never know for a poem.

The chapter on reproduction is not a dry analysis of transcription rules and techniques, but rather a further development of the problem of the confusion of the statement or the work with its physical reality. Tanselle insists that manuscripts and books are merely "objects of utility" (p. 40), this physical essence being combined with their forceful demonstration of the "human inability to do the same thing twice" (p. 49). There are some ironies to this condition, for since all copies are inevitably different (a version of Greg's "universal variation" law), the act of so-called preservation, whereby photocopies are made of decaying originals (which may then be destroyed) creates yet another witness and yet another stage of textual transmission, and preserves not the text but the work, and even that imperfectly. The situation Tanselle notes here (which he has developed more fully in his recent article on "Reproductions and Scholarship" for the 1989 *Studies in Bibliography*) is not dissimilar to the copying and destruction which took place during the other two great periods of textual transference—from roll to codex and manuscript to printed book—and is especially pertinent in these days when the new bibliographical canon, in the electronic media, is being created by our current curatorial activities. It is therefore quite proper that Tanselle should enlarge the textual/critical empery to include archivists and librarians, who have traditionally been excluded from textual concerns. With his usual ecumenical enthusiasm, Tanselle proclaims that "anyone who comprehends how documents in fact transmit texts, and how works are related to the texts of documents, will also see that everyone in the world of books is contributing to a single great enterprise" (p. 46). After this embrace, however, Tanselle concludes this section with one of his familiar complaints—against those who would "tamper" with such features as punctuation, noting (in his expected disdain for the claim of "readability") that "the reader's convenience is basically irrelevant" (pp. 61–62). In the *Rationale* the interdisciplinary, ecumenical Tanselle is in general control, but there is still the Tanselle of fixed opinions in matters of textual truth (he observes, quite soundly, that once one accepts that there is "no detail that is not potentially significant for interpreting meaning" [p. 62], then any such "tampering" will make the text "intentionally inaccurate").

The third chapter also contains its polemical sides. For example, Tanselle is obviously impatient with "persons [unnamed again] not interested in taking any of the historical approaches to literature" (p. 70) since they are confusing the medium that they are working in—regarding a literary text as a literary work and therefore treating it as if it were a painting. Later in the chapter he does allow such concentration on specific moments in the text's progress as a form of textual criticism (and even concedes that some of McGann's "bibliographical codes"—such as "poetic lines and indentations [or even poetic shapes and typographic patterns])" may have textual as well as purely historical significance (p. 91). But while he recognizes that "every aspect of the design of a document . . . can influence readers' responses to the text it contains" (p. 91), his emphasis is finally on that *containment*, not on the mutual identity. He would entertain McGann's position as an aspect of cultural history and reader response, but not as an embodiment of intention (except in rare cases) and not therefore as an accident of the "work," only of the "text."

The privilege still accorded to intention in such an ideology is present in the recognition of the distinction between "expectation" (what an author expects to happen to a text in the collaborative nature of publication) and "intention." The distinction (most convincingly dealt with in Shillingsburg's *Scholarly Editing in the Computer Age*), may be accepted by Tanselle as historically or socially accurate but is denied as a vehicle for reconstruction: "What will be done to the text by others can have no bearing on the reconstruction of an authorially intended text" (p. 77). He claims that following "expectation" is simply a confusing of two competing goals of textual criticism (the intentional and the social), and that while "social" textual criticism "is as valid as . . . recovering the author's intended text" (p. 85) the two cannot be undertaken simultaneously and have incompatible historical purposes. This is all fair enough, and I doubt that Jerome McGann would quarrel with the demarcation Tanselle is drawing. The problem of the distinction lies in the recognition and evaluation of intention, for there is a paradox in the "strict" Tanselle position: while according stated intention (even the details, such as punctuation, of that statement) a specific privilege in the adjudication of the "meaning" of texts, Tanselle repeats his denial of that privilege when it comes to adjudicating authorial "statements" on "collaboration," which "cannot be accepted uncritically" since they may be "attempts at self-persuasion" (p. 84). But if the self-persuasion has been apparently successful, and the author has consequently accepted not only the realities but the virtues of collaboration (presumably the condition Tanselle is referring to), then does not this "self-persuasion" fall into that same class of "misguided" revisions (p. 83) which, according to Tanselle's privileging of intention, *must* be accepted?

This final section, therefore (somewhat like the book as a whole), while seeming at times to offer an extremely liberal dispensation and a pluralism of approach and method, is still occasionally rigid in its implementation of that pluralism. Tanselle would, I am sure, argue that even in pluralistic societies there are nonetheless basic distinctions and codes of behavior available for judgment, and the society of textual critics is no different. Indeed, he would probably argue that the very title of his book (*"A"* [not *"The"*] *Rationale of Textual Criticism*) speaks to the pluralistic possibilities while at the same time recognizing that *rationale* is possible, and that there must therefore be some persuasions which are "irrational." But while taking his point as a rhetorical necessity, I do still feel that there are moments in this otherwise very hospitable and embracing work where traces of former privileges recur.

It is, however, this hospitality which remains in one's impressions of the book, for Tanselle challenges the disciplinary parochialism of much of contemporary academic writing, writing which, despite interdisciplinary claims, fails to overcome the prejudices of the "home" discipline. In general, the *Rationale* avoids this problem, for the discussions (for example) of the spatial integration of text and work in painting and sculpture (as opposed to the disintegration in "sequential" media) are entirely plausible. Thus the philosophical range and disciplinary scope of the *Rationale* are both impressive and provocative—even daring. But it is perhaps inevitable that any such attempt to link the ontological and epistemological grounds of the various media of transmission, from literature to music to painting and choreography, will occasionally run into trouble. While Tanselle's agenda needs this wide range of disciplines to prove his central thesis of their interrelationship, he is not always perfectly secure or authoritative in his undefended assertions or speculations, especially in the often parenthetical or elliptical treatment of the "non-verbal" media.

For example, his assertion that the reading of musical scores is "only a substitute for the experience of the works themselves, which exist in sound waves" (p. 23) would be supported (I am assured) by virtually no contemporary musicological theorists, for it fails to consider even such basic questions as Charles Seeger's distinction between prescriptive and descriptive notation (or indeed to make any historical distinctions around the increasing complexity and sophistication of notation in the last two centuries). Even Nelson Goodman's somewhat cranky speculations (e.g., on the musical work as a collection of performances in "conformity" to a score) might have helped Tanselle to articulate his generic taxonomies, and one misses any reference in the discussion of "instructions" to the continuing debate about musical notation as a metalanguage, or to silent reading as an abstract and analytical composition of the signs for the structure of the work (as opposed, say, to silent reading as an attempt actually to call up the sound). But leaving aside the omissions which render the musical speculations more simplistic than they perhaps should be, the assertions about the musical ontology are especially problematical, since they seem to contradict his earlier favoring of the "ineluctable entity" (more plausibly discovered in that silent reading which Tanselle disdains than in the grosser variability of individual performance, which comes closer to mere "reproduction"). Indeed, the digital encoding of music (or speech) on a compact disk would seem to overcome Tanselle's objection to "instructions" (i.e., that they cannot provide instructions precise enough "to eliminate ambiguity," even though these instructions are admittedly of a specific performance, in which Tanselle has otherwise invested the ontology of the musical work.

In other words, there are passages in the *Rationale,* especially in the discussions of non-literary media, where the range of theoretical implications has not yet been fully articulated, and where there remains some dubious thinking. Another example might be the following parenthetical reference: "(Cinematic works, though they consist of projected light and not of celluloid, do have a physical tie that the others [i.e., literature, choreography, music] do not, for a lost scene of a film, no matter how vividly someone remembers it, cannot be precisely refilmed; nevertheless, copies of film prints are like copies of printed books in their potential for variation and in their status as instructions for producing works)" (pp. 32–33). There is so much assumed and embedded in this aside that one would have wished for some further development and elucidation. For example, the dictum that film *consists* of projected light does not sufficiently consider the so-called classical position of André Bazin (that light is only the medium, and that the film actually consists microcosmically in the molecular structure of film stock, which is directly and referentially linked to the "actuality" of the real world), or the rejection of this argument by such figures as Noel Carroll, whose more formalistic analysis suggests that light and shadow are in themselves "meaningless" and therefore not part of the perception of the "work," which is a construction created out of formal alignments of image and not out of light itself. (The literary analogy might be that a literary work is not the morphemes or phonemes of its presentation, but the competence of the listener/reader to arrange these phonemes or morphemes according to the generated rules of composition within a given language and culture.) Tanselle's aside is provocative, but incomplete, and raises many more issues than can be settled in such a brief argument.

I point to such problematical areas, fully aware that it would have been impossible for Tanselle to have dealt with *all* of the competing theories in the various fields he considers, but in the hope that he might be led to a more comprehensive treatment in another encyclopaedic article. Whenever we stray into interdisciplinary speculation, there is some danger that the influence of our "home" discipline will produce some judgments which might look ill-formed or incomplete to practitioners in other fields: that is the danger, but it is also the excitement involved in interdisciplinary work, and there can be little doubt that Tanselle's short book has an air of such excitement about it, of new territories being brought into the purview of textual criticism and forced to give an account of themselves.

Some of this excitement is evident in the diction of the book. Tanselle has always been known for the clarity and precision of his prose, and sometimes for the polemics of his positions. But he has not, in general, been seen as a *passionate* writer, usually preferring the language of analysis and demonstration to that of a direct emotional appeal. But while the *Rationale* maintains these virtues of clarity and precision, it is a strangely evocative, even a moving book, a *rara avis* in textual circles. For example, there is a telling (and realistic) melancholy in his following the results of the "uniqueness" of "every written or printed copy of a text," noting that "these thoughts bring home to us with particular force the fragility of the thread by which verbal statements hang on to perpetual life" (p. 42). And this same melancholy informs his discussion of the author's (and presumably the editor's) role in attempting to overcome this physical law: "What every artifact displays is the residue of an unequal contest: the effort of a human being to transcend the human, an effort constantly thwarted by physical realities. Even a document with a text of the sort not generally regarded as art—a simple message to a friend, for example—illustrates the immutable condition of written statements: in writing down a message, one brings down an abstraction to the concrete, where it is an alien, damaged here and there through the intractability of the physical" (pp. 64–65). He goes on to speak resignedly of the "uncooperative" vehicles assigned to the attempted creation of "perfection" in art (from "neural pathways to pens and inks"), and recognizes that the apparent "calming and nourishing stasis" of documents is seductive but unreliable, for "we must also recognize, if we are interested in the verbal message [the document] bears, that it reflects the pulsing and tortuous underside of stasis, freezing into inanimate solidity one moment in the history of the attempt to transmit a work made of words" (pp. 65–66). Thus he can quite plausibly argue that editing is a "noble service," analogous to Melville's image of the creation of art as Jacob's wrestling with an angel (p. 66).

These are high aims for the enterprise of textual criticism, and they are high (and "noble") precisely because the physical and human condition is so imperfect and corrupt. There is thus an inevitable disparity between aim and performance both for the artist-writer and the artist-editor, but a disparity which should be seen as an incitement to action rather than a grim negativism. Tanselle can thus close his account of textual criticism's mediation between the "tissue of uncertainties" (p. 73) of the physical world and the "rage for order" (p. 68) of the human mind with a calm, beautifully articulated peroration that should be required reading for all critics, literary or textual—indeed, for all who are involved in the "single great enterprise" (p. 46) of the world of books and art:

Our cultural heritage consists, in Yeats's phrase, of "Monuments of unageing intellect"; but those monuments come to us housed in containers that—far from being unageing—are, like the rest of what we take to be the physical world, constantly changing. Verbal works, being immaterial, cannot be damaged as a painting or a sculpture can; but we shall never know with certainty what their undamaged forms consist of, for in their passage to us they are subjected to the hazards of the physical. Even though our reconstructions become the texts of new documents that will have to be evaluated and altered in their turn by succeeding generations, we have reason to persist in the effort to define the flowerings of previous human thought, which in their inhuman tranquillity have overcome the torture of their birth. Textual criticism cannot enable us to construct final answers to textual questions, but it can teach us how to ask the questions in a way that does justice to the capabilities of the mind. It puts us on the trail of one class of our monuments and helps us to see the process by which humanity attempts, sometimes successfully, to step outside itself." [p. 93]

Tanselle's *Rationale* is one further demonstration of the attempts to "step outside," for in its call to all the citizens of the great republic of arts and letters it allows us to overcome the narrow prejudices which we may have inherited and to put our scholarship and our criticism at the service of human communication in all its manifestations. This is the final polemic of the book, and it is an heroic one indeed. That it has succeeded so well, not least in its artfully modulated language, is a tribute to the comprehensiveness and liberality of the mind of its author.

Chaucer and the Stars

Derek Brewer

J. D. North. *Chaucer's Universe*. Oxford: Clarendon Press, 1988. xxi, 575 pp.

Professor North calls upon a lifetime's study of Chaucer's astronomical and astrological learning to create an impressive tome. He gathers up and frequently corrects all his earlier work, so that this is the indispensable reference book for all the massive learning he has brought to bear. The book takes the reader first through the elements of fourteenth-century astronomy and astrology, then applies them to numerous passages in Chaucer's poems. There is frequent reference to contemporary astronomical and astrological manuscripts, as well as to modern works.

Your reviewer has to confess that this is the most difficult book on Chaucer he has ever read, and that after long and painful struggle he has had to confess himself defeated on the scientific aspects. On the actual scientific details he is prepared to take North's word for what he asserts. This acceptance is rendered easier by North's readiness to advance certain corrections of his own earlier work and by the judicious and open cast of mind he everywhere displays. Perhaps in exculpation of your reviewer's failure on the scientific side it must be said that the exposition is often far from clear, even granted the complexity of the subject matter. Arguments often proceed crabwise, and questions are raised only to postpone discussion and then to show them mistaken or irrelevant. The author does not always explain the technical terms he uses. Some tentative enquiry of others suggests that North's historical science is valid, though as he himself very honestly shows, some of it must be speculative and controversial. Having accepted this with due gratitude, the principal questions must then center on the literary aspects.

North sets out to understand Chaucer in his own terms and follows no modern critical doctrine. He emphasizes Chaucer's competence in calculation and thus follows and extends the work of scholars such as Skeat in clarifying Chaucer's astronomical references and enriching our appreciation of his verbal texture. He is most helpful where Chaucer himself is most explicit, but where our own knowledge may be deficient. For example in *Troilus,* Books II and III, he fits the sequence of events into accordance with the movements of the stars. Pandarus starts out just after dawn on 3 May in Book II, and this seems to fit the year 1385. A convincing case is made out for placing Troilus's first night with Criseyde on 9/10 June 1385. We can thus appreciate a firm underlying structure in Chaucer's time scheme which might not have been so apparent before. Our understanding of Chaucer's art is to this extent enhanced. On the other hand, the timing tells us very little about the date of composition of the poem. One of the interesting facts that seems to emerge is that Chaucer used astronomical tables far more than he did observation. He could have worked out stellar configurations occurring in 1385 while writing in very different years. Chaucer's astronomy seems to be an important aspect of his literacy as opposed to that orality which he so often mimics. Numbers, like drawings, depend on writing. Tables of star-movements cannot be reported orally.

North amply proves his first and most important point: that Chaucer, poet of love, pathos, tender feeling, and bold bawdry was also a calculator of the stars' paths, however dessicated such calculation may seem in the eyes of Romantic or post-Romantic critics. Do accountants and arithmeticians write poetry? This one did, and turned his calculations to poetic effect.

He did it because the true science of astronomy was closely associated (to put it no more strongly) with astrology, the bogus science. Astronomy could calculate the time of day and measure the brilliant march of the stars. To do no more than that would have left the heavens a merely mechanical backdrop to the trivial human tragi-comedy. Even today few really advanced astronomers and mathematicians seem able to take quite so detached and positivist a view. They respond to the deep (and, to the non-mathematical, strictly incomprehensible) beauty of the cosmos which raises questions which tease us out of thought. This feeling for beauty and meaning in the heavens was even stronger in Chaucer and his culture. They were nearer than we moderns to the unfragmented concept of the mathematically structured yet morally sentient cosmos, in which astronomy was inevitably connected with astrology.

We broach here some very difficult questions. For rationalistic medieval theologians there was always a difficulty in agreeing to the unbroken connection between the "pure" though rarely simple calculations of astronomy proper, and the attribution of a controlling moral influence of the stars over the destinies of men. It was all very well to agree that weather, or even illness, might be the product of stellar control, for that was still in the realm of the material. The difficulty came with moral influence, which evoked serious problems of determinism. Full determinism asserts total materialism and abolishes free-will and moral responsibility. This is the conclusion that Troilus comes to (*Troilus*, IV 1078), and, like Wordsworth at such a crisis of scientism in his life, he gives up moral questions in despair.

Chaucer had a more than merely dramatic sympathy with Troilus's view. In *The Astrolabe* he propounds the orthodox astrological view that the stars control human beings. For example, the signs of the zodiac "hath respect to a certain parcel of the body of a man, and hath it in governance" (*Astrolabe*, Part I, Section 21, 70–80). No one has yet attributed *The Astrolabe* to a foolish Narrator and claimed that it is all ironical, to be understood in the opposite sense from what it appears to mean. As to horoscopes, the poet tells us that when Troilus was first wooing Criseyde, Venus was in a good position in the sky to help him:

> And soth to seyne, she nas nat al a foo
> To Troilus in his nativitee.
> *Troilus*, II 684–85

Current critical orthodoxy attributes almost everything in the poem to a foolish and muddled Narrator, and ought in logic to do that here: but consider *The Man of Law's Tale*, where the poet writes

> For in the sterres, clere than is glas
> Is writen, God woot, whoso koude it rede,
> The deeth of every man, withouten dred.
> *CT* II, 194–97

Possibly the same foolish Narrator of *Troilus* has somehow inserted himself into *The Canterbury Tales*, or the Man of Law is a fool, and they are both own brothers to the fool who wrote *The Astrolabe*. But it is critical orthodoxy which is foolish here.[1] There is no reason to doubt that Chaucer subscribed, at least to a considerable extent, to the belief in horoscopes, as North argues. There are too many other references in his poetry to doubt that.

Yet also in *The Astrolabe*, Chaucer *repudiates* horoscopes as "observances of judicial matter and rites of pagans, in which my spirit hath no faith" (Part II, Section 4, 56–59). North calls this a half-hearted rejection. Be that as it may, it is one of several major self-contradictions Chaucer offers us. In truth Chaucer is, like his whole culture, deeply ambivalent on this question; and we do well to agree with the remark in Professor Manzalaoui's brilliant and learned essay that "the division of astronomy into observational and judicial was to most medieval scholars apparently a sub-dividing of a subject they regarded as basically one."[2] This essay remains much the best summation of the place of science in Chaucer's work. Manzalaoui's commentary on North's earlier work remains, apart from details where North has now changed his view, equally valid for the book under present review. It is much to be regretted that North seems not to have known Manzalaoui's essay. It does not appear in the immense bibliography, which contains far less relevant works.

The general conclusion must be, it would seem, that the unitary view of the cosmos as a material, moral, and spiritual entity lies deep within Chaucer's mentality but that there was tentatively emerging in his mind the more specialized, fragmented, non-teleological view which characterizes modern science. I have elsewhere described this mixture of "archaic" or holistic with modern specialized attitudes as "Gothic." To do so seems to locate Chaucer's notable ambivalences and inconsistencies within a recognizable cultural frame, though it is to be doubted if any period of European culture is entirely free from mixed and inconsistent attitudes of this kind.

The question of individual interpretations of Chaucer's poems then arises. North has amply proved Chaucer's special astronomical knowledge, and his pleasure and interest in the subject. We can easily accept the obvious rhetorical adornment of astronomical references such as those which elaborately indicate the time. We can also accept North's exposition of Chaucer's mixture of astronomical and mythological embellishments. The outstanding example is *The Complaynt of Mars,* whose underlying astronomical structure as expounded by North is not in doubt. We can go further and accept that Chaucer may well, as in the passages from *Troilus* quoted above, adopt astrological aspects of astronomical phenomena for the sake of his story.

The next stage is crucial to North's enterprise, and where he carries much less conviction. In essence his argument is that the astronomical/astrological sub-structures which he detects are the controlling elements of many poems. He calls these stellar infrastructures "allegories," and he begs all sorts of questions. For example, why should *Parlement of Foules* be taken as a stellar "allegory"? The essence of allegory is that the covert or "real" meaning controls the overt, literal text. The pleasure comes from the tension between covert and overt literal levels. We seek covert levels when the literal meaning forces us to, either by open signals, such as the use of personifications as agents, or by sequences of action, or statements, which cannot be accounted for simply by recourse to the literal level.

None such signal appears in *The Parliament of Fowls.* There is an enigmatic reference to Venus, which North elucidates perhaps better than any scholar so far, but nothing to suggest that the whole poem is a stellar allegory. Why should we accept that the park in the poem signifies the sign Aquarius? North is learned and ingenious enough to find an analogy, but there is no signal in the text. Analogies, as North elsewhere recognizes, are no proof of authorial meaning. They are no more than a twinkle in the exegete's eye, liable to result in a rape of the text and a deformed offspring of interpretation. Arguments from analogy are all too common, and are usually based on approximate coincidents.

North thus reasserts his earlier argument that in *The Nun's Priest's Tale* Chanticlere's seven sister/wives represent the Pleiades. He quotes the medieval name for them, "gallina," and adds the sixteenth-century reference to them as the hen with chickens. But seven hens are not one hen, nor are the seven sisters a hen with her own chickens. The argument that the fox corresponds to Saturn is equally thin. Moreover, the hens play no part in the story, and the fox's behavior needs no stellar explanation, even if it were not a version of an oft-told traditional tale. The stellar "allegory" or analogy hardly fits and is anyway completely otiose.

The same difficulty arises with the numerological explanations to which North is drawn. No one doubts the numerological pattern of some medieval English poetry, notably *Pearl*. But Chaucer's poetry never quite fits. Either there are very general balances where precise numbers do not apply, or a mid-line in a poem is not quite in the middle, or an "invisible" (i.e., non-existent) line or stanza has to be posited to make the sums come out, or Chaucer is agreed to be very inaccurate or wonderfully flexible (p. 377). There are some curious coincidences it must be agreed, but the complete underlying schemes, if they exist, have yet to be found. The incontrovertible cases like *The Complaynt of Mars* and *Pearl,* far from being evidence that similar astrological or numerological schemes may be found in other poems, are so clear that they are arguments *against* any schemes not equally clear. At best we have only suggestions elsewhere of the presence of *failed* schemes. Perhaps that possibility should be kept in mind, for, if it could be proved, it would modify our understanding of the poetry, as the product in part of botching.

Any astronomical enquiry is perforce obsessed with dates. These do not add much to our understanding of the intended poetic effect. For the reason already noted they can only vaguely indicate the probable time of composition of a poem. North has now modified some of the more wildly improbable dates he assigned to Chaucer's poems in 1969 (e.g., that *The Parlement* was composed in 1394), but the kind of argument used is still the same, and the very fact of revision, though attractively fair-minded, serves to show how weak the reasons are.

As to *The Canterbury Tales,* he suspects that Chaucer attempted to arrange the tales symbolically in accord with the signs of the zodiac, but found it too hard and abandoned the attempt. As so often with the material in this book, one wonders why then bother with it? Even the evidence for failure is not conclusive. An astrological reading of the characters of the pilgrims similarly fails to convince.

North's final conclusion is that Chaucer practiced astronomically influenced writing between 1382 or 1383 and 1388, then 1392–94. The literary significance of this is said to be, rather bafflingly, that "on a number of occasions Chaucer was constrained by astronomical events to accept dates of no great calendrical importance" (p. 518). If not important to the calendar, are they to the reader? Is the sketchy influence of astronomy mediated through the choice of the star-name Elpheta for Cambyuskan's wife—otherwise of no importance to the story—of any greater importance to the reader?

Much of North's literary judgment seems to me over-simple, and much of his logic hard to follow. He anticipates the response of the "hardened sceptic" who will assign to Chaucer's astronomical references "only the value of rhetorical ornament" (p. 513). I assign a much higher value to rhetoric than North seems to, but, though I salute with some awe his learning, his labor and the sober sincerity of his arguments, I must regretfully confess myself, after making all the effort I can, unconvinced by his main literary thesis and many of his detailed arguments.

Notes

1. For an attempt to demolish the Narrator of *Troilus*, see my "History of a Shady Character: The Narrator in *Troilus and Criseyde*," in *Modes of Narrative*, ed. M. Nischik and B. Korte (Wurzburg, 1990), pp. 166–78.

2. M. Manzalaoui, "Chaucer and Science," in *Writers and Their Backgrounds: Chaucer*, ed. Derek Brewer (London: G. Bell and Sons, 1974), repr. D. S. Brewer (Cambridge, 1990), p. 227.

What's in a Text?

Marshall Brown

Jerome J. McGann. *The Beauty of Inflections: Literary Investigations in Historical Method & Theory.* Oxford: Clarendon, 1985. x, 352 pp.

Jerome J. McGann. *Social Values and Poetic Acts: The Historical Judgment of Literary Work.* Cambridge and London: Harvard University Press, 1988. xii, 279 pp.

Jerome J. McGann, ed. *Textual Criticism and Literary Interpretation.* Chicago and London: University of Chicago Press, 1985. xi, 239 pp.

For at least a decade, from say 1965 to 1975, romantic studies were the cutting edge of literary criticism in this country. The mantle has since passed to the Renaissance, and to nineteenth-century fiction. If romanticism has continued to some extent in the '80s to influence directions of thought generally, that is mostly due to two very different thinkers, Paul de Man and Jerome McGann. The McGann volumes under review here are the middle of an ongoing project of self-definition begun with *The Romantic Ideology* and *A Critique of Modern Textual Criticism,* both published in 1983. In them we can see the maturity of a Marxist critical orientation quite distinct from the cultural studies of a Jameson or a Said. The following pages attempt to determine the essence of McGann's many seminal contributions.

That is not easy to do, for McGann's work resists summation. His principles of active, engaged writing demand an adjustment and response to varied situations and contexts. The centered self, the interpreter's self-analysis are not for him. Even his first book, *Fiery Dust,* though a composed study of Byron's self-fashioning, "deliberately cultivate[s] a variety of critical approaches"[1]; Swin-

burne: An Experiment in Criticism (1972) is an elegant, multiperspectival critical dialogue; *Don Juan in Context* (1976) programmatically proliferates contexts; and the subsequent critical books have all been in effect collections of essays. The range in *Social Values and Poetic Acts* is particularly daunting. In support of general theoretical reflection of a kind he has seldom previously undertaken, McGann adds to his staple nineteenth-century repertoire (here represented chiefly by Blake, Kant, and Arnold) the Bible, the Greeks (Herodotus, Aeschylus, Plato), Pound and contemporary poets, and even *Ulysses*. *Social Values* and *The Beauty of Inflections* encompass extended close readings of poems in the context of contemporary history and social currents (among them a particularly impressive revaluation of *The Charge of the Light Brigade*), suggestions for new approaches to familiar poems (including the well-known essays on Keats and on the historically layered textual presentation of *The Rime of the Ancient Mariner*), career surveys of canonical and neglected authors (Crabbe, Christina Rossetti, and a rich overview of the interpenetration of life and history in Byron's poems), textual and bibliographical essays (including a fine one on the intellectual currents behind the format of Blake's *Book of Urizen*), a thematic essay ("Rome and Its Romantic Significance," which deals persuasively with Goethe, Mme de Staël and Stendhal, along with Byron), critical accounts of other theorists (Cleanth Brooks, de Man, J. Hillis Miller, Fish, Bakhtin, Habermas), defenses of poetry, and even a brief set of aphorisms ("Theses on the Philosophy of Criticism," in *The Beauty of Inflections*). Questions and concerns overlap and diverge to project a mind ever alert to opportunities (as well as to what prior critics have said), never closed in upon itself. The doctrinal center lies in Marxism, but the spirit—the capaciousness, the generous response, the claims for the preeminence of literature as a vehicle for distilling and communicating social forces, the sense of the past as a varied resource that can guide the present toward the future, the rejection of disengaged hermeneutics, and even the love-hate relationship toward reductive proverbs and inevitably premature totalizations (see *Social Values*, pp. 105–6)—seems to me closer to Goethe. Militant humanists both, Goethe and Marx have much in common—as do Goethe and Byron—but not enough to make Marxist doctrine and Goethean spirit easily reconcilable.[2] McGann encourages us to seek out the identifying divisions, or "rifts," in poets and critics alike; here is the split that, for me, gives his work its distinctive profile and that makes it hardest to sum up.

Contradictions energize. McGann values history for its contrasts: we need to salvage the past as ballast to the present. Poetry presents tensions, and does so "as a challenge . . . and not simply as a picture to be observed" (*Social Values*, p. 9). Under poetic totalizations, he contends, lie the incommensurate particulars that "in fact *make (and/or have made) a difference*" (*Social Values*, p. 128; all italics are McGann's unless otherwise indicated). Consequently, "sociohistorical criticism . . . holds that art imitates not merely the 'fact' and the 'ideal,' but also the dynamic relation which operates between the two . . . [and it] both assumes and seeks to display the *determinate* character of this dynamic relation" (p. 128).

McGann is too committed to change for him to be comfortable reducing his beliefs to formulas.[3] That is surely why he has been slow to embark on the propositional mode that prevails in much of *Social Values,* and why his theorizing can seem frustrating. His energy and Byronic flexibility seem to entail a certain slippage in the terms. By lining up the right excerpts, you can make McGann seem to be chasing his own tail. "Of all forms of communication, the poetic alone entails the *whole* of what is true" (*Social Values*, p. 92). That whole is not a Wordsworthian intuition, or "spot of time," but rather a Poundian compendium (p. 52). Totalization must not be idealized, as it is in the esthetics of Kant and Coleridge, for "any great historical product . . . is a work of transhistorical rather than so-called universal significance" (*The Beauty of Inflections*, p. 187). Hence McGann experiments in one essay with the notion of a "Mastercode," or "general fact" of a "political and social" nature (*Social Values*, p. 75) that "define[s] the poem's communication system" and "establish[es] the poem's particular set of sociohistorical interests and engagements" (p. 77). A typically tactical formulation (the essay's full title is "Poetic Ideology and Nonnormative Truth: To the Marxists"), McGann's Mastercode seems to substitute for the "master code," a "theme or 'inner essence,'" a "hidden master narrative," that Fredric Jameson reluctantly rejects.[4] The transhistorical, totalizing Mastercode thus proves to be the poem's particular situation—its spot of time—such as (here) the moment of composition of Juvenal's satires. The turn with this concept reproduces the discussion that finds Platonic truth to be not Ideas, but "a pursuit and an eventuality" (*Social Values,* p. 28). Ideology—if I set the accents right on some evasive passages—is at once the "permanent and originary meaning" which the Bible "struggle[s]" to "deploy" (p. 57), "a matrix of historical particularities" on behalf of which Tennyson undertakes "a quest and polemic" (*The Beauty of Inflections,* p. 182), a kind of "performativity" that "poetic performativity overtakes" as it "strives to thicken and realize the entire communicative field" (*Social Values,* p. 91), and thus indeed "illusions" and "ghostly shapes" that literature "dispel[s]" (p. 107). What matters throughout is not the position, but the resistance to fixity. So, finally, "meaning in poetry is neither the ideology of the poem nor the ideology of the critic; it is the process in which those ideologies have found their existence and expression" (*The Beauty of Inflections,* p. 10).

Such prose neither can nor wants to stand still. The occasional declarative passages are both inert and disorienting.

> This emphasis upon the determinate *is* fundamental if "what is" *is* to stand in a *natural* and scientific relation to "what should be." But because knowledge *is* a project rather than a possession, it falls short of a complete grasp of its objects. The determinate relation between "what is" and "what should be" *is* what Shelley had in mind when he spoke of "something longed for, never seen." The determinate *is*—in the alternative sense of that word—what exists by acts of determination. Knowledge as a project *is* knowledge grounded in a platonic *Eros,* which *is* in the end both determined and determinative, in every sense of those two terms. Kant's "categorical imperative" *is* an analogous concept, though it seems to me that subsequent readers of Kant have misleadingly emphasized the categorical rather than the imperative salient in his thought.[5]

Yet even such passages enact what they are meant to propound. We see in them what McGann terms the hermeneutic pseudo-dialectic of object and subject (or of realism and romanticism), whose hegemony screens out the "third world" of the voiceless and the invisible (*Social Values*, pp. 63–64), and we are driven to intuit in "literary work (poetry and philology)" "a network constructed to maximize contradictions and incommensurability, . . . mark[ing] an antithesis to forms of normativity and dominance" (pp. 55–56). De Man's work is for him the chief case in point: he claims that it erroneously pits nature against mind in order to argue that the poetic is the only realm where the two fuse—a false dichotomy, leading to a false reconciliation that hides the way literature "deploy[s] value" as "a concrete social institution" (pp. 102–3). Standing Hegel on his feet, McGann argues against merely conceptual resolutions that subsume "facts" under "interpretations," and in favor of human experience as "*events*—specific and worlded engagements in which meaning is rendered and used" (*Social Values*, p. 72). A literary work is "a dynamic event in human experience"; poems are "structures of social energy" (*The Beauty of Inflections*, pp. 108, 128).

II

It's a game of both ends against the middle. That doesn't always appear in the formulations as such, for not infrequently the treatment of tension or contradiction can verge on Cleanth Brooks's cohesive irony or on Coleridge's symbolic "translucence of the Special in the Individual or of the General in the Especial or of the Universal in the General."[6] But the logic of the argument, reinforced by the slipperiness (or dynamic urgency, or temporality) of the terms, saves McGann from the placid center and underwrites his claim that literature is "performative," not "representational" (*Social Values*, p. viii). "The Israel of Genesis is an island in a greater world, and the more it insists that it is the center of that world, the more it gives us glimpses of the actual, the whole, the objective truth. . . . Literary work is the art of multiplicities and minute particulars, the science of *un*buildings: one law for the lion and the ox *is* oppression" (p. 230).

He drives, then, in two directions. One is toward a broadening reflection on what he likes to call "the meanings of the meanings." The other is toward an ever more precise account of texts, their production, and the factors that condition composition and publication. Arguing against New Critics and their poststructuralist avatars, McGann insists that a "work" is more than a "text," for he is interested both in the work that poems accomplish and in the work that goes into generating them. Ideology critique and textual criticism are convenient names for the two directions, future and past the vectors that he wants to rescue from the stasis of momentary or eternal presence. (One section of *Social Values* is called "Literature and the Future of History." It includes the visionary teleology of "The Third World of Criticism," which contends that "in writing what amounts to an imaginative history of the present, every poem thereby constructs a past and a set of possible futures" [p. 229], encompassing insights into events after its composition.) The unacceptable alternative, he writes in his conclusion, would be to imagine literature "as occupying a world elsewhere, . . . a 'poetic' space redeemed from time and the agencies of loss" (p. 246). Even Genesis shows us— not through its doctrines, to be sure, but through the meanings of its meanings—that we must "relinquish an imperial imagination."

III

> Three times the concentred self takes hold, three times
> The thrice concentred self, having possessed
>
> The object, grips it in savage scrutiny,
> Once to make captive, once to subjugate
> Or yield to subjugation, once to proclaim
> The meaning of the capture, this hard prize,
> Fully made, fully apparent, fully found.
>   [Wallace Stevens, *Credences of Summer*, 99–105.]

It's suspicious that *The Beauty of Inflections* takes its title from that great visionary of the central imagination, Wallace Stevens. It may be harder than McGann wishes to decenter poetry. Between meanings and the meaning of meanings, between textual criticism and the critique thereof lies at best a very fine line. The more we scrutinize McGann's two moments, the ideological and the material, the more we realize that their core is textual after all. This is not to go back on his achievements: McGann's writings make it impossible to return to the negative idealizations of "the poem itself" or to confuse Stevens's problematic *Credences of Summer* with a positive creed. But it remains important to reaffirm the dialectical productivity of poetry in creating the possibility of the very critique that McGann undertakes.

What's in a poem? McGann argued lucidly in *A Critique of Modern Textual Criticism* that poems are not isolated products of the solitary imagination. Conditions of production and reception are both fundamental to what Habermas calls the communicative act. Scholars should abandon the notion that the author's manuscript, prior to editorial intervention, preserves the purest and truest state of a work, for "the fully authoritative text is always one that has been socially produced."[7] Hence "the study of texts is fundamental and primary" (*Social Values,* p. 99) in order "to restore the connection . . . between 'intrinsic' and 'extrinsic' literary investigations, between hermeneutics and scholarship, *verstehen* and *erklären*" (p. 16). In the conjoint critique of de Man and Fish (pp. 95–114), both are taken to propound self-enclosed systems, the former's exclusively intrinsic, the latter's exclusively extrinsic. Restoring connections means testing the poem's opening to the world. "The set of ideological formations imbedded in the poem at its historical inception will always remain part of the work's fixed dialectical pole with which the moving pole of the reader interacts."[8]

The nature of that embedding needs to be interrogated here, together with the curious fixity of the dialectical pole. What puts meaning into the poem? The long Keats essay in *Social Values* relates textual variants to the specific media of publication of several poems as elements of Keats's communicative situation. It argues that to know what Keats meant we must know what was meant by those who designed and published his books and the journals where his poems appeared, and it has been rightly influential in counteracting both the intrinsic philosophical allegories of critics of consciousness like Wasserman and Hartman and the extrinsic social and class allegories of critics like Benjamin and

Eagleton. But how, in the case of someone like Keats, do we distinguish significant choice from contingent opportunity? Did Keats intend the publishing options which he used? To what extent are they part of the meaning of his meaning? The essay has been emphatically attacked for neglecting to face these questions.[9] But it does face them implicitly, for the metaphor from Donne suggests where McGann will be seen to stand: the energy to encompass and circumscribe its worldly engagements comes from the work, not from the world.

In a notable essay inspired and praised by McGann, Marjorie Levinson has claimed that "'Tintern Abbey' finally represents mind . . . as a barricade to resist the violence of historical change and contradiction." How does the moving, extrinsic, worldly pole get attached to the fixed dialectical pole (the resistive barricade) of the text? To a large degree by conjectural inference: the essay bristles with formulations like these: "To a man of Wordsworth's experience and inclination, Tintern Abbey would have represented," "a poet given to historical perspectives could not but remark," "he must have felt," "the spoiled ruin would have figured," "surely." The moving pole of the reader, indeed. Yet Levinson shows the spirit of McGann when she rescues the argument from circularity by means of a textual sensitivity that, from within the poems, "bring[s] out . . . the aura of the enclosure in Wordsworth's authorial ideology."[10] The meanings of the meanings are the authorial ideology as its aura reaches out beyond the letter of the text.

The fixed pole of authorial ideology is the firm foot of McGann's readings, as of Levinson's. As "a social event," "every poem" may well entail a "dialectical relation" between intention ("the author's expressed decisions and purposes") and reception ("the critical reactions of the poem's various readers") (*The Beauty of Inflections*, p. 24). Yet our access to "the aesthetic domain which Cockney verse attempted to conquer" is "not merely the abstract *characteristics*, but the felt *qualities* of its poetic structure" (p. 28). The word that really should have been emphasized here is "felt." Textual intuitions govern our adjustments of text to context— ours and even McGann's. Thus, in the midst of contending that we need to consider the different publication formats of *Don Juan* in order to appreciate the poem's significance, he says, "The fact that Byron's *Don Juan* should have called out these two sorts of edition is one sign of its creative power" (p. 121). The text's power, in other words, precedes the editions and channels their impact. In the Mastercodes essay, McGann insists that reception defines the crucial extrinsic code, which must not be neglected: "That initial documentary situation highlights, by its concrete and positive differentials, the fact that later texts are equally marked, at the level of production, by specific ideological interests" (*Social Values,* p. 83). Yet it turns out that the "horizon of critical values" is never out of sight; "In fact, *of course,* the poem *always has* been read within that context" (p. 85; McGann emphasizes only "has"). In repeatedly denouncing "the modern fashion of referring to poems as 'texts'" (*The Beauty of Inflections,* p. 121) precisely in order to draw attention to their "many different textual constitutions" (p. 121), McGann commits a telltale terminological contamination. Much as he would like to pit intrinsic factors against extrinsic ones, the crucial dialectic remains intratextual.[11] What's in the poem is what's in the text, either as meaning, or as implication, aura, the meaning of the meaning. Reception history paves the way toward "a close textual 'reading'"; "its chief intention [is] to establish a framework within which the poem's more localized and particular details would be able to be reimagined."[12] Situations may exist where the textual constitutions and the reception history of a poem contribute essential meanings at odds with the text, but I don't think that McGann ever exhibits any. Indeed, I don't think that, deep down, he even *wants* to.

The fate of polarities in McGann is to be undermined. That's what gives them (like his prose) their flux and their energy. By his own yardstick, he becomes a critical thinker at the moment when his own categories suspect themselves. I will examine a strong essay where the reversal is explicit, and then, approaching my conclusion, a weak essay where it is shunned. (The weaker, by the way, is the more self-revealing.) Explicit dialectic guards appearances, and the polarized categories that are transcended nevertheless remain as apparitional—the term is McGann's—structures with an illusion of substance. Hence the strong essay is incomplete, whereas the tottering categories of the weak essay provoke more forthright response. McGann is an artist of what the Italian philosopher Gianni Vattimo has come to call "il pensiero debole." Like some of the authors he most admires, such as Herodotus and Montaigne, his writing is more than the sum of its parts, more suggestive by moments than rhetorically complete. And its true character lies in the confrontations that it evades. Thus it will take me back, at the last, to Stevens, and to Goethe—and to Wordsworth.

IV

"Some Forms of Critical Discourse" (*Social Values,* pp. 132–51) embodies McGann's yearnings for discontinuity. Taking off from an essay by Hayden White, McGann proposes some alternatives to the essay form that prevails among literary critics. (McGann characterizes the form—since the text matters here—"as a lecture or, more normatively, as an essay or monograph" [p. 135]. His book in fact contains six lectures—the first five numbered chapters and the last—surrounding five "more detailed and scholastically rigorous" chapters that "execute shifts in the formal continuities of the book" [p. ix].) Essays are narrative and hermeneutic, and hence discourage "true criticism," which "entails a self-conscious response to certain social and historical factors" (p. 149). By disrupting the link of mind to mind, we can rupture the illusory timelessness of poetic truth so as to gain a fuller appreciation of poetic acts.

Here we have to undertake some textual criticism. When the essay—and it is an essay—was originally published, McGann identified four "nonnarrative forms"—the hypothetical, the practical or injunctive, the array, and the dialectic, exemplified respectively by the scientific paper, by "a book like Euclid's *Elements,* or any cookbook," the bibliography (McGann's substitute for the historical annals that White discusses), and Montaigne's— yes—essays.[13] Now it is virtually a reflex of modern critical rhetoric that any of these forms ought actually to be decoded narratively.[14] I suspect that is the reason why McGann drops reference to the first two forms in the *Social Values* text. Deep down he knows that what matters is the internal workings of the particular text, not the external format. Formal nonnarrativity is merely an appearance; what really counts is the spirit within: "The *apparition* of such forms is not, however, a guarantee that the discourse will in fact be critical, only that it will exhibit the form of criticism."[15] Almost at the end, then, McGann adduces an "essay" of Geoffrey Hartman's, "The Interpreter: A Self-Analysis," as an almost successful critical and dialogic project. The essay's failure may be that it is "formally narrativized" as McGann claims (*Social Values,* p. 150), but more likely the failure is rhetorical, as his footnoted evidence demonstrates (p. 262, n. 16). After all, the same "fundamental question . . . must [be] put to every form of ideological discourse," namely, "How much genuine self-criticism does a scholar's or an ideologue's work seek after and encourage?" (p. 150). First and last, it is the spirit and the "scholarly climate" (p. 151) that matter, and the forms are at most only conducive to the true aims. Formalism is not ideological criticism, and the revision retreats in full self-awareness from the formalist illusion that seems to have prompted the essay initially.[16]

"Some Forms of Critical Discourse" ends by "speculat[ing] on the possibility that a critical edition . . . is now being assembled somewhere which will induce a major shift in scholarly understanding" (p. 151). Two essays later comes the opportunity which that conclusion had seemed to forecast. "*Ulysses* as a Postmodern Work" (pp. 173–94) reviews the new critical edition of Joyce's novel by Hans Walter Gabler. Here McGann erects the editor into a hero much as earlier textual critics idealize the author. The modernist *Ulysses,* he tells us, was a private and elitist work, "finished and monumental," "a limited edition and supported by subscriptions of the literati."[17] The postmodern *Ulysses* is a technological book and a process text. The editor's job is to lay bare the productive forces by determining the various layers of the text. Following several Continental precedents—McGann mentions editions of Hölderlin, Kafka, Flaubert, Klopstock, and Proust—Gabler has produced the first such edition in English.

To my mind this is the weakest of all McGann's essays, partly because the information is defective. The notion of Klopstock—

the arch-sentimental author of the mid-eighteenth century biblical epic, *Der Messias*—as postmodernist poet is untenable. And the notorious Frankfurt edition of Hölderlin, which aroused a storm of public debate on the politics of editing, is precisely an attempt to produce an image of continual change in order to counter the notion of determinate compositional process in stages in the monumental Stuttgart edition that preceded it. Behind these questions of fact lies a conceptual incongruity. Elsewhere McGann says that we live amid "an indeterminate flux of conflicted and competing possibilities" (*Social Values*, p. 246). Here, by contrast, he claims that the number of forms of a given text "will always be a small number *in actual fact*" (p. 182) and that "unstable 'texts'—texts that are 'in process' or 'indeterminate'—always appear in material forms that are as determinate as the most 'stable' text one might want or imagine" (p. 186). Popular ballads are a counter-instance to the former assertion, Verdi's operas to the latter.[18] As so often in McGann, the polarities—modern vs. postmodern, stable vs. determinate—won't work. Where poetic movement is the concern, textual fixation comes to seem a regression, or a bulwark.

A bulwark against what? I find it curious that in listing Continental predecessors and in calling Gabler's *Ulysses* "the first English-language work to illustrate these new European lines" (p. 186) McGann neglects a well-established project closer to home, the Cornell Wordsworth edition. The omission is not in itself a statement, since McGann is a known admirer of the Cornell text. But it calls attention to his general slighting of Wordsworth, and that is significant. Chapter 8 of *The Romantic Ideology* presents Wordsworth as a representative of romantic evasion and false consciousness. "Wordsworth's poetry elides history," he writes, as if the three poems discussed (*The Ruined Cottage, Tintern Abbey,* and the Immortality Ode) represented all that Wordsworth had to say.[19] Wordsworth also figures in the conclusion to *The Beauty of Inflections* as the exemplar of romantic displacement (McGann's term for sublimation, viewed negatively), to be admired for the "resistances . . . dissatisfactions and yearnings" (p. 337) that hedge in his utopian individualism and psychologism. Another essay depreciates Wordsworth in order

What's in a Text? 101

to praise Crabbe. Quantitatively, McGann's selections display an overwhelming preference for narrative poetry—for ballads or ballad-like lyrics. Lyric and reflective moments—the Wordsworthian inwardness—are kept on the margins, or out of sight.

To read Wordsworthian displacement "as an invitation to substitute interiorized spiritual values for social ones is, in my view, a travesty of Wordsworth's work" (*The Beauty of Inflections*, p. 340). I agree with the judgment here, but not with the terms. How does one distinguish interiorized spiritual values from social ones? Is not the lesson that we should draw from McGann's searchingly honest investigations that social values *are* spiritual, that the interior and the exterior are connected, that interpretation *is* critique, that reaction is a form of action, that thinkers are laborers, and that works work? The maker of the phrase, "the beauty of inflections," made other phrases that link up with it. "There is nothing beautiful in life except life." "It is life that we are trying to get at in poetry." "Art, broadly, is the form of life or the sound or color of life. Considered as form (in the abstract) it is often indistinguishable from life itself."[20] McGann likes to present himself in an antithetical or polemical Blakean stance. But the separation of life from thought, or of the narrative from the reflective, is an unreflected abstraction. It is the ideological moment exposed through McGann's endeavors.[21]

Stanley Fish and others have argued recently that theories have no consequences.[22] That holds for abstract theories and intended consequences. An example would be "the Anachronism of George Crabbe" in *The Beauty of Reflections*, pp. 294–312. Here McGann describes the formal characteristics of Crabbe's poetry, which is additive, non-totalizing, non-redemptive, empiricist, and scientific; these, he contends, reveal idealist illusions that the romantics share with the Augustans. To see that the meanings don't follow from the abstract pattern, you need only consider Clare, to whom all of these terms apply equally well, but who was an extreme Wordsworthian individualist. Forms indeed do not have a life of their own, apart from the spirit that lives in their concrete embodiments. Despite itself, and through its failure to confront adequately the romantic poet who should be central to it, McGann's work reveals the binding of form and content, substance and style, (hermeneutic) meaning and (ideological) meaning of meaning. Those interpenetrations are the Goethean essence of the totalizing ideal that McGann can never bring himself to renounce. He presents it in Lukacsian-sounding formulations like this: "The critical ideal must be a totalizing one, for literary 'works' *continue* to live and move and have their being" (*Social Values*, p. 125). But the polemical "must be" proves in practice to be an empathic "is"—a universal fact of our relation to the world. "For merely eyeing a thing is no help. Every look turns into a consideration, every consideration into a contemplation, every contemplation into a connection, and so it can be said that we always theorize with every attentive glance at the world. But to do and undertake this with consciousness, with self-knowledge, with freedom, and, to use a daring expression, with irony requires such a skill, if the abstraction that we fear is to become harmless and the desired result is to be alive and useful."[23]

Scratch the dialectician and you find the harmonizer. In Kenner's *The Pound Era* "expository form . . . rhyme[s] with the complexities of its subjects" (*Social Values*, p. ix). Arnold's "Sohrab and Rustum" is "a polyglottal text moaning round with many voices" (p. 89), but the effect is more a polyphony than a cacophony: "Arnold's book [*Poems* 1853] says one thing *and* (not *but*) means another" (p. 86). There is a "consonance between [Allen Tate's] interpretation of the Dickinson poem and his ignorance of its textual problems" (*The Beauty of Inflections*, p. 130). "Tennyson's verse style and form exhibit a genuine congruence and symmetry with his methods of production" (p. 178). It is not by chance that one of the most brilliant of the essays demonstrates homologies among Don Juan's life, Byron's life, and the history of the French Revolution. Like the Kant whom he criticizes, McGann finally has a correspondence notion of truth: "That the poem should have been transmitted and finally published in this way is in perfect keeping with every other aspect of its text and context" (p. 101).

And in practice, the text remains *primus inter pares*. For, scratch the ideologist and you find the stylistician. If, for McGann, "The poem is a social act" (*The Beauty of Inflections*, p. 21), it acts *as*

What's in a Text?

a poem, and that means, verbally, or, in the most extended of McGann's notions of the term, as a text. That isn't always what McGann says, but I don't think he speaks clearly, or consistently, or in his own best interest, when he asserts that "it is not 'texts' which act in the world, it is the men and women who formulate and deploy those texts and who have assented to the textualization of their lives" (*Social Values,* p. 16).[24] For many of his greatest triumphs as a commentator are actually with words. His mastery lies in both the knowledge of and the feeling for words, inseparably mixed. The knowledge that Dickinson's plural, "Horses Heads," indicates a funeral procession, not a bridal journey. The feel for the resonance of the word "world-wind" in a variant text of Keats's Paolo and Francesca sonnet. The knowing grasp of iconographic connotation in the wonderful reading of *The Charge of the Light Brigade*. The stylistic intuition to recognize that "bassoon" and "lighthouse" are anachronistically modern terms in *The Rime of the Ancient Mariner*—the crucial detail in McGann's historicizing account of that poem. Because he knows how saturated our languages are with meanings, with social values, and with history, McGann regularly and powerfully makes the totality of poetic acts depend on such punctual responses.

Like virtually all the poets with whom he has particularly identified himself, McGann is a connoisseur. His admiration goes out to the living world of incommensurates that are found on the textured surface of things. He is a great connoisseur, because his tact is controlled by vast and exact knowledge and empowered by ideological sophistication. He knows how to make the precise details that act on him count for us as well. As editor and as critic, he takes his mission to be saving the past. Distinctions and recognitions go hand in hand as we funnel past energies toward the future. "Thus," concludes the most theoretical of the essays in the earlier book, "in our differences do we learn about, and create, a community" (*The Beauty of Inflections,* p. 132). That is what's in a text.

Notes

1. McGann, *Fiery Dust: A Study of Byron's Poetic Development* (Chicago: Univ. of Chicago Press, 1968), p. viii.

2. See, for instance, *Social Values*, p. 91, where the issue is distilled. "Poetry is obliged, as it were, to present all sides of a question. This includes bringing forth, *within a sympathetic structure,* those details and points of view which are by ordinary measures incommensurate with themselves and with each other . . . . The consequence is a certain kind of nonnormative discourse: not a discourse *without* norms, but one in which we observe the collision of many different and even contradictory norms." I find the generally dialectical tenor hard to reconcile with the sovereign embrace of the phrase that McGann italicizes. On Goethe and Marx, see Marc Shell, "Money and the Mind: The Economics of Translation in Goethe's *Faust,*" *Modern Language Notes,* 94 (April 1980), 516–62.

3. "How one decides which parts of the strategic programme need to be emphasized in particular case studies is always a difficult question. I am not even sure that one can theorize these sorts of problem at all" (*The Beauty of Inflections,* p. 9).

4. Jameson, *The Political Unconscious* (Ithaca: Cornell Univ. Press, 1981), p. 28.

5. *Social Values,* pp. 128–29; my italics on the verbs. Since the categorical is, in fact, the determinative (*die Bestimmung,* in post-Kantian usage), the passage ends by rejecting the very emphasis that it began by declaring "fundamental."

6. Coleridge, *The Statesman's Manual,* in *Lay Sermons,* ed. R. J. White (Princeton: Princeton Univ. Press, 1972), p. 30.

7. McGann, *A Critique of Modern Textual Criticism* (Chicago: Univ. of Chicago Press, 1983), p. 75. For an excellent case study, see Peter J. Manning, "The Hone-ing of Byron's Corsair," *Textual Criticism and Literary Interpretation,* pp. 107–126.

8. McGann, *The Romantic Ideology: A Critical Investigation* (Chicago: Univ. of Chicago Press, 1983), p. 157.

9. See Paul Fry, "History, Existence, and 'To Autumn,'" *Studies in Romanticism,* 25 (Summer 1986), 215–16.

10. Levinson, *Wordsworth's Great Period Poems* (Cambridge: Cambridge Univ. Press, 1986), pp. 53, 32, 32, 34, 35, 36, 33.

11. See the forceful critique of would-be divisions of intrinsic from extrinsic factors in Lee Patterson's essay, "The Logic of Textual Criticism and the Way of Genius" (*Textual Criticism and Literary Interpretation,* pp. 55–91). McGann's basically intelligent reading of Kant's aesthetics as a cardinal instance of the individualist and idealizing "romantic ideology" is a case in point. When he criticizes de Man for "bracket[ing] our attention to the way 'Kant' performs . . . . in his sociohistorical field" (*Social Values,* p. 104), McGann overlooks both extrinsic and intrinsic factors that would *conjointly* condition his account. Externally,

What's in a Text? 105

Kant's political and theological reputation was generally radical, at the opposite pole from the later Coleridge. And, textually, McGann's proof passages from early in the "Critique of Aesthetic Judgment" should be registered as a transitional moment of idealism on the way back to the natural science of the "Critique of Teleological Judgment."

12. The quotations here come from a McGann essay-in-progress entitled "Four Characters in Search of a History."

13. McGann, "Some Forms of Critical Discourse," *Critical Inquiry*, 11 (March 1985), 399–417. The list is on page 399, the first two examples in the footnote on page 416, the others developed in the text.

14. See, for instance, the following: on scientific essays, Charles Bazerman, *Shaping Written Knowledge: Essays in the Growth, Form, Function, and Implications of the Scientific Article* (Madison: Univ. of Wisconsin Press, 1988); on Euclid, Gilles-Gaston Granger, *Essai d'une philosophie du style* (Paris: Odile Jacob, 1988), pp. 24–42; on cookbooks, Susan J. Leonardi, "Recipes for Reading: Summer Pasta, Lobster à la Riseholme, and Key Lime Pie," *PMLA*, 104 (May 1989), 340–47. With respect to the array form, Hayden White's essay needs to be consulted ("The Value of Narrativity in the Representation of Reality," *Critical Inquiry*, 7 [Autumn 1980], 5–27). McGann says that White narrates what is really a pseudo-progress from nonnarrative to narrative forms. He does not say that White demonstrates how we can actually read annals narratively, thus effectively effacing the distinction that McGann wants to make.

15. *Critical Inquiry* version, p. 414 (my emphasis). Symptomatically, the dialectic is attenuated in *Social Values*, p. 149: "Although these three types of critical discourse (array, narrative, dialectic) exhibit the *form* of criticism, that form is no guarantee that the discourse will in fact be critical."

16. See the change from the original uncompromising formulation: "the array and the dialectic offer especially clear contrasts with narrative forms of discourse, both critical and noncritical" (*Critical Inquiry*, p. 400), and the modified later version: "In this respect the forms of array and dialectic are particularly important, not merely as alternative critical modes, but as forms which cast an important critical light on the structure of narrativized discourse" (*Social Values*, p. 133).

17. This is not so pure a conception as McGann's text might seem to imply. For the material complexities—i.e., the social dimension—involved in producing the first edition, see Hugh Kenner, "'The Most Beautiful Book,'" *English Literary History*, 48 (Fall 1981), 594–605.

18. Verdi repeatedly added, subtracted, and recomposed material (musical and verbal) in response both to his own second thoughts and to aesthetic and political promptings from outside—a fairly normal situation for nineteenth-century opera composers, and not unparalleled in symphonic music (e.g., orchestration in Mahler, or in Schumann). Some literary authors have also been tinkerers producing uncontrolled textual forms—McGann's immediately preceding essay on *Urizen*, "The Idea of an Indeterminate Text: Blake and Dr.

Alexander Geddes," presents a great instance, Philip Gaskell's *"Night and Day: Development of a Play Text"* (*Textual Criticism and Literary Interpretation,* pp. 162–79) a minor one, not very interestingly analyzed. Other authors, like William Dean Howells and Thomas Wolfe, have written in complex collaboration with editors. And manuscript transmission, of course, is prone to unresolvable indeterminacies, like Dickinson's or Hölderlin's punctuation. (Heidegger's exegesis of Hölderlin depends crucially on an attributed line-end comma ["Des gemeinsamen Geistes Gedanken sind,/Still endend in der Seele des Dichters"] in a poet who characteristically neglected line-end punctuation.)

19. *The Romantic Ideology,* p. 91. There is a less dismissive reading of "A slumber did my spirit seal" in Chapter 6 (pp. 68–69).

20. Wallace Stevens, "Adagia," in *Opus Posthumous,* ed. Samuel French Morse (New York: Random House, 1982), pp. 162, 158.

21. For a challenging, unnecessarily difficult, but often profound extension of McGann's impulse into (among other things) the psychological dimension, see Marjorie Levinson, *Keats's Life of Allegory: The Origins of a Style* (Oxford and New York: Blackwell, 1988).

22. Stanley Fish, "Consequences," *Critical Inquiry,* 11 (March 1985), 433–58.

23. Goethe, *Zur Farbenlehre,* "Vorwort," in *Gesamtausgabe der Werke und Schriften* (Stuttgart: Cotta, 1959) XXI, ed. Reinhardt Habel, 15 (my translation).

24. More in McGann's spirit is Gerald M. MacLean's "What Is a Restoration Poem? Editing a Discourse, Not an Author," which argues that "authors are never entirely in control of their texts" and which brilliantly demonstrates how an unnormalized text can reveal significances hidden by emendation according to principles of authorial meaning (*Text,* 3 [1986], 339).

Art, Elitism, and Gender: The Last of the Aesthetes

Regenia Gagnier

Karl Beckson. *Arthur Symons: A Life*. Oxford: Clarendon Press, 1987. xi, 402 pp.

Arthur William Symons, the premier spokesperson for an autonomous and elite art in *fin-de-siècle* England, was born to a Wesleyan minister from a long Cornish line and the daughter of a Devonshire farmer. Raised provincially by religious parents, as early as his school days Symons crafted a myth of art and the artist that would greatly influence the high Modernism of Yeats, Joyce, Eliot, and Pound. Until he moved to London at the age of twenty-five, Symons lived at home with his parents, whose complete unconcern for his love of art was matched by his apparent indifference to their religion. By twenty-two, he had published books on or dedicated to Browning, Meredith, and Pater and was a prolific critic who insisted that his "life's work" would be as a poet. In 1890, he commenced the great mediation between French and English letters that would culminate in *The Symbolist Movement in Literature* (1900). In London, he also distinguished himself as one of England's first serious scholars of popular metropolitan entertainment, what Yeats called "a scholar in music halls" (p. 75). He cultivated a *grande passion* for a minor dancer whose surname, if she ever had one, has not survived, and he cultivated an even grander illusion of his own libido, an image his male friends ridiculed. He stood upon professional ethics in rebuking a reviewer of his verse for mistaking "a book which was manifestly written with an artistic intention and an artistic intention only" (p. 119) for a lurid depiction of sex with prostitutes. In 1895 he assumed the editorship of the notoriously short-lived art magazine *The Savoy*.

Perhaps to be expected of such a one, Symons's problems began or, more probably, were exacerbated in 1901 with his marriage to the daughter of a Newcastle shipbuilder, a marriage mutually described from the beginning as "a joining of two discontents" (p. 205). He suffered a mental collapse in 1908 on holiday in Venice and was manacled and imprisoned in a castle dungeon in Ferrara. Certified insane and committed to a hospital in East London, he was finally permitted and, with grants from the Royal Literary Fund and Civil List Pension, enabled to return to his quiet cottage in Wittersham. Thereafter the aesthete in his cottage and his wife in London each tried to succeed after his and her fashions: he remained prolific but was unable to reestablish his shattered career and increasingly came to remind people of a delicate ghost from the belle epoch; she remained mindful of her husband but failed to establish the public acting career she passionately desired. Like many of his compatriots of similar class and tastes, Symons spent his last years obsessed with imagined and unpaid royalties and sanguine about his debts to others. He died in 1945 in World War II, as the *TLS* obituary said, the last of the aesthetes. His last words ("Oh, mother!") were for the housekeeper Bessie whom his late wife had provided for his care.

Such is roughly the life of Arthur Symons by Karl Beckson, a quarter of a century after Roger Lhombreaud's *Arthur Symons: A Critical Biography* (1963). The two biographies dovetail in an apparently inevitable interpretation of Symons as incapable of disentangling a Methodist fear of sin from a Decadent capacity for desire. In other ways, however, Beckson's is a considerable advance in scholarship over the earlier biography, most notably in the several thousand letters of Symons, his wife Rhoda (née Bowser), and major literary and art figures of the period that Beckson has collected and meticulously documented to supplement the vast range of Symons's published and unpublished work. (Oscar Wilde said that a syndicate was responsible for the mass of printed matter under the corporate name of Arthur Symons.) In addition to the letters, which were unavailable to Lhombreaud and which considerably augment our view of the art world of the time, and the correction of some of Lhombreaud's factual errors, Beckson's biography provides an extensive treatment of the post-breakdown period, during which, among much ephemera, Symons composed his *Confessions,* partially published in 1930 and according to Beckson "a major document in the literature of madness" (p. 317). Although Beckson rigorously avoids the social and cultural aspects of British life of the period that did not directly impinge on Symons—this is not a "situated" life—there is much here of interest, even of fascination, to students of the "transition" period between Victorianism and Modernism beyond Symons's personal psychodrama, critical pronouncements, and uneven poetry. Although Beckson does not foreground the matter, it is clear that Symons's life contains more than one psycho*cultural* drama that go far toward domesticating our more exotic notions of the great aesthetes.

Symons's presentation of the art world and artist became one of the most underanalyzed *idées reçues* in Modernism. In the early 1880s, pressed by Reverend Symons to choose a profession that would provide a living, Symons always replied that he hated every profession, that he would rather starve than go into business, and that he would prefer to go on living as he had been, by reading and writing. In *Spiritual Adventures* (1905) he wrote, "It was not that I had anything to say, or that I felt the need of expressing myself. I wanted to write books for the sake of writing books. . . . It helped to raise another barrier between me and other people" (p. 14). In his essay on Verlaine in *The Symbolist Movement* he reformulated the Romantic protest against a bourgeois, utilitarian society: "It is the poet against society, society against the poet, a direct antagonism" (p. 194). When even respectable critics were beginning to be bullied into an acceptance of the autonomy of art from ethics and only in the most provocative cases felt driven to ask "why poetic art should be employed to celebrate common fornication" (p. 107), Symons developed, via Mallarmé, a position on nonrepresentational modes of language that Beckson compares to MacLeish's dictum in "Ars Poetica" that "a poem should not mean but be" and that many of our contemporary readers would rather recognize as postmodern *écriture,* or writing without a signature.

This separation of art from everyday life, however, led in the

1890s not to the death of the author—or the disappearance of the autonomous subject before the power of discourse itself—but rather, as Beckson points out, to aesthetic elitism, the Modernist distinction between high and low culture. In his impressionistic account of Edgware Road in *London: A Book of Aspects* (privately printed in 1909), Symons reveals the essentially undemocratic tendency of his religion of art, a tendency that would be most evocatively imaged in *The Waste Land:*

> As I walk to and fro in Edgware Road, I cannot help sometimes wondering why these people exist. Watch their faces, and you will see in them a listlessness, a hard unconcern, a failure to be interested. . . . In all these faces you will see no beauty, and you will see no beauty in the clothes they wear, or in their attitudes in rest or movement, or in their voices when they speak. They are human beings to whom nature has given no grace or charm, whom life has made vulgar. [p. 242]

Here, as in *The Waste Land,* the poor are aestheticized, i.e., used by the artist for aesthetic effect, while they are simultaneously excluded from the world of aesthetes, or taste. Such views, like those expressed in *The Symbolist Movement in Literature,* were pondered by the young James Joyce, whose early work was promoted through Symons's efforts and who had written in *The Day of the Rabblement* (1901), "No man . . . can be a lover of the true or the good unless he abhors the multitude; and the artist, though he may employ the crowd, is very careful to isolate himself" (p. 223). After his breakdown, Symons even enlisted Blake in his sublimation (and mystification) of the artist. "I was born, 'like a fiend hid in a cloud,' cruel, nervous, excitable, passionate, restless, never quite human, never quite normal," he wrote. "I am of all men the most Impenetrable / Some say that I am cold as stone" (p. 332). Finally in his *Confessions* he promoted his lifelong conviction that the artist was fundamentally abnormal. At this point we are far from the Romantic poet as either revolutionary (Blake, Byron, Shelley) or social antenna (Wordsworth): Symons's poet has little to do with society: he is (by his own account, of course, and by his own account only) as autonomous as his art. His personal relations as well as his work would suffer from this insistence—always, no doubt, connected with his illness—on autonomy from others.

Symons's unconventional pose of the artist was always in tension with a Methodist puritanism; nor was the contradiction ever dialectically productive of a higher state. This contradiction was most evident in his astonishingly commonplace (for many artists and writers of the time) attitude toward gender, an attitude which again reflected a separation between art and everyday life. Gender differentiation is perhaps our most long-standing and deeply held convention, and for Symons it was an obsession. Sex itself, he wrote in *Spiritual Adventures,* was prohibited by his Methodist upbringing and from his teens entirely divorced from his deepest "reverence for women" (p. 13): "Love I never associated with the senses, it was not even passion that I wanted; it was a conscious, subtle, elaborate sensuality, which I knew not how to procure" (p. 14). At the age of twenty, he considered publishing a book of poems entitled *The Legend of Women,* in which, he naughtily confessed to a former teacher, he would "typify various characters or aspects of women ... especially the Ambitious, Saintly, Heroic, and Desperately wicked," which is to say that he would represent madonnas and whores. The project was abandoned, however, because Symons's experience of women (outside of literature) was confined to his mother and his sister, who fell into none of these categories. His subjective "aesthetic" transformation of sexual women (or women he had sex with) into whores permitted him to feel victimized by them (as in *Amoris Victima* [1897]) and thus allowed him to assuage his guilt for his "elaborate sensuality."

Symons's appropriation of the dancer "Lydia" is most disturbing in this regard. Lydia herself, the illegitimate daughter of a Spanish father and English mother, is now a cipher to us: smiling out of dark eyes, wearing a simple pendant heart, her photograph gives little indication of the personal *mythos* Symons made of her in his art: a femme fatale to match the demonic in him. At the time of their affair, Symons privately recorded her resistance: "I am not strange; I am just like other girls; I don't want to be different from other people," she told him when he confessed his attraction to her "strangeness" (p. 102). Yet when she finally broke with him to enter a respectable bourgeois marriage, Symons, a mere Svengali-in-letters, transformed her in his *Memoirs* into his own *outré* fantasy. In the *Memoirs* she gazes at him "with those animal eyes of hers" and asks:

"Why Arthur, do you so often read of madness, speak of madness? I know I am not like other girls. I know you are not like other men, you have said to me I'm not quite normal; that's true, no more than you. There is something—oh, ever so many things!—in you that I can't make out. You are so inhuman. Then you become human: then back again comes your inhumanity. No, no, I also, am not altogether human." [p. 102]

"Am I really inhuman?" Symons asks, her "animal eyes" no more than a mirror for his self-absorption. Such appropriations of vulnerable daughters of exploited mothers raise the problematic of historical "representation." As with Symons's aestheticizing of the common people in Edgware Road, it is evident here that male privilege to appropriate women and aesthetic privilege to represent them are allied and oppressive.

Symons's profoundly unaesthetic, unplayful response to the conventions of gender is revealed in another case of contradictions amounting to a common double standard. Writing to an American girlfriend and singer, Katherine Willard, he crafted the legend of himself as Bohemian:

Do you know, I have no interest in what is proper, regular, conventionally virtuous. I am attracted by everything that is unusual, Bohemian, eccentric: I like to go to queer places, to know strange people. And I like contrast, variety. It used to amuse me to go to see Mme Blavatsky, & it would satisfy my sense of the piquant to call next day on Cardinal Manning, & then, leaving the arch-episcopal Palace with a volume of sermons, drop the book, with the portrait of an actress between the leaves, in the garret of a friend whom I was taking to the open-air ballet at the Crystal Palace. [p. 70]

Yet in the same year, he reveals the limits of his Bohemianism in his prim reaction to Willard's desire to go on the operatic stage:

I really shudder at the thought of all you would have to go through. I doubt if you quite realize what the opera bouffe stage is really like. Few people are fonder of the stage than I am, or more interested in everything theatrical, but I don't quite like the idea of seeing you on it. It is not the fact of the acting, but the associations of every kind. People to whom at present, you would indignantly refuse to be introduced, would be your companions most of the time. [p. 78]

The manuscript reader of Symons's *London Nights* (1895) at the Bodley Head praised the craft in the poems but observed that the range remained "limited, and, indeed, contracted, until the whole universe appears as an embodiment of desire . . . utterly loveless and unimpassioned—mere and sheer libidinous desire" (p. 112). Symons deplored the "kind of sterilisation" he found in "sexless" writers like Ruskin and Carlyle, and considered his "obsession" with sex the source of his creativity: "Sex—the infernal fascination of Sex—even before I actually realised the meaning of its stirrings in me—has been my chief obsession. One's own Vitality: that is a centre of Life and of Death. It is also the centre of Creation. Without the possession of women, how can one create?" (p. 83). Since he could not reconcile sex (the source of his artistic creativity) with love, his respectable marriage to a woman he "loved" initiated a crisis of his "self" as an artist. Although similar fears are often submerged in the literature of the 1890s, they have seldom been so nakedly expressed:

Have you ever thought of the frightful thing it is to shift one's centre? That is what it is to love a woman. One's nature no longer radiates freely, from its own centre; the centre itself is shifted, is put outside one's self. Up to then, one may have been unhappy, one may have failed, many things may seem to have gone wrong. But at least there was this security: that one's enemies were all outside the gate. With the woman whom one loves one admits all one's enemies. Think: all one's happiness to depend upon the will of another. [p. 217]

Beckson sees Symons's sexual psychodrama as fundamental to a manichean metaphysic, in which sense and ideal, or evil and good, play themselves out in a, as it were, bonsai Nietzschean struggle. He quotes T. S. Eliot's review of Symons's 1925 translation of *Les Fleurs du mal*, in which Eliot remarked upon "the childish attitude of the 'nineties toward religion, the belief—which is no more than the game of children dressing up and playing at being grown-ups—that there is a religion of Evil, or Vice, or Sin" (p. 313). Yet "Symons's attitude toward vice," Beckson concludes, "was considerably more complex than Eliot—or even Symons—knew, for, in part, it had contributed to the central disaster of his life" (p. 313). Since *Arthur Symons: A Life* is in fact organized as a chronological presentation of Symons's work and letters rather than an argument with a consistent analytic frame or theoretical standpoint, this intriguing metaphysic, like the analysis of Symons's psychology, is fragmentary and unsustained.

Beyond Symons's individual psychodrama (what some feminists and critical legal scholars would call a masculine quest for autonomy), his relationship with Rhoda reveals a general crisis in the Edwardian sex/gender system between Victorian patriarchal domesticity and New Womanism. Although Rhoda inherited a substantial income from her family in Newcastle, the couple's domestic agreement to live solely on Symons's earnings contributed to perennial worry and occasional hysteria over finances. His male friends attributed his breakdown to their economic trials and Symons's consequent overproduction—he published some sixty books and pamphlets, edited and contributed to more than seventy volumes, wrote more than one thousand articles and reviews, and translated plays, novels, memoirs, and poems—and this view was corroborated by certain statements of Symons's own. Yeats, John Quinn, and others continually railed at Rhoda for her extravagance, although from the time of Symons's breakdown in Venice in 1908 until her death in 1935, she never abandoned a husband who offered her only minimal physical, emotional, or intellectual companionship. The last twenty-five years of their relationship make a sorry tale indeed: Rhoda in lonely rooms in London, ceaselessly begging for minor acting parts, Symons obsessively recounting encounters with prostitutes in real or imaginary theatrical haunts: each consoling the other for their respective "failures." Perhaps most depressing amid the pathos of these lives contorted by the sex/gender system is the response of Yeats, Augustus John, and the artistic brotherhood. The couple's tragedy mainly elicited masculine outrage at the impecunious Rhoda and virile contempt for Symons's attempts to present himself as Casanova.

Of Symons's work, modern criticism has declined to accept the aesthete's estimation of himself as preeminently a poet. Although there are some considerable exceptions, the poetry that Beckson selects as exempla of Symons's elected art is mechanical, cliché-ridden, and entirely unself-conscious in its putative confession. On the other hand, from this biography as well as from the primary sources, it is clear that Symons was—true to the nineties' most perfect genre—a superior epigrammist, able to produce in trenchant phrases miniature descriptions of miniature social arenas, like the actors of the art world. His precise allusion to J. K. Huysmans's quintessential *tedium vitae* cannot be improved: "He leans back on the sofa, rolling a cigarette between his thin, expressive fingers, looking at no one, and at nothing" (p. 56). And Symons was a great critic, especially acute on artists and writers with whom he identified in fantasy or in fact. These included the French poets and playwrights in *The Symbolist Movement* as well as Huysmans and Casanova; the quote above on the destructive love of women was intended to refer to Keats and Fanny Brawne. He was also the herald of Modernism, including its worst excesses of elitism, solipsism, and the great divide between high and low culture; and he furthered that literary movement by making the work of Baudelaire, Verlaine, Mallarmé, and others accessible to British and American writers. In this line, one of Beckson's several contributions is the treatment of Symons's reception of Browning, which links the English poet with his French contemporaries.

Ezra Pound could write in 1911 that the "Gods" in whom he had found his "sanity" were "Plato, Longinus, Dante, Spinoza, Pater, and Symons" (p. 332). Now the late twentieth century can turn to Symons's *insanity* (as it has to Pound's) in his *Confessions,* in both the published and unpublished versions.[1] Several layers of dense signification are revealed when we add Symons's instability at the time of writing to the remarkable narrative of his flight from Venice to Bologna, his confusion in Ferrara, and his incarceration in the Castello Vecchio. As an earlier critic put it, "I do not think I have read anything so pitiable as these *Confessions of Arthur Symons;* for he wrote them when he thought himself sane, but he was mad" (p. 318). Scholars will be able to pursue these and other aspects of Symons's life and times in ELT Press's new volume in the 1880–1920 British Authors Series, *Arthur Symons: A Bibliography,* edited by Beckson, Ian Fletcher, Lawrence W. Markert, and John Stokes.[2]

It has become fashionable for critics to compare the *fin de siècle* with our own *fin.* Although Symons's capacities for blindness and insight apparently combined Jimmy Swaggart's and Paul de Man's, Beckson's biography will feed no such flames. In general, if *Arthur Symons: A Life* has a fault, it is that of Richard Ellmann's *Oscar Wilde* (1987): although they are impeccable in literary scholarship, both biographies downplay the world in which these artists operated, choosing rather to present them, according to the myths they themselves helped create, as isolated tragic heroes slouching toward their respective dooms, in both cases having to do with an "elaborate sensuality." Unlike Ellmann, who retained some pre-Foucaultian notions of one's "true sex," Beckson is indeed aware of the social construction of gender, as evident in his sympathetic treatment of Rhoda; but when World War II is introduced in the Epilogue, the world outside the art world enters with a shock of perspective, perhaps as it did to Symons himself. To write of artists, madmen, and criminals without substantial reference to their societies is as the sound of brass or a tinkling cymbal—to accept uncritically the autonomous aesthetics that even Symons himself, shortsighted as he was, occasionally saw beyond. Even if its theorists, like Richard Le Gallienne, perceived Decadence as "merely limited thinking, often insane thinking" (p. 95), scholars ought not represent it as an entirely anomolous event, disengaged from the broader forms of life of the period. As the problems of sex and gender so central to Symons's art and life are not simply psychological but cultural, so the problem of elite culture and democracy extends well beyond Symons's personal and overdetermined taste. The United States had Whitman, Germany had Heine, but the story of English poetry's relationship to democracy after Blake is still to be articulated. In his insistence upon elitist art, in his own case intimately related to gender dimorphism, Symons confronts us with the modern problem of a poetics for the people (including women) that Wilde, Edward Carpenter, and William Morris had discerned in Whitman and others and addressed in some of their lesser known works.

Beckson's *Life* reads as a chronology of Symons's letters and works. In several cases I could see no particular logic to chapter titles or divisions between chapters. I noticed only one error—Arthur Machan rather than Machen (p. 302)—in what is by current production standards a well-produced volume that will have a subtle but not insignificant impact upon its readers. Last week, in the lobby of a California motel on what could be called the ugliest street in the United States if there were not hundreds just like it, I noticed the complete *Memoirs* of Casanova (which Symons in part edited and translated) and was startled for a moment by my impression of their inappropriateness. Of course, Casanova's *Memoirs* are not inappropriate for a California motel in the Silicon Valley, their presence being merely a combination of sensation and Culture in an international marketplace. But my *impression* of their inappropriateness—my undeniable *feeling* that such things were merely simulated and dislocated in my (post)modern world—as well as my momentary and ungenerous disapproval of their commonplace surroundings I attributed to the subtle influence of this authoritative *Life of Arthur Symons*.

Notes

1. For the distinctions between published and unpublished versions of the "Confessions," see Alan Johnson, "Waifs of Memory: Arthur Symons's Confessions" in *Twilight of Dawn: Studies in English Literature in Transition*, ed. O M Brack, Jr. (Tucson: Univ. of Arizona Press, 1987), pp. 153–67.

2. Greensboro: ELT Press, 1989.

Reading Mary Shelley, Well—

L. J. Swingle

Paula R. Feldman and Diana Scott-Kilvert, eds. *The Journals of Mary Shelley: 1814–1844.* 2 vols. Oxford: Clarendon Press, 1987. Vol. 1, xlii, 427 pp.; vol. 2, x, 308 pp. Pages numbered consecutively.

Anne K. Mellor. *Mary Shelley: Her Life, Her Fiction, Her Monsters.* New York: Routledge, 1988. xx, 276 pp.

Emily W. Sunstein. *Mary Shelley: Romance and Reality.* Boston: Little, Brown, 1989. xi, 478 pp.

Karl Kroeber. *Romantic Fantasy and Science Fiction.* New Haven: Yale University Press, 1988. vii, 188 pp.

On the evening of 27 July 1814 Percy Bysshe Shelley, embryonic poet and author of a few radical tracts, was the twenty-one-year-old father of a one-year-old daughter; and his wife Harriet, pregnant again, was carrying their first son, who would be born in late November. On that same evening Mary Wollstonecraft Godwin, daughter of the famous/infamous mother who had died when Mary was born, was a sixteen-year-old girl, living a sort of Cinderella life (as she saw it) in the household of her stepmother and once-famous father. But at four o'clock the next morning Percy and Mary eloped. With that act they shattered the structures of their previous lives and commenced an intense, complex and sometimes strained relationship which would nurture or provoke the creation of some of the most important literary works of second-generation British Romanticism.

The elopement itself calls to mind the dreamscape of a Romantic poem—for example, the concluding scene in Keats's *The Eve of St. Agnes,* where Porphyro and Madeline cast aside the bonds of conventional human existence: "Arise—arise! the morning is at hand;— / The bloated wassaillers will never heed:— / Let us away, my love, with happy speed" (11. 345–47). But whereas Keats's poem teasingly prevents us from following its imaginary lovers once they flee away into the storm, human life among the molecules tends to leave traces of its passage.

After fleeing Godwin's house, Percy and Mary raced to the coast and crossed into France. In Paris they bought a green notebook. It was to be the start of "Shelley and Mary's Journal Book"; but it gradually became primarily, and then exclusively, Mary's journal. Percy, writing the initial entry in the new journal, captures the lovers' sense of the high drama of their venture:

July 28. The night preceding this morning, all being decided—I ordered a chaise to be ready by 4 o clock. I watched until the lightning & the stars became pale. At length it was 4. I believed it was not possible that we should succeed: still there appeared to lurk some danger even in certainty. I went. I saw her. She came to me. . . . a few minutes past she was in my arms—we were safe. we were on our road to Dover.—

Unlike Porphyro and Madeline, Percy and Mary left records of "our road to Dover"; and many of the records have been preserved. Yet a challenge arises with that word "our." As we seek via those records to peer into the life of storms past, can we keep our own modern inclinations, anxieties, and habits of thought sufficiently in check? What we should wish for is a picture of past life in which "*our* road to Dover" is less ours and more the closest approximation we can achieve of the road that those beings from the past actually travelled.

There used to be relatively little scholarly interest in Mary's road to Dover. Mary was treated mostly as a helpmeet for getting at the real meat, an understanding of Percy. But in recent years, thanks partly to feminist studies and partly to emerging recognition that our conception of British Romanticism ought to involve serious recognition of more than The Six Major Romantic Poets, Mary Shelley has become a subject for sustained scrutiny in her own right. Accordingly, much attention is presently being directed toward the task of developing a clearer understanding of this person—"I saw her. She came to me"—to whom Percy

Shelley with such fervour committed himself on the morning of 28 July 1814.

A considerable body of important primary evidence, beyond that which we glimpse through the veiled forms of Mary Shelley's imaginative writings, is now available in dependable editions. The third and final volume of Betty T. Bennett's *The Letters of Mary Wollstonecraft Shelley* (Johns Hopkins) was published in 1988. Bennett's edition, which gives us some five hundred more letters than had been previously published, is highly accurate; and Bennett provides careful annotations and thoughtful, substantial introductions to each volume. These letters contain our most direct evidence concerning the various sides of herself, and the evolution of those personae, that Mary Shelley presented to the people around her. And now with the publication of *The Journals of Mary Shelley,* edited in two volumes by Paula R. Feldman and Diana Scott-Kilvert, we have also our best evidence concerning the more private sides of Mary Shelley that she presented to herself (and, for the space of his life with her, to Percy).

To be sure, if we come to the *Journals* looking for spicy revelations, we may be at first disappointed. The entries do not reveal, for instance, whether Mary's flirtation with Hogg extended beyond mental intercourse. Nor do they tell us if Mary thought that—let alone knew whether—Percy and Jane/Clara/Clare/Claire were sexually intimate. Many of the entries prior to Percy's death are short records of events mental and physical—as, for example, that for 31 January 1815: "Shelley is out all day—work in the evening Clary to sleep as usual—Shelley reads Gibbon alloud to me—Hogg comes-he is not well—but will go home to sleep—work—H. goes at 1/2 11—" (*Journals,* p. 62). Yet in their frequently stark and abbreviated way such entries hint at matters beyond the mundane—as when the reference to Claire, "to sleep as usual," touches delicately on how sensibilities in this indefinitely extended family of intellectual migrants grated against each other. Further, in some of these entries we come upon passages that uncover, sans delicacy, unexpected and significant features of the young Mary Shelley's mind. In the entry for 28 August 1814: "We stopped at Mettingen to dine and there surveyed at our ease the horrid & *slimy* faces of our companions in voyage—our only wish was to absolutely anihilate such uncleansable animals" (*Journals*, p. 20). It is difficult to read this passage without wondering about the workings of Mary Shelley's mind two years later, as she was beginning to formulate her famous tale of Frankenstein and the creature whom he finds so despicably ugly. The journals themselves, though, resist our yearning to make straightforward discoveries concerning Mary's creative processes. During the *Frankenstein* period, the most we encounter concerning that startling exercise of imaginative creation is some occasional unremarkable remark: "We ⟨des⟩ arrived wet to the skin—I read nouvelle nouvelles and write my story—Shelley writes part of letter" (entry for 24 July 1816, *Journals*, p. 118). If we seek deep insight into the more private spaces of the young Mary Shelley's mind, therefore, we are generally forced to read these early journals somewhat at an angle, as if we were trying to follow a faint path in a forest.

This evidential situation changes somewhat in 1822, after Percy's death, when Mary Shelley begins to use her journal as a communicative substitute for the husband she has lost: "For eight years ⟨my soul⟩ I communicated with unlimited freedom with one whose genius, far transcending mine, awakened & guided my thoughts.... Now I am alone! Oh, how alone! ... White paper—wilt thou be my confident?" (entry for 2 October 1822, *Journals*, p. 429). During this latter period the journals become much more an extended and sometimes painfully intimate record, first, of Mary Shelley's fear, depression and doubt, but then, gradually, of her self-reconstruction into an independent human being and writer. They offer, accordingly, an invaluable source of evidence concerning the often neglected, complex subject of whom Mary Shelley became, once the half-protective and half-inhibiting shadow of Percy was removed from her life.

The new Feldman and Scott-Kilvert edition of the *Journals* clearly supersedes the 1947 Frederick L. Jones edition. Jones had worked primarily with Edward Dowden's copy of the mutilated version of the journals that appears in Lady Shelley's *Shelley and Mary*. Feldman and Scott-Kilvert, working with the manuscripts themselves, have sought to present "the text of the entries as far as possible as Shelley and Mary left them" (*Journals*, I, xxii); and they have also reproduced the endpapers of the notebooks. This new edition gives us, therefore, a transcription not only of the entries as the Shelleys actually wrote them, complete with authorial cancellations and eccentricities of spelling and punctuation, but also of much peripheral, intriguing life-clutter that found its way into the margins of the notebooks—lists of books read, medical prescriptions, addresses, even (so far as this form of publication can present them) drawings, doodles and impatient or pained slashes of the pen.

In addition, Feldman and Scott-Kilvert provide in their introductions, notes, and appendices a generous supporting text of their own that identifies persons, places, things, and issues necessary to an understanding of the journal entries. Their editorial stance in these materials is admirably conservative, as when, concerning the issue of what implications might be drawn from gaps in the journal entries, they caution that "it would be dangerous . . . to read too much into Mary's silences," because sometimes "the brevity of entries can be explained by the fact that she was extremely busy" (I, xviii). The editors obviously have sought to keep their own interpretive impulses in check; and they are concerned to restrain our impulses as well, in cases where evidence seems murky: "On only one of the seven occasions when Mary Shelley wrote the symbol [D] in her journal is it possible to be sure of why she did so" (p. 579).

Yet editors, whatever their ideal objectives, rarely can remain entirely objective. The Mary Shelley who emerges from the Feldman and Scott-Kilvert editorial apparatus is a woman inclined toward "habitual reserve" (I, xvi); and this inclination, as the editors picture it, shades in the direction of "*fits* of depression and lapses into reserve" (II, 587; emphasis mine). As these word choices imply, their Mary Shelley is at least slightly unstable, emotionally unsound; and such weakness is almost a constitutional affliction: "It is also true to say that Mary was *naturally* a reserved and secretive woman, to whom concealment was often an emotional necessity" (II, 580; emphasis mine). Now whether this is actually "true to say" must be debatable. The picture of Mary Shelley that emerges from the editorial apparatus in Betty T. Bennett's *Letters,* for example, exudes a significantly greater bloom of emotional health. Bennett, in fact, reviewing the Feldman/Scott-Kilvert *Journals* in the *Keats-Shelley Journal*, 37 (1988), has cautioned that, as "the editors are remarkably unsympathetic toward their subject," their footnotes should be read "more for data than interpretation" (p. 199). This does not mean that Bennett's Mary is more true than the Scott-Kilvert version. The point is, rather, that when we enter the territory of Mary Shelley's psychic health, we go beyond the boundaries of what evidence can be expected to tell us about what is "true to say." This need not imply, as John Locke likely would murmur, that we should back off and sit down in quiet ignorance of a matter we cannot sensibly discuss; but it probably does mean we should know and acknowledge when we have moved from relatively solid ground onto the more swampy terrain of interpretation.

When such difficulties concerning what may be true arise in connection with admirable editions of letters and journals, where the ambition has been to transmit primary evidences with a minimum of possible interpretive distortion, then how much more perplexing is the problem we are apt to encounter in studies, biographical and critical, that aspire to build up structures of interpretation out of primary evidences? The two most recent major studies of Mary Shelley, Emily W. Sunstein's *Mary Shelley: Romance and Reality* and Anne K. Mellor's *Mary Shelley: Her Life, Her Fiction, Her Monsters,* offer a dramatic case in point. Sunstein and Mellor develop fundamentally opposed portraits of their subject.

Sunstein tells us in her introduction that she had intended originally to present Mary Shelley in accordance with the "general view" that Mary was only "Shelley's satellite" and a somewhat contrary satellite at that, "the conservative daughter of a radical mother" (p. 7). But research into Mary's life, and the years following Percy's death, caused Sunstein to alter these assumptions. The Mary Shelley who emerges from Sunstein's study is nearly the opposite of "conservative." For Sunstein, Mary Shelley is fundamentally a radical sensibility who struggled to live the "romance" she believed in, until eventually, in the late 1820s, she sensed that "she had almost expended her capital of countercultural defiance" and began to accept "the 'cold reality' of human beings and the world as they were" (p. 290).

Reading Mary Shelley, Well—

The Sunstein version of Mary Shelley is a woman of "Promethean ambition" (p. 7), "claiming sexual fulfillment among women's rights" (p. 5), who was finally forced by poverty "to live in an England whose social system, moralism, and dullness she loathed" (p. 6). She "took female unorthodoxy and achievement for granted" (p. 41). She felt "scorn" for Maria Edgeworth, whose *Moral Tales* for girls picture young females "foolishly" attempting to combat "the system of social slavery" (p. 54). Mary, as Sunstein sees her, revels in such combat: "Even the world's hostility exhilarated Mary, as she, Shelley, and Clare were spotlighted in Byron's notoriety and became the scandal of the visiting international set" (p. 119). Sunstein is fond of gathering incidental details of the life Mary and Percy led together that call to mind links between the Shelleys and the eager, poignant radicalism of youth in the 1960s: "Like protesters against impure societies through the ages, [Shelley] abstained from meat and alcohol; she laid in a store of vegetarian foods, occasionally made him a passable pudding, without sugar, which they boycotted because it came from slave plantations" (p. 104). In sum, the Mary Shelley that Sunstein offers us "literally embodies the English Romantic movement." Mary's "concept of romance as supranormality" captures "what Romanticism meant at its height to many of her contemporaries" (p. 3).

Mellor disagrees. Mellor's study presents us with a Mary Shelley who stands firmly, even sternly, opposed to primary Romantic inclinations: "Mary Shelley understood that the romantic affirmation of the creative process over its finite products could justify a profound moral irresponsibility on the part of the poet" (p. 80). Mellor's Mary Shelley "believed that a poet must take responsibility for his actions" (p. 80). Committed not to a celebration but to a "critique of romantic Prometheanism," she thinks that a "Romantic ideology that represented its own poems as self-consuming artifacts" is not "a moral ideology" (p. 80). This factor of "moral ideology" is very prominent in Mellor's study. Mary Shelley, as Mellor pictures her, believes that "one must balance the abstract ideal one serves against a moral obligation to preserve the welfare of living individuals" (p. 85); she endorses "the ideal of the man of feeling as a moral exemplar" (p. 109); she thinks monsters can be produced by "uninhibited scientific and technological development, without a sense of moral responsibility" (p. 114); she advocates a "strenuous commitment to the preservation of a moral society" (p. 137). As these phrases suggest, Mellor's Mary Shelley is "no revolutionary herself" (p. 86). Mellor's fundamental thesis, in fact, is that Mary Shelley is nearly the reverse of radical. Mellor's Mary subscribes to an "ideology of the egalitarian bourgeois family" (p. 215). She is "essentially conservative" (p. 137). Further, and in accordance with this, she exhibits a literary consciousness that is more Neo-Classical than Romantic: "Mary Shelley endorsed a neoclassical mimetic aesthetic that exhorted literature to imitate ideal nature and defined the role of the writer as a moral educator" (p. 126).

This rather startling contrast between Sunstein's and Mellor's portraits of Mary Shelley generates stories about Mary Shelley's life that are shaded in very different ways. Both authors agree, for example, that the relationship between Mary and Percy, which had begun with such delight, matured into something less joyous. But for Sunstein Mary's life with Percy was, all things considered, more a boon than a bust: "Together they created an existence that, for all its punishments and tragedies, came closer than could any other to fulfilling her ultimate desires" (p. 83). During his life Mary "adored Shelley for his generosity and regarded his improvidence as rather fun" (p. 102); and after his death she mourned him sincerely, while she sought to build some sort of life for herself in his absence. But Mellor's Mary and Percy live a life together that is basically tortured. Percy, as Mellor presents him, "clearly did not share Mary's grief" over the death of their daughter—he seems, in fact, "to have been singularly unconcerned with the welfare of his female children, and unmoved by their deaths" (p. 32). And Percy's attentions to other women are a recurring anguish: "Mary more than ever needed reassurance from Percy of his primary commitment to her, to their love, and to the family she represented—this at just the point when Percy seems to have been most intensely involved with Claire" (p. 32); "Mary Shelley was of course fully aware of her husband's dissatisfactions and of his flirtations with Emilia Viviani and Jane Williams, but she was too weakened physically by her pregnancies and miscarriage and emotionally by her grief and ambivalence to confront him openly" (p. 146). Mellor's Mary is an angry, repressed woman in relation to her husband: "Perhaps she feared the consequences of her own liberated anger. Certainly that unacknowledged anger was deep and enduring" (p. 146). So, for Mellor, Mary's commitment to Percy's memory after his death is psychoanalytically suspect: "Mary Shelley's devotion to and idealization of Percy Shelley manifest her genuine love for him. At the same time, they exist in inverse proportion to the anger she wished to mask or deny. Unable to admit, in her intense guilt at having caused him to suffer, that he had faults . . ." (p. 147). Mary in the Mellor version is nearly as tormented by Percy in his death as she had been when he was alive.

What accounts for these radically opposed presentations of Mary Shelley? Sunstein and Mellor have very different orientations of mind. Sunstein, previously author of a biography of Mary Wollstonecraft, is primarily oriented toward the investigation of historical evidences, "trying to dig out all the facts," as she puts it (p. 7). Her book is grounded in an immense amount of information about events in and surrounding Mary's life—where Mary was at a given date, whom she was with, what was said, what was done; and Sunstein is concerned to embed these matters firmly in a sense of the socio-historical context of the period. The "facts" for Sunstein do not mean, principally, the evidences of the imagination as they may be revealed in Mary Shelley's fiction. For Mellor, however, who has previous books on Blake and on irony in English Romantic poetry, it is Mary Shelley's fiction, and principally *Frankenstein*, that grounds the discussion. Mellor has things to say about the life outside the novels—she speaks of "taking into account" unpublished archival materials in the Abinger Collection and "paying more attention" than previous critics to "contemporary cultural influences" on Mary's work (p. xii). But it is telling that of her eleven chapters six are on *Frankenstein*, while another is titled "Love, Guilt, and Reparation: *The Last Man*." Mellor's book is primarily a series of literary studies, combined and amplified with some biographical material.

I should mention here that Mellor's book must be approached with caution if one is looking for Sunstein-type "facts." I noted the following problems in the first thirty pages: Mellor has Mary's daughter Clara born 1 September 1817 (p. xvi), while the *Journals* (p. xxxviii) and Sunstein (p. 143) have the date as 2 September; Mellor writes that "Mary settles at Portman Square" in May 1829 (p. xviii), while the *Journals* tell us that Mary "moves" there in January 1829 (p. xli) and Sunstein tells us that May is when she signed a year's lease there (p. 295); Mellor has Godwin discovering Percy and Mary's relationship on 8 July 1814 (p. 21), while *Journals* quotes a letter by Godwin that gives the date as 6 July (p. 1) and Sunstein confirms, adding that July 8 is the date when Godwin confronted Mary with his knowledge (p. 75); Mellor has Percy and Mary fleeing "at five in the morning on July 18, 1814" (p. 21), while *Journals* (p. 6) and Sunstein (pp. 78–79) have four in the morning of July 28; Mellor has "nine separate sections . . . removed from Mary Shelley's Journal for the period January to May, 1814" (p. 30), while the *Journals* have themselves not beginning until 28 July 1814 (p. 6).

Further, one needs to be cautious about how Mellor uses facts; and one should be conscious of what sorts of facts she does not use. For example, both Mellor and Sunstein refer to the familiar anecdote about how Mary, worrying over the issue of Percy Florence's early schooling, reacted to Mrs. Butler's advice that he should attend a school where he would be taught to think for himself: "Teach him to think for himself? Oh, my God, teach him rather to think like other people!" Mellor, employing this anecdote in support of her thesis concerning Mary Shelley's "commitment to the bourgeois family," introduces the quotation as something Mary "is reported to have answered" (p. 211). But Sunstein, discussing the anecdote as a part of the "fallacious Mary Shelley legend," points out that it must be patently fabulous," since Mrs. Butler and Mary did not meet until 1837, when Percy went to Cambridge (p. 313). As this example suggests, Sunstein tends to think considerably more about intricate details of Mary Shelley's life than Mellor does. Her argument for Mary's fundamentally radical temperament, for instance, is supported by much discussion of the sorts of offbeat women Mary established relationships with throughout her life. Of these, the most strange is probably Mary Diana Dods, "a secret lesbian and sometime transvestite" (p. 273), who found literary success as "David Lindsay." Years after Percy Shelley's death Mary conspired with Dods in a bizzare scheme to rescue Isabel Robinson, a secret unmarried mother, by having Dods transform herself into "Mr. Sholto Douglas" and elope with Isabel to Paris (p. 280). This seems the sort of thing Percy, in a wildly Queen Mab mood, might have found appealing; and it seems very much not the sort of thing a woman committed, as Mellor proposes, to an "ideology of the egalitarian bourgeois family" would consider doing. Mellor's study makes no mention of Dods.

On the basis of the "facts," then, it would appear that Sunstein's picture of Mary Shelley has the clear edge. Perhaps it might be argued, nevertheless, that the *real* facts are secret, hidden, and that they unveil themselves only in the light of Mary's imaginative activity. It is the letter that should be trusted, not the outer fleshy envelope of life's facts. The question, then, would be whether Mellor's preferred evidential ground, her extensive analysis of the fiction, has substantial merit as a basis for her picture of Mary Shelley.

As the several chapters she devotes to the subject testify, Mellor's analysis of Mary Shelley's fiction has its primary ground in *Frankenstein*. And at the center of her analysis of *Frankenstein* is the point that the novel exhibits "Frankenstein's failure to mother his child" (p. 42). This is a touchstone for Mellor; and she touches it repeatedly: "But rather than clasping his newborn son to his breast in a nurturing maternal gesture, he rushes out of the room" (p. 41); "Frankenstein's failure to mother his child..." (p. 70); "Frankenstein callously fled from the outstretched arms of his loving, needful, freakish son" (p. 80); "Frankenstein's failure to embrace his smiling creature with parental love..." (p. 101); "Frankenstein's failure to mother his child..." (p. 215). Mellor's thesis here, as her phrasing suggests, is that Mary Shelley is building up an indictment of Frankenstein in the novel: her "ideological commitment to a mutually supportive, gender-free family functions in the novel as the ethical touchstone by which the behavior of Victor Frankenstein is found wanting" (p. 44). Frankenstein's behavior, resulting from a "failure of empathy" (p. 42), associated with the failings of his "Promethean Politics" (title of chapter 4), produces a drama of tension between "anxious and rejecting parent" and "abandoned child" (p. 44). As Mellor reads *Frankenstein,* this abandoned child is a version of Mary Shelley herself. Mary, at odds with the Promethean ambitions of her father and Percy, was a being, like Frankenstein's creature, "In Search of a Family" (title of chapter 1).

How substantial is this way of reading *Frankenstein*? It is a reading that, to my mind, is grounded in a number of questionable assumptions. Mellor assumes, first and most fundamentally, that Frankenstein's creature should in fact be thought of as a "child." It is this premise that allows her to introduce all those moral issues attendant upon human births and nurturings that connect with her idea of Mary Shelley's moral ideology. Mellor does note that in revising the manuscript Mary Shelley introduced the term "species," changing Percy's phrase "a new existence would bless me" to "a new species would bless me" (p. 66). And in chapter 7 ("Problems of Perception"), a chapter that seems to contradict or to have implications that contradict much of her previous argument about *Frankenstein,* Mellor does discuss how the creature is "a unique being," who thereby "functions in the novel as the sign of the unfamiliar, the unknown" (p. 128). But these matters do not seem to have led Mellor to think about whether Mary Shelley might have been presenting the Creature as an alien quantity, a non-human or even anti-human force, to whom we apply our human ways of thinking and valuing to our peril. Why not? Mellor also assumes that what the Creature says is what it is. For her the Creature is basically innocent and benign: she speaks of its "innocence" as "given" (p. 42). Why? She believes that Mary Shelley "identified with the orphaned creature" (p. 44). This assumption leads her, for example, to believe that the expression on the Creature's face, when it appears before Frankenstein, is benign. Significantly she wants to call that expression a "smile" (pp. 41, 101)—although at one point in chapter 7 this word choice slips: "As his creature, *grinning,* leans forward to embrace his father, Frankenstein sees the gesture as an attempt 'seemingly to detain me'" (p. 128; emphasis mine). "Grin" is in fact the word Mary Shelley uses in the crucial first encounter scene of the novel (chapter 4, 1818 edition); and "grin" perhaps suggests something less amiable or more ambiguous than "smile."

As these few examples may suggest, a good many assumptions underlie Mellor's reading of *Frankenstein*. We all, to be sure, carry assumptions into our reading of a text. But my uneasiness with Mellor's reading stems, I think, from the confidence with which Mellor proposes that something must be so—without appearing to have considered alternative possibilities. A final example: Mellor takes one of the things Frankenstein says—his speech to Clerval in chapter 3 (1818 edition), which begins with the assertion, "A human being in perfection ought always to preserve a calm and peaceful mind"—to be "both authorial credo and moral touchstone" for the novel (p. 86); and she keeps returning to this idea (pp. 124, 137). But why would one single out as "authorial credo" this particular speech more than other speeches that Frankenstein makes, as, for example, "Oh! be men, or be more than men. Be steady to your purposes, and firm as a rock. This ice is not made of such stuff as your hearts may be" (chapter 7, 1818 edition)? Frankenstein displays both anti-Promethean and Promethean moods in the novel. According to what principle does one determine that this mood rather than that mood reflects Mary Shelley's own beliefs?

It is not clear to me which is the chicken and which the egg in Mellor's version of Mary Shelley—whether, that is, she started with a conception of the person and then read the novel in such a way as to fit that conception; or whether she started with a reading of the novel and worked to the person. It may be significant, though, that her discussion of *Frankenstein* begins with this sentence: "From a feminist viewpoint, *Frankenstein* is a book about what happens when a man tries to have a baby without a woman" (p. 40). I am not confident about how to read this reference to "a feminist viewpoint." But it may suggest that in writing her study Mellor started with commitment to a particular ideological viewpoint herself and that she was not primarily concerned to ask what viewpoint Mary Shelley had. I speculate that this might account for what I take to be Mellor's most basic assumption. Mellor posits, it seems to me, that Mary Shelley thought that failure and unhappiness must be accidents—that they must be caused by some error or moral fault that occurred along the path to the ill result. This poignantly optimistic idea is often present in happy temperaments that subscribe to modern activist ideologies. Such temperaments suppose human beings ought to be able to make the world work out in desired human terms; and, if it doesn't, then this must be because particular human beings have been somehow morally deficient. But another, rather different idea operates among at least some people of the Romantic period. Sunstein in her study of Mary Shelley refers to it as a cultivation of "intensity not merely in love and sex but in all the passions; expressiveness, imagination, innovation . . . but also ordeal and woe—Lermontov longed to be as unhappy as Byron had been" (p. 3). For Sunstein, Mary Shelley has some of this temperament that finds profundity in loss, failure, and woe. To lose means that one has yearned mightily, perhaps spiritually, and differentiated oneself from the ordinary herd of humans grazing the ordinary pastures of the world. Mellor's version of Mary Shelley does not entertain the possibility of this viewpoint.

What vision of Mary Shelley, then, is the right one? It seems to me that Sunstein's argument in support of her portrait of Mary as Romantic radical is considerably stronger than Mellor's for Mary as conservative protester against Romantic Prometheanism. However, the possibility remains that better arguments might be developed for the conservative position. A sketch for one version of such an argument appears in Karl Kroeber's *Romantic Fantasy and Science Fiction,* wherein Kroeber's concern is to isolate and explore differences between the fundamental impulses of those two types of writing and thinking. Chapter 2 of Kroeber's study, centering on *Frankenstein,* invites us to read that novel as "prototypical of subsequent science fiction because it represents so powerfully how our modern, scientific, technological society dehumanizes itself" (p. 19).

In Kroeber's reading of what Mary Shelley is up to, the novel is, as with Mellor, a skeptical critique of Victor Frankenstein, whom Kroeber sees as "a full-blown monster . . . who climactically manifests [his] family's morbid traits" (p. 18). But the premise here is not that Mary Shelley is an essentially neoclassical moralist, at war with Romantic transcendental yearnings that endanger the human values of the bourgeois family. It is Kroeber's premise, rather, that Mary Shelley's protest against the Frankenstein mentality reflects a fundamental impulse of Romanticism itself. For Kroeber, Enlightenment culture bequeaths to the Romantics a "triumph of humanism" that, excluding the fantastic from life, develops a situation "that has become intolerable through the obliterating of any otherness in a world human beings have come to dominate with frightening completeness" (p. 7). Thus in *Frankenstein* "one observes how human beings have become the sole—but quite sufficient—threat to humanity" (p. 19). Mary Shelley, for Kroeber, is a conservative, but in the sense that her concern, a very Romantic concern, is to expose the "socially menacing self-deception" of an Enlightenment-produced mentality like Frankenstein's that defines "humanity in terms of an abstract universal such as one's species" (p. 20). In Kroeber's argument Romanticism, and Mary Shelley as Romantic, would have us recall and recover the sense of magic and otherness in the world that once preserved us from ourselves. A vision of Mary Shelley that develops in this direction, I suspect, would help us recognize the connection between the conservative and radical impulses that appear to mingle in her life.

Pound Among the Women

James Longenbach

Ezra Pound and Margaret Cravens: A Tragic Friendship. Edited by Omar Pound and Robert Spoo. Durham: Duke University Press, 1988. xvii, 181 pp.

Pound/ The Little Review: *The Letters of Ezra Pound to Margaret Anderson,* The Little Review *Correspondence.* Edited by Thomas L. Scott and Melvin J. Friedman, with the assistance of Jackson R. Bryer. New York: New Directions, 1988. xxxiv, 368 pp.

Ezra Pound himself did not write this rhyme, and neither did he know its origin.

> Ezra Pound
> And Augustus John
> Bless the bed
> That I lie on.

The "Virgin's Prayer," as it was called, circulated among the tonier artistic circles of pre-World War I London. Pound did not mind publicizing his sexual prowess, but he did mind being coupled with John, who was not tony enough. Having heard from Wyndham Lewis that John referred to Pound as a "coxcomb," Pound offered an anatomy lesson: "A coxcomb or cock's comb is the large red object which flops about on a rooster's head, this is carefully to be distinguished from the *small* red object placed at the other extremity of the rooster, i.e., and to wit, the cock's cock. I judge that Augustus is trying to distinguish between my temperament and his own, i.e., pointing out that I fly my flag over my intelligence (such as it is) whereas he flies his over his penis, (such as it is), or over his flies, or buttons."[1]

Incredible as it seems, Pound was serious about a kind of

pseudo-scientific sex-in-the-head. In the postscript to his translation of Rémy de Gourmont's *Natural Philosophy of Love* (1921), he ventured that "it is more than likely that the brain itself, is, in origin and development, only a sort of great clot of genital fluid held in suspense or reserve. . . . It would explain the enormous content of the brain as a maker or presenter of images." In Pound's fantasy of phallic creativity, "the power of the spermatozoid is precisely the power of exteriorizing a form": the role of women in the creative act of childbirth is decidedly marginalized, and all great works of art are likewise conceived of as essentially masculine, all resistance to the force of genius feminine. "Even oneself has felt it," Pound admitted, "driving any new idea into the great passive vulva of London."[2] Such effort demanded a great deal of genital fluid on the brain, and James Laughlin, Pound's publisher, has suggested that this fantasy of phallic power explains Pound's usual posture—seated in a chair, he would virtually recline, his head thrown back level with his torso: fluids don't flow uphill.

Pound also suggested in the de Gourmont postscript that because a woman is formless, a chaos, and not inventive, she makes "always the best disciple of any inventor."[3] And once a disciple, it would seem, always a disciple: "Not wildly anti-feminist," he wrote in 1918, "we are yet to be convinced that any woman ever invented anything in the arts."[4] Pound's words are chosen carefully: in his terms, a woman could never invent anything because women are by nature not capable of invention—they could be disciples to inventors or the objects of invention. Pound's friend and patron, John Quinn (the New York lawyer and art collector) agreed: "I don't mind the aberrations of a woman who has some openness and elasticity of mind . . . in whose excretions there may occasionally be cream; but, by God! I don't like the thought of women who seem to exude as well as bathe in piss, if not drink it, or each other's."[5] Quinn was raving to Pound about Margaret Anderson and Jane Heap, the editors of the *Little Review* (which Quinn was subsidizing and for which Pound was acting as foreign editor), and the fact that these two women were lovers riled Quinn most of all: they had excepted themselves from the phallic force which, in his mind as in Pound's, not only made the "chaos" of femininity tolerable but sustained civilization itself.

I begin with this material in order to make the obvious even clearer: Pound's anti-feminism was often as rampant and offensive as it could possibly be. And yet, as is usually the case with any aspect of Pound's behavior, there remain exceptions and contradictions difficult to explain away. "I distrust the 'female artist' as much as even you can," Pound told Quinn, but he made this remark by way of trying to convince Quinn to purchase the work of Gwen Baxter, a young sculptor whom Pound thought promising.[6] Both H.D. and Marianne Moore have testified to the oppression of Pound's tutelage (to take only the most famous examples), but they have also made a point of expressing their debts to him. Just as it is difficult to imagine Eliot's career without Pound's influence, so is it difficult to imagine the development of H.D. or Moore—even though their work transcended Pound's influence utterly. Given Pound's anti-feminism, it seems that it should be easy to cleave apart the work of male and female modernists, yet the separation isn't possible. The development of Pound's career is equally unimaginable without Dora Marsden, Harriet Shaw Weaver, Harriet Monroe, Jane Heap, and Margaret Anderson. Feminists all, these women edited the journals (*New Freewoman, Egoist, Poetry, Little Review*) in which appeared not only the work of Pound but of Yeats, Eliot, Stevens, Williams, Lewis, and Joyce. Joyce's work was serialized in the *Egoist* and *Little Review;* the *Portrait* was published by the Egoist Press; *Ulysses* was published by Sylvia Beach's Shakespeare and Co. For many years Joyce's work was subsidized by Harriet Weaver; and Margaret Anderson and Jane Heap watched their magazine suppressed and gleefully faced prosecution for publishing Joyce's prose. "It is some kind of commentary on the period," recalled Robert McAlmon, "that Joyce's work and acclaim should have been fostered mainly by high-minded ladies, rather than by men."[7] It is some kind of commentary on the period, but it's not clear just what kind. Many memoirs of the period, like McAlmon's, will appreciate the efforts of these women but only insofar as they acquiesced to Pound's editorial demands: the resistance put up by Harriet

Monroe or Margaret Anderson is dismissed as a shortsighted inability to see the value of modernism as Pound did. But the resistance was more often motivated by political rather than purely aesthetic concerns. The *Egoist* and the *Little Review* were conceived by their editors as radical magazines: some of Pound's radicalism matched their own—in spite of his anti-feminism—but some did not.

Two new collections of Pounds' correspondence, the first with Margaret Cravens and the second with Margaret Anderson, help clarify these convoluted interactions of modernism and feminism. *Ezra Pound and Margaret Cravens: A Tragic Friendship,* edited by Omar Pound and Robert Spoo, lives up to its subtitle. Covering the brief period from 1910 to 1912, Pound's letters to Margaret Cravens offer a compelling narrative, and the book reads something like a tale Henry James could have written. The book also includes appendices which reveal the presence of Margaret Cravens in several of Pound's poems and in H.D.'s unpublished novel "Asphodel." (Excerpts from "Asphodel" and from Alice Woods's *The Hairpin Duchess* [1924], in which Cravens appears, are also included.) Throughout the volume the editors' annotation is copious, enhancing the narrative which the letters themselves provide. The letters are embedded in an editorial commentary drawn from a thorough knowledge not only of Pound's career but of the social conditions of pre-war London and Paris; in one letter, for instance, the editors hear the full resonance of Pound's apparently offhand use of the word "technique," and their annotation directs us to a passage in "I Gather the Limbs of Osiris" that enriches our experience of the letter. Occasionally this assiduousness detracts. Anyone who reads this very specialized collection of Pound's letters will not require an extensive note on Ford Madox Ford, beginning, "His immense literary output included novels (two of them and part of a third with Joseph Conrad), essays, travel books, and poetry" (p. 56). Ford is not even mentioned in the letter to which this note is appended; the note helps to identify Ford's mistress, Violet Hunt, who was also a productive writer.

Margaret Cravens is far less well known even than Violet Hunt. She came to Paris from Indiana to study music, and Pound met her in 1910 through his friend Walter Rummel, a pianist who premiered several important works by Debussy. After just a few days' acquaintance, Cravens offered to become his patron. Her source of income was a trust that gave her $1,500 a year, and she offered $1,000 (equivalent to about $10,000 today) to Pound. Pound was astonished, but he accepted her generosity and left for Italy, where he was to complete *The Spirit of Romance*. "You have given me so much," he wrote to Cravens from Bergamo, "—I dont mean the apparent gift—but restoration of faith. Your 'largesse' in all that a forgotten word should mean!—and then the apparent gift comes, as a sort of sign from beyond that my work is accepted. It couldn't have come unless there was some real reason, behind us all, for the work to go on unfettered" (p. 12). This kind of "it's-bigger-than-both-of-us" rhetoric fills Pound's letters. On one occasion he associates Cravens with the Virgil who in the fourth canto of the *Inferno* leads Dante to Homer and the pantheon of great poets. One result of this glorification of Cravens's role as patron was to insure that she'd keep the money coming; and to borrow the terms of Eve Kosofsky Sedgwick's work on "homosocial desire," Pound is interested in her only inasmuch as she leads him to other men; the woman enters the masculine world as an element of "exchange."[8]

I think Pound felt a measure of real gratitude. Cravens was the first of several patrons from whom Pound would benefit, and she helped Pound to see the lost dignity of patronage. In 1915 he would characterize Quinn's patronage in the terms he developed for Cravens—"if a patron buys from an artist who needs money (needs money to buy tools, time and food), the patron then makes himself equal to the artist."[9] At the conclusion of "Patria Mia" (1912–13) when Pound appealed to "the American individual" to support the arts, he was thinking of the example of Margaret Cravens: "I suggest that a sane form of bequest would be an endowment of 1,000 dollars per year, settled on any artist whose work was recognized as being of value to the community, or as being likely to prove of value to the community provided it were left to develop unhampered by commercial demand."[10]

The point of Pound's "Patria Mia" is to inspire an American renaissance in the arts, and his letters to Cravens overflow with a young man's enthusiasm and sense of promise; at one point he admits their naivete; "imagine anything thinking it could turn America into a paradise of the arts" (p. 63). But that sense of wonder in the world's possibilities is what makes the letters attractive. Especially attractive is the wonder he had for Yeats. In 1910 he was thrilled about the developments in Yeats's verse. On one occasion he copied out "No Second Troy" for Margaret Cravens, and on another he explained the importance of the stylistic transformation that poem signalled.

> Yeats has been doing some new lyrics—he has come out of the shadows & has declared for life. Of course there is in that a tremendous uplift for me—for he and I are now as it were in one movement, with aims very nearly identical. That is to say that the movement of the '90'ies (nineties) for drugs & shadows has worn itself out. There has been no "influence." Yeats has found within himself spirit of the new air which I by accident had touched before him....
>
> His art can of course be no greater, but there is in it now a new note of personal & human triumph that will carry him to more people. [pp. 41–42][11]

In the notes to "Redondillas," a poem Pound cut from the *Canzoni* volume of 1911, Pound identified Yeats as a "specialist in renaissances."[12] To Pound, the Irish Renaissance was still going strong, and Yeats's achievement inspired him to think that something like an American Renaissance might be possible.

Margaret Cravens's "largesse" gave Pound the economic freedom to entertain such dreams in the first place. And while the nature of their relationship, beyond the subsidy itself, is unclear, it seems probable that Cravens was more dependent on Pound than he knew or would acknowledge. In the spring of 1911 she commissioned the painter Eugene Paul Ullman to paint portraits of herself and of Pound—but later that same year Pound would approach Henry Hope Shakespear, asking permission to marry his daughter Dorothy with the understanding that he had an income of at least $1,000: Cravens was floating Pound's literary ambitions and his love life. Pound tried to memorialize his feelings for Cravens by dedicating his Cavalcanti translations to her, but she refused; instead, two of Walter Rummel's settings of

Pound's troubadour songs were dedicated to her as "the Weaver of Beauty, the comfort of these forgotten strains redreamt" (p. 67).

To sit at the piano and play one of those songs was one of the last things Margaret Cravens did before she killed herself on 1 June 1912. It seems likely that her relationship with Pound (and with Rummel) had something to do with her despair. Pound had raised her to the heights of Virgil but only to assure that she would never be more than a handmaiden. A few days before the suicide, Pound left Paris for the south of France, and he sent Cravens a telegram that was discovered in her apartment after her death. The editors narrate this turn in the story: "In unpublished memoirs written more than forty years after the event, Alice Woods Ullman tells how her husband Eugene [the painter] found the message among Margaret's clothes and pocketed it before the police arrived. Its exact nature may never be known, since Alice chose to cloak the incident in mystery and innuendo, but the Ullmans clearly considered it very disturbing and never forgave Ezra for sending it. . . . Ezra may simply have requested or acknowledged a sum of money, as he had done before when traveling; the Ullmans might have misinterpreted this. On the other hand, it is possible that he wrote Margaret that he would not marry her. . . . Hilda [Doolittle] suspected that there had been 'kissing,' as she put it in 'Asphodel,' and so did others" (p. 112). The suicide note she left for Pound ended: "This letter would be partly to Dorothy if I knew her or had (I do). So to you both, all happiness and final attainment be yours" (p. 117).

H.D.'s "Asphodel" (1921–22), a sequel to *HERmione* (published in 1981), contains a dramatization of Cravens's suicide. H.D. knew well the price to be paid for Pound's attentions, and in her novel the suicide of "Shirley Thornton" embodies Hermione's fear that she too will be smothered by the powerful men who surround her. Of "George Lowndes" (the Pound figure in the novel) she says: "George had killed her certainly. It was Walter saying it, 'But we thought she was going to marry—George.' George must be blamed, scape-goat. He was a scape-goat. Kissing them all. Let all the sins of all the kisses be upon him. For this was a sin. Kisses that had killed Shirley" (pp. 162–

63). H.D. also knew that no suicide is so simply explained, and she circulates the blame among Walter Rummel, herself, and America. Margaret's aunt Drusilla Cravens laid the blame on Europe, and this Jamesian tale finds its coda in a letter she wrote to Pound a few months after the suicide.

> Margaret Cravens, Mr. Pound, was a comparatively *normal* girl until she overreached herself and was led so to speak—into deep seas. To you I can say in all sincerity that the girl was led to overestimate her own mentality and capacity. Brighter and far more apt than the average young woman, it was easy enough to be misled—influenced into believing her abilities were superior, and just this fact misguided her—I think. [p. 127]

One wonders if Pound agreed. His letters to Margaret Cravens give us some new details about his early career, and mostly they confirm what readers of Pound have already suspected: the real focus of interest in this book is the mysterious Margaret Cravens. Ironically, since Pound did not let her be more than a handmaiden to him, her presence in the book overwhelms Pound's completely—even though her only words in the book are her last.

Margaret Cravens's suicide was part of the beginning of the end for Pound. While his letters of 1910 are filled with promise and excitement, his letters of just eight years later are weighed down with bitterness and disappointment—as if he jumped from the energy of youth to the bitterness of old age without passing through maturity. The letters now available in *Pound*/The Little Review: *The Letters of Ezra Pound to Margaret Anderson* show Pound's slow decline. Published by New Directions, this volume joins others—Pound/Joyce, Pound/Ford, Pound/Lewis, Pound/Zukofsky, and Pound/Dorothy Shakespear—in "The Correspondence of Ezra Pound." (Volumes currently in preparation include Pound/Quinn and Pound/Williams.) This edition of Pound's correspondence has no general editor, so the format and the quality of each volume varies considerably. Any editor of Pound, especially the later Pound, has to make a tough decision concerning Pound's wildly idiosyncratic spelling, punctuation, typing, and page layout. Pound's early correspondence, written

Pound Among the Women

before he began typing his letters and considering their visual appearance, is less problematic. Working from handwritten letters, the editors of the Cravens volume choose to regularize Pound's letters somewhat, but the editors of the Margaret Anderson volume, working from typescripts, give us Pound's prose in all its chaotic glory, his irregular spacing and indentation preserved, and that decision sometimes results in pages that are nearly unreadable. That decision is defensible, but other volumes of the New Directions series are edited according to different principles: given the quality and importance of Pound's correspondence, I wish that it were being published under a more centrally watchful eye.

The annotation of the Pound/Margaret Anderson volume is almost as copious (if not nearly so subtle) as the Cravens volume. While it rarely obtrudes, there is no delicate narrative here for the editors to sustain; the letters mostly offer insight into Pound's professional life as an editor and artistic entrepreneur, and consequently the annotation is straightforward and not at all speculative or even imaginative as in the Cravens volume. (More than a dozen pages are given over to the lists of subscribers Pound sends Anderson: the sheer bulk and repetition of this dull material are at first tedious and then maddening.) Pound's letters to Anderson begin in 1916, when he first sent a poem by Jean de Bosschère to the *Little Review,* and continue through the years in which Pound acted as the magazine's foreign editor (1917–1919) to 1923, when regular correspondence stopped. The volume ends with several late letters from Pound at St. Elizabeths, and an appendix includes Margaret Anderson's replies to these letters (none of her correspondence from the early years survives). The volume begins with an introduction that surveys in general the role of the little magazines in the rise of modern literature and provides in particular a history of the *Little Review* and Pound's interaction with it. The terms of the history are somewhat one-sided. The editors quote Noel Stock (Pound's early biographer) on Pound's responsibility to the magazine: "to gather contributions worth publishing and to educate or if necessary to bully the editor into publishing them" (p. xvii). Even though Margaret Anderson's letters do not survive, Pound's responses to her reveal that she was educating Pound as much as he was educating her. Yet the editors of the correspondence sometimes reinforce Stock's dismissive view of Margaret Anderson. Noting that the early *Selected Letters of Ezra Pound,* edited by D. D. Paige, reprint several letters from Pound that Anderson published in her autobiography in truncated forms, they suggest that "one has the uncomfortable feeling that her gestures have been prompted by less admirable motives—a desire on her part, perhaps, to show Pound in a negative way or to soften his criticism of her" (pp. x–xi). They hope that the complete correspondence will set the record straight, and it does: No one shows Pound in a more negative way than Pound himself, and though Margaret Anderson does not emerge from the book as luminously as Margaret Cravens does from her volume, Anderson's presence is strong and hardly in need of protection.

Margaret Anderson founded the *Little Review* in 1914, three years before Pound got hold of it. The magazine would sometimes be criticized for its lack of focus, but in her initial editorial Anderson was adamant that her "point of view shall not be restrictive; we may present the several judgments of our various enthusiastic contributors on one subject in the same issue." Though she was open-minded, Anderson's politics were not diffuse: "Feminism? A clear-thinking magazine can have only one attitude; the degree of ours is ardent!"[13] Like her colleagues at the *Masses* in New York or the *New Freewoman* in London, Anderson's vision depended upon a wide conception of the word *political.* Dora Marsden and Mary Gawthorpe, the original editors of the *Freewoman* (later the *New Freewoman* before it became the *Egoist*), founded the magazine partly in opposition to suffragettes who limited their struggle for women's rights to the scope of liberal politics. To Marsden, the vote was only the goal in the public dimension of a battle for women's rights that should take place in all realms of culture, public and private; Gawthorpe explained that their magazine would "be essentially a thinking organ and will afford expression for all phases of feminism—not being politically inclined merely."[14] For Margaret Anderson as well as these editors, then, their feminism was compatible with many forms of radicalism—socialist, anarchist, spiritualist, and literary—whose goal was to disrupt the discourse of the dominant culture. In "The Challenge of Emma Goldman" (1914) Anderson explained that "radical changes in society, releasement from present injustices and miseries, can come about not through *reform* but through *change;* not through a patching up of the old order, but through a tearing down and a rebuilding." Unlike some anarchists, who saw violence as a necessary part of this process, Anderson's conception of the word violence was as wide as her conception of the political, and a "tearing down" of the old order could take place in intellectual as well as physical terms. Consequently, she is able to say that the anarchist Goldman is fighting "for the same things, concretely, that Nietzsche and Max Stirner fought for abstractly," summing up Goldman as "a practical Nietzschean."[15] A politically disruptive art was Anderson's goal, and in "A Real Magazine" (1916) she would go so far as to say that "Revolution *is* Art" and that Emma Goldman is "a great artist."[16] She ended a 1915 essay on "The Artist in Life" with this quotation from Nietzsche: "Art and nothing else! Art is the great means of making life possible, the great seducer to life; the great stimulus to life."[17]

On the one hand, the strength of Anderson's position is that she conceives of change as something that will make a difference in any cultural discourse, not just in the limited political sphere dominated by men. (Anderson would see just how little effect she could have in that world when at the *Ulysses* trial the judge refused to read the offending passages out loud because a woman—Anderson herself—was in the courtroom: when he was told that she was the publisher of the passages, the judge replied that she could not possibly have understood what she was doing.) On the other hand, the weakness of Anderson's expansive sense of political radicalism helped to thwart the consensus on which change so often depends. If Nietzsche and Stirner are compatible with her feminism, then—impossible as it seems—so is Ezra Pound. Nietzsche and Stirner were equally as important to Dora Marsden, who bolstered her feminism with the individualism of Stirner's *The Ego and His Own* (1844) even before she changed the name of her magazine to the *Egoist*. In a 1913 issue of the *New Freewoman* she explained why she didn't want to associate herself with something other feminists called the "Woman Movement": "A very limited number of individual women are emphasizing the fact that the first thing to be taken into account with regard to them is that they *are* individuals and can not be lumped together into a class, a sex or a 'movement.' . . . They are Egoists."[18] Ezra Pound could join forces with Marsden (though not unproblematically) because he too seemed to be an individualist. And he could become the foreign editor of Margaret Anderson's *Little Review* for the same reason. Nietzschean radicalism is slippery business, and it can underwrite both Pound and Anderson as it underwrites both Hitler and Derrida; the case of Paul de Man does not show that one side of this opposition must collapse into the other, but it does suggest just how difficult it is to maintain one position without harboring the specter of the other.

In "A Real Magazine" Anderson confessed that after publishing the review for two years she was dissatisfied with the work it contained. "Where are the artists? Where is some new Pater, and how will his 'She is older than the rocks among which she sits' sound to us? Where is some new Arthur Symons with his version of 'Peter Weyland'?"[19] She left thirteen pages of the following issue blank because no one answered her call. Then along came Ezra Pound, the artist who had modelled his literary mission on Yeats, Symons, and Pater themselves. In his opening editorial (May 1917) Pound seemed to sing just the tune Anderson longed to hear: "The shell-fish grows its own shell, the genius creates its own milieu. You, the public, can kill genius by actual physical starvation, you may perhaps thwart or distort it, but you can in no way create it. . . . There is no misanthropy in a thorough contempt for the mob. There is no respect for mankind save in respect for detached individuals."[20] There was some misanthropy in Pound's contempt and there was misogyny too. He shared with Anderson a Nietzschean faith in the radical power of the individual artist, but for Pound, that inventing artist was necessarily male. Given what I've already said about Pound's fantasies of phallic power, it is difficult not to read straight the sentence he wrote Anderson in setting out the terms by which he'd function as her foreign editor: "I want an 'official organ' (vile phrase). I mean I want a place where I and T. S. Eliot can appear once a month (or once an 'issue') and where James Joyce can appear when he likes, and where Wyndham Lewis can appear if he comes back from the war" (p. 6).

The arrangement was that Pound would edit a portion of the magazine while Anderson (along with Heap, who had joined the masthead as "Jh" beginning in 1916) continued to be responsible for the remaining pages; John Quinn agreed to pay Pound $750 a year for two years, $450 of which Pound would use to pay his contributors and $300 of which would go to Pound for his editorial duties. Pound wanted to start off "with a bang" (p. 15), and the biggest bang he knew was still Yeats: "I have spent all my splurge fund for the first six months on his two lots of poems," Pound told Anderson. "Which, BY GORD ought to act as an announcement that the L.R. is a vurry serious magazine" (p. 54). Under Pound's auspices, the *Little Review* did publish such high points of Yeats's career as "The Wild Swans at Coole" and "In Memory of Major Robert Gregory"; it also published many of Eliot's quatrain poems, several prose works by Lewis and Ford, and between 1918 and 1920 it serialized the first thirteen episodes of *Ulysses*. Pound's editorial achievement also included the anthology issue ("A Study in French Poets") and the great Henry James memorial issue (August 1918), in preparation for which Pound reread and commented upon James's entire corpus: his James essays remain one of the great critical acts of the century. Pound did publish several women writers—Iris Barry (a disciple whose work Anderson thought unworthy), Lady Gregory, Marianne Moore, and May Sinclair—and he tried repeatedly to persuade Edith Wharton to contribute to the James number (probably at the instigation of Eliot, who admired Wharton's work very much).[21] But the writer whose contribution to the *Little Review* amounted to almost nothing was Ezra Pound. Between 1917 and 1919 Pound's work appeared in almost every issue, but the writing was almost completely ephemeral: with the exception of the James essays, almost none of the prose is worth reading today, and what little poetry he published in the *Little Review* is equally negligible. This was a dry period for Pound. He knew it, and his bitterness infects his contributions to the magazine and his letters to Anderson. An "official organ" was precisely what Pound feared that he lacked.

Given Pound's anti-feminism and his fear that his own genital fluids were not flowing properly, it is surprising that he and Anderson and Heap agreed as often as they did. Yet the small demilitarized zones where their visions overlap are bordered by areas of violent conflict that reveal the contradictions supporting their tenuous agreements. Pound generally liked the work Jane Heap wrote for the magazine (signed throughout with only her initials), and he particularly admired her "Push-Face" (June 1917), an account of police brutality at an anti-conscription rally in New York. Pound echoed Heap's anti-war sentiments in a brief statement published the following October: Pound offered a "translation" of a phoney German document commanding all German men to "interest themselves in the happiness of the married women and maidens by doubling or even trebling the number of births."[22] One doubts that this humor was exactly what Heap had in mind; and one wonders just how seriously the subject of the "Virgin's Prayer" took his own joke—especially since the October 1917 issue also included Wyndham Lewis's story "Cantleman's Spring Mate," in which a British soldier seduces a young girl and rejects her when she becomes pregnant. The post office confiscated the October issue because of these contents, and despite the anti-feminism of both Pound and Lewis, Anderson would defend their writing as radically individualist: "*The Little Review* was founded in direct opposition to the prevalent art values in America. It would have no function or reason for being if it did not continually conflict with those values."[23] Like the editors of the *Partisan Review* in the 1930s, who in spite of their Marxist principles printed modernist literature by right-wing writers, Anderson and Heap were treading an ideological tightrope: fully committed to their feminism, they did not want their political beliefs to foster a narrow-minded dogmatism. Yet like the *Partisan Review*'s editors (whose equation of political change with avant-garde rebellion would ultimately weaken their Marxism), or the editors of the *New Freewoman* (who saw their feminist concerns swallowed up in the *Egoist*'s increasing focus on literary innovation), Anderson was in danger of becoming the victim of her own catholicity.

Occasionally, however, it was Pound who supported Anderson's feminist principles in spite of his own anti-feminist dogmatism. He was very keen on publishing Ford Madox Ford's work, and Ford gave him the incomplete manuscript of *Women and Men*. Not without his own unacknowledged ambivalences, Ford had supported the suffragettes for years. In 1913 he wrote a pamphlet called "This Monstrous Regiment of Women" for the Women's Freedom League (one of the organizations to which Dora Marsden objected on "individualist" principles), and Ford's attitudes toward women confirmed Marsden's doubts about the long-term effect of focusing feminist power exclusively on the realm of liberal politics: though he completely supported women's right to vote, Ford was far from sympathetic to women's struggles in less obviously political realms of British culture. (Violet Hunt, whom Ford treated miserably, pointed out in her story "Love's Last Leave" that like male soldiers, "women, who had no vote, fought too, for they worked too and endured the beastliness of living in what were practically beleaguered cities."[24]) Despite this blindness, the second installment of *Women and Men* offers a responsible and convincing critique of Otto Weininger's violently anti-feminist and anti-Semitic—and extraordinarily popular—*Sex and Character* (1904). And here Ford even seems to understand that the vote alone would not rectify women's place in British culture. He recalls that in 1906, when "Miss Pankhurst interrupted the late Sir Henry Campbell Bannerman at the Albert Hall," he joined a conversation of liberal young men who found her behavior appalling, though they conceded that her cause was just: "They were anxious to point out to me that they were the most advanced body of men that could be found in the world. Their sympathies with anything advanced could not possibly be doubted.... But when it came to Miss Pankhurst, they exclaimed all together that she was really a bad girl.... And then suddenly all their voices sank low together.... [T]hey were talking about Weininger."[25] Pound considered *Women and Men* to be Ford's "best work" (Pound would publish it again in book form in 1923), and he told Anderson that the book "wipes Weiniger [sic] off the earth" (pp. 37, 99). But Pound admitted to Quinn that he had never read *Sex and Character*—which contains theories of masculine dominance as crazy and offensive as Pound's—and one has to wonder how he would have felt about Ford's work if he had known the opposition.[26] To Margaret Anderson and Jane Heap, in any case, Pound's support of Ford's work must have confirmed their sense that Pound's vision was at least partially compatible with their own.

Quinn's uncontrollable rage at Anderson and Heap, though sexually motivated, emerged most often in his contempt for their editing principles. He wanted Joyce to be able to publish *Ulysses* in book form, and he saw every suppression of the *Little Review* as another strike against that goal. (After the suppression of the issue containing Lewis's story, the post office confiscated four issues containing episodes of *Ulysses* until the matter finally came to the attention of the New York Society for the Prevention of Vice and went to trial). Quinn also saw Anderson and Heap's unwillingness to censor Joyce (or simply to stop publishing work that would get them suppressed) as sheer stupidity (the chaos of femininity unmodified by the shaping power of men), and he warned them over and over again about their lack of "business sense." But Anderson saw this lack of conventional editorial caution and focus as part of her magazine's mission, and she knew what she was doing: "Most magazines have efficient editors and definite editorial policies," she said; "that is what's wrong with them."[27] In court, Quinn defended Joyce's obscenity by stressing that it was masculine, not feminine, a kind of phallic excrement—"strong hard filth" and not "the devotion to art of a soft flabby man like Wilde."[28] And as she sat in the courtroom, unable to speak ("My function is silence"), Anderson suspected that no man in the room could understand anyway. She described the trial to her readers: "The court opens. Every one stands up as the three judges enter. Why must I stand up as a tribute to three men who wouldn't understand my simplest remark?"[29]

By the time the *Ulysses* trial took place in 1921, Pound was no longer functioning as foreign editor of the *Little Review*. Though he would renew a loose connection with the magazine from April 1921 until the spring of 1923, he resigned formally in 1919, having forsaken his dream of an American Renaissance: "Must let it alone (I must). Must return to the unconcern with U.S.A.

Pound Among the Women

that I had before 1911–12."[30] Pound's disappointments at this time were manifold. His first "Three Cantos" of 1917 had seemed a dead end; "I get no poetries written," he confessed to Anderson (p. 212). In 1918 a publisher lost the manuscript of his Arnaut Daniel translations. Attack after attack on Pound appeared in the "Reader Critic" column of the *Little Review*. At the same time his *Pavannes and Divisions,* containing the ephemeral prose works that appeared in the *Little Review,* received uniformly dismissive reviews. When parts of his "Homage to Sextus Propertius" (his one great poetic achievement from the latter teens) finally appeared in 1919, they received excoriating notices. Soon afterward, *Quia Pauper Amavi,* a collection of poems including the Propertius sequence, was rejected by Elkin Matthews; Knopf backed out of a commitment to publish *Instigations,* another collection of prose. When Pound began his association with the *Little Review* he was already bitter from his experience with *Poetry* magazine, and the honeymoon with the *Little Review* was brief. In July 1918 he published his ultimatum in "Cooperation (A Note on the Volume Complete)."

> My net value to the concern appears to be about $2500; of which over $2000 does not "accrue" to the protagonist. It might be argued with some subtlety that I make the limited public an annual present of that sum, for the privilege of giving them what they do not want, and for, let us say, forcing upon them a certain amount of literature, and a certain amount of enlightened criticism.
> This donation I have willingly made, and will as willingly repeat, *but* I can not be expected to keep it up for an indefinite period.
> ... [E]ither the *Little Review* will have to provide me with the necessities of life and a reasonable amount of leisure, by May 1st. 1919, or I shall have to apply my energies elsewhere. [pp. 213–14]

Pound kept his word and resigned as foreign editor. Eighteen months later, he left England ("London is dead to deadish"), and as Dr. Johnson once said, he who is tired of London is tired of life; Paris seemed just as useless to Pound: "at any rate [Picabia] and Cocteau are intelligent, which a damn'd large number of Parisians aren't" (pp. 265, 264). Pound kept in touch with Margaret Anderson, and in April 1921 he sent her this oddly pathetic letter, headed "Private = i.e. you can read it to yr. friends but its not for print."

> Point I never can seem to get you to take is that I have done more log rolling and attending to other people's affairs, Joyce, Lewis, Gaudier, etc. (dont regret it) But I am in my own small way, a writer myself. . . .
>
> It is bad enough to have to look forward to Christ knows what means of paying for precisely my (as jh puts it) cup of coffee and shoes (say rather re-soles). . . .
>
> Joyce has the sense, or grit, or sheer imbecility to *DO nothing* but his Ulysses and let the world go hang. [pp. 266–67]

"I am in my own small way, a writer myself": this is not a tone one often hears from the mastermind of the Great English Vortex. Pound was deeply worried that he was just a patron—not an inventor. In a memoir of the war-time London years, Iris Barry cast Pound as a patron: "It was natural to him to encourage and groom young writers as though he—penniless enough himself—had been one of those patrons of the arts of whom Chesterton spoke when he reminded his contemporaries that it was the 'privilege of the privileged to assist the possessor of wit.'"[31] That was just the rhetoric that Pound used to dignify Margaret Cravens and John Quinn—but Pound himself was supposed to be the inventor, the phallic externalizer of form, and not the disciple or handmaiden. "May your erection never grow less," he told Eliot after reading the manuscript of *The Waste Land* late in 1921, aware that his poetry of the last several years was shapeless and therefore (in his own terms) "feminine": "I am wracked by the seven jealousies, and cogitating an excuse for always exuding my deformative secretions in my own stuff, and never getting an outline."[32] Pound still lacked his "official organ." Writing to Quinn at around the same time, Eliot agreed: "The fact is that there is now no organ of any importance in which [Pound] can express himself, and he is becoming forgotten. . . . I am worried as to what is to become of him."[33]

Beginning in 1922 Pound's letters to Anderson move from the pathetic to the downright weird. Sometime early in that year he sent her his cryptic "Little Review Calendar" (published in the spring 1922 issue), declaring that the "Christian era came to an end at midnight of October 29–30" (p. 282). The significance of that date is overdetermined: Joyce had completed *Ulysses* on the 29th, but the 30th had been Pound's thirty-seventh birthday. Not just the Christian era but something we've since come to call the Pound era had come to a close. After the calendar arrived, Margaret Anderson received this letter from Dorothy Pound, dated 14 April 1922—Good Friday.

Dear Miss Anderson
   I have sent you the photos of Ezra's death mask.
There is nothing more to be said.

   Yours sincerely
     D. Pound
The plaster mould of the features was taken by Mrs. [Nancy Cox] McCormack. [p. 283]

The mask had been made and the photographs taken (Iris Barry reproduces them in her memoir), but Anderson did not publish them in the *Little Review*. In later letters Pound complained: "I don't propose to die daily. I died once to satisfy the consolidated hecklery assn"; and again: "In response to repeated requests; requests for death, for crucifixion etc. etc. etc. etc. I finally die. Why the hell shouldn't I vary the bowling, and give this small drop of liquid pleasure to a long parched, long exasperated public" (pp. 284, 287). This hoax was Pound's last-gasp plea for attention, and when the *Little Review* did not run the photographs, it was a fate worse than death. Late in 1922 he sent Anderson a list of ideas for the magazine—a Duchamp number, a Ford number, and last but not least, a "Symposium on my death, and earlier actions" (p. 288). When Anderson moved to Paris in 1923 and finally met Pound after years of correspondence, this was her reaction: Pound gave her "somehow the sensation of watching a large baby perform its repertoire of physical antics gravely, diffidently, without human responsibility for the performance."[34]

Pound was much obsessed by death between 1919 and 1923, and the death-mask hoax is a grotesque literalization of "E. P.

Ode pour l'election de son sepulchre," the opening poem of the *Hugh Selwyn Mauberley* sequence (1920).

> Unaffected by "the march of events,"
> He passed from men's memory in *l'an trentuniesme*
> *De son eage;* the case presents
> No adjuncts to the Muses' diadem.[35]

Everything that had once sustained him now seemed dead: Paris, London, Eliot, Yeats, the Great English Vortex, the hope for an American Renaissance—and most of all Ezra Pound himself. Canto 7, completed in December 1919, is an elegy for all those lost hopes, but most of all it is an elegy for Pound: though it seems at first to be a wail against the decline of European culture, it is really the cry of Pound's own deadness—intellectual and sexual—and the walking dead that inhabit the canto are all externalizations of his darkest fears. Like the barren landscapes of *The Waste Land,* the sterility of this canto is in part a record of its author's impotence. After the ghost of Henry James appears ("And the old voice lifts itself / weaving an endless sentence"), Pound describes his own "ghostly visits" to Paris in 1919—his first visit to the city after the conclusion of World War I once again made travel on the continent possible.

> We also made ghostly visits, and the stair
> That knew us, found us again on the turn of it,
> Knocking at empty rooms, seeking for buried beauty;
> And the sun-tanned, gracious and well-formed fingers
> Lift no latch of bent bronze, no Empire handle
> Twists for the knocker's fall; no voice to answer.
> A strange concierge, in place of the gouty-footed.
> Sceptic against all this one seeks the living,
> Stubborn against the fact. The wilted flowers
> Brushed out a seven year since, of no effect.
> Damn the partition! Paper, dark brown and stretched,
> Flimsy and damned partition.
>   Ione, dead the long year.

Pound conflates the memory of two suicides here. Ione de Forest, a member of the *New Freewoman* group, shot herself through the heart in her Chelsea apartment on 2 August 1912; Margaret Cravens died by the same act in her Paris apartment on 1 June 1912. The turning stair that Pound climbs in Canto 7 is the stair to the place where Margaret Cravens killed herself, and the room he surveys is hers—her Erard piano remains but her ghost does not.

> Low ceiling and the Erard and the silver,
> These are in "time." Four chairs, the bow-front dresser,
> The panier of the desk, cloth top sunk in.[36]

When Pound could control his bitterness at his own failures, he could transform the loss into elegy. As the *Pisan Cantos* show best of all, the elegiac mode was always Pound's greatest strength; it is what Yeats called the note of nobility in his work, more often than not suppressed or obscured by Pound's ranting. What makes Pound's poetry attractive in these elegiac moments is that he puts down the mask of the virile poet, and as in his 1922 letter to Margaret Anderson ("I am in my own small way, a writer myself"), he lets his readers sense his vulnerability. It does not seem accidental that Pound wrote his postscript to De Gourmont's *Natural Philosophy of Love* in 1921 since it was at that time that he doubted the strength of what he needed to think of as masculinity most of all. A product of the same period, Canto 7 reveals not a different Pound but at least a Pound who felt, as H.D. did in "Asphodel," that his behavior might have been in part responsible for the deaths of these young women. And yet the suicides of Ione de Forest and Margaret Cravens stand for the act Pound would commit only on paper. In her suicide note to Pound, Cravens called her suicide an act "of extreme courage" (p. 116); in Canto 7, at the same time that he memorializes her death, Pound wonders if he lacks that courage, if these young women might not have been stronger than he all along. But that fear is dismissed too easily, and with Canto 8 we are thrust into the world of Sigismundo Malatesta, the first of the grotesquely phallic heros of the *Cantos*, and before long, Pound—sounding much like Otto Weininger—would be excoriating the feminizing force of women and Jews throughout the history of Western culture.

After remaining out of touch for nearly three decades, Pound resumed correspondence with Margaret Anderson in 1953 when her *Little Review Anthology* appeared. He asked her to visit him in St. Elizabeths. "Yes, I'd love to have some 'intelligent conversation,'" replied the understandably cautious Anderson, "but I'm convinced that my contribution to it might hold no interest for you" (p. 323). That remark stung Pound, as blind to his own excesses as ever, but it provoked him to respond with honesty and in the elegiac mode that marked this correspondence too infrequently.

> That yu shd/ write to me as if YU thought that I thought you a total idiot instead of the sole productress of, I will not say a spiritual home, but at least [the only] roof or awning ever provided me in this distressed and distressing country . . . . [p. 310]

Notes

1. *Pound/Lewis: The Letters of Ezra Pound and Wyndham Lewis*, ed. Timothy Materer (New York: New Directions, 1985), pp. 114–15.
2. Ezra Pound, *Pavannes and Divagations* (New York: New Directions, 1958), pp. 203–4.
3. Ibid., p. 213.
4. B. H. Dias [Ezra Pound], "The Tenth London Salon of the Allied Artists Association," *New Age*, 23 (1 August 1918), 223–24.
5. Quinn to Pound, 16 October 1920; this letter is quoted in the very suggestive chapter on Pound and Eliot in Wayne Koestenbaum, *Double Talk: The Erotics of Male Literary Collaboration* (New York: Routledge, 1989), p. 119.
6. Pound to Quinn, 9 February 1917; quoted in the introduction to *Ezra Pound and the Visual Arts*, ed. Harriet Zinnes (New York: New Directions, 1980), p. xxi. Timothy Materer is currently editing the Pound-Quinn correspondence.
7. Robert McAlmon, *Being Geniuses Together*, rev. with supplementary chapters by Kay Boyle (New York: Doubleday, 1968), p. 82.
8. See Eve Kosofsky Sedgwick, *Between Men: English Literature and Male Homosocial Desire* (New York: Columbia Univ. Press, 1985).
9. Ezra Pound, *Selected Letters*, ed. D. D. Paige (New York: New Directions, 1950), p. 53.
10. Ezra Pound, *Selected Prose*, ed. William Cookson (New York: New Directions, 1973), p. 140.
11. These letters concerning Yeats were quoted prior to the publication of the

complete correspondence in A. Walton Litz, "Pound and Yeats: The Road to Stone Cottage," *Ezra Pound Among the Poets,* ed. George Bornstein (Chicago: Univ. of Chicago Press, 1985), pp. 128–48.

12. Ezra Pound, *Collected Early Poems,* ed. Michael John King (New York: New Directions, 1976), p. 313.

13. Margaret Anderson, "Announcement," *Little Review,* 1 (March 1914), 2.

14. Quoted in Carol Barash, "Dora Marsden's Feminism, the *Freewoman,* and the Gender Politics of Early Modernism," *Princeton University Library Chronicle,* 49 (Autumn 1987), 40. Based on Dora Marsden's unpublished papers in the Princeton University Library, this essay offers an essential history of the *Freewoman*'s nominal and ideological transformations. On the tensions within the women's suffrage movement concerning the public or private nature of political conflict, see Susan Kent, *Sex and Suffrage in Britain 1860–1914* (Princeton: Princeton Univ. Press, 1987).

15. Margaret Anderson, "The Challenge of Emma Goldman," *Little Review,* 1 (May 1914), 6, 9.

16. Margaret Anderson, "A Real Magazine," *Little Review,* 3 (August 1916), 1.

17. Margaret Anderson, "The Artist in Life," *Little Review,* 2 (June–July 1914), 20.

18. Dora Marsden, "Views & Comments," *New Freewoman,* 1 (1913), 5; see Barash, pp. 46–47.

19. Anderson, "A Real Magazine," p. 2.

20. Ezra Pound, "Editorial," *Little Review,* 4 (May 1917), 6.

21. Eliot wrote a brief but laudatory review of Wharton's *Summer* (1917); see "Short Reviews," *Egoist,* 5 (January 1918), 10.

22. Abel Sanders [Ezra Pound], "This Approaches Literature!" *Little Review,* 4 (October 1917), 39.

23. Margaret Anderson, "Judicial Opinion (Our Suppressed October Issue)," *Little Review,* 4 (December 1917), 48.

24. Violet Hunt, *More Tales of the Uneasy* (London: Heinemann, 1925), p. 83.

25. Ford Madox Hueffer [Ford], "Women and Men II," *Little Review,* 4 (March 1918), 41–42.

26. See Pound, *Selected Letters,* p. 133.

27. Anderson, "Our First Year," *Little Review,* 1 (February 1915), 2.

28. See Jackson R. Bryer, "Joyce, *Ulysses,* and the *Little Review,*" *South Atlantic Quarterly,* 66 (Spring 1967), 158.

29. Margaret Anderson, "'Ulysses' in Court," *Little Review,* 7 (January–March 1921), 23.

30. Pound to Marianne Moore, 1 February 1919; *Selected Letters,* p. 148.

31. Iris Barry, "The Ezra Pound Period," *Bookman,* 74 (October 1931), 162.

32. Pound made these comments to Eliot in letters written in December 1921 and January 1922 (see *Selected Letters,* pp. 169–72). The passage including the phrase "May your erection never grow less" was deleted from the *Selected Letters;* it may be found in *The Letters of T. S. Eliot,* ed. Valerie Eliot (New York: Harcourt,

1988), I: 505; see also Koestenbaum, p. 124.

33. *The Letters of T. S. Eliot,* I: 358.

34. Margaret Anderson, *My Thirty Years' War* (New York: Covici, Friede, 1945), p. 243.

35. Ezra Pound, *Personae: The Collected Shorter Poems* (New York: New Directions, 1971), p. 187.

36. *The Cantos of Ezra Pound* (New York: New Directions, 1972), p. 25.

Pentimenti:
The Georgia Edition of Smollett

Hugh Amory

Tobias Smollett. *The Adventures of Ferdinand Count Fathom.* Introduction and Notes by Jerry C. Beasley; the Text Edited by O M Brack, Jr. Athens: University of Georgia Press, 1988. xlii, 479 pp., illus.

Twenty-two years ago O M Brack, Jr., announced "The Bicentennial Edition of the Works of Tobias Smollett," to be published under his general editorship by the University of Iowa Press; despite the title, the collection was originally restricted to Smollett's five novels, the *Travels in France and Italy,* and the *History and Adventures of an Atom,* as the writings by which "Smollett is still read and enjoyed."[1] This was in that golden Indian summer of the New Bibliography, when American universities vied to establish presses and bottle the wine of scholarship: it collapsed in the aftermath of the student revolution, the Vietnam War, and the deconstruction of the very reasons for which the proposed canon had existed for two hundred years. Battered by these misfortunes, the "Iowa Smollett" became the "Delaware Smollett" under the editorship of Jerry C. Beasley (Brack assuming the narrower duties of Textual Editor); and only now appears as the "Georgia Smollett," with the addition of Jim Springer Borck as Technical Editor. One of the pleasures of my association with the edition as "Advisor" has been Beasley's Newsletter, through which he coordinates the activities of an ever growing group of scholars: it is a model of its kind. My duties so far have been light. I criticized a draft of the textual introduction and apparatus before publication, but otherwise have had no opportunity to examine the text until now.

In the course of its vicissitudes, the canon of the edition has also grown. As now projected, it will include Smollett's miscellaneous writings—periodical essays, poems, and plays—and at least one of his translations, *Gil Blas*. These are not what we still read and enjoy, but they constitute some of Smollett's least available texts, essential biographical materials, and characteristic literary activities. His *Gil Blas* is surely as important a representative of the eighteenth-century English novel as *Peregrine Pickle*. Smollett's canon, which extends over such vast projects as the *Universal History*, Voltaire in English, and the *Critical Review*, is difficult to fix, but all scholars will applaud this expansion of the edition and admire the tenacity and courage with which Brack and Beasley have steered their growing charge through impossibly whelming seas. Indeed, only two of the volumes still retain their original editors.

The University of Georgia Press should also be congratulated on a handsome production: the appropriately "Scotch" typeface is, I think, more legible than the lighter Caslon used in the Wesleyan Fielding; and though the notes appear at the end of the text, they are at least in a reasonable nine-point size, a great improvement over the six-point type of the Wesleyan edition. A welcome innovation is the reproduction of Stoddard and Clennell's illustrations, which, though in no sense authoritative, provide interesting and appropriate evidence of the novel's reception in the late eighteenth-century and Romantic eras. Like most "definitive editions" of that *belle époque* in the 1960s, the Georgia Smollett appears in imperial octavo (9 1/4″) with the mandatory four-fold apparatus that has been standard since Bowers's Dekker (1952).

The design of the volume, in which I suspect that neither editor was directly involved, occasionally interferes with a proper understanding of the text. By hallowed convention, the general introduction appears at the front of the volume, denying Smollett's epigraph its conventional position in the preliminaries, and allowing the spooky but familiar illusion that he dedicated his novel "To Rita"—as Fielding, we have lately learnt, dedicated *Tom Jones* "To Ruthe." The facsimiles of the original volume title-pages and the addition of chapter references in the running titles raise other questions, to be considered later. If the text is not just Smollett's words, but also its material presentation (context), these are not matters that can be left to tradition and the designer in a critical text.

The bibliography of the lifetime editions of *Ferdinand Count Fathom* is fairly straightforward, though spiced with some unsolved and perhaps unsolvable riddles. The first edition appeared in 1753 under the imprint of W. Johnston, at the sign of "the Golden Ball, in St. Paul's Church-yard." Johnston licensed a Dublin reprint by R. Main before publication; that is, Main paid for advance sheets in order to secure first publication in Dublin, which the Irish booktrade recognized as copyright. Yet a third edition flaunts the parodic imprint of "London: Printed for T. Johnson, at the Golden Ball, in St. Paul's Churchyard, M,DCC,LIII"—seemingly, at W. Johnston's address, but actually published in Scotland, as bibliographers have agreed since Louella Norwood's Yale Ph.D. thesis (1928). "T. Johnson," not to be confused with the notorious Hague or Rotterdam pirate of the earlier eighteenth century, conventionally designates anything unmentionable;[2] fully 114 seventeenth-century London imprints are actually ascribed to "John Thomas," an exact equivalent.[3]

Norwood also questioned the date of "Johnson's" edition, but decisive evidence is still wanting. A contemporary date of acquisition in the Rothschild copy might put it as late as 1777, but 1753, 1760 (when an otherwise unattested second edition is advertised), and 1771, when *Humphry Clinker* revived the market for Smollett's novels, all remain possible. A little disconcertingly, Beasley seems unaware that the imprint is controverted and takes it at face value (p. xxv); whereas Brack attributes it to Scotland, and tentatively dates it after 1771, on stemmatic grounds (p. 449, n. 5).[4] It could be either, but it can't be both.

All three lifetime reprints, I believe, descend independently from the first London edition; and though the second London edition contains some useful and necessary corrections, none of them, it seems, is authorial. Smollett was in Italy at the time, and Brack plausibly suggests that a friend corrected the text. He therefore records only the variants of the second London edition, eliminating "T. Johnson" and R. Main's editions from the apparatus as wholly unauthoritative. In the standard Greg-Bowers rationale followed by the Georgia edition, the text is therefore a literal reprint of the first edition, emended (with record) and "typographically" normalized (e.g., for features like the long *s*, running quotations, etc.).

I gather from the acknowledgments that the editors proceeded on their task as follows: Brack selected the copy-text by collation and bibliographical analysis; Rita Beasley put it on disk and Brad Howard proofed it twice (against a photocopy?); Brack emended the printout and keyed his collation to it; and the resulting text went to the designer. The literal accuracy of the edition is good, if slightly lower than Damian Grant's text for the Oxford English Novels (1971). This is more a compliment to Grant than a reproach to the Georgia Smollett, however. I append a list of errata, for some of which I bear joint responsibility with Brack.[5]

I am more concerned that bibliography, criticism, and design seem to have gone their separate ways in the edition, each contributing a slightly different concept of the text. Editing, as its etymology implies, looks to publication, so that its object is not a text but a book. I would not say that the Greg-Bowers rationale of copy-text bent the textual twig, and the bough inclined, since there are also questions of practical judgment involved. I shall explore both together, because otherwise theory is of no earthly interest.

My discussion appeals, on the whole, to textual theorizing that has often sprung from a reaction to Bowers's synthesis, but which, as G. Thomas Tanselle has argued, is not always inconsistent with it in result. The field is littered with straw men, and one often feels that theory has permanently abandoned application. This is another reason to bring them together, to test the practical norms of much scholarly editing in America over the last thirty years. If the Georgia Smollett can, in my opinion, be criticized on theoretical grounds, it is not for want of some excellent company. As an advisor, I belatedly volunteer the following friendly and conjectural recommendations and frank practical grumbles. It is some vindication of my theory, though not of my practical usefulness, that I had to grasp these nettles only after publication.

The New Bibliography of Greg, McKerrow, and Bowers originated in the perception—itself an inheritance from classical textual stemmatics and *Quellenkritik*—that the varieties, classes, and descent of textual witnesses might be identified and established without recourse to criticism, in its most general sense of "interpretation." In Greg's classic formulation, "what the bibliographer is concerned with is pieces of paper or parchment covered with certain written or printed signs. With those signs he is concerned merely as arbitrary marks; their meaning is no business of his." By "meaning," Greg indicated not only sense and internal logic, but the location of the document in its historical and intellectual contexts. This is not to say that he and the other founders of the discipline neglected interpretation, but they posited it as a derivation from the bibliographical establishment of the sources. McKerrow is absolutely clear on this point, as is Bowers.[6]

In the past fifteen or twenty years, under the captaincy of D. F. MacKenzie, Jerome J. McGann, Michael Warren, and others, this divorce of bibliography and criticism has been increasingly questioned. Partly the very concepts of text and authority themselves, influenced by Barthes and Derrida, have become problematic and can no longer be simply equated with a particular document or class of documents. Partly we are coming to see that the signification of the text is a product of all aspects of its material production; that to lift a letter off a page, so to speak, and name it is not the innocent, "objective" act that Greg and McKerrow supposed, but a theft of fire, fraught with undisclosed consequences.

"Looking" and "reading"—or bibliography and criticism, if you will—meet in at least three ways that affect the production and reception of the Georgia text. First, I shall argue that Smollett censored *Ferdinand Count Fathom* before publication, to avoid suit for libel. This birth defect cannot be corrected, but explains certain weaknesses in the novel's construction. Second, Beasley implicitly equates the commercial and literary failures of Smollett's work. Though *Ferdinand Count Fathom* may not rank with Smollett's best, I shall suggest that it was not a commercial failure, given Johnston's commerce, and that its literary failure is easily exaggerated. Finally, I would like to free the relationship of the Georgia editors and their publishers from the wheel of stemmatics, which too rigidly categorize and hierarchize the overlapping functions of bibliography, criticism, and design.

Beasley's account of the composition of *Ferdinand Count Fathom* is essentially negative: "[Smollett's] surviving letters tell nothing of his work on the book; the manuscript disappeared long ago, and there are no printers' records to provide clues as to how or when he wrote it" (p. xxv). This is a fair summary, if we limit our notion of the text to a "copy-text," that is, the monogenetic development of the author's words from the archetypal fair final draft into print. In a broader view of the matter, however, the text is also evidenced by the responses of readers who saw the manuscript or early sheets before publication, even if they do not reproduce it. In this respect, I think we know more that Beasley admits of the novel's genesis, from at least two sources, neither adequately discussed.

The earliest notice of Smollett's *Ferdinand Count Fathom* is readily available in Knapp's standard biography. On 14 October 1752, Thomas Birch reported to Lord Hardwicke, his patron, that

Smollet . . . is trying his Fortune again as Writer of Romances, notwithstanding the ill Success of his *Peregrine Pickle* which ruin'd his Reputation among the Booksellers in general, against whom he breathes immortal Revenge; & one of them, Millar . . . is to have a large Share of Invective in the new Romance, in w[ch] Sir Geo. Lyttelton also is to be again introduc'd.[7]

This is only three weeks before William Strahan purchased a one-third share of the copyright from William Johnston, on 8 November 1752. In the published book, there is no hint of satire on the booktrade, and little enough on Lyttelton. Knapp accordingly dismisses Birch's report as unsubstantiated rumor,[8] and the Georgia editors do not mention it. I doubt that Birch was wholly mistaken, however. Though he occasionally made minor errors, reporting the title of Smollett's previous novel, for example, as "Jeremiah Pickle," in general he is an exceptionally well-informed observer of the literary scene.

Knapp indeed accepts Birch's account of Smollett's mood, which can be documented from other sources; but he supposes that Smollett restrained himself, for once, and never allowed his feelings literary (or as Birch says, "immortal") expression. Interestingly, the eminent counsel, Alexander Hume Campbell, seems to have referred to *Ferdinand Count Fathom* before it was printed.[9] Knapp and Beasley question this evidence as well because, as Beasley pleads, "It is unclear how Campbell could have seen a copy . . . several days before the novel's publication" (p. xxxviii, n. 17); true—of print; but the MS had been around since mid-October 1752. And what reason would a lawyer have to look at it, except with an eye to litigation? Putting two and two together, it sounds as though Lyttelton or Millar or both had threatened suit, and that Smollett removed or diluted the offending passages before publication. There is a limit to the testimony we can ignore, just because its explanation is obscure.

Now, the physical structure of the first edition and the Dublin reprint is absolutely regular and betrays no sign of cancellation.[10] It follows that any revisions must have been made in MS, and that they will appear, if at all, in vestigial inconsistencies and errors. Inconsistencies, indeed, have been evident to all readers since Ralph Griffith's notice in the *Monthly Review* for March 1753. Birch seems to be describing an analogue of the College of Authors in *Peregrine Pickle,* where Smollett savaged Lyttelton. The closest parallel in *Ferdinand Count Fathom* is the circle of King Theodore (chapters 40–41), where Fathom encounters those disappointed authors the French chevalier and Sir Mungo Barebones. These chapters are puzzling for a number of reasons: they seem to be a device for isolating a satiric target, and yet they have no very visible satiric tendency. They are lacunose, because Fathom "recognizes" Major Macleaver's cousin and her daughters (p. 192), though in the novel as we know it, they have never met. Smollett introduces these characters to the narrative in a way that promises more important developments for them than they ever receive, indeed (p. 185). And finally, the numbering of the chapters is disturbed, in "CHAP. XXXV [i.e., 38]" and "XLIII [i.e., 42]." We may well conjecture that these errors and lacunae are vestiges of one or more deleted chapters, containing Fathom's encounter with the Macleaver cousinage and the satire on Andrew Millar, but where?

Any precise diagnosis is complicated by the fact that Smollett must have added fresh material to make up for his deletions, if the misnumberings are vestigial. On a similar ground, one might argue that the misnumberings are printer's errors. This seems unlikely, however, since they reappear in all lifetime editions except Main's—so that they are not "obvious" errors, unless, like Main, you devise a table of contents. "XXXV" for "XXXVIII" is also no easy visual error. We can identify one very probable insertion in the episode of Celinda (chapter 34), moreover. Unlike Ferdinand's other female quarries, Wilhelmina, Elenor, and Monimia, all of whom reappear at the end of the novel, Celinda vanishes for good. Her seduction is just a device to move our hero from London to Bristol Wells; and our interest, I fear, centers more on the Aeolian harp as the latest in musico-sexual technique, than on Celinda's otiose misfortunes, which match Elenor's even to the formula with which Smollett dismisses them from the narrative (pp. 146, 163).

The evidence of revision is slight and ambiguous in itself, but adequate, I think, to show that Birch's report had substance; it is smoke to his fire. The numeration suggests redundancy before chapter 35, and that is where we find it; the lacuna suggests deletion around chapters 40–41, where Birch tells us to look. Lady Mary Wortley Montagu, a lover of "my Dear Smollot," as she called him, thought his invention "flag[ged] a little" in *Ferdinand Count Fathom,* compared to *Peregrine Pickle.*[11] If so, there were reasons; and this is exactly why we cannot regard his text as "pieces of paper . . . covered with certain written or printed signs," like an action painting. To do so, and reprint the result as the author's "final intention," canonizes the provisional, conditioned and—as here—thwarted work of the author in deadly immortality. One of the best features of Beasley's introduction and commentary is his awareness of Smollett's oversights; but these internal signs of textual instability and the external evidence are never brought together.

The study of the reception of a text is another area in which the claims and uses of bibliography have shifted since 1967. Beasley writes unhappily about Smollett's "commercial failure," "the critics' nearly total disregard for it," and "the few who bothered to read *Ferdinand Count Fathom* when it first came out" (pp. xxvi, xxxi). This is also the conclusion of the standard study, by Fred W. Boege (1947); but a fresh look at the evidence (some unknown to Boege) hardly supports it. I would dismiss at once the aristocratic groans of Mrs. Delany and Lady Mary—even if they were not partially offset by an enthusiastic anonymous poem of 1760.[12] Two *grandes dames* and a poet are no fair sample of Smollett's readership. One not wholly unfavorable review, in the only regular review of the day, hardly qualifies as "total disregard," moreover.[13] Measured against the only three readings we know of, it did not greatly affect reception: Mrs. Delany had already bought the novel when the review appeared, and the poet quite disagreed with it; Lady Mary, in Italy, perhaps never saw it. There remains only George Colman's representation of *Ferdinand Count Fathom* as popular circulating-library fare, in his novel *Polly Honeycombe* (1760). This is fiction, but Colman obviously thought it credible, and as such it is the only contemporary testimony directly in point. It puzzles Beasley (p. xxxix, n. 28) because it contradicts his conviction of the novel's failure: is it so surprising that Mrs. Delany and Lady Mary neither led nor followed the mob? or that the public thought better of Smollett's novel than the *Monthly Review*?

Like Boege, Beasley is confirmed in his opinion by a tally of editions, which seems to echo the siren voices of Lady Mary and Mrs. Delany. In order to explain away Colman's testimony, Beasley further suggests that Johnston was forced to remainder his "unsold copies" to the circulating libraries (p. xxxix, n. 28). And finally, he proposes that the book trade conspired to block the sale of *Ferdinand Count Fathom* (p. xxii). These conjectures must be assessed against what we know of book trade history. None of them is very compelling, however.

Remaindering is a practice that James Lackington claimed to have innovated in the 1780s, and it is quite atypical of the eighteenth-century trade, as a glance at the *London Catalogue* should show. Hundreds of antiquated titles are forever "in print." *Ferdinand Count Fathom,* indeed, sold more slowly than *Roderick Random* (five London editions, 1748–1754), but it was also pirated, an infallible indication that Johnston was not meeting demand—in Scotland, at any rate. And all failure is relative: both Fielding and Richardson produced such "failures" in the 1750s, and Andrew Millar concluded at the end of that difficult era—on the eve of *Tristram Shandy,* be it said—that "The Demand for that Species of Writing is over, or nearly so."[14]

Reprinting is as much a function of distribution as of demand; that is why there is a gulf fixed between Harvard University Press (say) and Signet or Penguin. In 1753, Johnston was still a newcomer to the trade, having entered business in 1748 with the acquisition of John Clarke's stock (including *Pilgrim's Progress*) for £3000. This massive investment set the pattern for a career in share-publishing, typically of established properties.[15] Before Smollett's novel, indeed, Johnston had published only one original piece of fiction, *The History of Jack Connor* (1752; 2d ed., 1753) by William Chaigneau. Compared to Millar, Dodsley, Lownds, or the Nobles, he never made many such ventures, and his sales followed a pattern very different from theirs. He might expect to recover his profit over sixteen years, on an average, whereas they would lose their investment if the edition was not exhausted in three.[16]

By implication, too, Johnston could hardly have offered Smollett "top dollar" like Millar, who, as Dr. Johnson noted, had "raised the price of literature." Indeed, Smollett may never have sold the entire rights, for *Ferdinand* never became a "share book" after 1780 (one year before copyright expired), when Johnston's properties were dispersed by auction.[17] Strahan, moreover, fails to appear in the imprint, though he owned one-third of the copyright; Smollett, then, might have been another silent partner. He is the most innovative of the great eighteenth-century novelists in his publishing arrangements, and we cannot assume, as Beasley and Brack do, that he followed common form, selling the property for a lump sum.

Ferdinand's sluggish movement in Johnston's hands has several causes, then: it entered the market when demand was declining;

the suspicious author would not entrust the publisher with the property, so that the publisher had relatively little reason to push it,[18] and the publisher was in any case new to the business of novels, and operated through commercial channels that were more accustomed to classics and reference works. We can only speculate, but there is no evidence of a general conspiracy of the trade against Smollett. Millar was quite capable of combining in restraint of trade, as Smollett alleged he did to ruin the sale of *Peregrine Pickle*,[19] but we have no reason to suppose that he wanted *Ferdinand*, or that Johnston would have refused him a share, if he had, and Smollett's silence on this score is deafening. Millar and other leading booksellers eagerly bought into Smollett's *Don Quixote* (1755), and an even larger group employed his talents in the *Universal History*. Thomas Lownds, proprietor of the largest circulating library of the decade, advertised all of Smollett's novels in his catalogue (1758?; reprinted, 1764?).[20]

The gradual establishment of *Ferdinand*'s popularity, which climaxed in 1760, is entirely consistent with what we know of Johnston's commerce. His other novel, *Jack Connor*, got a better start, but in the long run found far fewer readers. If I had to guess a date for "T. Johnson's" piracy, 1760 would be as good as any: the 1753 imprint still had magic worth imitating, and Johnston, predictably for his sort of bookseller, was unable or unwilling to meet the rising demand. The advertisement for an otherwise unattested "second edition" at this date must be connected—whether we take it as concealed publicity for the pirate, or as Johnston's belated, cheap riposte. The interloping hare made a quick profit, and the tortoise plodded on, replenishing stock eleven years later. The eleven or so eighteenth-century editions of *Ferdinand* after 1771, by such artists of the classic reprint as Harrison, Wenman, and Cooke, no doubt testify to Smollett's general reputation, built on such enduring titles as *Humphry Clinker, Don Quixote,* and *Gil Blas*. They also tell us that *Ferdinand* found enough initial readers to recommend it to the next generation. Even if it unwittingly anticipated the craze for Gothic novels, it was already a classic by 1790.

Like all publishers, Johnston had his mannerisms, one of which was to omit the table of contents; a feature so conventional that the Dublin reprint automatically supplied it—as does Damian Grant, in his edition for the Oxford English Novels (1971). Smollett controls the episodic structure of his novels by connecting the chapter headings in rhetorically discursive units, such as chapters 11–17, for example, or 35–37, which the volume division interrupts. These connections are often difficult to perceive in the text. Consider the following example, where the relative pronoun refers to *"noose"* (six pages earlier, in the Georgia edition), not, as it would in Fielding, to "CHAP. LVI.":

C H A P. LV.
After divers unsuccessful efforts, he has recourse to the matrimonial noose.

C H A P. LVI.
In which his fortune is effectually strangled.

The Georgia Smollett rigidly follows copy-text, which here means Johnston's intentions, as confirmed by his other publications, against those of the author. There is no table of contents, though the text implies that Smollett composed his chapter headings in a single continuous unit.

"The text," I would argue, is not something we are handed in black and white, but is implied in our response to the whole book. The Georgia designer understood this, but his or her response was inadequately informed by a reading of the text, for the edition parades the original *tomaison* in outsized divisional title-pages. The original division, however, arbitrarily cuts across the rhetorical unit of chapters 35–37, and the very distinction subverts Smollett's concept of the novel as "a large *diffused* picture" (p. 4; my emphasis). We have learned our lesson too well, from *Pride and Prejudice* and *Tom Jones*, that the original publishing units do indeed "speak volumes." They don't in Smollett.

In these respects, the presentation is too literal-minded; in others, it seems too indifferent to its "copy." The elevation of chapter references into running titles (*à la* Fielding) is part of a cumbersome linkage of footnote numbering and chapters; convenient for the editor and publisher, since the numbering does not depend on page make-up, but not for the reader. It does not appear in any of Smollett's novels, and it misleadingly implies that the chapter, rather than the episode, is the fundamental unit of narration. The 9 1/4" size of Bowers's Dekker pleasantly and appropriately alluded to Malone's Shakespeare, but it is not suitable for all texts; for Fielding or Smollett's duodecimos, a post octavo size (like Chapman's Austen) would be far more eloquent. What is a novel that cannot be cradled in one hand, or inserted (and often forgotten) in a pocket? Answer: a definitive edition. As in most books of the *ancien régime,* Smollett's dedication appears in larger type than the text. This *relative* difference, expressive of social distance, should not be silently subsumed in the absolute difference between the typography of the copy and its reprinting, as it always is. Either editors should note their departure or (my preference) we should insist that the designer follow copy.

Beasley's preface, a reworking of an article that appeared in *Papers in Language and Literature* (1984), is more original than he cares to admit. A coherent body of critical opinion on *Ferdinand Count Fathom,* as on many other eighteenth-century novels, is wanting: it is generally admitted to be a "failure," but that does not take us very far; otherwise, one must make do with *obiter dicta* of critics who were hurrying on to *Humphry Clinker,* or with specialized discussions of the novel's "unity" and style, which scarcely address the reader's real unease. *Ferdinand* is *sui generis* and thus difficult to locate in an appropriate context. Beasley is the first to tackle its problems of genre and poetic economy, and this alone represents an important critical advance, right or wrong.

His location of the novel in "criminal biography," indeed, inspires reservations. It may be the last gasp of a traditional comparison between *Ferdinand* and Fielding's *Jonathan Wild*—which he otherwise quite rightly rejects; a more appropriate parallel, surely, would be *Tom Jones,* though this too cannot be fully sustained. Borrowing a hint from Robert Alter's characterization of *Amelia,* I think we might more fruitfully see *Ferdinand* as a "problem comedy." Smollett's invocation of tragic precedent (p. 5) tells us more about eighteenth-century (mis)readings of Shakespeare than it does about his own novel. Ferdinand is no Iago, as Beasley suggests (p. xxx), unless we can imagine Iago repenting and marrying Emilia; he is not even Blifil, though they both end up in the North of England. Crime is a problematic concept in Smollett's world, and not just because his hero's schemes fail or return on his own head. That would-be poisoner Don Diego, for example, flourishes as a green bay tree, and a juvenile delinquent like Ferdinand is not as far from an adolescent menace like Peregrine as Beasley imagines (p. xxix). Their common ground is that, however improbably, they change *(experto crede Roberto)*.

Beasley's commentary is incomparably the fullest now available and obviates many obstacles to understanding. It occasionally fails to provide a rationale for annotation. If, as the preface argues, following the standard study of George Kahrl (p. xxxii), national differences are meaningless, why should the annotation touch on them at all? To provide "recognizable context," Beasley pleads (p. xxxiv), though what this context is, and what part of it is historical reality, and what part rhetoric, is not always self-evident. In short, annotation must verge on interpretation, a "privilege" that Beasley disclaims (p. xiv). As an alternative to any such self-denying "objectivity," and a plea for critical reading, I offer the following critique: a defense of Beasley the annotator against Beasley the theorist.

The hero himself, like Smollett "literally a native of two countries" (p. 8), begotten by a putative army of fathers on an English mother, adopted in turn by a German trooper and a Scotch-Hungarian count, and sporting a "Polish" title, is not a "universal character type," as Beasley implies (p. xxxiv), but that emphatic historical paradox, a True-born Englishman:

> *A True-Born Englishman*'s a Contradiction,
> In Speech an Irony, in Fact a Fiction.

Like the Huguenot Defoe, Smollett has no doubt of the superiority of the reality to the homegrown, John Bull fiction (which, with an added twist, he incorporates as fact in his novel). The predatory Scot and defenseless English—it's all *true*, he seems to say, God help us all! (He does, of course, including Ferdinand.) And what Samuel Johnson called "the casual distinction of country and condition" continues to drive the plot, where Spanish

Pentimenti: The Georgia Edition of Smollett 173

pride of lineage, English eccentricity, Scotch poverty, Irish "bulls," French *politesse*, and German phlegm all play their part. Locality is generalized out of all recognition, to be sure, but the Wars of the Spanish, Polish, and Austrian Succession dramatize and precedent Fathom's predations on society—which is no society, but a Hobbesian state of war. There is more at issue here than providing the narrative with washy details of "recognizable context"; the details are as thoroughly tendentious as the background of a Hogarth print. Dismissing their importance in favor of "a large, still picture intended to be seen all at once" (p. xxxiii), Beasley strips the novel of its dynamics. Even habitual moral turpitude is a transient condition, in Smollett's world; it is hardly "still."

In more mechanical matters, I found myself wishing that mere glosses had been relegated to a glossary, so that the text was not so cluttered with references. And there are inevitably occasional lapses: Lucian probably did *not* write "Lucian and the Ass," alias "Lucius, or the Ass" (chapter 1, n. 11); and Ali Beker's "Persian" beard adequately explains Ferdinand's failure to identify his face as that of Don Diego de Zelos (chapter 46, n. 3). The Spartans' habit of combing their hair before battle is attested by Herodotus and others, and hardly qualifies as a "murderous custom"; while the Malayan penchant for running amok is well known, indigenous, and uninspired by Western culture, crazy though it is in other respects (chapter 50, n. 4–5). Bear Key is the London Cornmarket (chapter 28, n. 12).[21] The phrase, "food (prey) for the beasts of the field and the fowls of the air" is Smollett's free paraphrase from the opening of the *Iliad* (chapter 13, n. 4, and chapter 46, n. 6), and also appears in *Peregrine Pickle* (1st ed., chapter 47). There is no end to nit-picking, but if I tried to convey how much is done right, I should never finish this review, which has grown to an unconscionable length. I may have unfairly emphasized the staidness of the edition, its unadventurous adherence to copy-text and received opinion; these are qualities that others will welcome in a reference work. This will certainly be the standard edition of Smollett for years to come, and we are lucky to have it.

Appendix: Treatment of Copy-text

Note: The lemmata and sigla are those of the Georgia edition; G = variant readings in Damian Grant's edition (London: Oxford Univ. Press, 1971). The agreement of the second edition is only noted where the reading of the first edition might be questioned.

26.20   sallacious] fallacious I
46.14–5   expressly] expresly I
49.29   re-echoed] II; re-ecchoed I
76.30   *career*] II; *carreer* I
77.21   stong] strong I
82.1   earrings] ear-|rings I

The hyphenation should also be recorded in "Word-division," sec. 2.

88.39   surrendering] II; surrendring I
90.11   demonination] denomination I
96.13   putting] II; put-|ing I

Emendation to II is surely defensible here, but requires record.

101.17   to rob] rob I
102.5   Apize] I–II; A pize G

Grant's emendation is certainly attractive.

132.10   aroused] ar-|roused I

The lemma might be defended as an emendation, but isn't. Cf. 136.23

136.23   haranguing] har-|ranguing I
155.15   where] II; were I
159.32   full] a full I
184.30   *beinseance*] *bienseance* II

The reading of the first edition may be authorial, but emendation may be preferable to explaining so tedious a conjecture.

185.11   Scripture] scripture I

The "down" style of capitalization of the text does not reflect Smollett's autograph, but a new typographical fashion emerging in the 1750s. The editor should feel free to emend, when the sense is affected; but it requires record. Cf. 219.39.

210.31   exlaim] exclaim I
219.39   orphan] I–II
   The sense would be clearer if this were capitalized; cf. the note to 185.11.
229.11   *PATIENCE*] P A T I E N C E I
   The eighteenth-century printer did not have italic small capitals, and it might be argued that it is permissible to normalize them; but the editor's freedom should be explicitly pleaded.
235.2   splendour] splendor I
241.10   Malayse] I–II
   A plural is certainly intended; which seems to rule out "Malayese" as an explanation of the occasional spelling (if that is what it is). If the editor wishes to defend it as an occasional spelling of either "Malays" or "Malayese," however, he should probably be explicit. Emendation may be a less intrusive alternative.
271.30   resine] refine I–II; repine G
   Smollett's meaning is obscure: Ferdinand would like to leave Mrs. Muddy to "refine at her leisure," i.e., to "improve," to bask in her moral superiority (cf. OED, sense 7; not, however, an exact parallel). Grant's emendation is appealing, but graphically unlikely.
279.14   himself] he himself G
   The typographical context of I ("which | himself") encourages an easy eyeskip; but Smollet's usage, which I have also observed in Fielding, is probably just archaic. Cf. OED, sense 3.
290.5   he] I–II
   "had" may have dropped out by eye skip; the auxiliary is required by "given" in the parallel clause.
290.31   blessing] blessings I
296.33   hand ˄ writing] ~ - ~ I
   The hyphen is clearly visible in the Harvard copies.

Notes

1. "The Bicentennial Edition of the Works of Tobias Smollett," *Books at Iowa*, 7 (1967), 41–42.

2. Beasley seems reluctant to believe that "Johnson" is a fiction (p. xxxix, n. 27); since he uses the same address as Johnston, I think we have no alternative. Certainly none of the possible names in Plomer are plausible candidates: the Hague or Rotterdam pirate (ca. 1715–1740); a possibly pseudonymous pamphlet publisher in Newgate St. (1742); and a Liverpool printer active ca. 1775. Henry R. Plomer et al., *A Dictionary of the Printers and Booksellers . . . in England, Scotland and Ireland from 1726 to 1775* (Oxford: The Bibliographical Society, 1932). Not surprisingly, no Scottish bookseller of this name appears either in Plomer, or in the supplements published by Carnie and Doig, *Studies in Bibliography*, 12 (1960), 131–59 and 14 (1962), 81–96, 105–20.

3. "Thomas, John," in Paul G. Morrison, *Index of Printers, Publishers and Booksellers in Donald Wing's* Short-title Catalogue. (Charlottesville: Bibliographical Society of the University of Virginia, 1955). Eric Partridge, *A Dictionary of Slang and Unconventional English*, ed. Paul Beale. 8th ed. (London: Routledge & Kegan Paul, 1984), does not record the sexual sense of "Johnson" and "John Thomas" before the mid-nineteenth century, but of course, this may just reflect the poor survival of such evidence.

4. The agreements in correction cited by Brack are probably less significant than two agreements in error: "expeded" (202.28) and "unluckly" (248.28).

5. See appendix; Grant's text shows only ten errors, of which three are substantive.

6. W. W. Greg, *Collected Papers*, ed. J. C. Maxwell (Oxford: Clarendon Press, 1966), p. 247; Ronald B. McKerrow, *An Introduction to Bibliography for Literary Students* (Oxford: Clarendon Press, 1928, reprinted 1951), pp. 2–3. For a catena of quotations from Bowers, cf. James Thorpe, *Principles of Textual Criticism* (San Marino: Huntington Library, 1972), pp. 94–95.

7. Lewis Mansfield Knapp, *Tobias Smollett: Doctor of Men and Manners*. (Princeton: Princeton Univ. Press, 1949), p. 119; corrected against B.M. Add. MSS. 35398, f. 104–5.

8. Knapp, *Smollett*, p. 151.

9. Knapp, *Smollett*, p. 157.

10. The collation of the London edition argues that the printer had four blank leaves left over in the final sheet, containing v. 1, π 1, a^4, and v. 2,[A]1, P^2, but they were not used as cancels, as the paper shows. The misprint "C o u n t" for "Count" in the running titles of v. 1, B-F 11/12r may be safely ignored. The Dublin edition collates [a]^{6}b^{2}B-R^6 (R5, 6 advts.); A^4 (-A4) B-U^6[X]1 (= A4?); the only irregularity in the running titles is the misprint "F r d i n a n d" in v. 2, B-D5r.

11. *The Complete Letters of Lady Mary Wortley Montagu*, ed. Robert Halsband (Oxford: Clarendon Press, 1967), III, 66, 78, and 180.

12. Knapp, *Smollett,* pp. 223–25.

13. Reviews in the *Gentleman's* or *London Magazine* are selective and rarely discuss novels; William Woty's *Journal britannique* is specialized for a scholarly audience. One would not ordinarily expect extended notices of a novel in any of these periodicals.

14. *New Books by Fielding: An Exhibition of the Hyde Collection* (Cambridge: The Houghton Library, January 12–March 6, 1987), pp. 34, 43; substantiating Millar's opinion from the publication of novels by the Nobles.

15. Plomer, *Dictionary,* p. 142. The fullest account of share-publishing is Terry Belanger, "Booksellers' Sales of Copyright: Aspects of the London Book Trade, 1718–1768" (Ph.D. diss., Columbia University, 1970).

16. [Docket title:] *A List of Books Printed by the Booksellers of London and Westminster . . . with the Number of Years an Impression of Each Is in Selling* [London, 1774], of which I know only the BL and Harvard copies, is conveniently reprinted in *The English Book Trade, 1660–1853,* ed. Stephen Parks (New York: Garland, 1974). These are all share books. For original publications, cf. David Hume to William Strahan, 25 March 1771, *The Letters of David Hume,* ed. J. Y. T. Greig (Oxford: Clarendon Press, 1932, reprinted 1969), no. 455: "I have heard you frequently say, that no Bookseller woud find profit in making an Edition which woud take more than three Years in selling."

17. The sale catalogue seems to be lost; but the sale is attested from the purchases of John Nichols, Cambridge University Library, Add. MSS. 8226 (though I have not checked to see if these include Smollett properties).

18. Cf. J. A. Sutherland, *Victorian Novelists and Publishers* (London: Athlone Press, 1976), particularly pp. 45–49 and 94–98, for the perhaps obvious but often overlooked truth that mutual trust and publishing arrangements have as much to do with sales as literary merit and demand.

19. Ernest Campbell Mossner and Harry Ransom, "Hume and the 'Conspiracy of Booksellers': the Publication and Early Fortunes of the *History of England,*" *Texas Studies in English,* 29 (1950), 162–82.

20. *A New Catalogue of Lownds's Circulating Library* [London: Thomas Lownds, 1764?] (copy at Harvard); on internal evidence, this is a reprint of a 1758 catalogue, with an appendix of additions to 1764. *Ferdinand Count Fathom* appears in the first section, no. 1756.

21. Hugh Phillips, *The Thames about 1750* (London: Collins, 1951), p. 39.

Dreiser's Long Foreground

Robert H. Elias

T. D. Nostwich, ed. *Theodore Dreiser's "Heard in the Corridors": Articles and Related Writings*. Ames: Iowa State University Press, 1988. xxiv, 155 pp.

T. D. Nostwich, ed. *Theodore Dreiser Journalism, Volume One: Newspaper Writings, 1892–1895*. Philadelphia: University of Pennsylvania Press, 1988. xiv, 398 pp.

Yoshinobu Hakutani, ed. *Selected Magazine Articles of Theodore Dreiser: Life and Art in the American 1890s*. Rutherford, N.J.: Fairleigh Dickinson University Press, 1985, 1987. Two volumes. 288, 257 pp.

Stories of genesis are compelling. Whether animated by religious, scientific, historical, psychological, archaeological, or biographical concerns, we are drawn to them by a need to move back in time, either to make the past as real as the present or to understand the present as a consequence of that past. Shelley is said to have caught up a newly born baby to peer into its face in the hope of discovering the secret of Origin or Being. In this spirit we conduct all our genetic inquiries, less intuitively, no doubt, but just as intensely. We cannot accept that anything particular exists in itself, spaceless and timeless. Everything is always *in situ*. We trowel for shards; we collect scraps; we rearrange bones. We try to penetrate the secrets of Origin.

Thus as literary interpreters do we peer into writers' earliest forms of verbal life to identify the genesis of accomplishments we have come to value. If we can find a Baby Book with Baby's First Words, what symbolic extrapolations we can produce with those expressions! If we can lay our hands on paragraphs written in the elementary grades, we can surely make much of them, too. And if we can discover early publications, we certainly feel that we can enter our author's mind and glimpse the emergence of his artistry.

It is, as my tone implies, tempting to scoff at such excavations and resurrections, until we look at our own careers. Can we readily dismiss our earliest verbal efforts, especially our written ones, as wholly unrelated to what we write now? Is there not a connection in tone, in topical preoccupations, in implied values? Sometimes, to be sure, we must struggle to establish connection. Whitman's "long foreground" that Emerson alluded to in his famous letter has challenged many an explorer. (What did Whitman *really* do in New Orleans and how does that explain everything?) With Theodore Dreiser, though, we do not have to be inventive. The career that he, himself, described and partially accounted for is now being so systematically and thoughtfully documented that there is no question about connection.

We do not have any Baby Book, and we appear to be without writings from school and college days. But we are well supplied with what Dreiser did as a writer for newspapers and magazines before he composed his first stories and *Sister Carrie*. And we have sympathetic scholars devoted to presenting the record in full.

Beginning with Walt Whitman's editorial stint in Brooklyn, the journalistic experience has provided a critical apprenticeship for many American writers—particularly, after the Civil War, for white, male writers of fiction, whose stories and novels are marked by close observation, devotion to detail, commitment to rendering faithfully, whatever their metaphysics or tone, the texture of Americans' lives. What, Why, When, How, Where, and Who—these were the concerns that shaped Dreiser's career.

Between June 1892 and March 1895 Dreiser wrote nearly three hundred articles, possibly even more, for the seven newspapers that successively employed him as he made his way from the Midwest to New York City. Some pieces could be classified as conventional reportage; some were brief theatrical "reviews," mere notes; others were interviews, anecdotes, sketches, and the kinds of features we label "human interest stories"—indeed, what characterizes most of Dreiser's newspaper writing, even the reportage, is the human interest, the way people look, talk, and react to predicaments. Sometimes there is admiration; sometimes humor; sometimes irony and compassion. Always there is a rendering of vitality, a felt reality, a largely urban landscape with moving persons in it. In the magazine articles written during the last part of that decade there is less variety but still an adherence to telling the human story.

Much of this material has long been available to researchers who could devote themselves to extended periods of archival excavation. And a handful of biographers have rewardingly availed themselves of some of those resources. Yet it is only now that a comprehensive view of Dreiser's earliest accomplishments has become possible for more than the few specialists. Thanks to the separate projects of T. D. Nostwich and Yoshinobu Hakutani, we can all read in book form the bulk of what Dreiser wrote during those years of apprenticeship.

I do not foresee a radical reassessment of Dreiser's achievement emerging from all this. But I do expect that we shall have an enhanced appreciation of the development of a practicing writer who wrote regularly, diligently, in a disciplined way, meeting deadlines, the writer that Arthur Henry detected at Maumee during the summer of 1899 and that we did not adequately understand as long as we let him persuade us that he came into being at that time without significant preparation.

The extent and range of Dreiser's preparation is what is most striking about the volumes recently published. Together with Donald Pizer's *Theodore Dreiser: A Selection of Uncollected Prose* (Detroit: Wayne State University Press, 1977), which includes a substantial selection of Dreiser's editorial reflections for *Ev'ry Month* during 1895–1897, these books fill in the eight pre-*Carrie* years with a wealth of examples of his ability to report facts, to embellish facts, to sketch character, and to pose questions about the human condition, quite often with a distinctive voice.

The most enlightening examples are those provided by the newspaper writings, primarily because they best exhibit Dreiser's style, tone, and preoccupations. Although much of what he routinely covered was necessarily assigned, he was a reporter whose nose for news often determined what the news was. In his newspaper writings we encounter fake auctioneers, mediums, clairvoyants, and practitioners of voodoo portrayed with an informal, frequently ironic touch—and almost always zestfully, especially when he is recounting follies and foibles. We encounter politicians, union organizers, teachers, whose statements and conversations Dreiser reproduces with sensitivity to cadence. And we encounter many whose luck has run out—"the poor, ignorant, and depraved" in Chicago's Cheyenne section, for example, the unknown dead, the deceased destined for Potter's Field, the man who blew out the gas flame. "Let the wise world ponder," Dreiser wrote on 24 July 1892 for the *Chicago Globe*. "Let human pity extend a helping hand." Explicit early in Dreiser's career, implicit always. "An unknown has no story," a morgue-keeper told him in those days. It obviously became Dreiser's commitment, as a reporter, later as a free-lance magazine writer, finally as a novelist and short-story writer, to make the unknown known.

In this context we naturally think of Hurstwood. But it is relevant to think of others, too, the ordinary men and women of the world, those who get along from day to day. They, too, Dreiser could view as unknown because taken for granted. A glimpse of their world emerges in the anecdotes that he contributed to what was mainly his column, "Heard in the Corridors," in the *St. Louis Globe-Democrat*. Here visitors, actual or fabricated by Dreiser, staying at local hotels relate paragraph-length experiences and discoveries that might illuminate existence, ranging from the way greenbacks can transmit germs to proof that domestic love is incompatible with worldly success and evidence that instinct works in human beings as surely as it does in animals. Most of these individuals were ordinary people. Almost always men, they were travelers standing in hotel lobbies, or leaning against a bar sipping lemonade, or pausing in a hallway to light a cigar or gaze out the window while holding forth. They conjure up for us the drummer's world that Drouet was at home in. Yet they also go beyond Drouet, to commentary, to a beginning of the sort of scrutiny that Dreiser later undertook as The Prophet in *Ev'ry Month*.

Still, though these were all individuals at home in the world, they were not the individuals who moved and shook the world.

They were not the power-brokers of Frank Cowperwood's milieu. The importance of the magazine articles that Yoshinobu Hakutani has compiled lies in their showing Dreiser not only observing rural scenes, little-noticed dramas of city life, and technological and industrial processes, but also encountering the movers and shakers in business and the arts, encounters that would have less effect on his style and attention to detail than on his ability to imagine what it meant to arrive—although Hakutani rightly notes that in these articles the writing has become less "broody," the syntax more effective, and the diction less repetitious than in Dreiser's earlier writing.

At the same time, Dreiser's voice here is surely less marked. There is a flat, almost formulaic tone that pervades the free-lance work. Understandably. The magazines' demands were pretty well tailored to readers' expectations. There was a way of writing about the homes of the famous, busy rivers, drainage canals, the making of stained-glass windows, and the achievements of caricaturists, harpists, and sculptors. And Dreiser, trained to satisfy the city desk, became adept at fulfilling editors' requirements. He also repeatedly managed in more than thirty systematic interviews to elicit from successful men and women stories of their rise, in fields ranging from literature and the arts to the law and finance. Adept again. Here, then, are Dreiser's accounts of the well known, material that he could draw on when he subsequently undertook to penetrate more deeply into the nature of success and failure.

As engaging or arresting writing, the somewhat more polished work for the magazines cannot match the earlier work for the newspapers. The wry detachment, the adversarial stance, the wonder at human frailty, pretension, and power, the fascination with natural processes—these seldom appear in the contributions to *Success, Demorest's, Ainslee's,* and the other periodicals to which Dreiser sold his articles. Yet the world whose values he explored does emerge; particularly in the biographical articles, we can infer the condition of the arts, the stature of various writers, and the standing of leading politicos and financiers in this country during the 1890s, matters of interest to anyone wanting to locate Dreiser historically.

Dreiser would, I know, have been delighted by the attention

given his apprentice work. I remember how pleased he was when I showed him the Orison Swett Marden volumes that John F. Huth, Jr., had demonstrated were actually compilations of Dreiser's unacknowledged interviews for *Success*. At the time he saw these volumes he had already come to want a collected edition of his writings, in the cloth of a uniform set, and perhaps, glancing backward over his traveled road, he glimpsed how the recovery of his early publications could make the desired set more complete than he'd envisaged.

The University of Pennsylvania, under the exemplary oversight of Thomas P. Riggio, is now faithfully carrying out Dreiser's wish, if not in uniform bindings, at least with the imagination and integrity he would have valued. Nostwich's edition of the first four years of Dreiser's journalistic work serves admirably to meet the editorial standards established by preceding volumes of the Pennsylvania edition, with their helpful commentary, precise yet ample historical and textual notes, and good index. The same praise is due Hakutani and his publisher.

Nostwich's "Heard in the Corridors" volume, though, well edited as it is, attaches a question mark to its value. By publishing a separate volume that contains a hundred and seventy-five of the column's pieces, along with some related writings, Nostwich has removed from its appropriate chronological position a substantial segment that ideally should have remained in place, and consequently included in the *Journalism* volume only six examples of that column. The excuse is that the cost of printing the 2300-page typescript that the complete edition of the journalism for 1892–1895 fills would be prohibitive. I am unable to challenge the cost estimates, but I cannot believe there were no better solutions. To set apart all those "Corridors" pieces may seem neat and convey the appearance of unity, but it isolates a single aspect of what Dreiser was doing, which was not a truly distinguishable phase but an integral part of a more versatile and complex achievement. Moreover, in his historical commentary for the Pennsylvania edition Nostwich has rather thoroughly cannibalized his introduction to the other volume, calling unhappy attention to the solution's flaw.

For all that, the flaw remains basically only a single flaw. Alert readers will know how to contend with it when they must. What most matters, after all, is that valuable material for the appreciation of Dreiser is finally within convenient reach, respectfully and sympathetically presented. Both Nostwich and Hakutani have thus accorded Dreiser recognition he did not consistently receive in his lifetime. They have chosen not simply to write *about* him, but instead directly to help his own words survive. Dreiser would indeed have been greatly pleased by the result.

Dictating Taste in the Eighteenth Century: New Lights on the Careers of Robert Dodsley and John Almon

Beverly Schneller

James E. Tierney, ed. *The Correspondence of Robert Dodsley, 1733–1764.* Cambridge: Cambridge University Press, 1988. xxxvii, 599 pp.

Deborah D. Rogers. *Bookseller as Rogue: John Almon and the Politics of Eighteenth-Century Publishing.* New York: Peter Lang, 1986. xvii, 151 pp.

The Dodsley correspondence and the Almon letters included in *Bookseller as Rogue* demonstrate in a new way that both of these eighteenth-century booksellers were ambitious men who brought the activity of publishing to new heights in their period. While these two booksellers shared some interesting personal similarities, their careers were quite different. Both Dodsley and Almon came to London from provincial towns to seek their fortunes; both were supported by influential men who financed their starts in the book trade; both were collectors and anthologists. Dodsley aspired to be a successful author; Almon was one. These two men, working at different times within the same century, greatly influenced literature, and through their accomplishments the perception of the bookseller as just a middleman was changed. Dodsley all but dictated what *was* literature from 1735 forward, and when Almon needed to turn from political publishing to something less controversial, he chose to imitate Dodsley's highly successful *Collection of Poems by Several Hands.* Moreover, Almon, because he was not afraid to challenge Parliament, increased the power of printers and publishers against censorship, thus earning Horace Walpole's description, "Almon, whom I know and have found to be a rogue."

James Tierney has recovered 393 of Robert Dodsley's letters written between 1733 and 1764 for the third volume in Cambridge University Press's recently launched series, "Cambridge Studies in Publishing and Printing History," an endeavor of potentially great importance to literary historians, textual scholars, and bibliographers. The two previous volumes in the series are John Feather's study of the English provincial book trade and Cohen and Gandolfo's edition of Lewis Carroll's correspondence with his publisher, Alexander Macmillan. Forthcoming volumes will address the fifteenth-century book trade, William Caxton's early printing career, and Samuel Johnson's *Dictionary*. Cambridge has done well in presenting this as the third volume of the series; Dodsley's was a very important career about which, thanks to Tierney, much more is known.

Dodsley's publishing career and his correspondence are familiar territories to Tierney, whose previous studies of *The Museum*, the poet John Gilbert Cooper, and the eighteenth-century periodical have appeared in journals such as *Studies in Bibliography, Papers of the Bibliographic Society of America,* and *The Library.* In his present volume, Tierney also includes the text of Dodsley's will, his list of copyright registrations in *The Stationers' Register,* and materials relating to James Dodsley's continuation of his brother's trade, all of them never before published. There are a chronological table of correspondence and a listing of letters according to correspondent, which make the volume easy to use. Tierney notes that there is always the possibility of finding more of Dodsley's letters and also that James Dodsley, after his brother's death in 1764, burned those letters which did not seem important. Still there is substantial data here to fully illustrate Dodsley's business practices and to enable us to better understand the man, who was at times very funny, at other times very humble, and apparently always in control of his destiny.

Robert Dodsley was born in 1703 and began his career in London as a footman. Because his father was a schoolmaster, it is certain that Dodsley and his brothers were literate. (Not all eighteenth-century booksellers were literate, nor were all typesetters, a fact which distressed many an author.) By 1732, Dodsley had made the acquaintance of Alexander Pope, who helped the young footman open his own book shop, Tully's Head, in Westminster in 1735. By 1732, Dodsley had received assistance in composition from Daniel Defoe, and his first collection of poetry, *A Muse in Livery; or, A Footman's Miscellany*, had been published. How Dodsley supported himself between 1733 and 1735 is not quite clear because of a conflict of dates which Tierney points out. He rejects the notion of Ralph Straus, Dodsley's biographer, that Dodsley served an apprenticeship with either Lawton Gilliver or Thomas Cooper, both of whom were Pope's publishers, because to have done so, Dodsley would have had to break his indenture to the bookseller. If Dodsley served no printing apprenticeship, he must have been a very quick study, and it is not clear just how he learned the trade and how he made contacts with the *literati* beyond those afforded him by Pope. Whatever the circumstances, the patronage of Pope gave Dodsley entrée to literary circles that would have taken him years to enter on his own. The extent of Pope's desire to see Dodsley succeed is evident from the first letter of the *Correspondence:* "I will do more than you ask me; I will recommend it [*The Toy-Shop*, Dodsley's first play] to Mr. Rich. I sincerely wish it may be turned any way to your advantage, or that I could show my friendship in any instance" (p. 65).

Dodsley's brief brush with the law and weeklong imprisonment for libel in 1739, when he published Paul Whitehead's *Manners,* may have turned him against political publishing and made him wary of controversy in any form. As the letters bear out, Dodsley was highly conservative and often hesitant to accept new projects. But such caution could have severely limited his publishing activities had Dodsley not engaged other booksellers, especially Mary Cooper, to issue those works about which he was unsure. Two well-known instances of Dodsley's use of Cooper to publish for him occurred in 1756, when she brought out the first part of Joseph Warton's *Essay on the Writings and the Genius of Pope,* which denies Pope's stature as a poet of the first class, and in 1759, when Cooper published the initial volumes of *Tristram Shandy,* about which Dodsley was uncertain until they became the rage. Because no one knows the precise terms of the collaborations between Dodsley and Cooper (or any of his other publisher-agents), Tierney endorses Michael Treadwell's speculation that Cooper was a "trade publisher."[1] This is an example of how the unexamined thesis perpetuates itself, right or wrong. Cooper's own book list, her trade sale catalogs, and her activities as a projector of periodicals belie the classification of trade publisher which by Treadwell's definition was a minor tradesman who worked mainly for other publishers and who owned few or no copyrights. It is possible that Cooper owned her own printing press, and she managed her own book shop, The Globe, in Paternoster Row, from 1743 to 1761. In the case of Cooper, Tierney is not well informed. Further, there are few imprints in the notes to the text bearing the joint Dodsley-Cooper names, and most of those provided are relegated to the appendix concerning Dodsley's copyright ownership. While admittedly it is often commonplace to omit or abridge eighteenth-century imprints, it is disappointing not to find complete imprints in this particular volume.

By the 1740s, Dodsley's reputation as a publisher of high-quality belletristic works was established. In addition to publishing poetry, drama, criticism, and some novels, Dodsley was a shareholder in *The London Chronicle* and the projector of two important literary periodicals, *The Museum,* edited by Mark Akenside, and *The World,* edited by Edward Moore. While projecting literary magazines was common to many booksellers, Dodsley's magazines were of uncommonly high quality. Dodsley also distinguished himself as an anthologist by bringing together first *A Select Collection of Old Plays* in ten volumes, begun in 1745, and then *A Collection of Poems by Several Hands,* begun in 1748. Many of the letters from the first decade of Dodsley's career are devoted to soliciting materials for his famous *Collection of Poems*. With few exceptions, these letters have never been published before and Tierney does an excellent job of annotating each piece of correspondence as fully as possible.

One of Dodsley's most frequent and petulant correspondents was John Gilbert Cooper, a poet, critic, and biographer. In 1748, he was engaged with Dodsley in the publication of his *Life of*

Socrates. Cooper's dealings with Dodsley are fairly well delineated, and something of the personalities of both men emerges as they haggle over bills, typographical errors, and the shipping of complimentary copies. Dodsley's letters to Cooper reveal his efforts to be diplomatic and to live up to his responsibilities to the authors he published. For instance, in addition to supplying complimentary copies to the author, the publisher had to send them to the author's friends, acquaintances, and benefactors. He also had to keep up with printing accounts and record whatever purchases the author might have made in the shop; to follow the author's directions for corrections if a new edition were called for; and to send reviews (especially from *The Monthly Review*). Dodsley's letter to Cooper in December 1749 is revealing: "I heartily beg your Pardon for not giving you an Account of the Expenses & Profits of this First Edition of ye Life of Socrates, which I should never have done had not You reminded me of our Conditions which had totally slipt my Memory till you recalled it" (p. 132). When there was a problem with an account, Dodsley was unfailingly gracious and humble. And Dodsley never writes about the profit he expects to gain from a particular publication—the quality of the literature was apparently his main concern. Thus, the few letters of rejection in the volume have more to do with the unsatisfactory quality of the offering than with its marketability.

Dodsley is at his most personal in the letters of the 1750s to his friend and associate William Shenstone, the poet. Dodsley wrote to Shenstone regularly, and Tierney's annotations show that Shenstone collected and dated Dodsley's letters when necessary. The most frequent subjects of their correspondence were Shenstone's health, Dodsley's need of new material for his *Collection*, and the quality of Dodsley's own poetical works. Dodsley always offered his works to Shenstone for critique, but, as Tierney remarks, he rarely used any of his esteemed friend's advice when it came to revising either his poetry or his play, *Cleone*. Dodsley also assisted Shenstone in landscaping the poet's estate, Leasowes, by buying swans and statues for the garden and pond, and in purveying London foods and liqueurs. The Dodsley-Shenstone letters provide more evidence of Dodsley's own tastes in food and art and more of his sense of humor than do any of the other letters in the *Correspondence*.

In the latter half of the 1750s Dodsley was consumed with the production of *Cleone*. The letters concerned with the writing of the play and Dodsley's efforts to have it performed provide an informative look at the difficulties some authors faced in trying to get a work staged and at the frustrations of dealing with theater managers, especially David Garrick. If Tierney better understood Mary Cooper's trade, he would not express surprise that she published John Hill's *An Account of the New Tragedy of Cleone*. Although it is conceivable that Cooper owed Dodsley some loyalty, she need not have been totally loyal to him, as Tierney seems to expect, and as an independent bookseller Cooper wanted to be a part of the publicity surrounding Dodsley's *Cleone*. In 1759, Dodsley turned the business over to his brother and partner, James, but his letters, especially to Shenstone, indicate how hard he worked in "retirement" to ready his *Select Fables of Aesop and other Fabulists* (which contained translated fables of Aesop and modern fables as well) and how he worked with John Baskerville toward the perfection of the Baskerville type. The last letter Dodsley wrote was to Elizabeth Cartwright, on 28 April 1764, detailing his travels with his friend, Joseph Spence. While on these travels, Dodsley died and was buried in Durham.

Tierney's edition of *The Correspondence of Robert Dodsley* is an interesting combination of textual scholarship and excellent research. While the general outlines of Dodsley's life have been available since Straus's *Robert Dodsley: Poet, Publisher and Playwright* (1910), the *Correspondence* greatly enriches our understanding of the accomplishments of this important bookseller, and it provides new insights into the workings of a successful eighteenth-century publishing house. Tierney also does an important service in presenting what information is available on the correspondence of James Dodsley, and his Appendix 5 will surely be the foundation for future scholarship on the brother's activities at Tully's Head. It is ironic that the *Correspondence* contains a few typographical errors, since Dodsley's authors themselves, the letters show, had serious complaints about their first editions. The error on p. 353, the inadvertent substitution of

"S.D." for "R.D.," might dishearten even a seasoned researcher of the eighteenth century.

The topic of Deborah D. Rogers's study of John Almon, Volume 24 in the Peter Lang English Language and Literature Series of American University Studies, is the impact of politics and legal proceedings on what a bookseller was willing to publish. John Almon is a good subject for such a study because he not only knowingly offended the administration of William Pitt, but he also openly supported the American Revolution, and he was well received by American *literati,* including Benjamin Franklin, as a bookseller sympathetic to their cause.

John Almon moved to London in 1759, when he was twenty-two. He began his career as a printer, and within three months he was hired by Charles Say to write newspaper essays to compete with John Newbery's publication of Oliver Goldsmith's "Chinese Letters" in Newbery's newspaper, *The Public Ledger.* Almon quickly established a reputation as an outspoken political pamphleteer. His 1762 *Review of Mr. Pitt's Administration* attracted the attention of Richard Grenville, Earl of Temple, and, through Temple, Almon met many prominent members of the Opposition Whig faction, not the least of whom was the controversial John Wilkes.

With the support of Temple and the patronage of his friends, Almon was able to open his first book shop in 1763, and, as Rogers says, for the next three years Almon's and Temple's careers were tightly interwoven. In 1764, Temple made Almon the bookseller to the Whig Club, the coterie, and promised him a political post, apparently in the Pay Office. When Temple broke with Pitt in 1766, Almon's hopes of preferment were dashed. Yet his position as the leading Opposition bookseller was firm, and his pretense of taking no money for copy but exacting money to cover a potential libel trial should the publication result in one, had earned him the reputation of "rogue."

Rogers shows that Almon was not just Wilkes's friend, but was also a leading source of national and domestic information for the exiled politician. Wilkes fled London in 1764 to avoid imprisonment for libel because of the *North Briton* #45, a paper questioning the rationality of the King. Rogers does not provide much detail about the *North Briton* affair, assuming it is well known. She does, however, provide a good bibliography of secondary sources so the reader can fill in; but without familiarity with the Wilkes affair, the nonspecialist may miss some of the significance of the early part of the book.

Quoting extensively from generally ignored letters from Almon to Wilkes, Rogers shows how Almon funneled information, both personal and professional, to Wilkes. The bookseller also kept Wilkes strategically before the public through his newspaper, *The Political Register,* to which Wilkes was a regular contributor. Writing to Wilkes in June 1767, Almon says: "I sent you (by the Dover postage) two of the Political Registers, the moment it was published & which I hope you have received. I think it will not displease you: & I assure you it will be carried on with spirit and in support of the true cause of Liberty" (p. 32). Almon's 1770 conviction for libel in reprinting the "Junius" letter in his *London Museum* remains significant as a representation of the law's efforts to manipulate the press. In a highly contrived trial, Almon was the only publisher of six to be convicted and fined. In her assessment of the verdict, Rogers apparently excludes printers from the term "publishers," as the printer of the *North Briton,* William Bingley, served two years in the King's Bench for refusing to apologize for his part in the publication. Almon's conviction was in part a reaction to his publication of Parliament's debates without abridgment or permission. The jury's ruling, that Almon was responsible for what he himself published and what he chose to reprint from others' publications, "would obviously have a bearing on the type of work that booksellers would be willing to support and sell, and, consequently, on the literature of the period. Indeed, Almon's situation provides a particularly dramatic instance of the influence of the law and politics on a bookseller and his output" (p. 48). In fact, Almon, under order of the law to avoid political publishing, ceased any overt political publishing, turning instead to collecting fugitive pieces of belletristic literature, on the model of Dodsley's *Collection,* which he published under the title, *The New Foundling Hospital of Wit.* Almon's collection is another index to public taste in the eighteenth century, and for the modern reader the value of his work persists as Almon collected lesser-known pieces by the famous authors Dodsley published.

In 1771, Parliament's ability to suppress newspaper publishers like Almon was questioned in a trial that became known as "The Printer's Case." Almon was of considerable importance in the proceeding's success, and he won greater freedom for the press by his boldness in challenging the authority of Parliament to prohibit the publication of Parliamentary debates. The bookseller's interest in politics, especially in Wilkes's return as M.P. for Middlesex, is evident in extant letters between Almon and the politician John Calcraft, which show that Almon, although forbidden to publish on political subjects, retained an active role in political matters and continued to supply and transmit information privately in correspondence.

Due to his and his wife's poor health, Almon retired temporarily from publishing in 1781, after over twenty years in the trade. During his last years as a bookseller, Almon had published pro-American Revolutionary War pamphlets; Rogers has recovered some interesting letters from grateful Americans and prints them as notes. Almon returned to London in 1784, and opened a second shop in Fleet Street. Little is known of Almon's final years as a bookseller except that he was fined for libeling Charles James Fox and then the King, and soon after he sold off his newspaper *The General Advertiser,* declared bankruptcy, and fled prosecution for failure to appear in court. After about two-and-a-half years at large, Almon surrendered, and, at age fifty-two, he was imprisoned and served thirteen months. For the remaining twelve years of his life, Almon lived at Box Moor and concentrated his literary efforts on such seemingly benign projects as his *Biographical, Literary and Political Anecdotes* (three volumes, 1797), an edition, with biographical memoir, of Wilkes's letters (1805), and the posthumously published edition of the Junius letters (1806).

Although Almon's publishing and association with Wilkes and the Opposition have been studied before, Rogers makes an important contribution in presenting Almon in the broader context of political repression and showing how it directly affected what a bookseller would or would not do. The letters she recovered from the British Museum, the Perkins Library at Duke University, and the New York Historical Society illustrate how Almon perceived himself as a pioneer in publishing, "making information available to the public." By restoring deleted parts of the Calcraft letters (elisions done by Almon himself) and closely examining the dealings Almon had with Wilkes and Temple, Rogers shows how Almon survived repressive attempts by manipulating the manipulators on their own playing field. No sooner was he prohibited from publishing political pamphlets in 1768, than he won "The Printer's Case" for freedom of the press. Through the *Eighteenth Century Short Title Catalog*, Rogers also illustrates the fact that Almon did not stop writing political pamphlets while under restrictions as was previously believed. Her publication of Almon's book lists, both the titles he wrote and the titles he published, increases the value of her book since future research into the patterns of his publishing is likely. Familiarity with Almon's imprisonment and struggles against the government makes it easier to account for Robert Dodsley's conservatism. Dodsley saved himself a great deal of time, money, and potential hardship by leaving anti-establishment work to others such as Mary Cooper, who unlike himself—for whom imprisonment was a sufficient lesson—was prosecuted and fined for libel on at least three occasions.

These two books are valuable additions to the literature on publishing history. Through them, we are able to understand the climate of publishing in the eighteenth century, the relationships between authors and booksellers, and the important role the bookseller could play in society if he were willing to take risks and uphold his convictions, whether political or literary.

Note

1. "London Trade Publishers, 1675–1750," *The Library*, 6th series, IV (1982), 99–134.

Through Forthrights and Meanders: Notes on Notes on Walking

Elizabeth Sewell

Jeffrey C. Robinson. *The Walk: Notes on a Romantic Image.* Norman and London: University of Oklahoma Press, 1989. xi, 139 pp.

Gonzalo lends me his words as we start our ambulation through this book on The Walk; lends some vestige of a persona, too, partly because he and I are probably about the same age, partly because Gonzalo is grumbling, mildly. Some time ago the invitation, "Lead off this ground!" was spoken and we fell in, he to search for a lost prince, we (searching also in our own way perhaps) to accompany an author through a peregrination of some 140 pages. Who would have thought that this undertaking would prove to be such surprisingly hard work? Not until much later did I realize that the first chapter opens with a midday walk in Denver and the last chapter closes with a midday walk on Sixth Avenue in Manhattan. I should have read the omens as well as the book.

It is far from easy to say what this book is about. Subject matter: this is the first of four categories I am going to take to try to keep myself from Gonzaloish garrulity, rambling on about walking; the other three are form, image, and author. We can ask the author's help: "What is this phenomenon, the walk that urges me to write? How have people in the past two hundred years written about it?" (p. 5). Shortly after, we come upon this:

I have written in the following pages commentaries on walking and on the literary history of walking: phenomenological inquiry, autobiographical or genetic touchstones for my relationship to the subject, analyses of literary and visual objects, surveys of types of walkers or particular historical or national literatures of walking, my own writing of a walk. [p. 5]

On page 6 Robinson calls his work "my meditation." Later we meet "writing walking" (p. 7) and "thinking walking" (p. 39) twice over. We are directed towards the walk as an image, "a quintessentially Romantic image," Robinson says (p. 5). One begins to try to hold all of this together. My already nascent sense of confusion is a little consoled by the fact that the Library of Congress Catalogue needs no less than five headings to categorize this short book: "1. English literature—History and criticism. 2. Walking in literature. 3. Romanticism. 4. Walking. 5. American literature—History and criticism." I am not the only one to perceive complexity.

If unified content fails the searching mind, can we turn to form as a means of providing unity or continuity? *The Walk* offers us thirteen chapters, all brief, frequently divided into shorter named sub-sections: The Foot and the Leg, The Walk as Comedy, Sidewalks and Streets, The Walk and Silence, and so on. Perhaps these could be considered as essays. Chapter 4 has as its title, "The Walking Essay and the Compulsion to Collect." Perhaps the whole book could be regarded as a long essay. But no, Robinson has chosen to call it "Notes." Notes suggest something provisional, of which one has no right to demand aesthetic unity. The walking essay, we read on page 33, can be looked at as a series of encounters. That may help to carry us forward.

For as we progress through these pages, this is indeed what meets us, a very large number of writers who walk, who write while walking, who write about walking, from the "vast and ever-expanding literature of walking" (p. 5). From memory now, let me put down some of those encountered here: Hazlitt, Hardy, Thomas Mann, Virgil, Socrates, Wallace Stevens, Virginia Woolf, Coleridge and the Wordsworths and De Quincey, Dickens, Valéry, Edgar Allan Poe, Hermann Hesse (whom Robinson takes a swipe at as he goes by), Dante, Sterne, E. V. Lucas, Homer, Rousseau, A. R. Ammons, Kafka, Marge Piercy, André Breton, Robert Louis Stevenson, Wollstonecraft, Aldous Huxley—and I hope your brain is spinning, for mine is, and there are many

Through Forthrights and Meanders 199

more. They, or we, go by so swiftly, a page or two apiece, half a page. Where a longer breathing-space is given, with Hazlitt for instance, or Basho (the extracts quoted are beautiful), or even that bounder Rousseau, there is real opportunity for profit and enjoyment. The author seems to be aware of the discomfort this too-muchness induces. He speaks of losing control over ideas "through the vertigo of profusion" (p. 39), and elsewhere of an impulse which keeps "blurring the edges of my ordinary good sense of when enough is enough" (p. 109).

There are two footnotes to this excess, this profusion. One of them is the author's; one is mine. His footnote, so to speak, is the bibliographical essay appended at the very end of the book, where we are given yet more, "some directions for further reading in a very large literature" (p. 135). My footnote is Gonzalo complaining, and this time with real feeling. "Some heavenly power guide us!"—for there is *no index* to this book. How are we ever to locate those thronging references, apart from the mere ten names which appear in chapter titles and hence in the table of contents? And since I have mentioned footnotes, this may be the moment to enter one more grumble: there are entirely too many misprints in this attractively produced little volume. And from a university press too, from whom we have the right, I would think, to expect something better than slipshod. Spelling errors show up, such as "repellant" or "double base" for the musical instrument, or "my principle object" (shades of freshman composition!). Proper names fare rather worse, "Linneaus," "Gaskill," "Susperia," "The City or Dreadful Night," "Marye Piercy," and "Williams Wordsworth" (which I rather like). All these peccant objects shall share one list of numbers: pp. 57, 107, 131, 73, 87, 133, 132, 128, 58.

Next, we can turn our attention to the Image as such, and with it, the imagination. If one is working with an image, that image should generate enough formative energy in the mind to make the subject matter cohere. This can be thought of as the very function of image and imagination working together. *Einbildung* in the German, our imagination, is in fact *In-eins-bildung*, forming-into-one, Coleridge maintains[1]. His etymologies are not necessarily reliable, but his point is clear. Is The Walk, the action of walking as such, not an image in the deeper symbolic sense, but a picture or reproduction of a human activity, essential enough—we note when small children take their first steps just as we do when they utter their first identifiable words—but devoid or symbolic meaning? I am not sure about this, and tried using other equivalents. The Swim—could one write cohesively, which is to say artistically, about that? The Dance, certainly. The Upright Stance, perhaps; one recalls Ovid's lovely half-line: "*et vultus ad sidera tollit.*" The actual pictures in this book, the illustrations, the Giacometti figure, Blake's Traveller, the Kertesz photographs, are rewarding, and there are interesting passages in the text about paintings: Constable, Gainsborough, van Ruisdael, I remember, and one whole chapter on the author's walk (he taking notes as he goes) through an exhibition of Degas' work at the Metropolitan Museum in New York.

Again looking for comparisons, this time of a book of multiple entries centred round an image, I came up with W. H. Auden's *The Enchafèd Flood*. The Sea is a coadunating image, no doubt, and Auden's book does wander as this one does, yet succeeds in holding together, partly because of power of image perhaps, or because he uses recurring and specific literary landmarks (seamarks?); the dream in *The Prelude, Moby-Dick, The Hunting of the Snark*. Robinson himself questions his own image at one point: "The image of the walk seems, so to speak, to undermine its status as image. It is not an image (like God, or the State, or Family) in which one can finally rest, even though many writers—particularly in the nineteenth century—may have tried" (p. 42).

Having mentioned Coleridge, I wonder whether *The Walk* might best be taken as a long "Conversation Piece," like "This Lime-tree Bower my Prison," where Coleridge imagines the walk his friends are taking, he himself being unable to accompany them because of an injured foot. Sitting with the book of Robinson underneath the bough, so to speak, I found this to be one of the chief virtues of this small but densely packed volume, the conjuring up in the imagination of walks stored up in the memory. It sent me back, and may do the same for other readers, to childhood and youth, in my case in England. Being taken for a walk (the indefinite article does seem more comfortable than the definite) was a steady part of one's young existence; long walks, often exhaustingly long walks—"Don't *drag*, child!"—crowd into memory, in Sussex and Surrey, school walks in small groups in Berkshire and Kent, long treks with my sister and later alone all over the wide heathlands where Dorset meets Hampshire, the edge of William the Conqueror's New Forest. For a time also in my childhood we lived in London, and walks were a delight there also, the Embankment along the Thames with the splendid bridges, the old houses in Cheyne Row, the rainbow colors of spilt petrol on a wet roadway. City walks come in for good measure in Robinson's book. Here enter the French, and one wonders: do the French really go in for walking at all except in Paris? It is Robert Louis Stevenson who takes, and then pens, "Travels with a Donkey in the Cévennes," which we read as a set text in school when we were twelve or so. Yes, there is one Frenchman at least who walks, Charles Péguy, but we will meet him a little later on.

Mulling over the nature of the walk, as this book invites or even compels one to do, I realized that for me the essence lies in the observation of what Blake calls Minute Particulars, which then become the ground of highly detailed and pleasurable memories. I am a picker-up of things—jewelry, money, a young neighbor's checkbook recently, a pass to a top-secret government department in London during the last war. It seems to me that I do not think at all when I take a walk. Robinson describes in himself and in fellow-spirits such as Hazlitt or Thoreau the process of walking as a process of thinking, critical, literary, sociological, philosophical. This seems to me very strange, because I belong to the other club, those who, to initiate and encourage thinking, demand solitude, a comfortable place to sit, silence. Whether one prefers to walk alone or in company, both of which Robinson discusses, seems to fit in here.

The other, connected, pleasure this book gives is that it stirs the memory of other walks in literature, beyond those many to which Robinson introduces us or of which he reminds us. Very sensibly he says he never intended to do a complete survey of all the riches here offered by other writers. His insistence on walking as a Romantic image sent me drifting back to Cowper, not a poet I know at all well, to read again what I had vaguely remembered, Books 5 and 6 of *The Task,* entitled respectively "The

Winter Morning Walk" and "The Winter Walk at Noon." The date is 1785, but despite the eighteenth-century air these poems have, they are after all only eight years earlier than Wordsworth's poem, "An Evening Walk," so Cowper conceivably belongs in that rather mysterious company we heard about in college, *Préromantisme*.

The invitation to search the memory for other literary walks is irresistible, despite the slight irritation audible in Robinson's remark, "No one has ever engaged me on the subject of walking literature who has not offered an instance that 'simply can't be left out'" (p. 5). I wanted to add to the author's stupendous collection the great walk of the Lama and Kim in Kipling's story and the magnificent description of the river of life on the Grand Trunk Road; the walk in Arnold's "Thyrsis"; Hölderlin's legendary walk across France into Germany and madness, and Edwin Muir's poem about that, "Hölderlin's Journey"; *Tobit* in the Apocrypha, young man, angel, and dog walking from Nineveh to Ecbatana, and James Bridie's charming dramatization of it in the thirties; Stifter's *Der Nachsommer* where the young hero walks and counter-walks his central European mountains as a means of self-education, and one day turns off the road to ask at the *Rosenhaus* for shelter from a threatening storm which in fact never arrives. I remember our German professor saying to us, "When you have read this you will spend weeks wishing passionately that the *Rosenhaus* existed and that you could walk to it and be taken in," and he was right. Dream-walks might form yet another sub-section of this subject, but we have enough apart from one name briefly mentioned a little while back—Charles Péguy. Péguy was a true walker, but what I have in mind here is a walk of a particular kind, recounted in his long poem, "Présentation de la Beauce à Notre-Dame de Chartres," the pilgrimage on foot from Paris to Chartres, 144 kilometers in three days, as he tells us. This pilgrim walks and (later) writes, observes, and describes, with realism and humor, but does not think so much as meditate or pray, if that is the right word here, the intentions toward God and Our Lady in that huge plain which almost annihilates the individual in its vastness, the walker spurred on through engrossing weariness by the sight of the exquisite spire on the far horizon, "la flèche unique au monde." There was a walk indeed.

In the end, however, I would cycle back to—above all others—Dorothy Wordsworth of the Grasmere Journal (not her German or Scottish journals, which are interesting enough but not magical); to the younger Coleridge and the wonderful walks of which the Notebooks between 1799 and 1803 are full; and one not mentioned yet, not mentioned by Robinson either, the Reverend Francis Kilvert who in his all too brief mid-Victorian life crossed and recrossed the beautiful country between England and Wales, among his beloved people, and recorded it in his diary. Great walkers all, they would fall under Robinson's criticism of the walk seen as Romantic idyll, he preferring dialectic as model for the inner nature of the walk, and he may link up here with Aldous Huxley's useful essay, "Wordsworth in the Tropics," where England, indeed all Europe, is claimed to be so "well-gardened" that it effectively conceals Nature's indifferent or even hostile otherness.[2]

Yet none of this literary talk explains or expunges what I have called "magic" above, a word to be used very sparingly and in the meaning of: a power one perceives and submits to but does not understand. Gonzalo would recognize it. Type of landscape (and cityscape) and one's relationship to it are certainly involved, and perhaps the activity of traversing those spaces as well, but I think the person of the author enters in also. "Author" was my last category for ordering these thoughts, I remember, and I have left it until much too late. It seems as if these especially appreciated walker-writers offer not just companionship but something more subtle and exhilarating. It could be that they make a second, congenial solitude available to one's own, and on those terms one would walk with them forever.

Notes

1. Samuel Taylor Coleridge, *Anima Poetae*, ed. Ernest Hartley Coleridge (London: Heinemann, 1845), p. 236.

2. Aldous Huxley, *Do What You Will* (Garden City, N.J.: Doubleday Doran, 1929), pp. 123–39.

Mr. Badman, Presented

Jim Springer Borck

John Bunyan. *The Life and Death of Mr. Badman: Presented to the World in a Familiar Dialogue Between Mr. Wiseman, and Mr. Attentive.* Edited by James F. Forrest and Roger Sharrock. Oxford: Clarendon Press, 1988. xlii, 188 pp.

There can't be any quarrel about the qualifications James Forrest and Roger Sharrock bring as editors for this, the last volume of the Clarendon John Bunyan. The history of their collaboration on Bunyan's "major" works is instructive towards an understanding of just how good the editorial standards of the *Mr. Badman* volume are. Forrest's 1967 New York University Press edition of *The Holy War* (1682) was the first reliable text of that work to appear in sixty years. Together with the still very frequently read *John Bunyan,* which Sharrock published in 1954 and revised for republication in 1968, it provides a scholarly rationale for this fourth and last volume in the edited major works, a project begun in the 1950s. Sharrock's individually edited volumes began appearing in 1960 with the appearance (then) of *The Pilgrim's Progress,* soon followed by *Grace Abounding to the Chief of Sinners* (1962), and eighteen years later by *The Holy War.* These volumes have appeared alongside Oxford University Press's thirteen-volume Miscellaneous Works and, like the volume under review here, share their format and editorial principles (though not their numbering in the volume series).

When in 1980, under Oxford's publication schedule for its edition of Bunyan's works, Forrest joined Sharrock to re-edit *The Holy War,* he augmented an already extensive introduction to the New York University Press edition (Louis Martz assisted him in authoring that introduction), and emended the editorial practices of his 1967 text. In his earlier text, Forrest had modernized the spelling, excised some of the initial capitals, and changed the punctuation to bring it "more into line with current practice."[1] By 1980, adopting stricter editorial practices, acknowledging the rhetorical purpose that pointings had for a seventeenth-century reader, and looking to present "a text that most fully accords with Bunyan's artistic conception,"[2] Forrest and Sharrock exhibit the flawless principles which have been extended to the 1988 *Mr. Badman*.

Though there isn't much of a problem in choosing the first edition of *Mr. Badman* as the copy-text for the 1988 edition, and though the date of the 1688 second edition might have been a graceful note for a tercentenary edition, the firm hand applied in selecting the British Library copy (C.59.a7) appears to have been correct. Forrest and Sharrock have added five woodcuts from a later state of 1696 (woodcuts which are also found in the second edition). Bunyan himself may have inserted these in a few copies; they are cuts which the editors note "were executed by an artist not noticeably scrupulous about accuracy of representation" (p. xxxix). The importance of these cuts, whether they inform the text or are curiosities, Bunyan and the editors appear to have left to their readers to evaluate. But it is generous of Forrest and Sharrock to have included them, perhaps for emblem study, however minor.

The history of Forrest and Sharrock's textual partnership is also important because it informs the reading of *Mr. Badman* they provide in the introduction and endnotes to the 1988 edition. That is, the somewhat narrow "allegorical" reading of the text in the earlier *The Holy War*, admittedly a different work than *Mr. Badman*, is expanded by a decade or so of scholarship, and by Sharrock's collaboration, to create a discussion of that volume's historical context, its epic structure, and a form "that might be called the typical second novel."[3] By 1982, Forrest and Richard L. Greaves had also collected and edited the G. K. Hall reference guide to John Bunyan, a very large task by any reckoning, as (for example) they estimate more than 1300 editions of *The Pilgrim's Progress* to have been printed by 1938, and the corresponding commentary is equally enormous.[4] This command of three centuries of public and private discourse which informs *Mr. Badman* recommends the 1988 introduction as an authoritative critical overview.

The text itself is forbidding, and a reader approaching it for the first time would do well to read Sharrock's thematic and characterological rephrasing of it in his *John Bunyan* (1954/1968), especially chapter 5, "Mr. Badman," pp. 106–17. Sharrock's critical approach in this chapter-length evaluation causes him to present *Mr. Badman* as "Bunyan's nearest approach to the novel" and to argue that it in some degree anticipates Defoe's own narrative style (pp. 116–17). By 1988 this novelistic emphasis is qualified further by the two editors' splendid discussion of *Mr. Badman* as a multi-faceted prose narrative, "the confluence of a number of literary kinds—the dialogue, the judgment-book, the picaresque, the exemplum, the posthumous, and even (by negative example) the conduct-book" (p. xxx). Viewed in this pluralist light, the text becomes less closed to our twentieth-century eyes, even though most readers of the Oxford text probably don't now share in quite the same way the moral, social, and theocentric values Bunyan sets before them. And despite our own day of iron-tower moralists who argue gender and social persuasions in the academy, perhaps the audience is a larger one than we might otherwise guess, for in the introduction Forrest and Sharrock establish a good case for considering this Puritan tract as literature.

One real value of modern editions of relatively obscure texts is their appeal to a specialized audience: they tend to generate dissertations, then articles, and then books. Though Bunyan would not have been aware of this scholarly progression, he did of course want his book to be studied albeit within the stern Christian literary genres towards which Forrest and Sharrock point us. Bunyan is quite clear about who he thinks his intended audience is *not:* "Reader if thou art of the race, lineage, stock or fraternity of Mr. *Badman,* I tell thee before thou readest this Book, thou wilt neither brook the author nor it, because he hath writ of Mr. *Badman* as he has" (p. 4). However fortunate his discrimination may be in filtering out possible extravagances in twentieth-century scholarly examination, it is within the context which Bunyan provides for his own contemporary reader that we garner an appropriate audience response for our own age, the wavering yet moral person who is tempted by the fast buck and/or those readers who have succumbed to the blandishments of, as W. H. Auden phrased it, a clever line or a good lay.

Bunyan tells his reader in relatively moderate doomsday terminology (moderate by seventeenth- and eighteenth-century apocalyptic written rhetorical standards of social commentators like Ebenezer Coppe or Samuel Cooke) that English civilization totters drunkenly at the brink of cultural collapse because of the million or so ("thousands of thousands") of Badman's relatives and friends who adulate him as a role model. And though Bunyan acknowledges that, because humans possess both sense and reason, perhaps some of those disciples can be changed from following Badman's example, he also seems to dismiss most of this horde ("turn my back on them") in much the same manner as the two narrators turn away from Mr. Badman—Mr. Wiseman by the beginning of the interlocutions, and Mr. Attentive by the dialogue's conclusion. In this light, Bunyan's persona is Wiseman speaking *with* Attentive, for he reserves his attention for the one soul who understands that "open rebuke is better than secret love." So the dialogue between Attentive and Wiseman is meant to be read as Bunyan's sermon delivered while Badman lies awaiting burial: "He is not buried as yet, nor doth he stink, as is designed he shall, before he lies down in oblivion" (pp. 1–10). Here too his colloquy isn't a posthumous one, just as Badman's history which follows Bunyan's "The Author to the Reader" isn't exactly an exemplum or a negative conduct-book in the traditional sense of those genres. To have been so would have made this edition much less valuable than it is to his audiences, however good the scholarly apparatus is—and it is good. Limited to one such literary mode, the chances are most readers of any period would have responded as did the Host of the Tabard Inn and the Knight to the Monk's dreary chronicles, and as do most thankful undergraduates to that interrupted Chaucerian tale.

Rather, the artistic merit of *Mr. Badman* lies in Mr. Wiseman's illustrative stories, for in them Bunyan argues that the world is structured by a series of unbreakable interactions between man and man, and man and God: "There is no man . . . that is sensible of the worth of one Soul, but must, when he hears of the death of unconverted men, he stinks with sorrow and grief" (p. 15). To lack feeling is to have a pathology, whether seventeenth- or twentieth-century. The dialogue as narrative structure parallels this world where an attentive audience can be found—one which listens to, and is affected by, instruction in how to remain a human being. Whether it is Chaucer's "Retraction," Swift's satiric verses on his own death, Jane Austen concluding her first novel by having Henry Tilney reprimand Catherine Moreland after Catherine's mistaken evaluation of the events surrounding his mother's death, Melville having Ishmael seize upon an unusual flotation device in the last chapter of *Moby-Dick,* or Hubert Selby, Jr., centering his New York novel around an apocryphal last exit to Brooklyn, Bunyan, like these authors, uses the inescapable honesty of a final departure to point an audience away from behavior which causes social death.

Literature is better at this than tracts, sermons, or self-help psychiatric booklets; as Chaucer sums up his tales in the "Retraction": "Fore our book saith, 'Al that is writen is writen for oure doctrine.'" That the life and death of Mr. Badman is the recollective history of a man who is an outlaw means that, paradoxically, his is the *bildungsroman* of a hero who, because he is psychologically dead, dies "two deaths at once" (p. 15). A merchant who lives by cheating his customers, a husband who is unfaithful to his wife and who marries for power, not love, and a human who cannot be trusted to make human responses to human situations, Badman is spiritually dead before he dies a chronological death. In addition to offering an example of the outsider in a theocentric society, *Mr. Badman* provides a wealth of historical data and observations taken from a mercantile and quite middle-class society. Bunyan gives rules for properly maintaining an employer/employee relationship (pp. 39–49, 79), to what uses a man may correctly invest his wife's dowry (pp. 65–69), and in what ways a retailer can morally turn a profit (pp. 87–117). Under this rather important trade-oriented umbrella, moreover, are to be found guidelines for rearing children, fostering long-term relationships with friends, and keeping oneself happily married (pp. 75–78, 126–32, and 69–75, 132–36), all directives which are supplied by Mr. Wiseman in details as fascinating as those found in Pepys's diary, Moll Flanders's various careers, the 1684 *Compleat Tradesman*, or, much later, Boswell's own journals.

Badman's death is, as his life has been, a bad one. Though his theocentric values are damning and his interpersonal values sociopathic, it is in his misuse of human language that the reader finds the most appalling absence of moral valuing. In Badman's youth, Wiseman concludes, he freely swore oaths and lies, primarily because "Swearing flows from that daring Boldness that biddeth defiance to the Law that forbids it" (p. 29), a defiance that extends into all areas of wrong discourse. Not merely do such men swear, Wiseman says, to be wicked in commerce, and "to get Gain thereby," but they "have little in their mouths but a sentence against their Neighbor" (pp. 29, 30). His wife suffers also, as have his parents, neighbors, and customers: "Upon a time, she was on a Lords day for going to hear a Sermon, and Mr. *Badman* was unwilling she should." Yet in a series of plaintive asides, all notched by the abused wife putting "on more courage than she was wont," she insists that her "Soul ought to be more unto me, than all the world besides" (p. 79). Following her defiance from a feminist perspective, or not, the reader is pleased when she continues to insist, even if Badman falls into a rage and gives her "an ugly wish," that "no man can stop me" (pp. 78–79, 141). Unable to love those to whom he is biocentrically, emotionally, or contractually bonded, it isn't surprising that in his pride he dies unconverted to goodness, expiring quietly in "blindness of mind, and hardness of heart" (p. 164).

The purpose of *Mr. Badman* extends far past the concerns of sociology, psychology, literary theory, and history, attractive as the concerns of those disciplines may be. Mr. Badman as a central character occupies a fairly unique place in literature in that he does not repent, even upon his deathbed. Because (in literature, anyway) villains usually recant their anti-social careers—Lady Macbeth, Blifil, Lovelace, Bill Sykes, and Jason Compson are a few examples—the closed-off world of the criminal serves to reassure the audience that the non-miscreant world is an ordered one, integrated and interdependent because human relationships with each other and to God demand kindness, honesty, and love. Sooner or later the outside world intrudes in such a manner that the misbehaving hero cannot ignore it, a moment which happens, say, either by a knocking at the castle gate during the Porter's watch or by a flat tire on a gravelly Mississippi road. No such moment happens in *Mr. Badman*, though a good deal of attention is hopefully extended by Mr. Wiseman to Badman's death, an attention which he gives, as Bunyan has posited in the author's preface, in "sorrow and grief" for the unconverted. And in the description of Badman's death, the reader is exposed to the conclusion which finishes a teleology of a bad man's life. The interpolated tales, the authorial asides, the interlocutory nature of Mr. Attentive's questions, and Mr. Badman's repellant history, in total present a biography of a wretched man.

In his darkness, Mr. Badman constructs for a modern reader a Sartrean hero in conflict with a world order which, though it will create a place for him, and materially reward him for his temporal objectives, will withhold the reward a humane individual might gain—the love of another when cold winds blow and night falls. It is a conclusion which points to why *Mr. Badman* is literature, and why the book retains for us, thanks to Forrest and Sharrock, its rightful place in that canon.

Notes

1. "Bibliographic Note" to *The Holy War* (New York: New York Univ. Press, 1967), p. xix.
2. "Notes on the Text," *The Holy War* (Oxford: Clarendon, 1980), p. xlvii.
3. "Introduction" to the 1980 Oxford edition of *The Holy War*, p. xxxv.
4. "Preface" to *John Bunyan: A Reference Guide* (Boston: G. K. Hall, 1982), p. vii.

Confronting Nightmares: The Dalhousie Manuscripts

Arthur F. Kinney

Ernest W. Sullivan, II, ed. *The First and Second Dalhousie Manuscripts: Poems and Prose by John Donne and Others: A Facsimile Edition.* Columbia: University of Missouri Press, 1988. x, 230 pp.

Editing the poetry of John Donne has always been notoriously difficult. When Donne died in 1631, only four of his poems had seen publication: *The Anatomie of the World* (1611), the "First Anniversary," republished as a part of *The First and Second Anniversaries* in 1612 with subsequent editions in 1621 and 1626, and the related "Elegy on Prince Henry" in 1613. In addition, his Latin verses on Ben Jonson's *Volpone* were printed in 1606–7. Yet there is substantial evidence that he had composed *Metempsychosis* around August 1601 and most of the songs, sonnets, verse epistles, and satires by which we know him best before 1620. Moreover, while there are plentiful manuscripts extant of various of his works, there is almost none that is holograph. Thus "No editor of Donne's poems," A. J. Smith notes in the preface to his Penguin edition of *The Complete English Poems* in 1971, "can be confident that he is printing just what Donne wrote."[1]

Nor does subsequent publishing history help us much. Six editions of the *Poems* were published in the seventeenth century, some shortly before Donne's death, but they present problems of their own. The monumental text published early in this century, that of Sir Herbert Grierson, is based on the first of these, that of 1633—indeed, "To vindicate the text of 1633" is Grierson's first principle—and while it is still thought to be the most reliable, it has problems.[2] For one thing, it is incomplete; the 1635 edition adds new poems. For another, it has an inferior ordering of some poems and inferior texts of others, both matters corrected in the text of 1635. Two additional sonnets appeared in 1649 and, unchanged, perhaps using the same sheets, these were incorporated into the edition of 1650, the first and only text edited by the younger John Donne, whose close personal relationship proclaims yet another kind of indisputable authority. Finally, the edition of 1669, according to Grierson, shows evidence of collation from new, independent, and superior manuscripts for some of its variants. The Westmoreland manuscript at the New York Public Library, for instance, which A. L. Clements finds "of high textual value," is "the sole authority for several poems not printed in [any of] the early editions, most notably for Holy Sonnets XVII, XVIII, and XIX."[3]

Thus we can readily understand Smith's frustration. "With a few possible exceptions," he continues, "Donne's own drafts of his poems never reached the press, and only one copy of an English poem in his own hand has survived. Indeed the evidence is that even the best of the early manuscript collections and printed editions we have stand at several removes from the original copies, and multiply copying errors or select by accident from the several versions of a poem that Donne himself had put about" (p. 13). Even the chronological ordering of poems is problematic, for we have no clear date for the composition of any of them. And the only contemporary clue—the biographer Izaak Walton's division of the poetry into types and genres—is really no clue at all; if we followed Walton, Donne would be composing several love lyrics while struggling with the very different *First Anniversary*. Conversely, though, contextual details suggest that in the spring of 1613 Donne was, in fact, writing, in succession, the erotic St. Valentine's Day *Epithalamion,* the pious *Good Friday, 1613. Riding Westward* and *The Primrose;* secular poetry followed the composition of the Holy Sonnets; and much of his best religious poetry, in Smith's judgment, comes from Donne's time at Mitcham when he was still anxious to attract patrons at court and just as stubbornly refusing to take holy orders.

We can add to such editorial problems Donne's notoriously complicated poetry. For the appreciative Coleridge, Donne was one

Confronting Nightmares

> whose muse on dromedary trots,
> Wreathe iron pokers into true-love knots;
> Rhyme's sturdy cripple, fancy's maze and clue,
> Wit's forge and fire-blast, meaning's press and screw.[4]

In his own time, Donne's contemporary Thomas Carew recognized perforce what C. A. Patrides has called his "robust metrical and linguistic calisthenics":[5]

> Our stubborne language bends, made only fit
> With her tough-thick-rib'd hoopes to gird about
> Thy Giant phansie.[6]

In between, in 1899, Francis Thompson paid tribute to his fellow poet Donne as "pungent, clever, with metre like a rope all hanks and knots."[7] Little wonder, then, that Patrides himself, in his 1985 edition of *The Complete English Poems of John Donne,* claims that "The text of Donne's poetry can vex an editor into nightmares" (p. 1).

Such vexed editors have confronted their nightmares in individual ways. For Grierson, who noted corruption in the precious 1633 edition when collated with various manuscripts, it was nevertheless a matter of retreat:

A short examination of the manuscripts convinced me that it would be very unsafe to base a text on any single extant manuscript [as Grosart had done in the nineteenth century], or even to make an eclectic use of a few of them, taking, now from one, now from another, what seemed a probable emendation [as Greg had done]. On the other hand it became clear that if as wide a collation as possible of extant manuscripts were made one would be able to establish in many cases what was, whether right or wrong, the traditional reading before any printed edition appeared.

A few experiments further showed that one, and a very important, result of this collation would be to confirm the trustworthiness of 1633 (p. v). For Helen Gardner, it could be a matter of various editions: in her 1952 edition of *The Divine Poems of John Donne* she took the initial twelve holy sonnets, in order, from 1633, four later interpolated in the 1635 sequence she took out and made into a separate grouping, and a third set she took from the Westmoreland manuscript;[8] while in *The Elegies and the Songs and Sonnets,* her 1965 text of the secular poems, she is wonderfully eclectic: "Donne is a great writer and a daring one, and I cannot think his editor should be timid. I have, therefore, felt at liberty to exercise my own judgement between the readings of Groups I and II [of the manuscript tradition] and have not automatically accepted the choice made in the edition of 1633. Again, in poems that are not found in the manuscripts of Group I and that the edition of 1633 took from a Group II manuscript, I have at times preferred the reading of Group III."[9] Her method switched again with the *Elegies.* "Of the fourteen that I print together, one was not printed until the nineteenth century; two appeared in 1635, one printed from the highly idiosyncratic *O'Flaherty,* and the other from a poor manuscript; and two were first printed in 1669, also from poor manuscripts. The text of these five poems has to be reconstructed from reliable manuscript tradition" (pp. xci–xcii). Another Clarendon editor, W. Milgate, edited his text of *The Epithalamions, Anniversaries, and Epicedes* (1978) by emending Grierson's text with subsequently discovered manuscript variants.[10] Equally eclectic is John Hayward, whose Nonesuch text (1929) reprinted by Penguin (1950–58) and the Heritage Press in the United States (1970) modifies the printed editions of both 1633 and 1635 with "a number of textually important MS collections which were in circulation while Donne was still alive [and] amended in a few places in the light of later knowledge or more mature consideration," which are presumably Hayward's own, he matching Gardner for boldness.[11] The most popular modern text, that of John T. Shawcross in 1967, is the most ambitious because it searches out all then-known manuscripts and builds its own "eclectic" and "somewhat subjectively based" version on his own best critical judgment.[12] The result, at the other end of the spectrum initiated by Grierson, he finds necessary because "a revision of Grierson's, eschewing certain misreadings which often seem to have arisen from delicacy and certain modernizations which obscure subtleties, has long been needed" (p. xxii).

It is just this gallimaufry of Donne's texts that Ernest W.

Sullivan, II, addresses in his magisterial edition of the first and second Dalhousie manuscripts, and from the first he makes no bones about it. The claims he sets forth for his work—claims on the whole justified—are at first sweeping and breathtaking. He says at the outset:

[This edition] revises our knowledge of the genesis and transmission of John Donne's poetic manuscripts by placing the Dalhousie manuscripts very early in the major Donne manuscript traditions. The discussions of the textual and critical significance of the Dalhousie manuscripts establish their importance to Donne textual and critical studies, and the textual apparatus provides the first complete listing of the substantive variants among Donne's seven, seventeenth-century collected editions/issues for the forty-six Dalhousie Donne poems. Further discovery that the Dalhousie I manuscript derives from papers preserved by the Essex family and that the Essex collection became the basis for the British Library MS. Lansdowne 740 and, ultimately, Trinity College Dublin MS. 877 suggests that Donne's patrons and poetical coterie, rather than Donne himself, may lie behind the major manuscript collections of his poems; and the deliberate nature of the Dalhousie collections has important implications for the study of Renaissance verse and culture generally. With this publication, the known manuscript locations for the Dalhousie poems are dramatically expanded, making it possible to trace the manuscript circulation of poems by several important Renaissance poets. [II, vii]

In one hugely significant gesture, Sullivan moves the old cosmos of textual editing into our contemporary world of the new historicism, showing how coterie demands and the tastes of patrons—directed or guessed at—shaped poems individually as well as motivated certain patterns and sequences of poems. Moving from Grierson, Sullivan would equally embrace the argument—compelling and dubious by turn—that Arthur Marotti has recently made for the political and social conditions behind many of Donne's compositions.[13]

To begin at the beginning: in 1977 the bibliographer Peter Beal discovered at the Scottish Record Office in Edinburgh two manuscripts in the depository of the Dalhousie family which contained poems by John Donne and his contemporaries. Both manuscripts soon arrived at Texas Tech University, where

Sullivan teaches and where he could work on them intensively. Dalhousie I, he found, suffered no harm in this transportation; it remained well-bound in very old reinforced paper stitched with "very old leather thongs," but since there is only slight water staining and a few worm holes, and since many pages are complete folio sheets (folded once) rather than loose leaves, it would seem hardly worn: this despite the fact that neither the binding nor the actual stitching is original. Sadly, the manuscript has been somewhat trimmed in the process, but happily no text has been lost and the crowded text on some pages matches this slimming of edges.

Dalhousie I (which he calls, for his university, TT1), has sixty-nine leaves constituting poems in five different hands, the work of these copyists unevenly distributed: 1A, folios 1–10, 11–20$_v$, 62$_v$–63$_v$; 1B, folios 10$_v$–11; 1C, folios 21–62; 1D, folio 62$_v$; and 1E, folios 64–69$_v$. Despite the scattered contributions, Sullivan registers no doubt that he has a manuscript with all the leaves properly reassembled.

Since TT1 has obviously been bound in its current order for a long time, and since its sheets lay unnoticed (and, presumably, undisturbed) for so long, the current order, despite the possibility of lost materials, likely approximates the original. Unfortunately, the presence of only three catchwords (two on rectos and one before a missing leaf!) and of twenty-three blank pages as well as an apparent effort by the copyists to keep poems from spanning more than one leaf prevents certainty in reconstructing the order and contents of the original TT1, particularly for the first twenty-three leaves. [p. 1]

Given the lack of final authority of ordering the leaves, these comments are dubious; and our doubt can grow when Sullivan attempts to reconstruct signatures or gatherings in which on occasion a single leaf is enclosed inside the normal double leaves of a single fold, such as this: "I hypothesize an initial, three-sheet quire with sheet 1/4 as the outer sheet, followed by 2/3, and then by a missing sheet containing the remainder of King James's reply to Archbishop Abbot. The catchword 'first.' on folio 2$_v$ of TT1 indicates that something other than the current blank folio 3 followed; and although 'first' is not the next word in the *State*

Confronting Nightmares 219

Trials version of James's reply, 'first' would appropriately continue his reply beyond where the missing leaf in TT1 cuts it off" (p. 1). Certain problems of pagination caused by missing or rearranged leaves and sheets thus lead to a questionable hypothesis. Sullivan is more persuasive when he is on surer ground—when poems run over from one leaf to another; and when the sequence is coherent, logical, or traditional, as in the later instances of Donne's *Elegiae* and some characters by Thomas Overbury.

The situation worsens, however, in the case of TT2:

> The Scottish Record Office catalog mentions "paper-covered volumes"; however, between the time that Beal saw TT2 at the Scottish Record Office and 21 July 1981, when it was auctioned at Sotheby's, all of its thirty-four leaves had been repaired, mounted on guards, and rebound with a dark blue cloth cover. In addition, its third leaf had been reversed (the earlier, penciled "3" in the same hand as the other modern foliation is still visible on the now verso side; a penciled "3" in a different hand appears on the now recto side). With all traces of the original binding lost and only the modern foliation, the order of the leaves in, and the contents of, the original manuscript remains problematical.
>
> Substantial evidence does suggest, however, that the current state of the manuscript closely approximates the original order of leaves and contents. [p. 3]

This "substantial evidence" is catchwords—one of the best kinds of evidence we have—but it seems especially secure because it is confirmed by the placement of watermarks in paper which Sullivan can identify as 12803 in Briquet and 469 and 471 in Churchill (paper made, that is, between 1580 and 1594). The case becomes a compelling one, moreover, when Sullivan finds what he calls "extraordinary parallels" among TT1, TT2, and Lansdowne 740—Sullivan's B78. This secures a line of textual transmission; at least as importantly, it secures a larger, composite text with social and political implications. Indeed, "The correspondences among the poem headings and ascriptions in the Lansdowne and Dalhousie manuscripts reinforce the connection implied by the contents and sequence" (p. 8).

The presentation of poems in the Dalhousie manuscripts is, then, for the study of the work of John Donne, of signal importance. But there are other equally important claims on our attention. For one thing, it would appear that both manuscripts were transcribed—and so probably circulated—during Donne's lifetime, thus awarding them textual and critical priority. Based on the first and last works in TT1—testimony of Archbishop Abbot and King James I concerning the divorce of Lady Frances Howard from Robert Devereux, third earl of Essex, on 12 May 1613, and an elegy on Ludovick Stuart, duke of Richmond, who died on 30 July 1624—Sotheby's dates TT1 between 1620 and 1625. Beal agrees, and the dating is supported, of course, by the paper watermarks. TT2 has two different transcriptions of a song entitled "*Carold for new yeeres day* 1624" (on fols. 21_v and 33_r), and this neatly falls between the first leaf of the collection, dated "the 28th of september the year of our Lord 1622" and the final leaf which bears "An Epitaph vpon the Duke off Buckinghame," referring to George Villiers, who died on 23 August 1628. No other text of this epigraph seems to exist, so it is unlikely to be a copy of a distant original; and the uniformity of the paper throughout TT2 argues a further coherence. In addition, allusions which constitute "internal evidence" (p. 4) suggest the texts are for the most part earlier than the works at either end of TT1.

The datable original versions of poems in the sequence are very early indeed: 1595 for the two Davies poems on Richard Fletcher, 1597 for Donne's "The Storme" and "The Calme," and 1602 and 1603 for the Roe poems. John T. Shawcross assigns all the Donne poems in this sequence (indeed, all the Donne poems in TT1 and TT2) dates earlier than July 1611 . . . , and even his July 1611 date for "A Valediction forbidding mourning" depends on Izaak Walton's unsupported account in his *Life of Donne* that Donne wrote the poem when he went abroad with the Druries. [p. 4]

Walton's account may be unsupported, but it is quite likely right:

The latest certain date for the Donne poems in TT1 and TT2 is 4 August 1609 ("Elegie on Mris. Boulstred"). In addition to the 12 May 1613 date for the divorce proceedings, evidence suggests that the material in TT1 up to folio 62 was transcribed before August 1617. [p. 4]

While there is no clear way to establish a *terminus ad quem,* 1617 is possible and not at all unlikely.

A second matter of additional importance is the connection of both TT1 and TT2 with the Essex family—lending the manuscripts a kind of social and political notoriety—and from this Sullivan moves, with some justification, to an identification of the copyist.

TT1 and TT2 provide a surprising amount of information about their compilation. Both verse miscellanies contain evidence in every gathering and in the work of every copyist that they derive immediately from documents consciously preserved by one or more members of the Essex family. Some of the poems may have been collected from the papers of Robert Devereux, Second Earl of Essex (1565–1601), statesman, soldier, poet, literary patron, and husband of Frances Walsingham, the widow of Sir Philip Sidney. Another possible collector would be Penelope Devereux (1562–1607), sister to the Second Earl, the Stella of Sir Philip Sidney's *Astrophel and Stella,* literary patroness, and indefatigable defender of her brother's reputation. The collection would have been continued beyond the 1601 and 1607 deaths of the Second Earl and Penelope by the Third Earl (1591–1646), of whom Robert Coddrington wrote: "And if ever any unseverer hours of leisure offered themselves in his study, hee would imploy that time in the perusall of some labourd Poeme, and having great judgment especially in the English Verse, it was his custome to applaud the professors of that Art, as high as their deserts and to reward them above it" . . . , or by Lady Lettice Carey and Mrs. Essex Rich, daughters of Penelope Devereux, to whom Donne wrote "A Letter to the Lady Carey, and Mrs. Essex Riche, From Amyens" in 1611, about the time the collection reached that state in which the Dalhousie manuscripts preserve it. [pp. 4–5]

The most likely copyist from the court of James would have been, according to Sullivan, Sir John Ramsay, Viscount Haddington and earl of Holderness (1580–1626), who had strong positions at both locations. Indeed, Ramsay had especially strong ties to the Essex family through his own; his nephew, William Ramsay, second baron and first earl of Dalhousie, signed the letter of covenant to the third earl of Essex on 19 April 1639 and later served with him in the Civil War against Charles I.

Sullivan amasses an amazing amount of material relating most of the authors in the Dalhousie manuscripts to the Essex family. Abbot's letter and James's reply concern themselves with Lady Frances Howard's divorce from the third earl of Essex. Other authors in the manuscripts have other connections. Edward de Vere, seventeenth earl of Oxford, saw the elevation of the first earl of Essex as Lord Great Chamberlain; Sir John Davies was Solicitor General for Ireland when Essex was Lord Lieutenant there; Sir John Harington, John Hoskyns, Richard Corbett, and Sir Henry Wotton all knew the second earl at the Inns of Court; Donne served with the second earl on the expedition to Cadiz in 1596–97 and worked for one of Essex's most important clients, Sir Thomas Egerton the elder; Sir Thomas Overbury, a close friend of the third earl, was murdered by Lady Frances Howard and her second husband, Robert Carr, earl of Somerset, for opposing their marriage: W. J. Paylor argues that some works in the collection, "A Very Very Woman" and "Her Next Part," are not only meant as the antithesis of a character called "A Good Woman" but are meant as specific attacks on Lady Frances.[14] Sir Walter Ralegh served with the second earl at Cadiz and in the Azores; Sir John Roe served with him in Ireland in 1599 and was knighted by him; Francis Beaumont's poem concerns Roger Manners, first earl of Rutland, who accompanied Essex to Ireland in 1599 and was also knighted there by him and later participated in Essex's infamous assassination plot of 1601. The only identified poet who is not clearly associated with the Essex family in TT1 is Joshua Sylvester. TT2 likewise contains poems by Donne, Davies, Harington, Beaumont, and Roe, but other poets—James Graham, William Herbert—may have little or no connection. Conversely, "The handwriting units within the Dalhousie manuscripts . . . connect the work of each copyist to the Essex family" (p. 6). Sullivan's conclusion follows:

> It would seem that the men who had served the earls in civil or military capacities sent their poetry to them in hopes of patronage and preferment and that the poems were then collected (and perhaps arranged) by one of the Essex family. The collection was subsequently copied at least twice, first by someone, perhaps Sir John Ramsay, connected to

Confronting Nightmares 223

the Dalhousie family and second into B78 by someone connected to the Cecil family (Penelope Devereux maintained good relations with the Cecil family). [p. 7]

The Dalhousie manuscripts have a third claim on our attention. As Sullivan notes:

Modern editors of Donne's texts have focused primarily on the seven seventeenth-century collected editions/issues of Donne's *Poems* and on a few major manuscripts that appeared to represent efforts to collect all of Donne's poems. This approach sidesteps the possibility that the collected editions and major manuscript collections of Donne's poems may derive from smaller collections, particularly groups of poems that circulated together, and that the texts of poems in these smaller collections (or even individual poems) of the sort that appear in verse miscellanies might be closer at least chronologically to Donne's originals than are the texts in the larger collections. [p. 7]

This larger question of primacy of texts contests Shawcross's more widely eclectic collection of manuscripts and directly challenges Helen Gardner's hypothetical "X" and "Y" manuscripts that she contends lie behind Group I and Group II manuscript traditions in Donne's work.[15]

Sullivan is also able to establish a convincing stemma. By comparing the texts of particular Donne poems, he argues that TT1 did not derive from the original of TT2 nor did B78. However:

Since B78 and TT1 have such an unusually close relationship, the fact that neither derives from the other implies the existence of a common source, probably "E"; however, TT2 derives from TT1 rather than from "E." The large amount of material missing from TT2, the relative uncertainty of the order of its remaining material, and the presence of two copyists in its main sequence make determining its derivation difficult; nonetheless, the omission of the same lines in the same poems . . . , the presence of eleven poems unique to TT1 and TT2, and the generally very close agreement between their texts of Donne poems . . . strongly imply that much of the material in hands 2C and 2D in TT2 derives from TT1 rather than from "E". . . . Yet not all of TT2 derives from TT1: not only does TT2 (admittedly in an incomplete state) omit much material from TT1, but it also has eleven poems not found in TT1. [p. 9]

Extensive differences between the texts of several Donne poems, moreover, even when they are in the hand of one of the two main copyists of TT2, do not derive from TT1. In addition, other hands make (obviously later) corrections in TT2, corrections which point toward later printed texts.

Finally, a fifth immeasurable gain through these manuscripts is better understanding of Donne's corpus.

As perhaps the earliest exemplars of an important Donne manuscript tradition, TT1 and TT2 provide authoritative evidence for Donne's canon. TT1 and TT2 are important witnesses for several poems now generally accepted as Donne's but not published in all or any of the seven seventeenth-century editions/issues of Donne's collected *Poems:* "Elegie: The Bracelet" (TT1, 27$_{r-v}$; TT2, 9–10) was not included until the 1635 second collection edition; lines 29–46 of "Elegie: Loves Warre" were first published anonymously in *The Harmony of the Muses* (1654), pp. 6–7, and the poem was not published in its entirety as Donne's until F. G. Waldron's *A Collection of Miscellaneous Poetry* (1802), pp. 1–5; and his *The Shakespearean Miscellany* (1802), pp. 1–5; "Elegie: Going to Bed" was first published anonymously in *Harmony* (pp. 2–3) and was not published as Donne's until the seventh collected edition of 1669; "Lecture upon the Shadow" first appeared in the second collected edition (pp. 66–67); and "Elegie: Loves Progress" was first published anonymously in *Harmony* (pp. 36–39) and did not appear as Donne's until the seventh collected edition. [pp. 10–11]

In addition, "The attributions and groupings in TT1 and TT2 also provide evidence for authorship for some poems mistakenly published as Donne's in the seventeenth-century collected editions/issues or frequently attributed to him in the seventeenth-century manuscripts of modern editions" (p. 11), such as "Song. Deare Love, continue nice and chaste" and *"An Elegie to M*^{ris} *Boulstred:* 1602" by Sir John Roe. Two special canonical problems are also addressed. The presence of "Elegie: The Expostulation" in a long sequence of twenty-six Donne poems in TT1 (44–56), broken only by single works by Beaumont and Hoskyns, and again in TT2 (fifteen poems from 22$_v$ to 29$_v$) broken only by one

Confronting Nightmares 225

of Beaumont's, supports the contention, in 1939, by Evelyn Simpson that this poem is Donne's.[16] The matter of "Faustus" is less clear. Because it appears in several sources as the work of JD, Shawcross assigns it to Donne, but it appears in no sequence of Donne poems in TT1 or TT2 nor is it similar in form to other Donne poems. Indeed, the variant text in TT1 from that appearing elsewhere suggests that TT1 corrects the text (as determined by a metrical test) and so weights the case of authorship against Donne.

Most of Sullivan's book consists of fine photographs of each of the leaves of the perfect TT1 and the imperfect TT2 with very literal transcriptions facing them; these transcriptions retain abbreviations, original spelling and punctuation, and all revisions (including crossouts and writeovers). The hands of the copyists vary considerably, but each transcription I have checked is painstakingly accurate and sometimes—at least with the blotted lines or bleedthrough in the photographs—remarkably so. The text is matched by equally extraordinary apparatus. There are the usual (but full) explanatory notes of persons, places, allusions, and unusual words; in addition there is a remarkable census of some 323 extant MSS containing poems from the Dalhousie manuscripts. Predictably, the largest collections of such manuscripts are at the British Library (90), the University Library at Cambridge (12), the Folger Shakespeare Library (20), the Houghton Library (11), the Huntington Library (8), the Bodleian Library (59), the Rosenbach Library (9), and at Yale University (8). All poems are keyed to this census, and there is also a useful subject index and first-line index.

Clearly, the Dalhousie manuscripts provide ample evidence for the importance of transcribing and studying miscellanies generally. Peter Beal has written:

Miscellanies can . . . throw extensive light on the process of textual transmission, on the general practices and assumptions involved in the collecting of verse in [the Renaissance], on the way contemporaries interpreted texts, and on the nature and provenance of sources. The selection and arrangement of poems by Donne in these MSS, and of accompanying poems by others, are vital clues to the collections from which they derive and to possible reasons for confusion over the canon. Individual texts in miscellanies may, in any case, derive not from large collections at all but from independent early copies of particular poems, and apparent "corruptions" may, in fact, sometimes represent different versions or states of revision of the text. In short, the potential and far-ranging significance of miscellanies should not be underestimated.[17]

Sullivan himself reaches even farther:

Ultimately, the chief literary significance of TT1 and TT2 may lie in the evidence they provide about the way verse circulated and was collected and arranged in the Renaissance. The discovery that verse miscellanies like TT1 and TT2 may not result from random circulation of verse but rather derive from a body of verse by a coterie of authors whose work was intended for the approbation of and deliberately collected by "culture-heroes . . . like Sir Philip Sidney and the (Second) Earl of Essex" (Marotti, p. 33) has profound implications not only for the study of the authorship, dating, manuscript circulation, and texts of Renaissance verse generally but also for our understanding of the function of verse in the aesthetic, social, political, and economic life of the Renaissance. [p. 12]

The exceedingly rich treasure that is the first and second Dalhousie manuscripts has been richly mined and extremely well served in this wide-ranging but meticulous edition.

Notes

1. A. J. Smith, "Preface" to *John Donne: The Complete English Poems* (Harmondsworth: Penguin, 1971, with corrections, 1983), p. 13.

2. Herbert J. C. Grierson, "Preface" to *The Poems of John Donne* (Oxford: Clarendon, 1912), p. vii.

3. A. L. Clements, "Preface" to *John Donne's Poetry: Authoritative Texts [and] Criticism* (New York: Norton, 1966), p. xi.

4. Samuel Taylor Coleridge, "On Donne's Poetry" (1818?) quoted in *The Complete English Poems of John Donne*, ed. C. A. Patrides (London: Dent, 1985), p. 14.

5. Patrides, p. 15.

6. Quoted in Patrides, p. 15.

Confronting Nightmares

7. Ibid.

8. Helen Gardner, "Preface to the First Edition (1952)" in *John Donne: The Divine Poems* (Oxford: Clarendon Press, 1978), p. vi.

9. Helen Gardner, "Textual Introduction" to *John Donne: The Elegies and the Songs and Sonnets* (Oxford: Clarendon, 1965), p. xci.

10. W. Milgate, "Preface" to *John Donne: The Epithalamions, Anniversaries, and Epicedes* (Oxford: Clarendon, 1978), p. v.

11. John Hayward, "Note on the Text" in *John Donne: A Selection of His Poetry* (Harmondsworth: Penguin, 1950), p. 15.

12. John T. Shawcross, "Introduction" to *The Complete Poetry of John Donne* (Garden City: Doubleday, 1967), p. xxi.

13. Arthur F. Marotti, *John Donne: Coterie Poet* (Madison: Univ. of Wisconsin Press, 1986).

14. W. J. Paylor, *The Overburian Characters* (Oxford: Basil Blackwell, 1936), pp. 109–11.

15. Helen Gardner, *John Donne: The Divine Poems*, pp. lxiv–lxv.

16. Evelyn Simpson, "Jonson and Donne: A Problem in Authorship," *Review of English Studies*, 15 (1939), 274–82.

17. Peter Beal, *Index of English Literary Manuscripts* (London: Mansell Publishing, 1980), I, 248–49.

The Not-So-Little Lower Layer

Michael Anesko

David S. Reynolds. *Beneath the American Renaissance: The Subversive Imagination in the Age of Emerson and Melville.* New York: Alfred A. Knopf, 1988. x, 628 pp.

It was Hemingway, of course, who narrowly traced the antecedents of modern American literature to "one book by Mark Twain called *Huckleberry Finn.*" But after pondering *Beneath the American Renaissance,* one can easily imagine David S. Reynolds reformulating that dictum to account for all the masterpieces of antebellum literary culture. It might seem a little bizarre to suggest that the most revered works of our canonical mid-nineteenth century authors—Poe, Emerson, Thoreau, Hawthorne, Melville, Whitman, Dickinson—come from one book by George Lippard called *The Quaker City; or, The Monks of Monk Hall* (1845), but that, in essence, is what Reynolds would have us believe.

Strange to say, he is right—or at least on the right track. The remarkable achievement of *Beneath the American Renaissance* is its encyclopedic reconstruction of a literary environment long since lost from view: an ephemeral world of print culture that served as a kind of popular substratum for the masterworks of the fabled American renaissance. Contrary to the commonplace belief that our great writers were marginalized by their society, alienated by the inescapable vulgarity of American life, Reynolds dares to suggest that these same writers were constructively influenced by popular culture. "The truth may well be that, far from being estranged from their context, they were in large part created by it" (p. 3). Far from being antithetical or antagonistic, the relationship between popular and elite culture "was one of reciprocity and cross-fertilization" according to Reynolds, "almost of symbiosis" (p. 4). The author's intention, then, is to quarry down into what Emerson called the "tough chaos-deep soil" of vernacular genres—newspapers, reform tracts, popular fictions—thereby securing for analysis a true cross-section of literary and subliterary expression.

The base of the cultural pyramid that Reynolds identifies is indeed broad. It covers much greater territory than Lippard's sensational exposé of urban corruption; but Reynolds knows this and shrewdly uses *The Quaker City* (and a handful of other frequently cited—albeit heretofore obscure—works) as representative of the popular idiom. That same idiom modulates—in Reynolds's ear—in a number of different voices, or styles, to which he assigns various descriptive labels. The author's wide-ranging survey divides our early national bibliography into three primary narrative groups. First are the Conventional narratives of moral uplift, so frequently deplored by cultural historians (and, more recently, celebrated by feminist scholars) as the dominant mode of literary expression. Such best-selling endorsements of domesticated or sentimental Christian piety as Susan Warner's *The Wide, Wide World* (1850) or Maria Cummins's *The Lamplighter* (1854) were the literary staples of their day. While recognizing the importance of this subgenre, Reynolds devotes considerably more attention to what he calls Subversive narratives, which, as a group, defied the norms of gentility espoused by Conventional works and made free use of irrational, violent, and frequently perverse subjects and language. John Neal, George Lippard, and George Thompson are Reynolds's favorite spokesmen in this category. A third subset is grouped under the heading of Romantic Adventure narratives, which bifurcates according to the ideological tendencies of the previous two groups into moral and immoral components. Cooper's novels exemplify the Moral Adventure narrative, and Natty Bumppo is its typical hero. Tales of Dark Adventure, on the other hand, relate the exploits of social outcasts and criminals with almost no corrective didacticism. The list of representative titles that Reynolds provides offers the best clue to their contents. *Wharton the Whale-Killer! or, The Pride of the Pacific, Fanny Campbell; or the Female Pirate Captain,* and *Mary Bean, the Factory Girl; or, The Mysterious Murder* are not likely to displace *Moby-Dick* or *The Scarlet Letter* from many college reading lists, but it is helpful to be reminded of their existence.

To some readers Reynolds's categories may seem arbitrary and the nomenclature wooden or theoretically unsophisticated; but it seems only fair to remember the scope of the author's undertaking. Unlike so many other recent "historical revaluations" of the antebellum canon—which, for all their provocative claims, usually end up confirming Matthiessen's stubbornly preemptive judgments—this study is supported by considerable (and, therefore, unfashionable) research. To all appearances Reynolds has read everything there is to read from 1830 to 1860, and that is no mean achievement. As a study of popular literature and culture from this period, *Beneath the American Renaissance* probably will not be superseded for a very long time. One can imagine Constance Rourke or Perry Miller having attempted to write this book—indeed, *The Roots of American Culture* and *The Raven and the Whale* seem close in inspiration—but such comprehensive intelligences are not all that common. And when it comes to popular culture, artlessness is long and life is short. All the more reason to be grateful for Reynolds's work.

To his credit and his credence, Reynolds can justify his efforts with numerous confessions from his primary subjects. Few critics are courageous enough to take Whitman at his word, but Reynolds attends very carefully to what he has to say in his exuberant epistolary response to Emerson (1856):

All current nourishments to literature serve. Of authors and editors I do not know how many there are in The States, but there are thousands, each one building his or her step to the stairs by which giants shall mount. Of the twenty-four modern mammoth two-double, three-double, and four-double cylinder presses now in the world, printing by steam, twenty-one of them are in These States. The twelve thousand large and small shops for dispensing books and newspapers—the same number of public libraries, any one of which has all the reading wanted to equip a man or woman for American reading—the three thousand different newspapers, the nutriment of the imperfect ones coming in just as usefully as any—the story papers, various, full of strong-flavored romances, widely circulated—the one-cent and two-cent journals—the political ones, no matter what side—the weeklies in the country—the sporting and sentimental novels, numberless copies of them—the low-priced flaring tales, adventures, biographies—all are prophetic; all waft rapidly on. I see that they swell wide, for reasons. I am not troubled at the movement of them, but greatly pleased.

This quintessentially Whitmanian catalogue describes very well the range of sources that Reynolds has consulted: text and context are made one. It is Whitman again who advises us that sensational fiction is "a power in the land, not without great significance in its way, and very deserving of more careful consideration than has hitherto been accorded it." *Beneath the American Renaissance* takes up where the solitary singer leaves off.

By taking Whitman at his word Reynolds has uncovered—or recovered—a vast quantity of neglected material. While the yield is noteworthy in itself, even more remarkable are the generic distinctions discoverable within it. By employing his criteria of descriptive content, for example, Reynolds calculates that the relative significance of genteel Conventional fiction actually declined from 1830 to 1860. If Hawthorne despaired of competing with a "damned mob of scribbling women" he pregnantly neglected to mention the increasingly voluminous output of sensational pulp journalists. "The claim that women's fiction began as a relatively sparse genre and then by midcentury assumed dominance of the popular scene has no basis," Reynolds writes. "The reverse, in fact, was true. . . . The sentimental-domestic fiction that is thought to have conquered the popular market actually ran a distant second to more sensational genres" (p. 338). Is it possible, then, that all the recent inflated claims made for *The Wide, Wide World* (e.g., Jane Tompkins's) are wide, wide of the mark? If so, how should one describe the "cultural work" done by these other, apparently more popular genres?

Unfortunately, perhaps, *Beneath the American Renaissance* cannot provide the answer to such a question because Reynolds does not ask it. For all of its archaeological richness, this book does not address its constituent materials in fashionably anthropological terms. To admit this, however, is not to diminish what Reynolds does accomplish: only to suggest that to readers of a particular stripe the book will prove disappointing. Even these readers, it might be worth pointing out, will ignore Reynolds's work at their peril; if his book is not abstractly theoretical, it recovers an enormous quantity of data for which theory must now unavoidably account. The astonishingly successful resuscitation of many works by "popular" women writers, for example, may prove cheap comfort indeed when confronted with new statistical evidence of their negligibility. The ranks of the suppressed and uncanonized, at least in Reynolds's tabulation, are overwhelmingly male.

An even larger disappointment, however, awaits the reader who still cherishes Matthiessen's optative assertion that the strongest common bond among the writers of the American Renaissance was their shared commitment to the possibilities of democracy. Because he insists that the masterworks of the period both assimilate and transcend popular literary forms, an unavoidable consequence of Reynolds's approach is the denigration of the very types of "subliterary" expression that inform superior works of genius. If, like Emerson, he urges us to embrace the low, in the final analysis it is still held at arm's length. For this reason (and in direct contrast to Matthiessen) Reynolds does not shy away from Poe, whose contempt for his more popular contemporaries (and for the gullibility of the reading public at large) was unmistakable. Poe's attitude may have been more virulent than Thoreau's, or Hawthorne's, or Melville's, but the logic of Reynolds's argument does not allow him much room for discrimination on this score. "Sensationalists like George Lippard and George Thompson enjoyed immense popularity," he claims, "because their fiction openly projected the common reader's most savage impulses and fantasies: violent antielitism, identification with monstrous outcasts and justified criminals, eroticism and gory violence, bizarre nightmares with revolutionary overtones. It was precisely these kinds of intensely democratic excesses that Poe constantly censured in his critical writings. In his fiction, he was like his own 'natural aristocrat,' using the tools of the rabble but not soiling his hands with them" (p. 230). The cool response toward the 'democratic excesses' of popular writing carries over, in Reynolds's view, from Poe to the other major writers of the period. Hawthorne's work, for example, affords "serious treatment of topics [such as marital infidelity and clerical hypocrisy] that in popular sensational literature had become matters of mechanical prurience and shallow irreverence" (p. 265). After identifying a predominant character type of popular fiction—the "b'hoy" figure, a kind of urban yeoman—and establishing his links to working-class politics in such works as Ned Buntline's *The B'hoys of Boston* (1850) and George Foster's *New York in Slices* (1849), Reynolds goes on to assert that "when assimilated by the major writers," the b'hoy "became a source of egalitarian sympathy but lost direct connections with political activism" (p. 466). The author's conclusion indicates a kind of wholesale depoliticization of several major works (notably *Leaves of Grass*), putting intolerable strain, as it were, on Matthiessen's patience and perhaps on the living reader's credulity.

It would probably be simple in a work as long as this to isolate stylistic infelicities or parade embarrassing lists of typographical errors. The latter are surprisingly few; the former, perhaps, easier to produce. Even after admitting the difficulties inherent in the admirable scope of his enterprise, Reynolds's critical vocabulary is not especially supple. As it recapitulates similar trends in the works of various authors, the book occasionally sounds like an echo-chamber. This is partly due to the author's self-imposed terminology, but also to simple and sometimes inelegant repetition. This is, in every sense, an over-determined book—which speaks to strengths as well as weaknesses. Still, there are moments when one almost yearns for another quotation, if only to relieve the pattern, however convincing, of programmatic demonstration. And does it really help to be told (on p. 128) that "A lot of cultural water had gone under the bridge between 1841, when Hawthorne left Brook Farm, and 1852, when *The Blithedale Romance* was published"?

Every reviewer is entitled to record a list of irritating peccadillos, and I hope the brevity of mine here will suggest the measure of my admiration for what David Reynolds has done. Like Matthiessen's exemplary predecessor, *Beneath the American Renaissance* may well prove to be a volume that will be consulted more often than read, but that is hardly an embarrassment. It is an archive and a catalogue in one. It is unique in scope and form. It will be consulted and, yes, it will be read.

Reading Wharton's Letters

Katherine Joslin

R. W. B. Lewis and Nancy Lewis, eds. *The Letters of Edith Wharton.* New York: Charles Scribner's Sons, 1988. xiv, 654 pp.

Leon Edel went to meet Edith Wharton in the early 1930s when she was a pleasant elderly woman of seventy and he an eager young man of twenty-four. Over the course of the afternoon, he found her quite a different woman than her legend would have it; in 1966, he detailed the events for an audience of Newporters at the Redwood Library and Athenaeum. "I mention these matters mainly to suggest to you," he explained, "that Mrs. Wharton, whose image is constantly evoked for us as a rigid, snobbish, society woman who happened to have written some books, was quite the opposite of this: she was—at any rate in her 70's—a warm, mellow woman who talked easily and with alertness."[1] Before lunch was served, the great woman of letters retired to change from her "knitted suit and one of those off-the-face hats of the 1920's" into a fresh "frock." Edel, both the young man and the older scholar, was amused by her change of outfit, even bemused by the ritual she so naturally performed. He went on to note, in differentiating her talent from Henry James's, that Wharton was a social historian: "She recorded the manners, humors, tragedies" of her society "with unfailing truth and in prose of great lucidity and clarity." James's art, however, belonged "elsewhere": James transcended the immediacies that Wharton so meticulously chronicled; he moved toward "moral essences" and "symbolic values." In both instances, the style of dress and of writing, Edel read the woman as he would read a man. Henry James would not have changed his frock for lunch, just as he would not have written merely to detail the local habits, the customs of a country. But a woman, especially a woman of

Wharton's social class and literary inclination, might very well do both.

Last year, Wharton's biographer R. W. B. Lewis and Nancy Lewis edited *The Letters of Edith Wharton*, giving the public a fresh look at the writer previously reserved for scholars who travelled to her archives, especially to the collection in the Beinecke Rare Book and Manuscript Library at Yale University. The edition includes only 300 of the perhaps 6,000 Wharton letters known to be in existence. Even such a small sampling offers scholars and readers a fuller portrait of the wealthy, talented, forceful woman of letters than we have had. Yet the picture of Edith Wharton that emerges from the carefully selected letters places her largely in a community of publicly successful men. The private side of her personality, especially in her friendships with publicly overlooked women, has been neglected. The Lewises, perhaps constrained by limiting the edition to one volume, have slighted her less dramatic epistolary exchanges with women rather than exploring the nature and importance of such friendships.

Edith Wharton wrote thousands of letters over the course of her life, several a day, to hundreds of people: publishers, writers, psychologists, historians, journalists, lawyers, and numerous friends, both female and male. Her letters differ in voice and content in virtually every case. Those alterations—shifts in tone, mood, subject matter, even diction from correspondent to correspondent—are the literary equivalent of changing her frock. We all, to some extent, alter our literary voices to fit the occasion, but Wharton's gender, social class, and artistic talent gave her a heightened sense of the relationship between language and situation. "People talk more for themselves, apparently, & write more for their correspondents," she once explained in a letter to her friend Bernard Berenson (p. 391). Certainly Wharton felt the presence of her audience and, on occasion, incorporated that voice into her own. Her change of voice, even at times the hesitation of her voice, has continued to confuse those who have been in charge of disseminating and evaluating her letters. In the introduction to the *Letters*, for example, the Lewises have the same problem Leon Edel had. Although they obviously value the letters and spend a good deal of time discussing Wharton's many epistolary voices, they conclude that the surviving letters to Henry James are her best: "Absorbing the Jamesian voice into her own, Edith Wharton had never expressed herself more handsomely" (p. 23). They too listen for the male ring of her voice, not the female one.

Percy Lubbock had first crack at Edith Wharton's letters. When she died in 1937, her literary executor and close friend Gaillard Lapsley sought Lubbock's professional advice; after all, Lubbock had edited Henry James's letters, knew the skills required and the value of such a publication. He, too, had known Edith Wharton over many years and had at one time admired both her intellect and her art. Lubbock squirmed. He wrote to Lapsley that the traumatic breach in his friendship with her would seem to have put editing her letters out of the question.[2] Yet he wanted to get hold of Wharton for himself. The truth is that Wharton had quarreled with Lubbock over his marriage to Sybil Cutting Scott, a woman who charmed the hearts of perhaps too many of their male friends. As a result Wharton cut them both, refusing during the last ten years of her life to talk to either of them.

It was Lubbock who had the last word. He argued that no satisfying book could be made from her letters. Instead of publishing them immediately after her death, he devised a plan for a memoir, *Portrait of Edith Wharton* (1947), built not around her letters but around letters from her friends "in the form of recollections, reflections, notes of all kinds—freely placed at [his] disposal to be used in any manner that should accord with the design of the book."[3] Lapsley agreed that letters from others, most of whom were not literary people at all, would be more representative of the writer than her own letters would be. Can one imagine them dismissing James's letters in such fashion? By suppressing Wharton's letters, Percy Lubbock managed to silence her voice for fifty years. He even destroyed her letters to him.

According to Lubbock and Lapsley, Wharton "was not one to whom letter-writing was a natural overflow of herself and her talk—her letters would give no living picture of her, to speak for itself."[4] As Edel and the Lewises would do later, Lubbock and

Lapsley believed that Edith Wharton did not measure up to Henry James; she did not talk with a characteristically consistent voice as James and others of their male friends did. Lubbock, of course, had personal reasons for silencing the voice of Edith Wharton. But beyond that, he failed to understand Wharton's voice as a woman's voice. Her voice might well have been hesitant with him and yet comfortable with someone else; as a woman, she selected her epistolary voice as she did her frock for lunch. Lapsley might have had his own reasons, as well, for agreeing with Lubbock. It would seem that male camaraderie came before his personal and official obligations to Edith Wharton; in selecting Lubbock, he clearly went against her wishes. But beyond that, at least some of her letters might have seemed to Lapsley inappropriate for publication. For example, she wrote in a 1923 letter to him not included in the Lewises' edition, "I don't write often because I can hear your groans from here at the sight of one more."[5] Although with certain men, at certain times, Wharton's letters seem relaxed, there is often a sense that she believed her own pronouncement in *French Ways and Their Meaning:* "Women (if they only knew it!) are generally far more intelligent listeners than talkers."[6] We can hear her apologetic tone, for example, in a letter to Edmund Gosse in 1911: "I never, if I can help it, send a superficial letter to a Man of Letters."[7] (This letter too is not in *Letters.*) The dread of seeming female, superficial, incompetent with language made its way into her letters to some of her close male friends. Especially in her later life she wrote many notes, what Lubbock and Lapsley considered merely "tokens," that pleaded for a visit and promised a good story or joke, some pleasant conversation, in return.

Edith Wharton's letters, despite Lubbock's suppression of them, have at long last made their way into print under the direction of eager editors. The publication in 1985, by the *Library Chronicle,* of many of Wharton's letters to the colorful, bisexual, meandering lover of her middle years, Morton Fullerton, has preempted the Lewises' edition. And the Lewises have brought on the ire of Mary Pitlick by preempting her planned collection of Wharton letters, a project she has been working on since the seventies when she was a research assistant for R. W. B. Lewis's *Edith Wharton: A Biography* (1975).

Reading Wharton's Letters

During the last few months, the *Times Literary Supplement* has published charges and counter-charges over the handling of Edith Wharton's letters and over the Lewis version of her life. Pitlick and another Lewis researcher, Marion Mainwaring, have accused him of fuzzy thinking, lapses of memory, and misinterpretation of data. They have further charged that the generation of scholars coming out of Lewis have propagated his errors. The most serious distortion, Pitlick claims, is Lewis's chapter on Wharton's "breakdown" or "nervous collapse" from 1894 to 1896. Lewis uses as proof a letter from Wharton to Scribner's, pleading illness as the cause of her failure to produce an expected volume of stories. Pitlick agrees that during that time "Wharton did have occasional illnesses: respiratory problems, influenza and a bout of 'peritonitis' that could have been a miscarriage" (another popularly held belief is that her marriage had been sexless).[8] Other letters from the period show her, in Pitlick's words, "an ebullient woman going back and forth to Europe." Lewis, in a subsequent letter in the *TLS*, has stuck by his interpretation of the "breakdown," but welcomes reinterpretations written in "a calmer and less hostile manner." Both of Lewis's former researchers are about to publish their versions of Wharton's life: Mainwaring's *Mysteries of Life*, actually a study of Morton Fullerton, and Pitlick's *Edith Wharton's Formative Years*. What all the clamor means, beneath the heated rhetoric, is that Edith Wharton has become big business indeed. The project Percy Lubbock scorned has, in part, been completed; some of Edith Wharton's letters have come into the light. And I hope many more letters will follow.

Perhaps no writer has understood better than Edith Wharton what such literary fame might cost a writer in personal terms. Her early novella *The Touchstone* (1900) tells the story of a dead writer, Margaret Aubyn, whose former lover sells the love letters she wrote to him for cash in order to afford a marriage to his current lover. It is as though, long before she ever wrote her first letter to Morton Fullerton, she knew how her own story might end. Although she pleaded with Fullerton at the conclusion of their affair to return her letters, he perversely saved them all, presumably for someone later to make a profit. The novella registers Wharton's horror at the prospect of becoming public property, of having her "woman's soul, absolutely torn up by the roots."[9] She would have seen the irony of her position, of course. The first voice heard after over fifty years of silence was her most tentative, vulnerable, wounded. The adulterous love affair of her forties with the slightly younger Fullerton has such dramatic power because it belies earlier accounts of her, all stemming from the tainted Lubbock portrait. Edith Wharton, strong-jawed, hawk-like, corseted, fur-draped, belonged to the repressions of the nineteenth century; ideologically conservative and emotionally aloof, she had not before figured as an impulsive, sensual heroine. Yet here she was, in the Fullerton correspondence, a woman in the flesh:

And if you can't come into the room without my feeling all over me a ripple of flame, & if, wherever you touch me, a heart beats under your touch, & if, when you hold me, & I don't speak, it's because all the words in me seem to have become throbbing pulses, & all my thoughts are a great golden blur—why should I be afraid of your smiling at me, when I can turn the beads & calico back into such beauty—? [p. 135]

What we learn from these letters is that though she may have repressed emotion earlier in her life, she was by her mid-forties a fully passionate, extraordinarily articulate woman.

Although her billets-doux have captivated readers of the 1980s, other correspondents might, in the end, prove more significant than one philandering lover. This shy, controlled woman of letters was capable of strong, tender emotion with more than one person. "I can't say too often that I am yours affectionately" (p. 66–67) she wrote in 1902; and later, "I think of you constantly & tenderly."[10] To another friend, she wrote in 1914, "Poor muddled hustled rag that I am, I still felt I should blossom in purple & red when I saw you."[11] And later, "I can only say that *you* are to me the life-giving spirit that you say I am to *you!*"[12] (None of these last three letters is included in the Lewises' edition.) More noteworthy than the fact of her strong feeling, especially in light of all the attention given the Fullerton affair, is that these lines come from her letters, not to men, but to women, specifically to Sara Norton and Margaret Terry Chanler. She wrote to them as "Edith or Pussy as you please" in the day when

Sara was "Sally" and Margaret was "Daisy." Often using such "pet" names, these women carried on supportive, nurturing epistolary friendships that centered on the quotidian world of homes, gardens, pets, travels, friends, books, and health. Percy Lubbock completely dismissed the Norton letters as unimportant in themselves.[13]

If we are to feel the flutter of Edith Wharton's presence within her correspondence, we must look as closely at her relationships with women as we have at her relationships with men. At a conference on the *Letters* in New York City, Nancy Lewis agreed that Wharton's "most interesting letters were not those to Fullerton or to Bernard Berenson or to Henry James, but the ones she wrote to her female friends, especially Sally Norton."[14] Wharton wrote to Norton and Chanler in a voice she never used with Lubbock or even Lapsley, Berenson, or James, an intimate voice sure of the shared nature of their experiences. It is that story of similarity, of her relationships with women, that seems overshadowed by the current interest in difference, in her friendships and love affairs with men. The overshadowed story sheds light as well on the claims that Edith Wharton was a misogynist, that she preferred the company of men, drew cruel portraits of women, even denied women an equal voice. That bias, too, comes from Percy Lubbock's account: "It is hard to speak of a chill, a check upon the swiftness of the sympathy that so many found in her; but certainly those who looked to her for a flow of deep communion heart speaking to heart—and I suppose they might be mostly women—wouldn't find it."[15] What this means for Lubbock, I suppose, is that women speak heart to heart only with their own gender and that Edith Wharton could not commune with her own kind.

In spite of Nancy Lewis's avowal that Wharton's letters to women are her most interesting, the Lewises selected only thirty-eight of the 240 letters to Sara Norton in the Beinecke collection, and a scant twelve letters to Margaret Terry Chanler, along with another fifty to various other women, adding up to a third of their edition. The letters to women chronicle the story of female concerns, a story of similarity, not difference. Such a tale of continuity and kindness is perhaps not as dramatic as the tale of disruption and deceit one finds in the Wharton/Fullerton letters. The dramatic rhetoric of the Fullerton letters is why, I suppose, critics have read them with such enthusiasm and assigned the erotic passion of her forties such a large role in Edith Wharton's psychological and literary development. In the face of that fascination, I can hear Wharton's own voice insisting that "the 'heart-interest' need not always predominate" (p. 59).

The early letters to Norton illustrate that Wharton's "awakening" to intellectual life came in her contacts with women as well as with men. Wharton began her correspondence with Sara Norton in March 1899, after Norton wrote her an encouragingly admiring letter about her fiction. "I am so lacking in self-confidence & my work falls so far short of what I try for that I am almost childishly grateful for the least word of approval."[16] In this letter (not included by the Lewises) Wharton was using a self-effacing tone she would employ throughout her life when commenting on her work. She found with Norton a camaraderie she never found with Fullerton. "It was so pleasant to find," she confessed in 1901 in another unincluded letter, "that we were *d'accord* on the more inaccessible subjects . . . that form either a barrier or a bridge to real friendship—such as I should like ours to be."[17] She discovered that special bridge with few women during her life, but it formed the basis of her strong attachments to Norton and Chanler. From the beginning of their friendship, Wharton wrote about her illness, the "hysteria" or "neurasthenia" she suffered over the first several years of her marriage. Like many of the intellectual female members of her social class—Jane Addams, Charlotte Perkins Gilman, and Alice James, for example— Wharton suffered from the inactivity forced on leisure-class women. Indeed the "rest-cure" of Weir Mitchell's clinic, where Wharton sought treatment over the years of her illness, reinforced traditional female behavior. In 1908 when Elizabeth "Lily" Norton, Sara's sister, showed signs of illness, Wharton wrote:

Tell Lily, if it's any comfort, that for *twelve* years I seldom knew what it was to be, for more than an hour or two of the twenty four, without an intense feeling of nausea, & such unutterable fatigue that when I got up

I was always more tired than when I lay down. This form of neurasthenia consumed the best years of my youth, & left, in some sort, an irreparable shade on my life. Mais quoi! I worked through it, & came out on the other side, & so will she, in a much shorter time, I hope. [pp. 139–40]

As Wharton was coming out of her long dis-ease at the turn of the century, her letters to Norton painted an isolated, lonely life far different from the social, intellectual life she gradually created. In May 1901, Wharton claimed that it would be an act of philanthropy on Norton's part if she would visit her:

I seldom ask people to stay because I am obliged to lead such a quiet & systematic kind of life that the house is a dull one for visitors; but as you know Lenox & feel at home here I do not feel so shy about inviting you, especially as I think there are many things *we* enjoy talking of together. [p. 46]

Wharton made such overtures to Norton with the assurance that their similarities as isolated, intellectual females would draw them together. Although they were anomalies in the society surrounding them—Wharton seems to say—they need not feel that difference in their own friendship.

In her response to an annual birthday letter (Norton always remembered her friend's January birthday), Wharton first made the obligatory complaint about middle age. "I excessively hate to be forty," she wrote. But then she discussed a more significant problem they both faced:

Don't I know that feeling you describe, when one longs to go to a hospital & *have something cut out*, & come out minus an organ, but alive & active & like other people, instead of dragging on with this bloodless existence!! Only I fear you & I will never find a surgeon who will do us that service. [p. 55]

Certainly that sense of difference from other women struck intellectual women of their day. The "organ" that made them different, that made them literally and figuratively ill, was the intellect.

Her intellect and literary talent could be "alive & active," however, in her homes, a series of retreats she built and remodeled in her middle and old age. Many times she expressed to Sara Norton her delight in refuge. "Two souls, alas, do dwell within my breast, & the Compleat Housekeeper has had the upper hand for the last weeks," she wrote as she moved into The Mount in 1902 (pp. 72–73). Lenox had "a tonic effect" on her, she explained to Norton: "It is great fun out at the place, now too—everything is pushing up new shoots—not only cabbages & strawberries, but electric lights & plumbing" (p. 66). While away from The Mount in 1903, she lamented the effect of the separation in another letter the Lewises omitted: "How I miss that beautiful white silence that enclosed us at The Mount and enabled me to possess my soul."[18] Sara Norton would presumably understand how necessary a house can be to a woman's sense of control. The "Compleat Housekeeper" in Wharton used the exterior gardens and the interior rooms to shield herself from Old New York, a society that she clearly felt differed from her in aesthetic appreciation, intellectual acuity, and moral probity. Silencing the outer world and its demands on women allowed Wharton to write, to give literary voice to her thoughts.

Her friendship with Margaret Chanler began in 1866 and developed over a considerable length of time. Not until 1911 did Wharton write to Norton that Chanler "is one of the people I am fondest of" (p. 264). By 1931 she claimed Chanler as her "usual travelling companion" (p. 539). During the years between, they wrote and saw each other off and on until the 1920s; thereafter Chanler took Norton's place as the chief female correspondent (Sara Norton died in 1922). One thing that accounts for the timing of their intimacy is the fact that Chanler married and had children. In her letter for Percy Lubbock's *Portrait,* Chanler explained the difficulty she had with her friend over the claims of her family. "With all her great intelligence she knew nothing of the natural pleasure our children give us; she interpreted maternal devotion as heroic self-sacrifice—indeed she seemed to look on all family life as more or less of a calamity."[19] When the children were older and Chanler had more time for their friendship, they often travelled together. It is clear from Chanler's account, in passages that Lubbock edited out of his memoir, that Wharton was a true friend to some women, that friendship was her cult and her joy. Percy Lubbock did not want to tell that story, even to see that side of the Edith Wharton who had iced him. Chanler noted Wharton's sense of humor and her kindness in their friendship, but those passages too were excised. In her own memoir, *Roman Spring*, Chanler referred to Edith or "Pussy" Wharton's "abounding gift of friendship."[20]

Wharton's letters to women are less dramatic, more episodic, full of the often minor incidents that make up the day. That general fact may account, in large part, for the strong focus on her letters to men, letters full of the more dramatic events of her life. Another significant reason, I suppose, her critics and she herself have explored and featured her associations with men is because those men held high places in the intellectual and financial world around her. That is to say, Edith Wharton's status is enhanced by such alliances. To place her with Sara Norton or Margaret Chanler is less dramatic; such female associations have done little to elevate her status in the public, professional, intellectual world she, almost alone in her class of females, entered in her middle years. Consider the Lewises' introduction of Sara Norton as "a woman of considerable literary taste and knowledge, and the daughter of Charles Eliot Norton, the distinguished professor of fine arts at Harvard, and an internationally renowned scholar and man of letters" (p. 28). Is it only in her connection to her father that she has a clear identity? Or take Margaret Chanler, herself a writer, "a devout Catholic" (p. 19), "one who belonged to the same richly be-cousined venerable American society, and to the same community of the extremely well read" (p. 21), but finally, "the daughter of the expatriate American painter Luther Terry" and wife of "Winthrop Astor Chanler, sportsman and traveler" and mother of "seven surviving children" (p. 64).

What seems clear from Edith Wharton's published avowals of male intellectual superiority to women and her private claims of hatred for "little girls and dolls" is that she wanted to identify with men and male activities. In her autobiography, she did as much as Percy Lubbock later did to place herself in the shadow of

Henry James. Wharton would probably have agreed with the Lewises that her letters to publicly important men are more significant to the general reader than her letters to privately important women. The private world, however, may add as much to our understanding of a writer as the public world. Wharton's letters to women suggest her ambivalence over being a woman; she wanted intellectual stimulation and felt she found it more often with men, but at the same time she found pleasure in more relaxed conversations with women, discussions of the details of everyday life.

The Lewises have done Wharton scholars a service by making so many letters available; the selection appeals, as well, to the more casual reader. Wharton's letters, as arranged in the edition, draw a fuller portrait of the woman and the writer than the general public has yet seen. We can begin to see how she changed her voices in her letters as she changed her frocks for meals. Still we need more letters, especially more to women; and I for one look forward to a complete collection. Edith Wharton, a large, powerful, many-sided literary figure, is in the midst of a reconsideration and revaluation. We need now to listen to her epistolary voices with an attitude that allows us finally to hear what a woman has to say.

Notes

1. Leon Edel, "Henry James, Edith Wharton, and Newport," An Address at the Opening of the Exhibition Held at the Redwood Library and Athenaeum, Newport, Rhode Island, July and August 1966. This article and all other letters and manuscripts are housed in the Collection of American Literature, Beinecke Rare Book and Manuscript Library, Yale University. I quote from this material with the permission of Patricia Willis, Curator of American Literature.

2. Percy Lubbock to Gaillard Lapsley, 14 November 1937.

3. Percy Lubbock, *Portrait of Edith Wharton* (New York: Appleton-Century, 1947), p. vi.

4. Lubbock, *Portrait*, p. v.

5. Wharton to Lapsley, 5 February 1923. I quote from Wharton's unpublished letters with the permission of William Royall Tyler, her literary heir.

6. Wharton, *French Ways and Their Meaning* (New York: Appleton, 1919), p. 25.

Reading Wharton's Letters

7. Wharton to Edmund Gosse, 18 February 1911.

8. Mary Pitlick, Letter, *TLS*, 30 December 1988–5 Jan. 1989, p. 1443. See also, Marion Mainwaring, "The Shock of Non-recognition," *TLS*, 16–22 Dec. 1988, pp. 1394 and 1405. For Lewis's response, see *TLS*, 17–23 Feb. 1989, p. 165.

9. Wharton, *The Touchstone* (New York: Scribner's, 1900), p. 67.

10. Wharton to Sara Norton, 19 October 1908.

11. Wharton to Margaret Terry Chanler, 2 January 1914.

12. Wharton to Chanler, 22 November 1928.

13. Lubbock to Lapsley, 8 February 1938.

14. Nancy Lewis, quoted in "Lewises Discuss the Letters," Alfred Bendixen, ed., *Edith Wharton Newsletter*, 6 (Spring 1989), 1.

15. Lubbock, *Portrait of Edith Wharton*, p. 55.

16. Wharton to Norton, 1 March 1899.

17. Wharton to Norton, 3 June 1901.

18. Wharton to Norton, 30 December 1904.

19. Lubbock, p. 148.

20. Mrs. Winthrop Chanler, *Roman Spring* (Boston: Little, Brown, 1934), p. 122.

Bernard Shaw on Progress

Henry J. Donaghy

J. L. Wisenthal. *Shaw's Sense of History.* Oxford: Clarendon Press, 1988. viii, 186 pp.

The primary paradox about Bernard Shaw is that, though he found no evidence of human progress in the course of history, he continued until the end to be a foremost apostle of such progress. For him, the nineteenth and twentieth centuries were the nadir of human existence. Despite our telephones and typewriters and trains and planes, he believed that the Middle Ages, even the so-called Dark Ages, were far superior to modern times. In this latter belief he had much in common with G. K. Chesterton, and to compare these friendly adversaries is to help understand the Shavian paradox. Like Shaw, Chesterton thought modern capitalism, a two-party system, and the loss of a religious foundation were responsible for a steady retrogression since the thirteenth century. So similar was their thought in this respect that Shaw, believing that Chesterton should have written *The Apple Cart,* long attempted to have him write a play on current politics and economics, and even helped him by writing a scenario for a tentative *The Devil and St. Augustine,* in which the saint returned to twentieth-century England and was duly scandalized by its loss of a Christian spirit. The scenario seemed certainly more appropriate for Chesterton than for Shaw since his solution to the current plight was to return to a distributist utopia, to a time before the commons were inclosed, when all had some small claim to the land. For Shaw this part of Chesterton's thinking was romantic nonsense. We had to go forward into the future. When challenged repeatedly by Chesterton to play fair and give a depiction of his utopia, as Chesterton had of his, Shaw produced *Back to Methuseleh,* an ultimately bloodless civilization which showed how much Shaw despaired of the human race. We had to produce something different if we were to save ourselves.

J. L. Wisenthal's fine study helps us understand the basic paradox in Shaw. It helps us see too that what often appear to be inconsistencies in Shaw's thought, and sometimes are, helped him to be the successful dramatist that he was, able in an engagement of ideas to present opposite sides convincingly. Finally, however, Wisenthal resolves the majority of these inconsistencies into a coherent philosophy of life.

To help us understand Shaw's view of history, Wisenthal compares him not with his contemporary Chesterton, but with Thomas Carlyle and Thomas Babington Macaulay, those two antithetical thinkers of the Victorian period, and shows his intellectual kinship with each. In so doing, he dramatizes the polar opposites embraced by Shaw's view of history. With Carlyle, Shaw shared the belief that history showed constant change but no upward movement. Both Shaw and Carlyle treated contemptuously the typical Victorian belief in man's own progress. For example, the comparison Carlyle makes in *Past and Present* between a twelfth-century monastery and nineteenth-century industrial England, to the latter's disadvantage, is echoed in Shaw's *Saint Joan*. Shaw also shares Carlyle's very Victorian respect for the heroic in history. Though Shaw gradually lost some of his regard for such military heroes as Napoleon, and though his heroes, unlike Carlyle's, are not heroic through and through but great in one direction and commonplace in another, he shared with Carlyle the belief that to portray the hero was a religious act in that it inspired people to have their reach exceed their grasp.

What then did Shaw share with Macaulay, a Whig optimist? Both admired technological improvement. Shaw always wished to be current. He did not, however, share with Macaulay the belief that scientific improvement was a sign of humanity's progress. Like Macaulay he, too, preferred the future (if not the present) to the past. When Caesar is chided in *Caesar and Cleopatra* for wanting to destroy the past in burning the library of Alexandria, he answers he will gladly burn the past "and build the future with its ruins." Like Macaulay, Shaw at least believed in the possibility of progress in the future. Though history had seen no progress, we could hope.

The source of Shaw's hope for the future was Creative Evolution. Unlike Darwinian evolution, which Shaw despised for its determinism, this essentially Lamarckian evolution was built upon will. When the giraffe realized it could not eat of the fruit at the top of the tree, it willed the growth of a neck that could accomplish its goal, and over eons of time it grew a longer neck. Likewise mankind can will over time to improve itself, to realize for example that our lifespan is too short. Our bodies are decaying and dying when we are just arriving at the maturity necessary to govern ourselves. The increase in lifespan over the past century might support Shaw's argument that we can realize a deep-seated need and will the means to meet that need. And Shaw did not stop with mankind's ability to will longer life. He saw the possibility of working toward infinity, toward what Teilhard de Chardin called an Omega Man. In the beginning, intelligence had taken on matter to improve itself. Eventually it could shuck matter and return to a spiritual existence. Shaw's effort to flesh out his ideas dramatically, as he did in *Back to Methuseleh,* was a herculean task, as Chesterton knew it would be, and it failed dramatically.

Wisenthal does not focus on Creative Evolution or on the Life Force, Shaw's version of the Holy Spirit that is driving evolution toward its goal. Most of Shaw's heroes are persons who, by being true to themselves, are attuned to the Life Force and help it in its upward movement. It is this attunement to the Life Force that makes Shaw celebrate characters whose ideas are sometimes quite different from those of other characters he has celebrated or from Shaw's own ideas expressed elsewhere. For example, the attraction Shaw shows for the Middle Ages in his preface to *Saint Joan* seems at odds with the saint who represents the new forces of individualism, protestantism, and nationalism, but, whatever her ideas, her will played a part in bringing on a change that at least initially had much to recommend it. Without treating Joan as a manifestation of the Life Force, Wisenthal attempts to explain the inconsistency in the play by asserting that, since Shaw wrote it after World War I, he was a disillusioned man and saw

Joan as both a saint and a threat. Again, when he wishes to discuss Marchbanks's religious impulse in flying out into the night at the end of *Candida,* Wisenthal attributes it to Shaw's attraction to nineteenth-century medievalism rather than to Marchbanks's uniting himself to the Life Force to work for a purpose greater than himself.

When Wisenthal discusses Shaw's growing disenchantment with the Great Man, he likewise has some difficulty explaining Shaw's continuing, if occasional, praise for Mussolini, Stalin, even at times for Hitler. Only Shaw's admiration for willpower and for what it could do to advance the Life Force and Creative Evolution seem to me adequate for explaining Shaw here. Still, I do not wish to fault Wisenthal for not discussing Shaw's ideology. His subject is Shaw's use of history, and he treats his subject thoroughly, even brilliantly, and with thorough honesty. He grinds no theses. When he advances an argument and realizes that Shaw is hard to pin down, he admits it. To cite one example among many, Wisenthal argues very effectively that as a historian Shaw is in Hegel's tradition of ideological historian rather than in von Ranke's tradition of merely factual historian. Shaw was interested in using his characters to show what their stated beliefs would have been, if they could have articulated them. He is interested in essential truth, not external veracity. Yet Wisenthal cites the conclusion to *Everybody's Political What's What?* to show that Shaw occasionally sounds Rankean: "'Though history is adulterated with lies and wishful guesses, yet it sifts and sheds them, leaving finally great blocks of facts'" (p. 40).

In all Wisenthal singles out ten history plays for discussion: *The Devil's Disciple, Caesar and Cleopatra, Saint Joan, The Six of Calais, The Man of Destiny, The Glimpse of Reality, The Dark Lady of the Sonnets, Androcles and the Lion, Great Catherine,* and *In Good King Charles's Golden Days.* However, he does not stop at discussing Shaw's view of history in these plays. Shaw brings the historian's perspective to most things he writes, and Wisenthal argues convincingly that at least half of Shaw's plays attempt to show the dynamics of an age in much the same way as the history plays *stricte dicta.* These other plays Wisenthal calls "present history" plays. *Heartbreak House,* for example, demonstrates that England is just another country, enjoying no special favor from God. *Back to Methuseleh* attempts to shake our usual view of our time by showing how we will appear when regarded from the future. *Misalliance* argues that there is no existing social group worthy of taking control of the country. Even Shaw's view of the Ring of the Niebelung in *The Perfect Wagnerite* is that Wagner created an allegory of the nineteenth century. Most of Shaw's plays, then, treat the present as a historical period so that we will not misinterpret our times or see them as somehow exempt from the judgment we make of other times. Finally, however, as Wisenthal points out, Shaw's purpose is not to teach a moral Lesson but, as Shaw himself said, " 'to interpret life by taking events occurring at haphazard in daily experience and sorting them out so as to show their real significance and interrelation' " (p. 168).

Part of the plays' real significance, of course, is to point us toward the future. We have, as a species, botched things, but there remains hope if we can be honest and will a different future. Chesterton's view of an ideal past can be attacked as a romantic falsification of fact. Shaw's view of the future cannot be so attacked, but, while it can win our minds and our hearts, it has not yet won our imaginations.

Exploring the Dialogue

Peter J. Manning

Theresa M. Kelley. *Wordsworth's Revisionary Aesthetics.* Cambridge: Cambridge University Press, 1988. xiv, 249 pp.

Paul Magnuson. *Coleridge and Wordsworth: A Lyrical Dialogue.* Princeton: Princeton University Press, 1988. xiv, 330 pp.

Nicholas Roe. *Wordsworth and Coleridge: The Radical Years.* Oxford: Clarendon Press, 1988. xvi, 306 pp.

The conjunction of the three books under review invites one to meditate again on the very different ways literary criticism now conceives its object of study. If *object* seems an outdated term, the oddity already measures the distance traveled since New Criticism. In recent years autonomous poems have been absorbed into intertextual fields, autonomous subjects have been revealed as author-functions or sites of sociohistorical conflict, and the canon and the center have ceded to the suppressed voice and the margin. In a self-conscious age the proposal of what to study is never innocent and always significant.

Despite substantial differences in scope and method the three books here joined share certain assumptions which locate them in neighboring territories of the current critical geography. Wordsworth and Coleridge denote for each critic definable historical individuals, developing in exchange with the persons, ideas, and events around them, in trajectories of reflection, choice, and reaction which provide the narrative plots about which the studies are organized. If all three critics place the literary text in the animating network of the author's life, they nonetheless fix the boundaries of the network at notably distinct ranges. Though each finds dialogue at the center of the critical enterprise, the number and the nature of the participants each identifies varies widely. Even as these books vividly display the advantages of the methodological free-for-all of our discipline, they prompt questions about how we determine the contexts through which we envision texts.

Paul Magnuson's *Coleridge and Wordsworth: A Lyrical Dialogue* joins an extended tradition of studies of the formative interaction between the two dominant figures of English Romanticism. The last two decades alone have benefited from the accounts given by Stephen Prickett, William Heath, Thomas McFarland, Lucy Newlyn, and (subsequent to Magnuson) Gene Ruoff.[1] This heritage obligates and enables Magnuson to articulate his procedures with exemplary clarity. The wealth of material made available by the new editions of Coleridge from Princeton University Press and of Wordsworth from Cornell University Press, he remarks at the outset, "offer the opportunity of developing a new methodology of reading their poetry as an intricately connected whole, of reading their works as a joint canon, and of understanding the generation of their greatest poetry" (p. ix). Magnuson acknowledges the practices of Harold Bloom and Mikhail Bakhtin as analogies for his own, but he abjures the agonistic competition emphasized by the former and the parodic strategies of the latter. His poets begin on common ground, and he shapes their successive utterances into a dialogue "constructed on the formal principles of lyric turn, transition, and sequence" (p. 19). As each poet profits from and positions himself against the other, the poems progress through the tropes of denial, negation, revision, and relocation.

Magnuson keeps a shrewd eye on the "fears of amalgamation"—the phrase was Thomas Poole's—which flowed between Coleridge and Wordsworth, but he is less concerned to track them into psychobiography than to illuminate the texts which they produced. From the pairings in his second chapter, "First Readings: 1793–1797," of "Religious Musings" with Wordsworth's Salisbury Plain poems and *Osorio* with *The Borderers*, Magnuson advances chronologically by such antiphonal analyses: "The Ancient Mariner" and "The Discharged Soldier" in Chapter 3, "The Ruined Cottage" and "Christabel" in Chapter 4, the conversation poems and "Tintern Abbey" in Chapter 5.

Magnuson argues that the dialogue between the poets was born from the failure of actual collaboration on "The Rime of the Ancient Mariner," and it is through the logic of such argument that disagreement is interpreted into stimulus, divergence into coherence of a more complex kind. Coleridge and Wordsworth, will-they nill-they, cooperate in building up a single grand ode.

The force of this demonstration does not rest on the seductiveness of its premise alone. Magnuson unfolds the echoing transformations Wordsworth and Coleridge worked on each other's verse, and he makes telling use of the compositional histories, retitlings, and rearrangements of the texts from one published collection to the next. It is no small praise to say that Magnuson shows how the plenitude of information presented by the new editions upon which he draws can be used to deepen and shade anew a narrative we thought we knew well. One is also grateful for a writer capable of such lucid, witty compressions as the characterization of "Frost at Midnight" as "the most important poem Wordsworth ever rewrote" (p. 156). Magnuson astutely compares Coleridge's habitually abstract and figurative language—a phrase like "intellectual breeze," for example—with the greater materiality images of nature held for Wordsworth (pp. 143–44), and highlights the structural difference between Coleridge's self-abnegation in the conversation poems and the increasing centrality of the self for Wordsworth.

Indeed in the tale Magnuson relates that Wordsworth's growing self-absorption after 1799–1800 gradually effects a shift between the two poets which relegates Coleridge to second place. He is particularly adroit, however, in disclosing how Wordsworth is most indebted to Coleridge just as he frames his myth of autogenic genius in the early drafts of *The Prelude:* "When he seems to be the most personal and individual, he comes close to ventriloquizing Coleridge's voice and appropriating his texts" (p. 194). Magnuson discreetly but firmly opposes those critics who have seen in the "spots of time" the essence of *The Prelude,* stressing instead the acts of connection by which Wordsworth constructed his self. As the title of chapter 6, "The Search for 'Perfect Form,'" indicates, Magnuson depicts the Wordsworth of the Goslar period not as a middle-aged man uncertain of his future in pursuit of a past but as a poet in search of what will suffice:

> The issue of isolation, which seemed in "Tintern Abbey" and in individual lyric moments of recollection in the drafts to be overcome by the forging of a psychic connection to childhood as the source of order, became in the early work on *The Prelude* a question of the arrangement of the text itself and not at all a matter of memory—a contextual, not a psychological, problem. [p. 199]

Magnuson entitles chapter 7 "A Farewell to Coleridge: Grasmere, 1800." Settled with Dorothy at last, Wordsworth sought to establish a context for his poetry within his own work and to obscure its uncanny implication in, and dependence on, that of Coleridge. From the lyric and retrospective genres they had shared, he turned to prospective and narrative ones; while Coleridge labored in London as a political journalist for the *Morning Post,* he withdrew into a nature subservient to the imagination of the "Poems on the Naming of Places." As Magnuson reminds us, Wordsworth intended to call the second edition of *Lyrical Ballads* "Poems by W. Wordsworth," and though the intention was not carried out, the effacement was thorough; "the second volume," he observes, "might well have been entitled *Home at Grasmere,*" so completely is the landscape Wordsworth's (p. 245).

Even the breaking-off of "Home at Grasmere" did not modify Wordsworth's course. "In the absence of new inspiration for intense lyric," Magnuson writes, Wordsworth returned in 1801–02 "to a reordering of material already written, a process that he recognized, two years before, would give intelligibility and purpose to his poetry" (p. 278). Thus, when chapter 8 reaches 1802 and what has heretofore seemed its finest instance, "The Dejection Dialogue," the exchange between Coleridge and Wordsworth was already almost over. It is the achievement of *Coleridge and Wordsworth: A Lyrical Dialogue* to have demonstrated the subtle twists, and the extent, of the web from which "Dejection: An Ode," "Resolution and Independence," and the "Intimations" ode emerged.

Transience, Magnuson writes in his conclusion, is the limiting if enabling condition of lyric, but "transience and trance would end in utter silence were it not for the generating turns of dialogue" (p. 319). His own master narrative, however, ends with "Wordsworth's determination to become his own origin" (p. 317), to generate from the renewed work on *The Prelude* in 1804 "the long poem that imitates the form of its own generation" and so appears, at some cost, to stand self-sufficient (p. 323).

Though consumed in the end, the modeling of the self-reflexive turns of the encounters between Wordsworth and Coleridge on the form of the ode is valuable. From his trope Magnuson derives the backbone of a narrative line without the constrictions of a reductive thesis. The discontinuities and abrupt shifts which the form licenses engender a shifting and reversing movement quite different from the emphasis of Stephen Prickett on "the poetry of growth," which is both the theme on which he concentrates and the teleology which governs his representation, or from the passage Thomas McFarland relates from symbiosis to fragmentation.

Expansive as Magnuson's formulation of dialogue proves, however, it is avowedly inward-turning. The poems, if not solely the canonical major ones, and the poets talk only to each other. The restriction to a single interlocutor occasionally leads to a strained interpretation, but that is less important than the overall consequence of Magnuson's intensiveness. Speakers beyond Coleridge and Wordsworth never intrude upon the conversation or disrupt its focus. To choose one example, the artistic single-mindedness Magnuson conveys in Wordsworth is heightened by the exclusion from this account of such matters great and small as Annette and Mary, the Lowther inheritance and the disputes with his lawyer brother it brought, the inconveniences of Dove Cottage and the Napoleonic wars, all of which demanded Wordsworth's attention, occupied his letters, and affected, if obliquely, his poetry. If one decides *a priori* to treat a dialogue as the stanzas of an ode, the random distractions which threaten but enliven daily existence are banished. "Mr. Wordsworth is not to be interrupted," Mrs. Wordsworth is said to have said to Keats: life rarely affords such a privilege.

Every author should be granted his premise, especially when sustained as *Coleridge and Wordsworth: A Lyrical Dialogue* sustains

Magnuson's. I am less concerned to challenge its central trope than to distinguish its elected limits. The citation of Bakhtin, for example, might have pointed to a less intentionalist, more socially inclusive notion of dialogue: Wordsworth and Coleridge together as competing for moral authority with other forms of discourse, such as the press or the law, or as embodiments of class or political interests. For Bakhtin the horizon of dialogue extends beyond the situation of utterance to the society at large.[2]

A mutually instructive contrast falls to hand in the dedication of Nicholas Roe's *Wordsworth and Coleridge: The Radical Years* "to the memory of John Thelwall, Citizen, Poet, Prophet, 1764–1834." Thelwall, the notorious radical lecturer whose visit to the poets at Nether Stowey and Alfoxden in 1797 alarmed the neighborhood and whose retreat from politics Roe foregrounds as emblematic of his generation, Magnuson mentions only in passing. Roe both complicates and confirms the picture E. P. Thompson gave twenty years ago of the erosion of the youthful revolutionary sympathies of Wordsworth and Coleridge.[3] Thompson's celebrated brief essay could only suggest a program for further investigation; in Roe's book we have the thickest description so far of the milieux in which Coleridge and Wordsworth moved in the 1790s.

The subtitle of Roe's introduction, "Voices from the Common Grave of Liberty," a phrase inspired by William Godwin, and the title of his second chapter, "'Europe was Rejoiced': Responses to Revolution, 1789–1791," manifest the amplitude of the dialogue Roe conceives Romantic poetry to enter. Because Coleridge later deliberately falsified and Wordsworth minimized the shared reformist views which Roe argues first drew them together, his task has been to reconstruct the aspirations and audiences their works addressed. Patient research into unfamiliar and unpublished sources has enabled him vividly to portray Wordsworth and Coleridge, despite their whitewashed reminiscences, "in much the same company, at the epicentre of British radical life" (p. 14).

The London to which Wordsworth came in 1791 was a hurly-burly of revolutionary sympathy and radical activity, and he rapidly immersed himself in the circles spreading around the unitarian Samuel Nicholson, Joseph Fawcett, and the radical printer Joseph Johnson. The Wordsworth who declared to William Mathews in 1794 in connection with their planned journal, *The Philanthropist,* that he belonged to "that odious class of men called democrats" had been affiliated for many years with members of the Society for Constitutional Information and the London Corresponding Society.[4] Roe's linking of the earliest stages of *The Recluse* with the Painite creed of natural rights plays strikingly against the conservative tenor which overtook Wordsworth's perpetually unfulfilled major project, and it is equally salutary to consider Coleridge's philosophy of the One Life as "a transcendent justification of Paine's 'system of principles as universal as truth and the existence of man'" (pp. 34–35).

Roe's second chapter, "'Pretty Hot in It': Wordsworth and France, 1791–1792," is still more revelatory. Roe has brought to light the proceedings of the revolutionary club at Blois, *Les Amis de la Constitution,* and so reconstructed the heady atmosphere in which Wordsworth apprehended the revolution. In his retrospective account in *The Prelude* Wordsworth honors Michel Beaupuy, whom he probably met at the society, as his mentor, but Roe documents as well the influence of the president of the society, the regicidal Bishop of Blois, Henri Grégoire. "It was from them," he argues, "that Wordsworth derived the militant republicanism of his *Letter to the Bishop of Llandaff* and the prophetic authority . . . first heard in the concluding lines of *Descriptive Sketches*" (p. 51). Seen through this lens, the Wordsworth of this period appears considerably closer to the violence of Robespierre than to the moderate he later made himself out to be (p. 39). The excitement of Blois and Paris and the enthusiasm of the radicals at home explain the shock Wordsworth experienced when he had to confront the outbreak of war shortly after his return to England in December 1792 (p. 83). If the triumph of the Jacobins tempered Wordsworth's trust in democracy, leading him after 1793 from millenarianism to the regeneration of the individual mind and the relocation of "Effort, and expectation, and desire, / And something evermore about to be" (1805 *Pre-*

lude, VI. 541–42), from the sphere of revolutionary action to that of imagination, Roe has detailed the itinerary he followed.

"Long before they met each other," Roe shows, mutual friends among "the dominant Cambridge presence in metropolitan radical circles" brought Coleridge and Wordsworth into the same orbit in 1794–95 (p. 93). By a series of capsule biographies of such figures as George Dyer, William Frend, John Tweddell, James Losh, and Felix Vaughan, Roe assembles a convincing group portrait of the reformist aims and ultimate frustration of this cohort by such repressive measures as the Treasonable Practices and Seditious Meetings bills, rushed through by an alarmed government at the end of 1795. A second, overlapping pattern of contacts emanated from William Godwin, not yet the gradualist of later editions of *Political Justice,* opposed to all organized political activity, but the "hero of the reform movement" whose pamphlet *Cursory Strictures* had been instrumental in the acquittal of Thomas Hardy, founder of the LCS, Horne Tooke, and Thelwall on charges of treason in 1794 (p. 190).

The implicit dialogue between Wordsworth and Coleridge Roe unpacks is shaped by these pressing controversies. While Coleridge's emphasis on the emotions and the domestic attachments of love and family drew him apart from Godwin's rationalism, Wordsworth relinquished his belief in revolutionary action and approached Godwin's reliance on the individual mind. Through succinct examination of the revised "Salisbury Plain" of 1795, *The Borderers,* and the "Baker's Cart" fragment of 1796–97, Roe follows the evolution of Wordsworth's poetry "as an inverse ratio of its explicit political purpose until in *The Ruined Cottage*" specific injustices have "receded into a background of incidental detail" (p. 132).

For both Wordsworth and Coleridge, Robespierre loomed as the dangerous avatar of Godwinian reason abstracted from feeling. The traumatic loss of faith in Godwinian principles to which the Terror Robespierre inaugurated drove him, Wordsworth figured through Rivers in *The Borderers* and recounted directly in *The Prelude.* In chapter 6, "'A Sympathy with Power': Imagining Robespierre," Roe amplifies the poet's own narrative by setting it against the drama jointly written by Coleridge and Southey in

1794, *The Fall of Robespierre*, and the alternatives to Robespierre elaborated by Coleridge in his 1795 Lectures.

By his persuasive, cumulative delineation of cultural crisis, mapped on a scale both national, even international, and particular to the work of the two writers and the subculture of Cambridge radicals in which they traveled, Roe reveals the rich soil from which the extraordinarily fertile interaction between Coleridge and Wordsworth stemmed when they met at last in the autumn of 1795. Roe's careful preparation makes clear how Wordsworth's fall into despair had left him "in need of precisely the intellectual and philosophic guidance that Coleridge could bring him"; the One Life asserted by Coleridge became a "redemptive possibility" upon which he could reconstitute the revolutionary hopes he had felt in France in 1792 (p. 233).

The withdrawal apparent in this reconstitution has turned the government's assignment of a spy to watch Coleridge and Wordsworth at Alfoxden in August 1797 into comedy for later eyes. Roe makes evident the causes of the government's suspicion: Thelwall, who arrived in July, had been tailed by James Walsh, the spy, since 1792, and Wordsworth and Coleridge, observing the landscape and jotting down their observations, had already aroused the suspicion of the locals and of a ministry who viewed the French landing in Pembrokeshire in August as the harbinger of invasion (p. 248 ff.). Whether English Jacobins or French spies, Coleridge and Wordsworth were persons to watch, and Roe restores the contemporary reputation that Coleridge was at pains to deprecate when in the *Biographia Literaria* he reduced the incident to the mishearing of "Spinoza" as "Spy Nosy."

Coleridge's poems of spring 1798, "France, an Ode," "Frost at Midnight," and "Fears in Solitude," nonetheless show the split between the public realm of politics and the private world of subjective meditation. In a reversal like that descried by Magnuson, Roe counterpoints the "disabling inversion" of "Fears in Solitude" (p. 267) with the "idiom of assertion and simultaneous reservation" which characterizes "Tintern Abbey." In the achievement of a rhetoric which "quietly re-enacts the more violent oscillations of his political and philosophical opinions in early years," Roe reads Wordsworth's reply to the paralysis of creativity attendant upon Coleridge's shattered confidence (p. 270). "Tintern Abbey," Roe concludes, "is grounded in Wordsworth's radical years," and in its distinctive hesitations he discerns

> the context of a lasting vulnerability—"And so I dare to hope"—that was the common legacy of revolution to Wordsworth, Coleridge, and their contemporaries. Wordsworth's consciousness of human weakness and fallibility, "The still, sad music of humanity, / Not harsh nor grating, though of ample power / To chasten and subdue"—was the hardest lesson of revolution, but for Wordworth it proved most fruitful. More than the aspiration he felt with his generation . . . it was failure that made Wordsworth a poet. [pp. 274–75]

The now-converging, now-diverging evolution of the two chief figures of *Wordsworth and Coleridge: The Radical Years,* and the number of actors whose individual careers Roe collects into an inclusive social history, inevitably produce some hiccoughs and repetitions in the narrative. Yet Roe executes his ambitious design with aplomb, and if his argument recurrently requires inference from their contemporaries to Wordsworth and Coleridge themselves, the process enlarges rather than restricts the bearings of the works under discussion. The quotation above from the final paragraph of the book suggests Roe's admirable critical tact and the judiciousness of his conclusions. Dispassionate scholarship here recovers the passions which Wordsworth and Coleridge brought to their writing.

I place Theresa Kelley's *Wordsworth's Revisionary Aesthetics* last in this survey in part because its inquiry into the "rhetorical competition" (p. 1) between sublime and beautiful figures in Wordsworth's aesthetics casts light on the commitment of all three studies to narrative as a mode of criticism. What models command their allegiances? The end enforced by Magnuson's story is artistic complexity: as Wordsworth searches for the perfect form to encompass the fragments of his output, so today's readers are urged to apprehend the diverse productions of Wordsworth and Coleridge as parts of a whole. The moral of Roe's book I might have summed up twenty years ago as "keep the faith," for Roe's sympathetic exposition of the permutations of his revolutionary ideals resists the condemnation poured upon Wordsworth by more ideological critics. Kelley's own study is based on a conflict model: the foremost dialogue of *Wordsworth's Revisionary Aesthetics* is Wordsworth's with himself.

Kelley presents a Wordsworth whose investments in the sublime were always checked by a countervailing respect for the second pole of eighteenth-century aesthetics, the beautiful. The dynamic Kelley describes arises from the career-long contest between "the wilful self-aggrandizement of the revolutionary or Satanic sublime" and advocacy of the "communicability and a sense of known limits in art as well as society" intrinsic to the beautiful (p. 3). In Wordsworth's repeated staging of "sublimity and beauty as successive, then competing, categories" (p. 3) Kelley locates the distinctive feature of his aesthetics, and in the dramatization of the rhetorical implications of these aesthetic differences his "singular poetic achievement" (p. 2). Since by definition the sublime eludes articulation and can only be expressed by a language which undermines its "otherness," it always yields to the figures which represent it. More than any previous critic, Kelley transfers attention from the initiating sublime moment to the acts of containment it provokes. Arguing that Wordsworth was "as much interested in how the mind defends itself against the sublime as he was in the sublime itself," she reinscribes it as instrumental to composition: "The sublime is important because it is an occasion for rhetorical and figurative strategies that enable the poetic effort to retrieve (or not to retrieve) it" (p. 10).

The altered status of the sublime signals the magnitude of Kelley's claim. The post-New Critical revival of the Romantics depended on privileging the sublime; although Geoffrey Hartman's *Wordsworth's Poetry 1787–1814* depicted a Wordsworth divided between *apocalypse* and *akedah,* all the glamor belonged to the former. Harold Bloom's *Blake's Apocalypse* and *The Visionary Company* were works representative of the times, and the same priorities governed Frances Ferguson's *Wordsworth: Language as Counter-Spirit* and Thomas Weiskel's *The Romantic Sublime.*[5] The "revisionary" of Kelley's title applies not only to a process in Wordsworth but, polemically if obtrusively, to the contribution of *Wordsworth's Revisionary Aesthetics* to the dialogue of critics.

Kelley's work is revisionary in a further sense as well: in the texts it treats. Chapter 2, "Archeologies," contrasts Wordsworth's fragmentary essay, "The Sublime and the Beautiful" with his *Guide to the Lakes*. With impressive historical imagination Kelley shows how the stratigraphy of the Lake District as formulated by eighteenth-century geological thought offered Wordsworth a model of the mind in which the operations of time smooth the sublime into the beautiful; the rough outcroppings of the landscape are archaic survivals, like eruptions from the psychic depths. If the fragmentary essay insists that aesthetic categories are learned, not found in nature, its form is homologous: awe at the sublime is the reaction of youth or an untrained sensibility, from which "as we advance in life, we can escape upon the invitation of our more placid and gentle nature" (quoted on p. 24). For Kant the mind's astonishment at the sublime in nature triggers a saving recognition of the still greater powers of reason, but for Wordsworth reason functions "as the agent of the beautiful" (p. 32). From the fearful self-sufficiency of the sublime Wordsworth "escapes" into The Progress of Beauty. The sequence Kelley identifies is thus cannily double, supplying both the development in perception which furnishes the plot of the Wordsworthian text and the ruling principle of the revisions to which Wordsworth subjected his texts, of which she makes good use throughout. She illustrates these characteristic strategies by examining successive editions of the *Guide* (first independently published in 1820). The ascent of Scawfell which Wordsworth added to the 1822 edition marks the quest for the sublime as the first phase of an aesthetic education, but beauty gains the last word in the excursion to Ullswater added in 1823, its dominance underscored by the "Ode: The Pass of Kirkstone" placed after it in 1835: "In announcing his farewell to the 'desolate domain' of the Pass of Kirkstone so that he might celebrate the neat, fixed personifications of Hope, Joy, Faith, and human life, the speaker of the ode reduces the sublime to a dispensable antechamber" (p. 41).

The paradigmatic "scene of aesthetic instruction," as Kelley names it in chapter 3, proceeds from Wordsworth's imposition of "a literary topography of sublimity and beauty upon a natural one" (p. 37) and his "persistent confusion of actual places with rhetorical ones" (p. 43). The concept again and again proves its worth by the range of material to which it restores interest. Wordsworth's transition in eight lines of the "Prospectus" to *The Recluse* from "the darkest Pit / Of the profoundest Hell" to "beauty, whose living home is the green earth" is familiar; so too Wordsworth's attempts to fashion the sublime experiences recorded in "Tintern Abbey" and Book I of *The Prelude* into narrative order and a coherent self. Though Kelley's handling of such passages bears out her thesis, the broad agreement of the critical tradition renders these pages less exciting, say, than her brief discussion of a little-considered poem from *Poems, in Two Volumes* (1807), "Fidelity." The poem lauds the faithfulness of a dog who had remained for months by the corpse of his fallen owner in an isolated spot in the mountains. Kelley concisely demonstrates how throughly representative is Wordsworth's taming of the starkness of the incident by positioning at its center the domestic affection of the dog, deflecting a severely sublime scene into an *exemplum* of "love sublime" (pp. 46–47). Without inflating the significance of "Fidelity," she employs it to open up the canon and reveal its pervasive traits.

If it is a far cry from the agonies and exultations prized by devotees of the sublime to the assurances of "Fidelity." The critique of the sublime Kelley disengages compensates by breaking the exclusive hold of Wordsworth's major poems and The Great Decade, broadening and extending in time the picture of the poet. Moreover, chapter 4, "Revolution and the Egotistical Sublime," and chapter 5, "Revisionary Aesthetics in *The Prelude*," abundantly attest the "political and semiotic hazards of the sublime" (p. 7) events forced upon Wordsworth. Unlike Kant, Wordsworth could not quarantine his aesthetics from "the pressures of history and human failure" (p. 6). The disruption of "the well-ordered surfaces of society and language" by "the chaotic energies of the sublime" in *The Borderers* (p. 72), Kelley, like Roe, diagnoses as the contaminating explosion of the French Revolution into violence. The satanic Rivers—"self-aggrandizement in the name of transcendent freedom"—who "assumes the 'sublime' voice of the autobiographical speaker of *The Prelude*" (p. 77) provides Kelley with the bridge to Wordsworth's campaign to master the sublime in the account of his own life. From the clearest opposition between beauty and the sublime, the episode of the Drowned Man, through the interpolation of the Carthusian monastery in Book VI to suggest a "reverential sublime" which counters the "soul-debasing" sublime terror of Book V, to the spots of time in Book XI, Kelley traces Wordsworth's arrangement of the troubling experiences of his past into the steps of an aesthetic education. "By a progress everywhere marked with suppressions and retrievals," she comments, "he has come to the place that so frequently lies unacknowledged beneath beautiful surfaces" (p. 124). Kelley's emphasis falls on *progress;* where suspicious critics have largely seen disguises and concealment, for Kelley "suppression" is an inevitable component of "retrieval":

Like Freud, who urged himself down through the layers of mind . . . here Wordsworth's speaker seeks that place within the mind's progress where human expression approaches the sublime. To have retrieved this much is the signal achievement of the expanded *Prelude*. Wordsworth's revisions of the Book XI "spots of time" reveal the partial settlements the heart must make and remake in order to meet what it knows and what it has been. [p. 124]

Kelley acknowledges the costs to the final books of *The Prelude* of "avoiding or domesticating the sublime," but argues that Wordsworth was developing, not betraying, the Romantic imagination: "He inaugurates the Romantic effort to re-define the imagination as something more than sublime vision" (p. 126). In her long view even the "unrelenting . . . management of sublime figures and values" in *The Excursion*, comprehensible in the aiming of the poem at "a larger, public audience whose ambivalent response to revolutionary and Napoleonic France mirrored Wordsworth's earlier reception and rejection of the sublime," stands as an interim position rather than a dead end (p. 133). The

Exploring the Dialogue 269

vanquishing of the sublime exhausted one mode but engendered another: "a version of the beautiful that dramatizes the cultural force of ideology (whether radical or conservative). By undermining those sublime figures or speakers that purport to act outside ideology and thus outside history, the beautiful insists that it structures and is structured by history and culture" (p. 136).

I have quoted at length because it is one of the great virtues of *Wordsworth's Revisionary Aesthetics* thus to have grasped the influx of energy which fed Wordsworth's continued productivity. T. S. Eliot dismissed Wordsworth as lacking in that "historical sense" he proclaimed "nearly indispensable to anyone who would continue to be a poet beyond his twenty-fifth year," but Kelley's resurrection of the late work witnesses that it was precisely the thoughtfulness Eliot sought which underwrote a career that closed only with a volume published in Wordsworth's seventy-second year.[6] Kelley's narrative generously concludes with Wordsworth's enduring vitality.

Chapter 6, "The Aesthetics of Containment," carries beyond *The Excursion* to Wordsworth's hollowing-out of chivalric romance in *The White Doe of Rylstone,* stabilizing the world of *The Borderers* and creating a space for the beautiful to inhabit, and to the rearranging of his works for the 1815 edition, bringing earlier poetry into fresh relations and stimulating readers to pursue the reverberations struck by the new sequences and categories. As an instance of these self-revising gestures (the habit Magnuson also scrutinizes), Kelley deftly illustrates how the placement of the ode "Composed upon an Evening of Extraordinary Splendor and Beauty" (1817) before the "Intimations" ode (1804) to which it alludes shapes the reader's response to the earlier poem. "Buried fears are not just suppressed or displaced," Kelly argues of Wordsworth's art of arrangement; "they are thoroughly re-contextualized" (p. 169).

In the final chapter, "Family of Floods," Kelley turns to the images of floods, torrents, and waterfalls in which Wordsworth repeatedly figured the instability of the sublime. A probing consideration of the Rhinefall sonnet, first published in the 1822

Memorials of a Tour of the Continent, devoted to a scene Wordsworth had first visited in 1790, demonstrates the extent to which Wordsworth's changing representations of the sublime were influenced by the history in the landscape he observed. Drawing for comparison upon guidebook engravings of the spot and Turner's controversial 1806 painting, *Falls of the Rhine,* Kelley brilliantly reveals how Wordsworth's—and Europe's—experience of the intervening thirty years transformed a *topos* of the sublime into a symbol of "Swiss resistance and French Tyranny" (p. 173).

The "aesthetics" Kelley limns bring her surprisingly close to recent New Historical work on the Romantics, and to such traditional historicist studies as Roe's. From her vantage, accordingly, those who most need persuasion are critics for whom "aesthetics" is a closed system, and language non-referential. Such gains in understanding as the discussion of the Rhinefall sonnet provide are the evidence which supports her plea:

> For some writers, including Wordsworth, the world beyond the text is implicated in the text. Those who have argued to the contrary have claimed that signs refer only to other signs or to other texts.... Wordsworth's response to the Rhinefall and other "torrents" suggests instead that signs exhibit visual and aural resonances that extend beyond the texts in which those signs appear. For this reason, they cannot be read as self-contained, self-consuming artifacts. As vehicles that support several contexts and tenors within and without his poetry and prose, Wordsworth's "family of floods" shows how things in the world are *significant* in the radical sense of this term.
>
> In Wordsworth's later poetry the dizzying, empty detours and countersigns which are the errant sign language of the sublime yield to the beautiful, which sanctions and extends the task of gathering inferences and echoes from several frames of meaning—in this case, an extensive one which binds the history of Napoleonic Europe to the history of Wordsworth's career. [p. 191]

By folding history into the language and formal shape of texts Kelley accomplishes a task that has too often proved elusive: a criticism at once genuinely literary and fully alert to historical conditions. *Wordsworth's Revisionary Aesthetics* is a capacious study, recapturing the dialogue in (and between) Wordsworth's texts as well as with the culture in which they came into being, and fostering renewed reflection on the literary theories through which we listen to them.

Notes

1. Stephen Prickett, *Coleridge and Wordsworth: The Poetry of Growth* (Cambridge: Cambridge Univ. Press, 1970); William Heath, *Wordsworth and Coleridge: A Study of Their Literary Relations in 1801–1802* (Oxford: Clarendon, 1970); Thomas McFarland, *Romanticism and the Forms of Ruin: Wordsworth, Coleridge, and Modalities of Fragmentation* (Princeton: Princeton Univ. Press, 1981); Lucy Newlyn, *Coleridge, Wordsworth, and the Language of Allusion* (Oxford: Clarendon, 1986); Gene Ruoff, *The Making of the Major Lyrics, 1802–1804* (New Brunswick, N.J.: Rutgers Univ. Press, 1989).

2. In recent work, such as the talk on "The Politics of 'Frost at Midnight'" delivered at the 1989 convention of the Modern Language Association, Magnuson investigates the cultural conflicts in which volumes of poetry are situated.

3. E. P. Thompson, "Disenchantment or Default? A Lay Sermon," in *Power and Consciousness*, ed. Conor Cruise O'Brien and William Dean Vanech (London: Univ. of London Press, 1969), pp. 1–13. For Thompson's somewhat querulous review of Roe's study, see the *London Review of Books*, 8 December 1988, pp. 3–6.

4. *The Letters of William and Dorothy Wordsworth*, ed. Ernest de Selincourt, 2d ed., *The Early Years 1787–1805*, rev. Chester L. Shaver (Oxford: Clarendon, 1967), p. 119.

5. Geoffrey Hartman, *Wordsworth's Poetry 1787–1814* (1964; Cambridge: Harvard Univ. Press, 1987); Harold Bloom, *Blake's Apocalypse* (Garden City, N.Y.: Doubleday, 1963) and *The Visionary Company* (1963; Ithaca: Cornell Univ. Press, 1971); Frances Ferguson, *Wordsworth: Language as Counter Spirit* (New Haven: Yale Univ. Press, 1977); Thomas Weiskel, *The Romantic Sublime* (Baltimore: Johns Hopkins Univ. Press, 1976).

6. T. S. Eliot, "Tradition and the Individual Talent," in *The Sacred Wood* (1920; London: Methuen, 1960), p. 49.

Market Studies and Book History in American Literature

C. Deirdre Phelps

Michael Anesko. *"Friction with the Market": Henry James and the Profession of Authorship.* New York: Oxford University Press, 1986. xiv, 258 pp.

Cathy N. Davidson. *Revolution and the Word: The Rise of the Novel in America.* New York: Oxford University Press, 1986. xiv, 322 pp.

Michael T. Gilmore. *American Romanticism and the Marketplace.* Chicago: University of Chicago Press, 1985. x, 178 pp.

Christopher P. Wilson. *The Labor of Words: Literary Professionalism in the Progressive Era.* Athens: University of Georgia Press, 1985. xx, 240 pp.

R. Jackson Wilson. *Figures of Speech: American Writers and the Literary Marketplace from Benjamin Franklin to Emily Dickinson.* New York: Alfred A. Knopf, 1989. xvi, 300 pp.

Within the last few years, studies of authors in relation to their readers or markets have proliferated, and while they are now understood to be part of a new socio-cultural history, there is as yet no sufficient recognition in literary studies of their relations with studies in the history of the book, an area that ranges from older traditional work in literary culture and the book trades, and the specific modern form of cultural book history, or *l'histoire du livre,* to textual criticism and analytical bibliography. The relations of all of these with literary theory are still to be determined; a welcome step in that direction has been taken by the market studies now appearing, but so far it is a conceptually limited step. The books here, the most recent of which treats the whole of the nineteenth century, and the others of which examine the four successive quarters of it, illustrate various partial uses of book history in the interpretation of American literature. A survey of their methods may help those critics who wish to assimilate such work in future studies and to recognize it as part of a distinct field with its own evolving knowledge and theory.

The "history of the book," or *l'histoire du livre*, has arisen mainly in the work of French social historians who have applied it to socio-cultural studies. In 1958, in *L'Apparition du livre*, Lucien Febvre and Henri-Jean Martin provided an important comprehensive study of the production and dissemination of books throughout history. More recently, this work has been developed in the impressive multi-volume *Histoire de l'edition francaise*, edited by Martin and others, and similar histories are planned for British and American book production, in which individual studies have proliferated.[1]

These studies have encouraged the appropriation of book history by literary students, but have also helped to restrict it to forms of social interpretation. Febvre himself, in the preface to *L'Apparition*, said that it might as well have been called "The Book in the Service of History"; since then, Robert Darnton's work has helped to define book history in cultural rather than literary terms. Literature of course has its place in history and culture, but in the interest of detailed analysis of specific works, literary students might be more properly concerned with the book in the service of literature, or history in service of the book.[2]

Writers past and present on the history of books and culture, whatever their fields, agree that the production of a book involves a complex set of interrelated activities. Robert Escarpit emphasized the importance of a three-part system of author, trade, and audience, in contrast to the literary student's usual approach only to author and reader. In this country that configuration was delineated by William Charvat, the writer who has done the most to give literary work a basis in the history of the American book trade. Robert Darnton has developed a chart of "The Communications Circuit" which diagrams the interaction of these factors with social, political, and intellectual influences.[3]

Critics who attempt to mix cultural studies with the book trade are easily led to misrepresent or ignore it by unbalancing these three factors. The devaluation of the author in recent theory can lead to the exclusive audience focus Cathy N. Davidson maintains, while market studies that include the author, like those of Michael T. Gilmore and R. Jackson Wilson, can still be made without adequate recognition of the book trade itself as part of that market. By contrast, I instance Christopher Wilson's *The Labor of Words*, with its balanced focus on authorship that exists in conjunction with a socially determined, yet carefully specified and individualized book trade, as a model of the way an understanding of the book trade can illuminate our reading of literary works. This is true in spite of the fact that he too seems unaware of current trends in book history. The limitation of Davidson's work, on the other hand, results from her very use of new work, which she appropriates on its own purely socio-cultural terms.

As the study of the history of books moves to merge with the Anglo-American tradition of literary publishing history, bibliography, and textual criticism as well as with American and European critical theory, it cannot be adopted only on those social terms that have been most useful for historians whose primary interest is culture itself.[4] Book history must include not only fundamental kinds of authorial autonomy but also the physical or material forms of any given text. Until now, study of these forms has fallen mainly within scholarly literary studies, and it will continue to do so, but we cannot afford a polarity between *l'histoire du livre* for cultural studies and bibliography and textual criticism for literary ones. The complex nature of the book requires that both be understood as parts of a broadly defined book history. Davidson appropriates physical text forms for social purposes, and they too are, ultimately, socially determined. But once they are recognized as discrete parts of book history that in analysis can be separate from social factors, they become open to a much greater range of interpretation. Of the critics here, only Michael Anesko, with his narrower, single-author focus and abundance of archival material, makes adequate use of documents of publishing history and physical bibliography, while also incorporating all three social factors—audience, trade, and author—into interpretation of James's novels (although he also fails to acknowledge recent work in book history).

Since the critics here all do make use of the book trade in their interesting, even enlightening interpretations of literary texts, my purpose is to consider first how comprehensively they understand its social configuration and then how they have used it in their readings. Finally, I consider whether they incorporate those other interpretive factors in the history of a book—its material forms. Because Christopher Wilson's and Michael Anesko's books succeed in their application of a more fully conceived book history (and have been reviewed previously in this journal), I will refer to them here primarily for comparison with the other three.[5]

In *Revolution and the Word*, Davidson analyzes popular historiographical, sentimental, picaresque, and gothic novels in the early part of the nineteenth century to locate structures and themes that fall within her Marxist and feminist focus. The "revolution" of her title includes, besides the historical conflict, the industrial revolution that helped make novels available to the mass of readers, the "reading revolution" of increased literacy (leading to the acceptance of the theretofore denigrated novel form itself), and the current critical interest in new history. The novels she takes up are revolutionary in the ways they encouraged education and underwrote new female and democratic initiatives.

Davidson begins with a careful and comprehensive survey of the trade, but her principal use of it is as background for the concept of the audience, to whom she finds her novels principally respond. Thus she actually does not include those necessary other factors in the social configuration of book history, the publisher or the author (although she clearly acknowledges Charvat on this point), but limits herself to the old dialectic of work and reader (albeit now the reader is concrete rather than abstract). Her authorial and publishing references quickly become reader references—the writer writes what appeals, and the publisher promotes it. This is entirely in keeping with Davidson's expressed purpose, and she has used her materials to create a study of real strength of the American popular novel's coalescence with the social conditions of the period. But the aim of restoring neglected works to serious consideration would be better served on the whole by a balanced attention to the trade complex. More to the point, if studies with such a special emphasis represent the uses of book history in literature, they may limit its theoretical understanding.

Davidson quotes Darnton on the use of book history to understand "how exposure to the printed word affected human thought and behavior during the last 500 years" (p. 4) and Geertz on the use of thick description to learn "about the society in which it is found, and beyond that, about social life as such" (p. 10). This is indeed socio-cultural history first, and literature and literary history second. She limits her analyses too by opposing the cultural focus of book history, as she sees it, to poststructuralist "codes and rules of fictive discourse" (p. 4) in her texts, when book history should include forms of the text itself. She argues that "literature is not simply words upon a page but a complex social, political, and material process of cultural production" (p. viii). Indeed it is, but the effect on it of the trade she has surveyed so well is not considered in her analyses, and thus she establishes a methodological separation that she herself has disavowed. The novel, she says, results from the publisher's intentions as much as the author's, but those intentions affect the writing of the text as well as audience appeal. Her semiotic analysis, which she sees as the formalist, "perhaps even ahistorical" complement to her cultural application of book history (pp. 4–5), becomes the location of words and structures that evoke only the social ideas she discusses. In fact each of her approaches, historical and linguistic, offers more than the purely social interpretation she chooses. Having chosen only the social aspect of each, it is no wonder that she can find them only "different from," and not in opposition to, each other (p. 4).

Gilmore's retrospective of his period is a broader one, of general market conditions, with briefer references to the book trade, but in his analyses of Emerson, Thoreau, Hawthorne, and Melville he can be as effective in locating his authors' market interests as Davidson is in locating the interests of their readers. While the questions he asks are also social ones, his focus is "on the literature and not on societal change" (p. 5). His approach may illustrate the danger of trade history becoming identified with a social approach like Davidson's. To Gilmore, it may seem that a "literary" study would therefore leave out the details of the trade, thus halting the progress of the synthesis Charvat initiated. In fact, the trade must be used in both approaches, but in different ways. As it is, Gilmore's book shows both the potential and the problems inherent in the interpretation of "the market" for literary works, and his compelling arguments suggest but do not acknowledge many connections with the book trade that should be integral to them. He has read Charvat, and may feel that this work has been done, but his notes do not cite arguments of Charvat that are directly relevant to his own, and in any case the field is wide open for the enlargement of Charvat's premises.

R. Jackson Wilson, an historian, is also interested in texts as evidence of authorial response to the market. In his cultural contextual studies, on Franklin, Irving, William Lloyd Garrison, Emerson, Dickinson, and in a pendant on Whitman, he argues that these authors invented transcendent romantic literary personae or "figures of speech" in opposition to the realities of the market. His readings are of lives as much as texts, and one half or more of each study is taken up with his authors' experiences of family, friends, and general occupations.

Wilson represents the context of the trade well when he occasionally illustrates specifics of his writers' involvement with it, but their presumed view of it as primarily an anonymous mass commercialized audience means that it remains largely generic and abstract. Thus while Davidson's trade material dissolves into only the audience view, Wilson's disappears in the author's. His studies do reflect the market insofar as its conditions coincide with this one-dimensional view. But his readings of idealized lives and literature, separate from the market, limit what might be a conception of his authors as developing professionals within it, and can force readings of texts as falsified answers to it.

Michael Anesko's evidence significantly revises the idea of James as an *artiste* who rejected the market by demonstrating his close interaction with it. In *The Bostonians, The Princess Cassimassima,* and *The Tragic Muse,* Anesko traces James's professional preoccupations. Anesko's attention to publishing history and textual and bibliographical detail cannot be matched by the other books here, and should stand as an example of their possibilities and requirements. He does not attempt much correlation of his material with the abstractions of current literary theory, but as I noted that area is only beginning to be explored.

The focus of Christopher Wilson's book falls between the individual author and broader questions. He divides his material evenly between aspects of authorship in the trade (in newspapers, magazines, and books), and his authors' relation to that trade (Jack London, Upton Sinclair, David Graham Phillips, and Lincoln Steffens). His study of both is so balanced and integral that neither can be said to be background for the other, and neither lacks the necessary depth.

Adequate use of book history in any critical analysis requires understanding it as a continuum in which period emphases must be set. That continuum can be discovered only through the complementary histories that make it up: of historical bibliography and scholarly textual studies, publishing and printing history, art history, and library and reading histories. Empirical studies must be balanced with newer cultural studies, with broader interpretive works like those of Raymond Williams, and then of course with literary history and current critical theory. The writers here depend on some of these secondary references and primary documents that serve their immediate purposes, but that can appear randomly chosen when they should be identified with and located in current studies in book history.

Davidson's use of such sources is the most comprehensive, and she is fully aware of recent trends, having conducted much of her research at the American Antiquarian Society and other institutions closely involved with American book history. She refers clearly, but briefly, to studies in *l'histoire du livre* (p. 4), and readers may still miss its encompassing significance. She has carefully surveyed the important standard sources, and has integrated with them the theoretical work of Escarpit and many others. From her audience perspective, she adopts a Bakhtinian "history of texts" equated with the "archaeology of reading" (p. 6), to form a narrative of the social concerns of the period. There she makes good use of physical evidence of ownership, readership, and trade records for analyses of women readers in particular.[6] But a real history of texts must also depend on studies that are most connected with the author and the publisher—of textual revisions and the publishing history of contemporary and later editions of which, admittedly, little evidence survives for the works she considers. Where it does, as with Royall Tyler and Brockden Brown, she too may feel that such work has been done, but leaving it aside not only undermines her analysis but gives the appearance of excluding it from the epistemology of book history.

Although he notices the book trade less, Gilmore uses his sources to some good advantage. He occasionally employs production histories where they are available, such as in critically edited works like the Centenary Edition of Hawthorne, but such information could well be central to a market study.

R. Jackson Wilson's notes show that he appreciates critical editions and composition histories, even if he does not always use them. He cites Haskell Springer's "fine modern edition with copious apparatus" (p. 78, n. 10) of Irving's *Sketch Book,* but quotes instead from the 1819–20 New York edition without explanation. He might prefer it, for instance, because it was Irving's first effort, but Irving substantively altered later editions, and it is the critical edition which has the purpose of representing the creative process most fully. Wilson credits both Charvat and Raymond Williams for his inspiration, and seems to be aware of important book-trade studies and concepts but often cites them only for incidental reference; there are odd gaps, and he relies on older or English trade studies when there are more recent or American ones. He occasionally makes use of publication data, for instance with Emerson and Irving, but seems at times to regard trade information as a useless restraint on his work. "In any case," he says, "what counts for an understanding of writers like Irving is not the facts of literacy or even of book production and sales but the perceptions of authors and booksellers" (p. 99, n. 35). But his efforts elsewhere to see behind "masks" show that he must know such facts are inextricably woven with those perceptions; even booksellers can "invent" their professional lives.

Period studies and narrowly conceived stratifications such as "elite" and "popular" still need to be challenged by the histories we have, old and new, of print production and circulation.

David J. Reynolds has recently suggested some important lines of integration of popular with better-known works (although he hardly notices the trade on which both literatures are based), while historians such as Mary Kelley have helped to explain the literature of a class.[7] Davidson's cultural context includes, besides the better-known works of Susanna Rowson, Hugh Henry Brackenridge, Charles Brockden Brown, and Royall Tyler that she analyzes, the entire class of popular novels, as well as other forms of writing to which they were connected. Gilmore, with a perspective skewed perhaps by the specific studies that have received recent critical attention, primarily opposes women to the "elite" writers he takes up, when he might also include popular male writers, journalists, blacks, or writers in areas of special expertise such as law, science, or scholarship, especially since he studies Emerson. R. J. Wilson, whose textual examples range among autobiography, letters, journalism, and essays as well as fiction and poetry, commendably suggests that problems of genre be superseded by developing "a way of studying people for whom writing of *any* sort is a principal vocation" (p. 16).[8]

The very choice of the kind of work to analyze can appear to be a definition of a period. Davidson and Christopher Wilson choose "popular" works while Gilmore and Anesko define their canonical works by opposition to the popular. R. J. Wilson chooses essentially "romantic" writers. The determinism of those choices can make us mistake them for the whole, and easily throw off market analyses. The status of literary art appears to shift accordingly, so that as Davidson establishes the importance of popular works, literature appears to have achieved a market value that is only to dissolve in the middle part of the century with the canonical writers. At the end of the century, Christopher Wilson's writers actually partook in "an imaginative identification with common people" (p. 114), and authorship became a kind of "democratic service" (p. 152) united with art that seems not at all unlike the moral lessons of Davidson's novels, as she interprets them. Wilson is able to show, however, that social politics in the late nineteenth century appeared in fiction not as an implicit structure to be uncovered by critics, but as an accepted form for literary art to take.

Markets in literature are not general. They are instead specific markets that develop around the trade in books. Critics who attempt to extrapolate the principles of a broad Marxist economic philosophy, or who do not fully explore the connections between book-market factors, may find themselves unwittingly blocked by the esoteric nature of the book trade. In spite of the advanced commercialism of the trade in his period, Christopher Wilson clearly differentiates literary industries with their peculiar vagaries from other professions, and can still find the perpetuation of an artistic, amateur, and private authorial tradition.

The generous space Davidson devotes to the book trade in her period helps to place it correctly in perspective. She comments that the new commercialism of the mass market that had been achieved by mid-century (pp. 16, 53) "has been refined but not substantially altered down to our own day" (p. viii). The subject of the other three period books here, however, is the very disruptive nature of that "refinement."

Gilmore is very much aware that the commodification of the market was a gradual, complex, and contradictory process, and in fact his authors' ambivalent reaction to it constitutes his thesis. But in his actual analyses he does not allow that trade the same ambivalence he grants to his authors, and seldom finds it necessary to specify it, referring to it on the whole as if it were unequivocally commercial. As important as are the examples he gives of authorial interaction with the trade, its sporadic appearance makes his evocation of every other commercial enterprise seem ironic. He discusses the obvious ones of Thoreau and agriculture, Melville and whaling, Hawthorne and the trade at the custom house, in small shops, and in scribal clerking, all of which perhaps makes his correlations with Marxist theory more workable, but how much more immediate would a market study be that concentrates on that real market—for the books themselves? Gilmore says that unlike Leo Marx, who opposed Thoreau to technology, he makes technology part of the whole market society (p. 160, n. 3), but technology itself includes the printing trades that embody literary production, and they are absent from Gilmore's discussion. Critics still find it easy to take trade, author, and work as interchangeable terms and set them together opposite some completely external form.

R. J. Wilson assumes too general a commodification over his long period from Franklin to Whitman, although he counters it with "personal" market alternatives for his authors, such as Garrison's small-town journalism career. But if Wilson's market were understood to be more specifically the literary one, these experiences would become author-specific points, not of opposition to a general social market, but of developing authorship within it, that shift as the other factors in the trade complex do. A writer of a column in a national journal might develop a more personal tone, and hear from more readers, than a news writer in a local one.

Even if the book trade over the century was wholly commercial, it could not be maintained that literary works functioned in the same way as other products. Davidson, usefully citing Lewis Hyde's *The Gift,* introduces the idea of the book as two things that are "not the same"—the commodity and the carrier of meaning. With this opposition established she purports to be able to separate the two by treating first the market, where the book functions only as "material fact and economic entity" (p. 15). In fact it maintains its other nature even while being traded, as her own example of Isaiah Thomas's marketing of *The Power of Sympathy* shows—it was promoted directly through its nature as a producer of meanings (pp. 37, 86–91).

Gilmore instances an isolated comment by the publisher Evert Duyckinck as evidence that books were treated as other commodities. Over the century such statements were part of a contradictory rhetoric that varied according to the likely profit advantage to be gained or lost from a host of government regulations, and none of it should be taken as evidence of the actual function of the book in the market. Citing Marc Shell, *The Economy of Literature,* for the concept of use value and exchange value, Gilmore locates in the nature of any commodity both the material and the spiritual (pp. 15–16). He finds that Emerson's *Nature* avows that duality in what it says, but misses the fact that it also avows it in what it is—that is, a book. As Emerson says himself, not only words but things are emblematic, and Gilmore's valuable discussion of commodities and symbolism could easily be extended to the historical idea of the material book as symbol.[9] R. J. Wilson does understand Emerson's sense of the book as both commercial and spiritual but still treats it as a typical capitalist commodity:

> In fact, the effect of the marketplace on writers was not, in the end, very different from its effect on other people. The new system of mass production for exchange—the production of books or lectures as well as shoes or stoves—tended to make everyone's experience (as Marx put it) "atomic." [p. 206]

This equation of markets can result only from a failure to recognize the book trade as specific and its product as a personal one, both of mind and production.[10]

When he comes to discuss *Bartleby the Scrivener,* Gilmore concedes that the legal profession was an exception to the disappearance of apprenticeship, when he might have noted that the entire book market exemplified exceptions to it in its various crafts for much of the century. Unlike Gilmore in his discussion of *Bartleby,* Anesko and Christopher Wilson equate artisanry with artistry. Anesko connects the bookbinder Hyacinth Robinson in *The Princess Cassimassima* with James as a "craftsman of words," as well as with James's "abiding concern about the technical standards of the book trade" (pp. 111–12). Later, Wilson points out, the approach of a writer such as Jack London was that of an artisan in apprenticeship to the trade (p. 96).

R. J. Wilson makes important use of Emily Dickinson's correspondence with T. W. Higginson, but builds a problematic argument on it. Because in his "Letter to a Young Contributor" Higginson moves from the idea of editors as mediators to that of only the author and the public, Wilson concludes that this editor and tradesman was portraying a market that included no concept of apprenticeship, so that by repudiating it Dickinson was free to remain an apprentice forever, turning out only exercises. But all professional writers are continually "practicing" and refining their work, and have a counterpart in the concept of book market apprenticeship.

Gilmore finally recognizes the artisanry in the literary work/book when he comments on Melville's citation of bibliographic terms for whale sizes and the varied makeup of *Moby-Dick*. Missing is the acknowledgment that this is a quality of all literary works, and especially those that go into production for the market. Here too, an entire range of craft associations from the history of bookmaking could be directly connected with the sense of authorship as a craft, as it might be practiced by printer-authors such as Twain, Howells, or Whitman.

R. J. Wilson indeed identifies Franklin, Garrison, and Whitman as printers, and credits the trade for facilitating their ascension to authorship status. He usefully notes James Sappenfield's work on the relationship of Franklin's journalism to his writing, but does not himself seriously consider for his authorial persona Franklin's absorption in the trade as art, craft, and *métier*, and his definition of himself first and last not as a writer, but as a printer. As Sappenfield noted, "In his mind, writing was part of the printing trade—fundamentally neither more nor less important than composing or presswork."[11] Wilson paints an absorbing picture, however, of Garrison setting italic and capital "I" types for his early dramatic first-person exhortations. He sees his move from local news editing to national reform work as a change from artisanal production to a market economy of language, but must therefore deny the artisanry of any work in the larger market (p. 146).

Approaching Irving's stories, Wilson dismisses the use of the point that Irving actually had a printer named Van Winkle (p. 110, n. 46). But if Emerson can be seen as incorporating references from his ministerial activity into his writing, why should there be no value in words signifying Irving's practice of authorship in its production relations? In fact, since sermon printing was such a staple activity of both printing and preaching, Emerson can be connected to the craft as well. If Wilson were open to it, the idea could support his argument about Irving's work, since he makes a case for Rip Van Winkle's death and rebirth, and his role as teller of tales, both relatable to the traditions of literary work itself as the offspring of the author, and the printer as the re/producer of literature.

One difference of book markets is the interaction of authors and publishers as producers who share both artistic and commercial aspirations. While the critics here have an interest in establishing the growing separation of the author from the publisher, the collaborative nature of their enterprise should not be understated. The character and motivations of the publisher may vary as much as those of the author; choices of action on the part of each at specific moments in a work's history can determine individual success. Gilmore maintains that "Under the market system, there is no way for an author to exert influence to a significant degree without attracting a popular audience" (p. 50). But what does significant influence mean here? For whom? What about varieties of markets? And the kinds of authorial involvement in that "attraction"? Christopher Wilson allows for these questions in terms that apply not only to his own period, but to all:

Book publishing suggests that the "linkage" between publishing imperatives and authors' actual practice was often indirect, subject to personal idiosyncrasy, even fluid—though undeniably detectable. Certain authors, at different stages of their careers, with different values and resources, might respond to the market in different ways; nor was the market the only source of status and power. Writing, to put it baldly, is not simply analogous to work in heavy industry: it is not directly supervised in all cases, nor is the editor's power always supreme in individual cases. [pp. 89–90]

The mixed nature of this interaction also subverts arguments about canonization. R. J. Wilson laudably supports exploration of practical authorial activities to challenge the "grounds on which writers have conventionally been elevated to importance" (p. 19). But although he is well aware of their real interaction, his identification of his writers' idea of the market as essentially anonymous leads him to treat their relation to it as unmediated.

This enabled writers to think of success as something that they could earn as a result of their quite solitary efforts. But it also meant that failure could not be laid off on the whimsy of a patron or the bigotry of an institution. [pp. 13–14]

But the modern trade institutions actually stood in the role of patron for authors, and it has always been too common (for authors as well as critics), to identify the publisher as a benevolent collaborator if a work is successful, and an opponent and exploiter if it is not. A survey such as W. S. Tryon's of the daily activities of a publisher like James T. Fields, for instance, who represented and promoted Hawthorne and many others, male and female, calls into question Jane Tompkins's recent selective array of supposedly male-biased promotional networking.[12] Anyone who writes on canon formation should have read Robert Escarpit on the various ways a publisher can influence the public, and consider authorial complicity in them.[13] Davidson pictures Susanna Rowson working readings and discussions of *Charlotte Temple* into her stage performance. Gilmore succinctly considers Thoreau's publication circumstances and his correspondence with Greeley as his literary agent, as well as his failure in relation to his own choice not to accede to the popular market. He notes that the "influential writers praised by Thoreau" enjoyed advantages not available to him, such as patronage (p. 50). But how did they get to be influential? R. J. Wilson's picture of Franklin's creative skill in accommodating a still personal market is a good one, but the association of nineteenth-century writers with the trade could also mediate their anxiety about commercialization. Once having identified the market not as a trade component but as a part of general society, Wilson postulates too automatic an alienation of the writer from it.

Irving's amateur writing status is opposed by Wilson to the professionalism of his later career, so that the earlier experience is made to seem more positive and personal than the later, when in fact his authorial experience was a mixed one at each level. Seeming to dismiss the value of a careful study of the context of professional development, Wilson concludes about Irving: "It would be a waste of time to try to decide whether the poses or the inert facts they were crafted to deal with are finally more suggestive about him or about the more general problem of the man of letters in the nineteenth century" (p. 85). He seems to understand the interaction of speaking, promotion, and publication in Emerson's lecture career, but artificially divides it from the supposed inaction of his early authorial career, and so cannot see his ministerial preaching as part of the larger market.[14] Gilmore misses the related point that the decline in Emerson's attacks on trade, and his endorsement of wealth, can be related to his mass market authorial success, to imply professional, if not actually popular, sympathies rather than the elitism he too readily attributes to it; such successes presage the actual identification of art with popularity that Christopher Wilson finds in the Progressive period.

The support Garrison accepted from wealthy reformers was a measure of his market success, as Wilson sees, but as such it was like the patronage a writer has from a large reading public through his publisher, gained in part from his complicity in the process of publicity. Although such success cannot be automatically identified with artistic capitulation, Garrison is portrayed finally as hypocritically compromising himself with those patrons.

Publishing always offered both benefits and hazards to authors. Anesko points out that trade development meant both "opportunity and threat to authorial integrity" (p. 34), and follows James's careful maneuvering within it. Christopher Wilson shows that new trade regulations earned new controls for both authors and publishers. If new legislation meant no fewer authorial conflicts, it also meant greater complicity in them, demonstrating again the ambivalence of the market even in the intensification of its commercialism.

Authorial reactions in a text to a sense of the market can include any reference to the author's awareness of his or her own role, to books, libraries, writing, or the publishing process. Subject, plot, structure, and characters may appear to evoke the author's professional role or concerns. These references need not always be in conflict with the market, but the critics here are mainly concerned with the traditional opposition between artistic and marketable writing, with which comes a host of correlations that have usually been treated selectively: the romantic vs. the realistic, the private vs. the public, the outcast vs. the *engagé*, and then either the feminine-artistic vs. the masculine market or the masculine writer of art vs. the feminine producer of popular non-art. Any of these may characterize an artist-figure in a text who suggests the author's concerns.

Although Davidson's theoretical approach dispenses with such authorial tensions for analysis of socio-political conflict, the fact that they are readily identifiable in her studies can illustrate how these critical works are each only complementary parts of a larger history of books than is portrayed by any one of them. In Royall Tyler's *The Algerine Captive,* Dr. Updike Underhill could correlate with the outcast artist-author: he has trouble telling his story, and the fragmentation that results might represent conflicts based on the author's uncertainty of the market. The conflict between country innocence and city decadence in *The Contrast* would make another common alignment with artistic hopes and the corruption of the market. Davidson maintains that Tyler was writing for two different audiences with different requirements—the aristocratic one of the theatre, and the popular one of the novel. But plays were not solely aristocratic forms, and part of *The Contrast*'s popularity derived from newspaper accounts and the circulation of printed copies, falsifying Davidson's contention that novels differed from plays because they could be read personally.[15] The authorial conflict here would indeed be a relatively formalist one—of the ways Tyler might change his words and style for the sake of the dramatic form, in hopes of the widest acclaim, rather than for a questionably separate dramatic audience.

Gilmore's intriguing identification of figures who reflect Hawthorne's own market conflicts includes Giovanni, the student and "reader" in *Rapaccini's Daughter,* who is trapped between the transcendental artistic view of Beatrice and the daylight one of the garden as the practical market, where the poisonous plants represent the corruptions of capitalism. In *The Scarlet Letter* Hester Prynne is "the first full-length representation in American literature of the alienated modern artist" (p. 85). In *The House of the Seven Gables* the artist-figure of the daguerreotypist and picture-maker (whose profession itself might be suggestive of the book trades with its reference to illustration, printing, and reproduction) represents the discrepancy between the artistry of Hawthorne's private "portraits for engraving" and public "pencil sketches passed from hand to hand" (p. 98).

With *Bartleby the Scrivener,* Gilmore moves from the question of the isolation of the author-artist to that of the new poor, who are kept from public view. This choice of one of any number of possible social questions is however brought back into authorial focus with a thoughtful discussion of *Moby-Dick*.[16] Many of the points Gilmore then makes could also, for consistency, have been applied to the authorial question in *Bartleby*. The public-private correlation means that wherever a work contains a window, a veil, a screen, or any obscuring feature, a critic can make it a symbol of the author's separation from the public, and many do. The walls Gilmore sees as barriers to a view of the poor can also liberate an author from the constraints of observation, or market presentation (the very limitation cited in *The Scarlet Letter*). Bartleby is, after all, a kind of writer, and his employer says he has "a style not easily to be matched," which suggests some artistry and pride of craft, although Gilmore says this is only a comment on his commodity value as a producer (p. 135). When he does finally equate Melville with Bartleby, it is only with the debased market side of literature—the copyist as the maker of cheap, easily reproducible fiction (p. 144). Like that of any other writer, Bartleby's work is a mixture of artistry and market constraint.

Although art in general is the traditional counter to the market, it has been the purpose of modern book trade studies to show that literary art itself becomes social in its interaction with its practitioners, purveyors, and purchasers, so that the work, no more than the author, can be unilaterally opposed to a wholly separate market.[17] While the other critics here find in their texts a mixture of both artistic and commercial experience that represents the mixture of it in the author's career, R. J. Wilson establishes a polarity in his readings where his writers within their texts produced only idealized artistic efforts (often also mirrored in their lives), in opposition to a market that remains entirely external to it.

In his idea that authors saw mainly an anonymous market, Wilson does offer some mixture of views—of vast audiences, success and freedom, and also fears of failure. But they also felt, Wilson tells us, that this market was so interested in culture that "what mattered most was that art and literature be understood as undertakings that dealt only with 'ideal' or 'spiritual' things like truth and beauty" (p. 16), and that therefore the only way to appease it and become successful was to palliate it with poetic, artful expression. This means first that Wilson must find any reality or sense of social interaction in the work to be consciously excluded, and must select in his readings only the poetic. But even in the Romantic writers the real must often appear, if only to be transformed, and Wilson contends too that his authors are interchangeable with any others (p. 17). Second, he must deny authorial reports that the ideal in the work is based in the real, to show that it has been fabricated for market demand. This art without life and life without art can work as long as it is cast in an artificial schema of clearcut oppositions, confined to the abstraction of the single idea. But Wilson's study is supposedly of the practical literary market, and what can be made out to be denials or fabrications when compared to a generalized commercial society can be revealed as legitimate professional activity when the trade is specified and the market itself becomes complex.

Opposing to their writing the action of "real" work in society, Wilson sees Garrison, Emerson, and Dickinson as having failed since their separation from the world renders their figures "ineffectual" (p. 13). He finds that admonitions to "observe" like those in Emerson's Phi Beta Kappa address are failures to act, but if seen instead as assertions of action proper to creative authorial work, in conjunction with Emerson's own incipient trade involvement, they might confirm the social role of author equivalent to the other trades Wilson says Emerson could not emulate, and make it possible to see Emerson's intended representation of the American scholar as a successful one. Wilson passes over Emerson's frequent affirmations of authorial activity, as in the section on the functions of the scholar, whose "task" or job (however unhonored or unpaid) is observation. The scholar engages in creative reading as well as writing. In *Nature,* Emerson finds that "An action is the perfection and publication of thought." In *The Poet,* he makes the author in his job of transformation a sayer, a namer, an architect, and a doctor. While he also opposes these to "doing," in the context of developing professional authorship this representation of doing becomes an action itself. Emerson specifies that "Words are also actions, and actions are a kind of words," and "Homer's words are as costly and admirable to Homer, as Agamemnon's victories are to Agamemnon." While he concludes that the poet must abdicate from life, and allow others to speak for him, this certainly could not apply to the author in his own business of publication. The proposal of a concept of inactive idealism still necessitates actions to indite and promote those concepts. So it is Wilson here, and not Emerson, who cancels the dualism Gilmore discusses, and the careful balance Emerson establishes again and again between the real and the ideal. True, Emerson ends in *Nature* with the poet as an idealist, but one who shows things to be "not different from what we know them, but only lifted."[18] Furthermore, the abstractions through which Emerson invests the scholar with spirit are really the same as he would recommend to all other professions, so also equating their work with his. In all of this, we are certainly not prevented from still placing what is really transcendent in Emerson in opposition to commercialization, whether in society or publishing, but we can then recognize the mixed nature of his experience with the literary market.

Once Wilson admits that Emerson was really active as an author, when he is more successful, Emerson becomes a wholly commercial figure himself, opposed to his own writing. The reading of Garrison's reform work as a compromise of spirituality and ambition is an interesting one, but is set in opposition to his earlier career as if he had given up writing for speaking. His continued use of personalized rhetoric is treated as a feint to gull the anonymous audience, not as a qualification of that anonymity itself, which would represent a literary market of varied character. Opinions by engaged authors that the expansion of trade was contributing to cultural growth are rejected as conscious falsehoods.

Because Wilson sees as apprenticeship Dickinson's legitimate professional writing ability to experiment, he condemns her expression of contradictory ideas as the practice of an amateur in which only form, not meaning, matters and in which her thoughts and feelings cannot be read. But professional poets have the ability to see and translate the world in a multi-faceted way. As for an audience, it was not that she lacked one, but that hers was limited to her personal and private addresses. Even if she rejected the larger market, her correspondence with Higginson was still part of it, and as Wilson shows, she exercised artistic freedom in it. And Higginson did not ask her to alter her letters for publication.

It was of course not just the physically separated Dickinson, but many other writers who remained ideologically at odds with commercialization as they tried to accommodate it practically through the developing profession of authorship. And of course they studied, and worried about, ways to best create the ideal. But by focusing on an idea of public acceptance, and originating with the public what is really a personal ideological motivation to represent the common man, Wilson too often reads his texts as deliberate falsifications for the sake of an egotistical self-preservation in the market. Bald statements that Emerson, for instance, purposefully filled his writing with abstractions not because they meant anything to him, but because he thought that was what market success would require, are hard to accept (pp. 172, 224). In his introduction Wilson disavows any such unwarranted faultfinding, and in his studies sometimes concedes his authors' genuine poetic feeling. But while personal documentary statements such as Franklin's autobiography, Emerson's journal, or Irving's and Dickinson's letters are plausibly considered to be as creatively written as literary works, Wilson's exposures of his authors' often "unconscious" motives (e.g., p. 231) are not always more convincing than the documents. To give just one example, his arguments qualify but do not falsify (contrary to his strenuous contentions that they do) Irving's account that personal unhappiness led to his writing career. For instance, Wilson relegates to "myth" (p. 96) Irving's copious reports of painful hardships in overseeing his bankruptcy in London, offering only his own supposition that there was no good reason for him to take the collapse of business and family matters to heart. Instead, Irving is said to have invented a pose in order to make "furtive gestures" toward professional independence (p. 97). After first denying Irving really suffered, Wilson chooses to believe his account of his problems establishing himself in London, treating it, however, as a psychic defense. He ends by proving what we already knew, that setting out as a professional author was a difficult thing to do, and we could have taken Irving's word for it to begin with.

Since the general market does cause constraint, Wilson's identification of what is poetic can work as long as it does not deny the specific market. Thus Whitman and Dickinson are said to have declared freedom in their poems because in the market they were not free (pp. 274–75, 282). This at least can be true, although it cannot be said, as Wilson tries to say, that their work was free of constraint, or their market experience devoid of art.[19] With Dickinson, Wilson does not need to invent, only to recognize her playful obscurity, for instance in what he calls her "masked minuet" with Higginson (p. 260, n. 31). In the stories of Rip Van Winkle and Ichabod Crane, Wilson, like Gilmore, discovers characters whose occupational experience in fiction was as complex as their author's in life.

While Wilson reasonably rejects readings that seem to be simple reflections of lives as given by their authors, the specific professional view would be both more representative of the literary market and more complex than the polarized readings he artificially constructs. Accepting the ambiguities of it, both without and within their texts, leads to additive, not detractive, interpretations. Carefully correlating them with publication circumstances, Anesko and Christopher Wilson find these ambiguous conflicts in texts and lives, for instance in Jack London's compromise between the "school of God" and the "school of clod" (p. 95). Although by the end of the century audiences might have been able to equate the popular with the literary, writers still found no resolution of the two. But even if some of the market portrayals here are only partial, these critics have all made important contributions to our consideration of its character and effect.

There are still other ways to use the evidence of the history of the book in literary interpretation, and they depend on expanding theoretical use of physical book forms and publication circumstances. Those who have followed recent discussions in textual criticism will be familiar with some of these suggestions, but they have not often been specifically identified in cultural or market studies. Textual critics have shown the value of reading individual works as multiple forms based on composition and publication histories, in which resulting fragmentation, for instance, has wide theoretical implications.[20]

Gilmore finds market influence in the personal appearance and then disappearance in their texts of Hawthorne, Melville, and their characters. The shifting and disappearing narrative voice in *Moby-Dick* ultimately vitiates the positive audience relation of the authorial voice, one that introduces a fragmentation Gilmore sees as indicative of Melville's pleasure in his workmanship. He finds Melville's bibliographic whale sizes to be part of the positive "array of literary forms" in the text (p. 120), although the array itself can be a disruptive form.[21] But it is questionable whether later, without the authorial presence, the now "obscure and devious" style of *The Confidence-Man* becomes a "deliberate act of hostility toward the public" (p. 150), and therefore fails entirely.

There is also a potential contradiction in Gilmore's argument that in later works, in *Benito Cereno* and *The Confidence-Man*, the reliance by Melville on documents is another form of effacement and retreat because of the implied reduction of his role to that of compiler or editor, in comparison to what is in fact an equally fragmentary and document-based *Moby-Dick*. In fact, it could be argued that editing is more "professional" work for an author than novel-writing with its ties to the amateur, and so its very practice can be evidence, however implicit, of authorial presence. In another sense, as Christopher Wilson's authors exposed in their work market conditions based on personal archives of factual experience, their presence was asserted as they edited those materials to create art.[22] R. J. Wilson wisely rejects the idea that a positive audience reaction depends on the visible naming or speaking of the maker of literary work, and points out that all texts have some kind of authorial presence (p. 10).

Criticism based on market relations alone needs to incorporate a systematic study of revisions, reception, and publisher interaction. Gilmore, for instance, speaks only of Hawthorne's own decisions about *The Scarlet Letter*, mentioning Fields only as a recipient of Hawthorne's letters, when his own to Hawthorne are equally important. But he allows for Thoreau's changes to *Walden,* and is sensitive to Melville's inclusion of the epilogue in the American edition of *Moby-Dick* (pp. 45, 49, 129). R. J. Wilson does pay attention to forms such as Franklin's manuscript style and Dickinson's home-made fascicles. His appreciation of critical editions is somewhat qualified, however, by his efforts to prove that Franklin's *Autobiography,* as evidence of his beneficial relation with a personal kind of market, was a unified whole. No one would deny his contention that Franklin had the ability to make it so, and Wilson's readings of connections between the manuscript parts are thought-provoking ones. But if he considered that the establishment of conceptual connections need not controvert the evidence of inscriptional disjunctions, he would not find it necessary to deplore the book's publication "with four awkwardly separated parts—the decision of the book's many editors, not Franklin" (p. 31—Wilson himself is one of those editors). But editors have decided only to give the actual inscription rather than a hypothetical publication; the divisions are indeed Franklin's decision, at the point where the historical record of his authorial experience stops. Leo LeMay's exemplary genetic text with its important scholarly detail of that experience is not mentioned, and other critical readings of the fragmented text as authorial evidence are discounted, when they could be incorporated along with Wilson's suggestions for Franklin's intentional unity to better reflect the complexity of the author's market response.[23]

To disclaim Whitman's poetic sense of popular empathy Wilson asserts, "The plain historical fact is that the earliest editions of *Leaves of Grass* did not reach the multitudes at all, but only a small body of readers, many of them manifestly eccentric in one way or another" (p. 281). Is Emerson meant to be in this group? The plain historical fact is that successive editions did reach a large body of readers, but Wilson has already discounted his own limited point, saying that in any case the poem is not the poet, as if in this sense there was no relation between reception and a writer's life of progressive work.

The relation of a work to the market is also often inseparable from the visual presentation of its type and binding, and the illustrative artwork that may accompany it. The book's very physical nature as a vehicle for intellectual "art" becomes the axis of the author-publisher relation, and just as much sales rhetoric of book marketers capitalizes on the material product in artistic terms. Any work may experience different kinds of market success depending on the different physical forms in which it appears (hardcover, paper, journals, anthologies), but little work has yet been done on the implications of such comparative reception. Anesko shows that in the "architecture" of the New York Edition James meant to "frame his goods in distinctly marketable form" (p. 144), but that market constraints meant James had less control over the final contents of the edition than Edel and others have assumed. Davidson employs the publishing history and visual material of the physical book to suggest kinds of audience response, but these also have connections to the producer and the trade that could illuminate many other critical approaches. R. J. Wilson opens each of his studies with interesting analyses of his authors' contemporary portraits, some of which appeared in their books. But in his preface he says that a book's characteristic "markings" (cover and jacket, authors' names, etc.) obscure its nature as a social product (p. xiii), when they rather reveal its social nature as a particular kind of product. It is remarkable that there are so many studies of fine art and literature while these artistic questions so immediately related to literary texts have been so little explored.[24]

Since even Anesko's detailed work in publishing history is used mainly to support the location in James's texts of social-authorial ideas, none of the books here can be said to move beyond the social sphere to a real rapprochement with the historical textual process itself. The history of books can certainly contribute much to social studies of texts, but significant work remains to be done on textual histories that explore all the unique facets of a work, as a book, in light of current studies in both the history of the book and critical theory.

Notes

1. Lucien Febvre and Henri-Jean Martin, *L'Apparition du livre* (Paris: Albin Michel, 1958). Trans. David Gerard, ed. Geoffrey Nowell-Smith and David Wootton as *The Coming of the Book: the Impact of Printing 1450–1800* (London and New York: Left Books, 1976). *L'Histoire de l'edition francaise*, Henri-Jean Martin, Roger Chartier, and Daniel Roche, gen. eds. 4 vols. (Paris: Promodis, 1981–86). For the latter work, see the review essays by Ian MacLean in *The Library*, 6th ser., 8 (1986), 365–73, and by Ruth Mortimer in *Papers of the Bibliographical Society of America*, 80 (1986), 471–76.

The extension of book history studies to American topics has been represented in part by the Program in the History of the Book in American Culture sponsored by the American Antiquarian Society, which has produced, for instance, a collection of essays on *Needs and Opportunities in the History of the Book: America 1639–1876*, ed. David D. Hall and John B. Hench (Worcester: American Antiquarian Society, 1987).

2. In "Literary History and Book Trade History: The Lessons of *L'Apparition du livre*," *Australian Journal of French Studies*, 16 (1979), 488–535, Wallace Kirsopp showed that Febvre's conception was broader and more literary than his comment would imply, but his ultimate purpose was still the use of such material by historians. Kirsopp provides a useful survey of trade and reading sources, commendably calling for further study, but does not extend his discussion to questions of textual analysis.

Darnton's frequently cited article, "What Is the History of Books?" *Daedalus*, 111 (Summer 1982), 65–83, is largely a commentary on the application of book history to questions of French culture. Darnton also advances socio-cultural studies as the foremost concern of book history in "*Histoire du Livre. Geschichte des Buchwesens*. An Agenda for Comparative History," *Publishing History*, 22 (1987), 33–41.

Hugh Amory discussed the question of the imperialism of social history in this regard in "Physical Bibliography, Cultural History, and the Disappearance of the Book," *Papers of the Bibliographical Society of America*, 78 (1984), 341–47. For my commentary and his response, see C. Deirdre Phelps, "History and Bibliography" (Letter to the Editors), in *PBSA*, 79 (1985), 107–9. For a recent, if oddly biased commentary, see John Sutherland, "Publishing History: The Hole at the Center of Literary Sociology," and the corrective response by G. Thomas Tanselle, in *Literature and Social Practice*, ed. Priscilla Parkhurst Ferguson, Philippe Desan, and Wendy Griswold (Chicago: Univ. of Chicago Press, 1989), pp. 267–87.

3. Robert Escarpit, *Sociology of Literature*, tr. Ernest Pick, 2d ed., with an introduction by Malcolm Bradbury (London: Cass, 1971). A representative collection of Charvat's work appeared as *The Profession of Authorship in America, 1800–1870: The Papers of William Charvat*, ed. Matthew J. Bruccoli (Columbus: Ohio State Univ. Press, 1968). See especially p. 284 for his publishing configuration. Darnton's chart is in "What Is the History of Books?" p. 68.

4. For a discussion of the influence of French work on English book history,

see John Feather, "Cross-Channel Currents: Historical Bibliography and *l'histoire du livre*," in *The Library*, 6th ser., 2 (1980), 1–15.

5. "Glimpses of the Henry James Who Earned His Living," rev. of Anesko by Hershel Parker, *Review*, 10 (1988), 211–17; "Authorship in America during the Progressive Period," rev. of Wilson by James L. W. West III, *Review*, 8 (1986), 149–56. From one point of view, Parker might be justified in deploring Anesko's mixture of interpretation with his scholarship, but the singular advantage of both his and Wilson's work is to demonstrate by their close incorporation of the two the value of a sound foundation for such interpretation.

6. An unfamiliarity with bibliography is evident in a minor point, when Davidson mistakes in a note G. T. Tanselle's article on "Press Figures in America" for a reference on the numbers of books produced, which Tanselle does consider in the other article she cites, "Some Statistics on American Printing, 1764–1783" (p. 269, n. 9).

7. Reynolds, *Beneath the American Renaissance: The Subversive Imagination in the Age of Emerson and Melville* (New York: Knopf, 1988). Kelley, *Private Woman, Public Stage: Literary Domesticity in Nineteenth-Century America* (New York: Oxford Univ. Press, 1984).

8. For a useful recent commentary on this question, see Lawrence Buell, *New England Literary Culture* (Cambridge: Cambridge Univ. Press, 1988), pp. 39–44.

9. Ralph Waldo Emerson, *Nature, Addresses, and Lectures*, ed. Robert E. Spiller and Alfred R. Ferguson (Cambridge: Harvard Univ. Press, 1971), p. 18. See, for instance, the section on "The Book As Symbol," in E. R. Curtius, *European Literature and the Latin Middle Ages*, trans. Willard R. Trask (New York: Pantheon, 1953). For one view of the modern book as both commodity and symbol, see Walter Benjamin, "The Work of Art in the Age of Mechanical Reproduction," in his *Illuminations*, trans. Harry Zohn, ed. Hannah Arendt (New York: Schocken, 1969), pp. 217–51.

10. It is of interest to note the qualification to early European market depersonalization offered by Stephen Greenblatt, whose contextual approach to reading authorial personae, although more comprehensively formulated, is the same one Wilson adopts: "Distance from the scribal hand, production in relatively large quantities, mechanisms of distribution far distant from the author and printer, refusal of subordination to a ritualized verbal transaction, the very lack of aura—all that we may call the *abstractness* of the early Protestant printed book—gave it an intensity, a shaping power, an element of compulsion that the late medieval manuals of confession never had." Greenblatt himself relies on Elizabeth Eisenstein's important, if flawed, *The Printing Press as an Agent of Change*, and on Benjamin's "The Work of Art," in *Renaissance Self-Fashioning from More to Shakespeare* (Chicago: Univ. of Chicago Press, 1980), p. 86.

11. *A Sweet Instruction: Franklin's Journalism as a Literary Apprenticeship* (Carbondale: Univ. of Southern Illinois Press, 1973), p. 2.

12. W. S. Tryon, *Parnassus Corner: A Life of James T. Fields, Publisher to the Victorians* (Boston: Houghton Mifflin, 1963); Jane P. Tompkins, *Sensational Designs: The Cultural Work of American Fiction, 1790–1860* (New York: Oxford Univ. Press, 1985), pp. 6–34.

13. Critics can still leave such a crucial factor as the book trade out of discussions of canon formation. John Guillory, in his valuable if pretentiously wordy argument, "Canonical and Non-Canonical: A Critique of the Current Debate," *ELH,* 54 (1987), 483–527, speaks in passing of "institutions such as the salon" that "produce and reproduce vernacular literary language" and the coffee-house, which helps in the "appropriation of the pedagogic apparatus by a hegemonic bourgeoisie whose administrative and ideological needs require the dissemination of a vernacular standard (a project enabled also by the technology of printing)" (p. 515). Such an offhand reference fails to recognize the pervasive importance of printing, publishing, and bookselling institutions that select works and undertake and define that dissemination.

14. Wilson does recognize this relationship in his discussion of Garrison, but only for itinerant preachers or national lecturers (p. 146). Gilmore makes the connection of preaching and authorship for Thoreau, citing on p. 43 Lewis P. Simpson's *The Man of Letters in New England and the South: Essays on the History of the Literary Vocation in America.* See also Walter J. Ong, *The Presence of the Word; Some Prolegomena for Cultural and Religious History* (New Haven: Yale Univ. Press, 1967).

15. Davidson's sources refer primarily to the theater of the Revolution. But in his critical biography of Tyler, which Davidson cites, G. T. Tanselle notes, "The kind of theater which Tyler encountered in 1787 was different from the pre-Revolutionary one: attended by all classes of people, it was a force for national unity" (*Royall Tyler* [Cambridge: Harvard Univ. Press, 1967], p. 50). Walter J. Meserve also makes this point in *An Emerging Entertainment: The Drama of the American People to 1828* (Bloomington: Indiana Univ. Press, 1977).

16. Charvat showed that Melville in himself represented a full progression of art-market conflicts, creative, public-private, and economic, but Gilmore does not note this. See *Profession,* pp. 204–82.

17. To admit this interactive understanding is not to confuse it with the individual autonomy and authority with which the author is vested in the act of writing, in his decisions to inscribe certain words. The essentially social nature of the publication process that Jerome J. McGann argues for in *A Critique of Modern Textual Criticism* (Chicago: Univ. of Chicago Press, 1984) is qualified for editorial practice by G. Thomas Tanselle in "Historicism and Critical Editing," *Studies in Bibliography,* 39 (1986), 1–46.

18. "The American Scholar" and "Nature" in Emerson, *Nature,* and "The Poet" in Ralph Waldo Emerson, *Essays: Second Series,* ed. Alfred R. Ferguson and Jean Ferguson Carr (Cambridge: Harvard Univ. Press, 1983), as follows: *Scholar,* pp. 62, 58. *Nature,* p. 28. *Poet,* pp. 5, 6 ff., *Nature,* p. 31.

19. As one example, Anesko notes the historical association of the printing trades with social activism (p. 112), a point Davidson and Gilmore might have noted as well. As a printer and as a writer, Whitman's sense of this activity can in fact be found in his work, a possibility Wilson rejects in favor of his idea of the poet as ineffective observer. Davidson cites Sean Wilentz, who delineates this

Book History in American Literature 301

connection in *Chants Democratic: New York and the Rise of the American Working Class, 1788–1850*, but only as a reference for general social unrest (p. 215).

20. Only a few citations in this continuing discussion can be given here. Important arguments appear in Jerome J. McGann's *Social Values and Poetic Acts: The Historical Judgment of Literary Work* (Cambridge: Harvard Univ. Press, 1988), and *The Beauty of Inflections* (Oxford: Oxford Univ. Press, 1985). See also the essays in *Textual Criticism and Literary Interpretation*, ed. Jerome J. McGann (Chicago: Univ. of Chicago Press, 1985). Criticism connected with the history of composition and production has evolved in France as *la critique génétique*; see for instance Louis Hay, "Genetic Editing Past and Future," in *Text: Transactions of the Society for Textual Scholarship*, 3, ed. D. C. Greetham and W. Speed Hill (New York: AMS, 1986), 117–34. Connections between textual criticism and reader-response criticism are discussed in Steven Mailloux's *Interpretive Conventions: The Reader in the Study of American Fiction* (Ithaca: Cornell Univ. Press, 1982). Other important discussions include D. F. McKenzie, *Bibliography and the Sociology of Texts* (London: British Museum, 1988); Hershel Parker, "The 'New Scholarship': Textual Evidence and Its Implications for Criticism, Literary Theory, and Aesthetics," *Studies in American Fiction*, 9 (1981), 181–97; Hershel Parker, *Flawed Texts and Verbal Icons* (Evanston: Northwestern Univ. Press, 1984); Peter L. Shillingsburg, *Scholarly Editing in the Computer Age: Theory and Practice* (Athens, Georgia, and London: Univ. of Georgia Press, 1986); G. Thomas Tanselle, *The History of Books as a Field of Study* (Chapel Hill: Univ. of North Carolina, Rare Books Collection, 1981), also printed in the *Times Literary Supplement*, 5 June 1981, pp. 647–49; G. Thomas Tanselle, *A Rationale of Textual Criticism* (Philadelphia: Univ. of Pennsylvania Press, 1989). Some of the essays in *L'Histoire de l'edition francaise* address the effect of physical forms on meaning.

21. See McGann's discussion of biographical documents and bibliography itself as forms of the array, in his *Social Values and Poetic Acts*, pp. 139–45.

22. One discussion of the interaction between authorial and editorial functions (at least in scholarly editing), and a view of any documents on which a writer works, including revisions of fiction, as biographical documents, appears in Klaus Hurlbusch, "Conceptualisations for Procedures of Authorship," in *Studies in Bibliography*, 41 (1988), 100–35.

23. J. A. Leo LeMay and P. M. Zall, eds., *The Autobiography of Benjamin Franklin: A Genetic Text* (Knoxville: Univ. of Tennessee Press, 1981).

24. For one example of the relation of typography to the text, see D. F. McKenzie's *Bibliography and the Sociology of Texts*. Such a critical approach would be based in the voluminous literature of printing history and the arts of the book, as well as art theory and criticism.

Realism Revisited: Darwin and Foucault Among the Victorians

Peter Allan Dale

George Levine. *Darwin and the Novelists: Patterns of Science in Victorian Fiction.* Cambridge: Harvard University Press, 1989. x, 319 pp.

With this, his second comprehensive book (in less than a decade) on the development of Victorian fiction, George Levine takes his place as perhaps the foremost scholar of the subject writing today. The earlier book *The Realistic Imagination: English Fiction from Frankenstein to Lady Chatterly* (1981) was essentially a study in literary history that in its conventional diachronical organization as well as in its final theoretical embrace of realism set itself against the postmodernist readings of Dickens, Thackeray, George Eliot, Hardy, et al. which by the 1970s dominated American critical discourse on narrative (J. Hillis Miller's *Fiction and Repetition* came out almost simultaneously in sharp, deconstructivist contrast to Levine's project). "To take the word *realism* and the idea of representation seriously," Levine argued against the grain in 1981, "entails a challenge to the antireferential bias of our criticism and to the method of deconstruction that has become a commonplace."[1] Whatever else it means, "realism always implies an attempt to use language to get beyond language, to discover some nonverbal truth out there" (p. 6). And while no major Victorian realist was ever oblivious to the presence of literary and linguistic convention mediating between the text and the real, he or she worked in the common faith that the continuous disruption of convention, which is the realist's primary objective, could gradually put us "in contact with the world out there" (p. 8).

The Realistic Imagination takes the reader from Austen's pioneering effort to make the novel's "words comfortable to reality, and particularly, to the reality of social action" (p. 35) to Conrad's agonized perception of a hopeless "disparity between language and being" (p. 49), which effectively marked the demise of the nineteenth-century realist project.[2] In *Darwin and the Novelists*, Levine returns to the same literary ground—Austen to Conrad—but with an entirely new historicist agenda, both more ambitious and more daring than what had gone before. It is no longer simply the *internal* history of Victorian realism that occupies him, but its *external* history, and, in particular, the single most important ideological force that he conceives drove its development, namely (as his subtitle indicates), the era's "patterns of science."

Thus baldly stated, the project may not seem particularly new. The scientific pattern that Levine focuses on is, of course, Darwinism, and we have had a series of books on the subject, many of them outstanding, stretching back for at least half a century.[3] Recently, however, there has been a revitalization of interest in and approaches to the subject under the impact of postmodernist literary and cultural theory, the most eminent example of which (among literary scholars) is Gillian Beer's groundbreaking study of 1983, *Darwin's Plots: Evolutionary Narrative in Darwin, George Eliot and Nineteenth-Century Fiction*. Such studies move beyond the conventional identification of Darwinian ideas "encapsulated" (the metaphor is A. O. Lovejoy's) in literature in at least two revolutionary directions. On the one hand, they seek to expose the socio-economic and literary presuppositions generating Darwin's scientific work; on the other, they try to show the effect of the Darwinian revolution on the structure and institution of literature (as opposed to its ostensible "message").[4] This new way of writing about the relation between science and literature, Levine, as we shall see, presses to new levels of theoretical sophistication.

Though he himself tends to downplay the connection (p. 276, n. 9), there is little doubt but that the principal inspiration of Levine's revaluation of the relation between nineteenth-century science and literature is Michel Foucault. What Levine seeks to

Realism Revisited

trace are what he variously calls the "imaginative possibilities constructed by the [Victorian] culture" (p. 12), the "gestalt of the Darwinian imagination" (p. 13), and the "conventions of nature and of the possibilities of its representation in language" (p. 269). The structuralist metaphor implicit in these phrases looks directly to Foucault's "archaeology" of virtually subconscious cultural codes or "epistemes" that delimit human knowledge and, what follows, human praxis in any given historical period. No less important to Levine's conceptualization of the past is Foucault's insistence on the *discontinuity* of epistemes, the caesural shifts from one code or gestalt to another, that occur in time but without discernible logic. The story Levine tells is essentially that of the collision between two scientific-cum-cultural epistemes, Darwinism and natural theology (the latter theoretically epitomized in Levine's argument by William Whewell, 1794–1866, Knightbridge professor of moral philosophy at Cambridge and the preeminent British philosopher of science in the first half of the century): "The lay model for understanding the natural and human world before Darwinism was natural theology"; in challenging that model Darwinism becomes a "radical dislocator of the culture's understanding of nature and of the self" (p. 16). But one needs to go further, for it is clear that Levine is not writing about the last century without reference to the present. Just as Darwinism disrupted early nineteenth-century epistemes, so Foucault now disrupts the epistemic assumptions of Darwinism and modern science in general: "Darwin played . . . the role in relation to traditional views of history and the creation that Foucault plays now in displacing the Darwinian vision and disrupting conventions of coherence and continuity" (p. 8). We have here in miniature the metahistorical pattern underlying Levine's argument. Darwin displaces the Enlightenment episteme which we call natural theology and replaces it with an evolutionist (Levine will prefer to call it uniformitarian or gradualist) one that even now is being displaced by Foucault. As we see, Levine has come quite a ways further down the postmodernist road from where he stood in 1981.

Among those whose critical intelligence is not instantly paralyzed by the realization that a critical argument has been enabled by Foucault, Levine's historical presuppositions will immediately raise problems. One of these, at least, we can briefly dismiss and that is that literary scholars in search of cultural contexts can afford to ignore the influence of science. The objection goes back to the neo-Kantian division of knowledge into the methodologically exclusive realms of *Naturwissenschaften* and *Geisteswissenschaften* in the late nineteenth century, and insofar as it continues to control our notions of what kind of knowledge does and does not matter to the understanding of literature, it is nothing so much as a residual prejudice of New-Critical aestheticism.[5] Over a century ago, T. H. Huxley tried hard to tell contemporary apostles of culture that the "distinctive character of our . . . times lies in the vast and constantly increasing part which is played by natural knowledge. Not only is our daily life shaped by it; not only does the prosperity of millions of men depend upon it, but our whole theory of life has been influenced, consciously or unconsciously, by the general conceptions of the universe, which have been forced upon us by physical science."[6] Huxley was right, and what is more, Matthew Arnold, the man who famously responded to him on behalf of culture, whatever misgivings he may have had about the implications Huxley drew from that historical proposition, did not doubt the correctness of the proposition itself (as we shall see in a moment). It has taken some time for the point to infiltrate traditional humanistic discourse, but it has at last arrived, together with a number of other long-marginalized intellectual interests, and should need no further apology. Indeed, Levine himself could have afforded to be a little less apologetic: "Perhaps more intensely than in any prior period [the imaginative possibilities of a culture] were conditioned by the discourse of science which had begun to assume almost exclusive responsibility for reporting on the real . . ." (p. 12). All due scholarly caution notwithstanding, there seems to me no "perhaps" or "almost" about it.

A much more significant historiographical problem resides in Levine's meaning of "period" in the sentence just quoted, for one thing that is bound to be controversial about his book is the way in which he has deliberately pushed the widespread cultural efficacy of the scientific episteme back to the (Romantic) beginning of the nineteenth century. What Huxley said about the power of scientific thought in 1881 we have little difficulty with, but would it have been right if uttered some seventy years earlier when Austen, Levine's first exemplar of the impact of scientific knowledge on British fiction, was coming into her own as an artist? Would it have been right even in the 1850s and 1860s when Dickens and Trollope, Levine's representatives of the heyday of Victorian realism, achieved artistic maturity? Given certain critical adjustments in our concept of "scientific," it seems to me that it was right, for Austen's "period" as well as for Dickens's and Trollope's though far less apparently so than in the 1880s.

As Walter F. Cannon has argued, the close alliance of natural science and religion "sheltered under Newton's great name" seems to have led to the establishment of the "normative role of science" in British culture very early on in the nineteenth century.[7] John Stuart Mill's monumental codification of that norm in the *System of Logic,* when it appeared in 1843, reposed on a long-standing social belief in the power of scientific knowledge, which is what made it the single most influential philosophical text of the Victorian era. Levine's assumption of the power of science as an arbiter of early Victorian and even Romantic "imaginative possibilities," strange as it may seem to many literary scholars, is quite plausible. What one may more fairly complain of is the fact that he has left his historical point too much of an assumption, too little documented. The notion that *Mansfield Park*'s well-ordered social world depends somehow on Whewell's well-ordered natural world must come as a surprise to most readers. It is almost certainly a correct notion, but we need more intellectual history to make it convincing.

Having postulated the presence of a powerful scientific episteme operating on the novel throughout the nineteenth century, Levine's concern is to distinguish two very different expressions of it that come into conflict in the mid-Victorian period, again, natural theology and evolution, Whewell *versus* Darwin. It is the triumph of the latter that decisively separates science from religion as a form of knowledge and, as Levine believes, redefines the nature of narrative.

"For to imagine a system in which disorder, dysteleology, and mindlessness are constitutive, and, indeed, the source of all value, is to turn the Western tradition . . . on its head. . . . Darwin's world required a new sort of [literary] imagination" (p. 94). Where we first find this new sort of imagination—and here we come up against what is bound to be the most controversial aspect of Levine's argument—is in Dickens and Trollope. He claims, that is, to find evidence of a "Darwinian pattern" in novels which were written before the publication of *The Origin* (e.g., *Bleak House* [1853], *Little Dorrit* [1857], and *Dr. Thore* [1858]), and by writers who had not read Darwin and/or had virtually no interest in science.

Levine is entirely conscious that he is flying in the face of ordinary historical logic, conscious, as he says, of the "counterchronological" (p. 3) nature of his argument. The key to his defense lies in the concept of "pattern" which figures prominently in his title as well as various cognates—"model," "gestalt," "code," "structure," "paradigm"—throughout the text. Darwin the individual is not so much the inventor of a new way of thinking as "the most powerful codifier" (p. 9) of a "whole movement" of scientific thought that emerges in the second quarter of the century. From this standpoint "Darwinism" becomes a name we give, in effect, to the crucial changes in scientific thought that produced the codification Darwin puzzled over for twenty years before actually publishing in 1859. The structuralist, specifically Foucauldian, dismantling of individual agency in history is, of course, not far to seek in this way of understanding Darwinism. What we must altogether eclipse, Foucault insists, is "that form of history that was secretly, but entirely related to the synthetic activity of the subject. . . ."[8] From this perspective, Darwinism can and does exist in some meaningful, if incompletely articulated form, before Darwin. As we used to say, thinking of Lamarck, Lyell, Chambers, et al., Darwinism was "in the air." But the phrase hardly does justice to the originality of Levine's position. "In the air" meant others were on the right track but the revolution had to wait for the genius of a single man. By Levine's account the essential shift in scientific paradigms was well under way before Darwin published, transforming not only his attitudes towards natural order but those of the imaginative artists who were his contemporaries. "We do not need a particular scientist named Darwin and his particular book to account for [these] changes in attitude" (pp. 8–9).

Darwinism, Gillian Beer acutely notes, "has been so imaginatively powerful precisely because all its indications do not point the same way.... Darwinian theory will not resolve to a single significance.... It is essentially multivalent. It renounces a Descartian clarity, or univocality."[9] Levine shares this understanding of Darwinism, and with a greater thoroughness than Beer herself analyzes the several (ten in all) aspects of Darwinism multivalence (pp. 13–20). What he then, in effect, does is break down Darwinism's imaginative effects on the novel into two broad categories, one that undermines the preceding religious episteme without seriously disorienting man's moral vision of himself and one that does radically disorient that vision. Beer in her book and Peter Morton a year later (*The Vital Science: Biology and the Literary Imagination, 1860–1900*) concentrate on the second, better known effect of Darwinism, that undermines design and teleology and leaves the human mind alienated in a universe governed by chance. This reading of Darwin goes with the more conventional historiographical approach which limits the discussion of his influence on literature to writers who actually read and/or knew what was going on in the *The Origin* or *The Descent of Man*, writers like George Eliot, Meredith, Hardy, and Conrad. There is a reason for this. *The Origin*, and still more *The Descent*, makes explicit (and difficult to refute) disconcerting possibilities that were only tentatively presented in the scientific debate that preceded 1859. When one commits oneself to an account of the emerging "pattern" of Darwinism in the early nineteenth century, however, it is other, less conspicuous, aspects of its move against natural theology and human values one needs to emphasize. The special contribution of Levine's study is that it foregrounds, as no previous work of literary history has done, this less celebrated, but crucial, side of Darwinism.

Drawing on Levine's own breakdown of the Darwinian "gestalt," we see that what this amounts to, essentially, is "uniformitarianism" (also referred to as "continuity" and "gradualism"). Uniformitarianism, of course, is the doctrine that the world of nature operates according to unchanging laws, which it is science's business to formulate. The debate between uniformitarianism and catastrophism (which posits periodic divine intervention in the natural process to create, for a notable example, species) occurs preeminently among geologists in the first quarter of the century. Darwin's teacher Charles Lyell was a uniformitarian, Whewell, a catastrophian. There is no occasion to rehearse here this pivotal conflict within the scientific community.[10] The important thing to note, as John Burrow has observed, is that uniformitarianism is, finally, an argument against natural theology for the simple reason that uniformitarianism persistently replaces divine or providential agency in nature with impersonal, abstract, rational law. "Much in nineteenth-century thought," writes Burrow, "can be interpreted on the assumption that the Uniformity of Nature had acquired for many intellectuals a logical status and numinous aura which made it a substitute for God."[11] Lyell's geological uniformitarianism, as his antagonist Whewell well knew, was the narrow end of a formidable epistemological wedge destined to separate science from religion, nature from God. Uniformitarianism was at the very foundation of Darwin's thought, and *The Origin,* as Levine means to indicate, established it more decisively than any other contemporary text as the *sine qua non* of scientific thought.[12]

Ultimately, the most threatening thing about the triumph of uniformitarianism was not the substitution of natural law for God. It was the application of the principle to "the human subject" (another aspect of Levine's Darwinian gestalt; see p. 14) or, put another way, the increasing inability of scientific logic to countenance the notion that the human mind, of all things in nature, was specially created and, what followed, specially endowed with an authoritative moral vision. "I will never allow," wrote Darwin in his notebook as early as 1838, "that because there is a chasm between man . . . and animals that man has a different origin." Though it took him another thirty years before he felt he could publish this view, the general point that man could be finally understood only as a product of nature, was already well established in the public mind by the 1840s.[14] This particular implication of Darwinism (though Levine does not precisely make the point) is what one imagines mattered most to contemporary literary artists. Natural law, as the scientists' substitute for God, does not truly become a problem until that can no longer be personified or anthropomorphized as *moral* law. Matthew Arnold, who early absorbed the Victorian scientific episteme, making it the foundation of his greatest philosophical poem, *Empedocles on Etna* (1852), spent a career trying to wean his contemporaries from their anthropomorphic, supernatural deities in favor of a nature that was, its failure to give us joy notwithstanding, still a thoroughly moral entity. As he argued in his most popular work, *Literature and Dogma* (1873), we must read the God of the Bible "in a scientific way," that is, as an impersonal natural force, a "not ourselves, which is in us and in the world around us." But he needed to add that this was a natural force which "makes for righteousness,"[15] thus at a stroke deconstructing his painstaking "scientific" case against anthropomorphism. He had to keep the human spirit at the center of things; nature as moral (righteous) is, after all, an "ourselves." Needless to say, Arnold was not alone in his moralization of the new god nature, as we see when we look at such real scientific thinkers as J. S. Mill, Herbert Spencer, G. H. Lewes, John Tyndall, Lord Kelvin, Leslie Stephen, and so on, into our own century. These anthropomorphic holding actions notwithstanding, the extension of uniformitarianism to the human spirit contained from the outset the implication that nature must at last define the limits of man's moral being, not the other way round.

It is time now to turn to Levine's use of this emerging scientific pattern to elucidate the history of the nineteenth-century novel. What we initially see is that the distinction between Whewellian and Darwinian scientific epistemes leads him to make a significant distinction in "realisms" that was not made in his earlier book. There Austen's fiction in its parody of romantic excesses was the "inception" of a "dialectical process . . . in the realists who follow"—Thackeray, Trollope, George Eliot, and Hardy (p. 67). Dialectical process, in which one convention or ideology is read, demystified, and replaced by a more realistic one is no longer the model of history in *Darwin and the Novelists*, as we have seen. Rather it is a Foucauldian discontinuous shifting of structures. Austen's fiction (specifically *Mansfield Park*) is no longer the inception of a new realism but the closing off of an old one: "That is to say, Austen's realism (consonant with the world described in natural theology), resists the consequences of the later realism (consonant with Darwin's antiteleological vision) in which the moral and material are severed" (p. 82).

The new realism, the centrally Victorian realism appears most prominently in Dickens's later career (Dickens, who was only marginally present in the earlier "dialectical" reading of realism, has price of place here). Dickens "dramatizes the loss of an unambiguous sense that the world makes sense and is ultimately ordered and just. He yearns for a 'nature' that is indeed God's second book, as in the tradition of natural theology. But like Darwin, he describes a world that resists such ordering" (p. 119). Dickens feels the uniformitarian separation of God from nature. Throughout his work we see nature, as pastoral, in precarious alliance with God, with whom Dickens is always ready to dispense whenever that God becomes too sectarian, too Chadbandian, which is almost always. But the crucial, Darwinian turn comes when the novelist begins to lose his ability to affirm not just the theological but the moral interpretation of nature, when he, unlike Arnold, can no longer be sure nature is an entity that "makes for righteousness." This turn Levine places between *Bleak House* and *Little Dorrit*. The earlier novel for all the disorder of its human, urban world, closes on Esther's country idyll where man's moral goodness rediscovers its essential ground among the green trees and clear flowing water. In the suffocating, carceral world of *Little Dorrit,* however, the sun, always Dickens's symbol of morally transcendent nature, scarcely has energy enough to filter through the image of Christ on a church window for the inevitable wedding. Indeed, the marriage celebration is virtually blocked out rhetorically by the subsequent image of the "Marshalsea and all its blighted fruits." As Levine says, "The courage of *Little Dorrit* is its confrontation of the possibility that the religious [I think *moral* is more to the point] account [of nature] could not stand against the pressure of those irrefragable [scientific] laws, denying both God and self . . ." (pp. 175–76). Had Levine chosen to move on to 1860 and Dickens's first novel written after the publication of *The Origin,* he might have further confirmed the development he has discerned in *Little Dorrit. Great Expectations* opens, one recalls, with a "universal struggle" for existence and ends beside a "ruined" garden. Blighted fruits and ruined gardens may stand with Darwin's "tangled bank" as powerful synecdoches of a collapsing theoretical order.

Trollope, for Levine, is the most Darwinian of mid-Victorian novelists, and this for two closely related reasons. First, although he has little to say about man's place in nature, he has everything to say about man's place in society, and what he says effectively establishes the scientist's principle of uniformitarianism (or gradualism) as the model of social and historical process in the novel. "He lays out the [uniformitarian] assumption of the Darwinian world view as they tended to be applied analogically to social and political matters" (p. 178); with "uniformitarian plodding movement," he shows how the conventions or forms of the human world evolve or merge into one another with no other logic than the historical one (p. 201). Second, Trollope, like Darwin, "gives us, rationally, a world not only impelled by irrational energies, but irrational in structure" (p. 193). The famous (or infamous) Trollopean irony towards both aesthetic and social forms, admirably explicated in *The Realistic Imagination*—"Trollope is free to treat violators of the rules with compassion because the rules have for him not a divine but only a social sanction and are thus, like everything else, rather a mixed, rough and ready business" (p. 199)—now takes on a Darwinian meaning. As Darwin undermines the assumption of design in the natural world, so Trollope undermines it in the human world.

For Levine, this willingness to acquiesce in a society that is without a determinate, authoritative design makes Trollope finally more Darwinian than Dickens, who always strives to wrench his chaotic society back into providential shape. But it also, says Levine in still riskier judgment, makes him more Darwinian than George Eliot who knew her Darwin inside out but, unlike Trollope, could not accept the application of his scientific model to the "human subject," with "the detachment and distance of the uniformitarian scientist" (p. 203). In the mature Trollope, notably in *The Claverings* (1866), Levine finds the Darwinian conclusion that George Eliot persistently resisted: "Chance, not providence, here determines rewards and punishments and thereby invalidates the conception of rewards and punishments" (p. 207). This is, when one thinks about it, a rather remarkable rearrangement of the two novelists' conventional places in the Victorian *Zeitgeist.* The age's greatest tragic novelist comes out less able to cope with the disturbing implications of the new science than its greatest comic novelist. But Levine is probably right. In the end, there may well be a little more than a certain phlegmatic unwillingness to pursue an uncomfortable theme between Trollope and the thoroughly Darwinized Hardy.

Before bringing his account of Darwinism and the novel to its conclusion with a discussion of Conrad, Levine breaks the progress of his historical argument to indulge in what appears to be a gratuitous Foucauldian digression on "The Perils of Observation" (Chapter Eight's title). The unscientific notion of "observation" as perilous comes, of course, from the later Foucault, specifically *Discipline and Punish,* where the focus of concern is less historiological and methodological than political. Here we learn of a "common matrix" between penal institutions and the institutions of human knowledge, in which "the technology of power [is seen to be] the very principle both of the [apparent] humanization of the penal system and of the knowledge of man." More particularly, for our present purposes, Levine draws on Foucault's critique of the distinctively scientific institutions of observation. "The exercise of discipline," writes the French philosopher, "presupposes a mechanism that coerces by means of observation; an apparatus in which the techniques that make it possible to see induce effects of power."[16]

Levine's discussion of scientific observation as power, as I say, seems at first sight gratuitous, but it develops logically from the preceding reading of Trollope. Darwinian uniformitarianism in Trollope, in addition to the consequences we have just noticed, also has a political implication. "Trollope," writes Levine, "is perhaps the best Victorian example of the way post-Darwinian assumptions fed into a political and social conservatism, that could ... only be disrupted ... by a recognition that there is no moral or social imperative embedded in the evolutionary scheme, or anywhere in nature" (p. 179). The thesis here is not an unfamiliar one: scientific philosophy or positivism, ultimately, underwrites political conservatism. Levine's chapter on the perils of observation brings the argument up to date, as it were, by reference to Foucault on discourse (as opposed, say, to the neo-Marxians on technology): "Observation of any kind, but particularly what might be taken as objective and disinterested observation, becomes, as Foucault understood it and as nineteenth-century narratives seem frequently to testify, an institutional or socially sanctioned act of power and aggression . . ." (p. 212). Darwinism, announcing uniformitarianism and continuity as the way of nature and anchoring its world view in the authority of "objective" observation, now emerges as a conservative, radically anti-revolutionary episteme, and the literary realism it conditions, as we see in both Dickens and Trollope, operates on the mind of the reader with a comparable political force. Victorian realism tends "to induce passivity, to deny identity itself, to cut off creative or free action . . ." (p. 234); it "constructs reality so that ideological antagonism to revolution is implicit in its very form" (p. 241).

We need to pause for a moment and consider what an extraordinary intellectual distance Levine has travelled from his earlier reading of realism. There the dialectical development of Victorian narrative was towards the progressive realization of positive human values through the critique of stultifying ideologies. In this context the political value of a Trollope lay precisely in his skepticism about aesthetic and social conventions: "Trollope's realism . . . reveals the arbitrariness of the [social] system," and this is very "healthy" (*The Realistic Imagination,* p. 202). Also healthy, it seems, is the way Trollope's (and others') realism tends to "absorb" the rebellious ("monstrous") energies that disrupt "community." Now revisited as an expression of the scientific episteme and under the lamp of Foucault's critique of power, Trollope's realism (and Victorian realism in general) has a distinctly "dangerous and unpleasant" (*Darwin and the Novelists,* p. 226) side to it, one which in the name of cultural continuity seeks to "reabsorb the aberrant into the uniformitarian movement or expels it for its refusal to surrender its personal ideal for the sake of an obviously irrational and arbitrary tradition called society or history" (p. 239). Levine's chapter on observation, far from being a digression in his story, goes to its heart. The new Darwinian pattern of knowledge began by liberating the modern mind from a constraining theological episteme only to subject it to a far more subtle, but no less powerful and repressive scientific one.

Having thus revaluated Victorian realism, Levine concludes with an account of the modernist reaction, which here, as in *The Realistic Imagination,* is harbingered by Conrad. In the earlier study Conrad disrupts the realists' project of bringing language and social convention into conjunction with truth by insisting upon an insurmountable "disparity between language and being" which, in turn, implies an absolute alienation of mind from reality, and, on a political level, individual from community (pp. 47–54). This "stark pessimism" issues at last in a direct confrontation of suicide and anarchy as mankind's remaining option. "The artist," concludes Levine, "may imagine such a position; he cannot live in it." Nor, presumably, can the critic (not to mention the man on the street), which takes us back, one surmises, to the quarrel with deconstructivism with which *The Realistic Imagination* begins.

In *Darwin and the Novelists* modernism comes to us not as pessimism or anarchism, but as a new form of liberation, a welcome "shift from belief in observation as authority to deep distrust of it" (p. 235), and Conrad in turn becomes, as Arnold writes of Heine, something of a "brilliant . . . soldier in the war of liberation of humanity." "The modernism in which Conrad participates . . . developed narrative strategies that, in exploding Victorian conventions of nature and of the possibilities of its representation in language, actually affirm the inevitability of revolution. . . . His is part of the last step of Western culture in the dismantling of the project of natural theology: he disrupts the Victorian analogy between nature and society by revealing with an almost nauseated disgust the blind arbitrariness of the bourgeois, gradualist society" (p. 269). This does not mean—a pivotal point—that Conrad has abandoned the Darwinian episteme. He, still more than Hardy before him, realizes in his narrative form the darker destabilizing aspect of Darwinism, the aspect with which, as I have noted, we moderns are more familiar than the uniformitarianism Levine has been emphasizing throughout the book. This, again, is the Darwinism that rationally undermines the concept of rational order and reduces the mind of man to an accident of evolution (p. 265). But Levine's larger, essentially deconstructivist, point is that the scientific episteme contains within itself, within its very rationalism, the seeds of its own overthrow both as a form of knowledge and of power. "The support that Darwin's theory gave to the realist novelist's [conservative] program could also threaten the stability it affirmed. Its rigorous exclusion of design and of the divine hand tended toward an unredeemed secularity that made experience meaningful only in the trivial sense that it could be explained by laws. But on the logic of the theory, laws are not universally applicable after all because the generating power of the new is chance." (p. 250). My earlier application to Conrad of Arnold's liberalist notion of individual soldiers in the war of humanity's liberation is, of course, a misapplication in this context, an instance perhaps of the way one's humanistic education tends to obscure the real dynamics of history. Conrad as an individual, a human subject, is not what matters here but the contradiction within a structure of knowledge which must inevitably issue in the collapse of that structure.

So what wisdom does Conrad's situation, the post-Darwinian situation, offer us? One well-known response to the recognition that human knowledge and the social structures that rest upon it are arbitrary, authorized by neither God nor nature, is that of aesthetic withdrawal. One recalls Walter Pater's bittersweet discovery of "that thick wall of personality through which no real voice has ever pierced on its way to us." In such an alienation of mind from the world and from others "our one chance" lies in the "love of art for its own sake. . . . For art comes to you proposing frankly to give nothing but the highest quality to your moments as they pass. . . ."[17] One need not pursue the question of how important this aesthetic wisdom has been over the years in shoring up the human subject's self-respect against the consequences of the scientific episteme (consequences which were unquestionably the cause of Pater's invocation of it a century ago). Nor is it necessary to point out that Conrad has been seen as a follower of that wisdom (by Levine himself, in *The Realistic Imagination*). It is enough to note that the novelist now comes to stand for a diametrically opposed wisdom.

If on the logic of Darwin's theory all knowledge is arbitrary or relative, the response need not be an aesthetic acquiescence in the inability to know, mitigated by the pleasures of the groundless text. On the contrary, it can take the form of a revolutionary attack on arbitrary and unauthorized structures of knowledge that restrict one's freedom. Thus for Conrad, as Levine now reads him, genuine "engagement with history means violence and destruction" and art becomes a "protector," a way of evading the recognition that beyond theory, beyond language exists not reassuring natural order but a reality governed "by irrationalities, by forces incomprehensible to human consciousness" (p. 267). Or put another way, if on the logic of Darwin's theory, the origin of the universe is neither providential nor rational, but fortuitous, then chance, not law becomes the arbiter of history. Against this background we see clearly enough the point of Levine's closing contrast between Scott's *Old Mortality* and Conrad's *Under Western Eyes*. Both novels centrally deploy the theme of assassination in their explorations of historical process. For Scott assassination is a monstrous human anomaly that the ongoing continuity of history will eventually efface in the interest of continuity as the elements obscure the Covenanters' tombstones at his narrative's outset. For Conrad, ushering in the modern, assassination is neither monstrous nor anomalous, but the norm of history, the very type of its ineffaceable discontinuities. In such a (Foucauldian) world "our one chance" lies not, as Pater has it, "to give nothing but the highest quality to [our] moments as they pass"[18] but, as Conrad's Stein has it, "in the destructive element [to] immerse." Having started out in the consummately civilized world of Austen, Levine leaves us at last, with Conrad, in distinctly uncomfortable proximity to the precarious grounds of all civilization—more uncomfortable, one might add, than we have lately been among the Derrideans. Perhaps we are not a little relieved to find him retreating in his closing sentence back behind the protection of his own art: "Nevertheless, our way of telling stories, of creating meaning, of distrusting both phenomena and language owe much to Darwin and the writers who absorbed, extended, and reacted to his imagination" (p. 272). We are talking, after all, about a way of telling stories, not necessarily about a way of living.

At the close of one of the last century's finest expositions of the critic's art, Oscar Wilde, having tried very hard to preserve that art "from being a sterile thing," fell back, as Victorians (even when they are aesthetes) do, on the meaning of the historical moment. "The nineteenth century is a turning point in history simply on account of the work of two men, Darwin and Renan, the one the critic of the Book of Nature, the other the critic of the books of God. Not to recognize this is to miss the meaning of one of the most important eras in the progress of the world."[19] Insofar as Renan stands in a hermeneutical line running from Hegel to Heidegger that problematizes not only the relation of scripture to reality but of all inscribing to reality, one may fairly say that modern critical discourse has not missed the point of the revolution in thought his name implies. Until recently, however, we have been considerably less perspicacious about Darwin. The reason, as I suggested earlier on, is that his discourse, being an interpretation of nature rather than of books, has not seemed continuous with ours. One of the sterling accomplishments of *Darwin and the Novelists* is that it brings home to literary criticism, as few other books have done, the intimate relevance of scientific thought to literary art from the turn of the nineteenth century on. It is difficult to know how humanistic readers can leave Levine's book with their presuppositions about the gap between the "two cultures" still intact. Certainly no less significant is the way in which his use of scientific discourse in general, Darwinism in particular, has resulted in an original, and provocative, reordering of our presuppositions about nineteenth-century fiction itself. On both counts Professor Levine has wonderfully preserved criticism "from being a sterile thing."

Notes

1. George Levine, *The Realistic Imagination: English Fiction from Frankenstein to Lady Chatterly* (Chicago: Univ. of Chicago Press), p. 3. Future citations will be given in parentheses in the text.

2. J. Hillis Miller, significantly, begins his story with Conrad's narrative structure "which has no beginning, no foundation outside itself" (*Fiction and Repetition: Seven English Novels* [Cambridge: Harvard Univ. Press, 1982], p. 25) and reads the Victorians backwards, as it were, tracing their anticipations on the deconstructive turn.

3. See, for example, L. Stevenson, *Darwin among the Poets* (1932), L. J. Henkin, *Darwinism in the English Novel* (1940), A. E. Jones, *Darwinism and Its Relationship to Realism and Naturalism in American Fiction, 1860–1900* (1950), G. Roppen, *Evolution and Poetic Belief, a Study in Some Victorian and Modern Writers* (1956), A. Ellegård, *Darwin and the Darwinian Revolution* (1959), M. Peckham, *Man's Rage for Chaos: Biology, Behavior and the Arts* (1965).

4. Two recent anthologies, *Languages of Nature: Critical Essays on Science and Literature*, ed. L. J. Jordanova (New Brunswick: Rutgers Univ. Press, 1986) and *One Culture: Essays in Science and Literature*, ed. George Levine (Madison: Univ. of Wisconsin Press, 1987), present a good range of examples of new work in the field.

5. See the first chapter of Frank Lentricchia's *After the New Criticism* (Chicago: Univ. of Chicago Press, 1980).

6. T. H. Huxley, "Science and Culture," in *Science and Education* (New York: Appleton, 1894), p. 105.

7. Walter F. Cannon, "The Normative Role of Science in Early Victorian Thought," *Journal of the History of Ideas*, 25 (1964), 488.

8. Michel Foucault, *The Archaeology of Knowledge and the Discourse on Language*, trans. A. M. Sheridan French (New York: Pantheon Books, 1972), p. 14. Foucault's well-known objection to being associated with structuralism should be taken with a significant grain of salt. See, e.g., J. G. Merquior, *Foucault* (London: Fontana Press, 1985), chapter 1.

9. Gillian Beer, *Darwin's Plots: Evolutionary Narrative in Darwin, George Eliot, and Nineteenth-Century Fiction* (London: Routledge and Kegan Paul, 1983), pp. 8–9.

10. The classic study is Charles C. Gillispie's *Genesis and Geology: A Study in the Relations of Scientific Thought, Natural Theology, and Social Opinion in Great Britain, 1790–1850* (New York: Harper, 1959). R. M. Young adds significantly to the history of the debate in "Natural Theology, Victorian Periodicals, and the Fragmentation of the Common Context," in *Darwin to Einstein: Historical Studies on Science and Belief*, ed. Colin Chant and John Fauvel (Harlow, Essex: Longman, 1980).

11. Cited by R. M. Young, "Natural Theology, Victorian Periodicals, and the Fragmentation of the Common Context," p. 76.

12. How the uniformitarian doctrine found its way into social theory is the subject of J. W. Burrow's *Evolution and Society: A Study in Victorian Social Theory* (Cambridge: Cambridge Univ. Press, 1970); see especially chapter 4. Levine's book, in effect, makes Burrow's point with regard to literary art.

13. Cited by Howard E. Gruber, *Darwin on Man: A Psychological Study of Scientific Creativity*, 2nd ed. (Chicago: Univ. of Chicago Press, 1974), p. 41.

14. My own book, *In Pursuit of a Scientific Culture: Science, Art, and Society in the Victorian Age* (Madison: Univ. of Wisconsin Press, 1989), develops this point in the first chapter in its discussion of Auguste Comte and J. S. Mill.

15. Matthew Arnold, *Literature and Dogma* in *Complete Prose Works*, ed. R. H. Super (Ann Arbor: Univ. of Michigan Press, 1961–77), vi, 171, 182, 188–89.

16. Michel Foucault, *Discipline and Punish: The Birth of the Prison*, trans. Alan Sheridan (New York: Pantheon Books, 1977), pp. 23, 170–71.

17. Walter Pater, *The Renaissance: Studies in Art and Poetry*, ed. Donald L. Hill (Berkeley: Univ. of California Press, 1980), p. 187.

18. Ibid., p. 190.

19. *Oscar Wilde,* ed. Isobel Murray (Oxford: Oxford Univ. Press, 1989), p. 296.

The British Stage Corrected, 1660–1737

Robert Adams Day

Peter Lewis. *Fielding's Burlesque Drama: Its Place in the Tradition.* Edinburgh: Edinburgh University Press, 1987. viii, 220 pp.

We are apt to forget, in celebrating Fielding the novelist, that had it not been for Walpole's Licensing Act of 1737, which nipped his career as a dramatist not in the bud but in florid bloom, we should probably not have had the novelist at all. And we are equally apt to neglect, in considering his fictions, the influence which comic drama must have had upon his conception of character and his confection of striking scenes and complex plots—compared by Coleridge, after all, not with earlier prose fictions but with *Oedipus Rex* and *The Alchemist*. The appearance of this volume, then, is, if nothing more, a timely reminder to do our homework. Its emphasis—not on Fielding's dramatic work as a whole, but on his burlesque dramas and the surprisingly rich if short-lived English tradition in which they are placed and from which to some extent they derived their form, mode, and subject matter—is equally welcome. In contrast to the novelists and the major poets, the dramatists of the eighteenth century have had relatively little attention of late; and while this fact undoubtedly reflects the relatively poor quality of eighteenth-century English drama in general, a search for unrecognized literary merit can never be without its uses, especially now that popular culture is claiming a place among the innovative fields of contemporary criticism. Burlesque, too, is a subgenre of comic drama that has suffered recent neglect. If to our taste the age was absurdly infatuated with the grandiose, the sentimental, the bathetic, with the sillier specimens of *opera seria,* worn-out mythological and classical plots and personages, sudden conversions, gory death scenes, it is well to be reminded that it equally enjoyed laughing at these when a little enlarged by caricature, and was furnished with authors who were glad to provide ammunition for attack and topics for mirth. Banks, Cibber, Dennis, Dryden, Lee, Lillo, Otway, Ambrose Philips, Rowe, Shadwell, Theobald, if admired in various degrees, were also pilloried by a succession of writers, some minor, some of the stature of Gay and Fielding, who provided their own correctives for the theatrical follies of their times.

Fielding's Burlesque Drama begins with a sensible discussion of the definition of burlesque and of its connections with and differences from comedy, satire, parody, and travesty. This is followed by a thorough analysis and placing of Buckingham's *Rehearsal,* justifiably seen as the *fons et origo* of the subgenre, with its devices, such as the play within a play, the rehearsal plot, the overinflated and huffing superhero, the preposterous denouement. Chapter Three concerns itself with an account of minor burlesques in the Restoration and early eighteenth century: *The Female Wits,* the plays of Thomas Duffett, Cibber's burlesques. Peter Lewis discusses these with a thoroughness which will be useful to the student, though whether it will encourage further investigation or make it seem superfluous will largely depend on the reader's taste. There follows an extended and original treatment of the dramatic burlesques of John Gay, which may be the most valuable section of the book. *The What D'Ye Call It* assumes a hitherto unrecognized importance and literary value (one wonders whether Hofmannsthal could have used it as a source for *Ariadne auf Naxos,* and would certainly like to see it produced); the successes and failures of *Three Hours After Marriage* are accounted for in detail (especially its supercomplex plot, which defeats its own purpose as a satire of excesses in the intrigue plot); and a very important discussion of *The Beggar's Opera* specifically as a satire of the conventions and extravagances of Italian opera will add a new dimension to our appreciation of the richness and wit of this work.

There follow equally extensive and detailed accounts of *The Author's Farce, Tom Thumb, The Covent-Garden Tragedy, Pasquin,*

The British Stage Corrected

Tumble-Down Dick, Eurydice, The Historical Register for the Year 1736, and *Eurydice Hiss'd.* Each of these is provided with a production history, an evaluation of its intention and the extent of its connection with comedy as such, distinct from burlesque, and a liberal sampling of burlesque verbal turns and visual effects, together with a meticulous tracking down and comparison of these with their specific sources in other plays and in topical allusions. There is an equally liberal provision of passages quoted *in extenso* from Fielding and from his specific targets for burlesque—Cibber, Dennis, Thomson, and many others.

The book's principal virtue lies in its thoroughness. There could hardly be a better basic text for the reader who wants to begin with a solid grounding in a subject on which secondary materials are still scanty, and primary materials hard to come by. We are given the basic facts surrounding the composition, production, reception, and orientation of a play in politics both national and theatrical, together with a detailed plot summary and an enumeration of its burlesque devices and its merits and defects. Valuable ancillary materials include a general history of Italian opera in its early English period, and pantomime—its characteristics, extreme popularity, and decline. Moreover, the reader is copiously furnished with summaries of the opinions of critics and scholars on matters large and small, together with Lewis's evaluation and agreement or disagreement.

Unfortunately, however, these practical virtues are accompanied by their complementary aesthetic defects. *Fielding's Burlesque Drama,* whether it is so or not, has all the earmarks of a doctoral thesis which has been published with little or no revision. A candidate must satisfy his examiners that he has done his homework: hence, the scrupulous citation of one's predecessors even on matters seemingly trivial or obvious, with agreement or refutation; the cautiously timid backing up, by a reassuring reference to authority, of points where we should be able to trust the author; the equally cautious dismissal of opinions clearly superficial or impressionistic. These have their uses, at least for the student if not for the professional reader; but the student's task is not lightened by the volume's heavy-handed laboring of the obvious and its nearly total lack of a sense of humor. Do we need to be told as follows, regarding the preposterous reprieve at the end of *The Beggar's Opera,* "to comply with the Taste of the Town"?

What makes the burlesque more caustic than the similar burlesque of peripeteia in *The What D'Ye Call It* when Peascod is saved from execution by a last-minute reprieve is the completely gratuitous nature of Macheath's reprieve. Whereas Peascod is a maligned innocent, Macheath is an incorrigible criminal whose guilt is unquestioned. He does nothing to earn his reprieve and there is no evidence that it will transform him morally.

And a list of such passages would be very long indeed.

These qualities, however, do not impair the book's value for the serious but non-expert reader. It is elegantly presented and carefully proofread (I noticed very few typographical errors). There are seventeen pages of attractive plates, some familiar (one from Hogarth's *Harlot's Progress,* for example), others new even to the specialist; all are instructive and relevant. The index is handily and usefully analytical.

Contributors

HUGH AMORY is Rare Book Cataloguer at The Houghton Library, Harvard University.

MICHAEL ANESKO is Associate Professor of History and Literature, and of English and American Literature and Language, at Harvard University.

JIM SPRINGER BORCK is Professor of English and Editor of *The Eighteenth Century* at Louisiana State University.

DEREK BREWER is Emeritus Professor of English and formerly Master of Emmanuel College in the University of Cambridge.

MARSHALL BROWN is Professor of English and Comparative Literature at the University of Washington.

PETER ALLAN DALE is Professor of English at the University of California, Davis.

ROBERT ADAMS DAY is Professor of English and Comparative Literature at Queens College and the Graduate Center, CUNY.

HENRY J. DONAGHY is Professor of English at Mississippi State University.

ROBERT H. ELIAS is Goldwin Smith Professor Emeritus of English Literature and American Studies at Cornell University.

WILLIAM E. FREDEMAN is Professor of English at the University of British Columbia.

REGENIA GAGNIER is Associate Professor of English at Stanford University.

D. C. GREETHAM is Professor in the Ph.D. Program in English at CUNY Graduate Center.

KATHERINE JOSLIN is Assistant Professor of English at Western Michigan University.

ARTHUR F. KINNEY is Thomas W. Copeland Professor of Literary History at the University of Massachusetts, Amherst, and President of the Renaissance English Text Society.

JAMES LONGENBACH is Associate Professor of English at the University of Rochester.

PETER J. MANNING is Professor of English at the University of Southern California, Los Angeles.

JUDITH MILHOUS is Professor in the Ph.D. Program in Theatre at CUNY Graduate Center.

C. DEIRDRE PHELPS is a Ph.D. candidate in the Department of English at Boston University.

BEVERLY SCHNELLER is Assistant Professor of English at Millersville University.

ELIZABETH SEWELL is a poet, novelist, and critic. She resides in Greensboro, North Carolina.

L. J. SWINGLE is Professor of English at the University of Kentucky.

MICHAEL WEST is Professor of English at the University of Pittsburgh.